SCHOLARS' GUIDE TO WASHINGTON, D.C. FOR CARTOGRAPHY AND REMOTE SENSING IMAGERY

SCHOLARS' GUIDE
TO WASHINGTON, D.C.
FOR

CARTOGRAPHY AND REMOTE SENSING IMAGERY

(MAPS, CHARTS, AERIAL PHOTOGRAPHS, SATELLITE IMAGES, CARTOGRAPHIC LITERATURE AND GEOGRAPHIC INFORMATION SYSTEMS)

RALPH E. EHRENBERG

Preface by
ALAN K. HENRIKSON

Consultants
JOSEPH W. WIEDEL
JOHN A. WOLTER

Editor
ZDENĚK V. DAVID

WOODROW WILSON INTERNATIONAL CENTER FOR SCHOLARS

SMITHSONIAN INSTITUTION PRESS
WASHINGTON, D.C.
1987

Scholars' Guide to Washington, D.C., no. 12

This work was developed under a grant from the U.S. Department of Education. However, the content does not necessarily reflect the position or policy of that agency, and no official endorsement of these materials should be inferred.

Library of Congress Cataloging-in-Publication Data

Ehrenberg, Ralph E., 1937–
Scholars' guide to Washington, D.C. for cartography
and remote sensing imagery.

"Woodrow Wilson International Center for Scholars."
Bibliography: p.
Includes index.
Supt. of Doc. no.: SI 1.20:Sch 6/7
1. Map collections—Washington (D.C.)—Directories.
I. David, Zdeňek V. II. Title.
GA193.U5E37 1987 026'.912'025753 86-600371
ISBN 0-87474-406-7
ISBN 0-87474-407-5 (pbk.)

CONTENTS

FOREWORD

This guide is sponsored by the Woodrow Wilson International Center for Scholars, the nation's "living memorial" to its twenty-eighth president. It is the twelfth volume in a reference series describing the scholarly resources of the Washington, D.C. area. Begun in 1977, these *Guides* were inspired, in part, by the accumulated lore about scholarly materials that was developing among fellows in the Wilson Center.

Though the Center has no special program in cartography or remote sensing imagery, it is aware of the importance of cartographic materials for most projects pursued by fellows and guest scholars in its eight current programs. These programs cover all the disciplines of the humanities and social sciences. Seven are geographical or thematic: Program on American Society and Politics, Kennan Institute for Advanced Russian Studies, Latin American Program, Asia Program, International Security Studies Program, East European Program, and West European Program. The eighth, broadly defined program—History, Culture, and Society—accommodates fellows who work on geographical regions not represented by the other programs (e.g., Africa and the Middle East), on comparative studies that cut across several global areas, or on projects with theoretical, philosophical, literary, or theological dimensions.

Taken as a whole, the series of *Guides* exemplifies the Wilson Center's "switchboard function" of facilitating connections between the vast resources of the nation's capital and those who have scholarly or practical needs—or simply curiosity. These *Guides*—like the Center's annual fellowship program—are designed to serve the national and international scholarly communities. Each year, at least 20,000 visiting scholars come to Washington from elsewhere in the United States and abroad to pursue serious research. The *Guides* are designed to inform scholars about the possibilities for engaging in research on particular topics in Washington. The *Guides* cover the accessible organizations of the metropolitan area of Washington, but they are not merely of local importance. In the city's libraries, archives, and data banks, in its universities and research centers, and especially in the federal agencies and international organizations concentrated here, Washington holds resources that are of national—indeed of worldwide—significance.

The series of *Guides* is under the general editorship of Zdeněk V. David, the Wilson Center Librarian, who has devised the basic format. Elizabeth Dixon is largely responsible for the book design and liaison with the publisher. Consultants for the preparation of this particular *Guide* were Joseph W. Wiedel, Associate Professor of Geography, University of Maryland at College Park, and John A. Wolter, Chief, Geography and Map Division, Library of Congress. Wilson Center staff members providing advice and assistance were Peter Braestrup, Prosser Gifford, and George Liston Seay. The author of this volume, Ralph E. Ehrenberg, is currently Assistant Chief, Geography and Map Division, Library of Congress. A special feature of this *Guide* is the prefatory essay,

"Frameworks for the World," by a former Wilson Center Fellow (1978–1979), Alan K. Henrikson, now professor of Diplomatic History, Fletcher School of Law and Diplomacy at Tufts University.

The Center thanks the United States Department of Education for its indispensible financial support of the *Guide's* preparation (under the authority of Title VI, Section 602, NDEA).

The Center has now prepared *Guides* for scholars in the fields of Russian/Soviet (2d rev. ed. 1983), Latin American and Caribbean (1979), East Asian (1979), African (1980), Central and East European (1980), Middle Eastern (1981), South Asian (1981), Southeast Asian (1983), and Northwest European (1984) studies, as well as *Guides* covering film and video collections (1980), and audio resources (1985). All were published by the Smithsonian Institution Press (P.O. Box 4866, Hampden Station, Baltimore, Maryland 21211). A forthcoming volume will survey resources in the Washington area for scholars interested in Southwest Europe, including France, Italy (with ancient Rome), Malta, Portugal, Spain, and the Vatican.

Washington, D.C.
March 1, 1986

James H. Billington, Director
Woodrow Wilson International Center for Scholars

FRAMEWORKS FOR THE WORLD

Through maps and charts, and through these graphic representations virtually alone, the earth and its regions have acquired the shapes by which we know them. Not only the outlines, or physical and political boundaries, but also the sizes, distances, and directions of the world's territorial and maritime expanses generally are apprehended first through the logical structures and vivid images of cartography. Long before they actually are visited, the world's remote geographical areas usually are visualized, correctly or incorrectly, in the mind's eye.

The principal sources of our world vision, and much of our factual knowledge of the earth and the happenings upon it as well, are the terrestrial map, the nautical chart, and, increasingly, the high-altitude aerial photograph and satellite image. With the advent of geometrically correct satellite imagery, it now is possible to map vast areas in all their detail at a single step, translating multitudes of information about places into proper cartographic form.[1] Perhaps no other medium of communication enables us to comprehend so much, so accurately, so quickly.

For the study of foreign areas and international relations, as well as for the practice of diplomacy itself, an understanding of cartography is more important than commonly is realized. "The world we have to deal with politically," as Walter Lippmann wrote many years ago, "is out of reach, out of sight, out of mind. It has to be explored, reported, and imagined." Like denizens of Plato's Cave, officials immured in government bureaucracies can only perceive outside events indirectly. Makers of foreign policy and military strategy are at a particular disadvantage in this regard. For them, most of the political world that is relevant lies outside their country's borders and jurisdiction. They must rely on their subjective cartography of it. "Their persistent difficulty," noted Lippmann, "is to secure maps on which their own need, or someone else's need, has not sketched in the coast of Bohemia."[2]

In order fully to understand the behavior of statesmen, one must try to form an image of the world as they imagine it, to visualize the global setting as they envision it, and to sense the environment as they experience it—that is, to read their "mental maps."[3] The same kind of imaginative projection into the geographical situations of others is required in order to understand the societies that are the objects of statesmen's policies and actions. There is no *better* evidence of these unique cognitive and perceptual worlds, I suggest, than the actual, cartographic maps that nations have used.

Foreign policy and diplomacy are, at the most basic level, manifestations in behavior of statesmen's conceptions of the world and of their own countries' particular places within it. No less a political figure than Napoleon asserted that "the policy of a state lies in its geography."[4] In this political context, "geography" means more than topographical irregularity or climatic variation, more than the distribution of mineral resources or patterns of settlement, and more than the cultural differences of peoples in diverse locales. It signifies the mental spatio-temporal frame, centered on a point of origin within the core of a country, by conscious or unconscious reference to which the activities of that nation are organized. The foreign thrusts as well as the domestic initiatives of a nation thus are guided. In order to have a political plan, statesmen first must have a geographical plan. Because the world cannot be known directly, even by the most peripatetic of leaders, they must have cartographic projects as well.

What sort of map plans do statesmen—whose spatial ideas inform the behavior of their countrymen—have? It is not true, as sometimes is asserted, that every country considers itself to be "the center of the world" and, accordingly, places itself at the middle of its world maps. Some countries sense that they are, in objective geographical, economic, political, and cultural terms, "marginal." Even psychologically, some countries may feel, in a sense, peripheral to themselves. One of the unfortunate characteristics of the colonial mentality, for instance, is that those who are afflicted by it believe that "the center" lies elsewhere, in the metropolitan capital of the imperial power. It is not surprising, therefore, that one of the first steps of leaders of newly independent nations is to try to assert their own centrality, or self-worth and self-importance, by building a new capital city, shifting its functions from one site to another, or, at the very least, changing the name of the old colonial seat of government to a more "authentic," native name. A new capital gives a society a feeling of having a nucleus, independent of external control. Hence, an inland city, rather than a port, often is chosen for the capital role.[5]

Within the realm of diplomacy, a new government typically attempts to reorient itself internationally from the basis of a new capital. It not only breaks most of its ties with its former colonial ruler. It also sometimes engages in diplomatic dalliance with the metropolitan country's adversaries. In order to increase its weight and influence, it may, in addition, join with other newly established countries in forming a regional or worldwide bloc of neutrals. All of these changes of relationship can affect, and be affected by, a country's global picture.

The history of the changing place of the United States in the world, as well as its sense of location on global maps, illustrates these points. Americans have gone through three major phases of cartographic self-imagining. These shifts in the perceived position of the United States in the world are correlated with the perceived geographical and political situations of other countries. Hence an examination of the changes in the place of the United States on world maps, actual and imagined, tells us much about international relations in general during the past two centuries.

The first phase of American cartographic history was the emergence of the United States within the "Western Hemisphere." This cartographer's abstraction became a category of thought and, eventually, the basis of a foreign policy. "America has a hemisphere to itself," wrote President Thomas Jefferson to Alexander von Humboldt, the German scientist and voyager to Latin America. "It must have a separate system of interest[s] which must not be subordinated to those of Europe."[6] This possessive notion of a separate "American" hemisphere, with a proposed new prime meridian that would run through the newly built U.S. capital of Washington, D.C., was the geopolitical premise of the 1823 Monroe Doctrine, a tradition that continues to influence American thinking to the present day.

The decisive crisis of hemispherist thinking, associated with neutrality and isolationism, occurred just before the entry of the United States into the Second World War. During that critical period, President Franklin D. Roosevelt and his advisors had to decide whether to continue to base the security of the United States on a limited strategy of Western Hemisphere defense or to acknowledge a more vital strategic interest in keeping the transatlantic sea lanes open. Under the peacetime Selective Service Act, Congress had stipulated that U.S. forces raised could not be employed "beyond the limits of the Western Hemisphere." Roosevelt's device for escaping this constraint, which lasted until the attack on Pearl Harbor made all such subterfuge unnecessary, was that of creeping hemispherism—that is, arbitrarily redefining the limits of the Western Hemisphere to permit ever wider naval patrols. Even the precautionary landing of troops in Iceland, conventionally considered part of Europe, was justified on hemispherist grounds.

By the end of the war, hemispherism, as the premise of American security doctrine, was dead. As S. Whittemore Boggs, the Geographer of the State Department, declared in 1945: "The limiting meridians of this so-called 'Western Hemisphere' have no political, historic, geographic, or economic significance."[7] The hemispherist idea survives today mainly as a symbol of the solidarity of the Pan American movement. The concept periodically is given cartographic expression, as in the American Geographical Society's classic "Map of the Americas, 1:5,000,000" or the continuing mapping work of the Pan American Institute of Geography and History, affiliated with the Organization of American States in Washington, D.C.

The second phase in American cartographic self-imagining, with even wider international consequences, was the shift to an "Arctic focus" during the Cold War era. The emergence of the Soviet Union as the looming danger, not only to the United States but also to the rest of the Free World, was related to two new developments in technology: long-range aviation and the atomic bomb. This new specter haunting America foreshadowed an "atomic Pearl Harbor" delivered by air from over the North Pole. As General Henry H. ("Hap") Arnold warned, "A surprise attack could readily come from across the roof of the world unless we were in possession of adequate airbases outflanking such a route of approach."[8] The need for such bases was one reason for the negotiation of a system of alliances, notably the North Atlantic Treaty Organization and bilateral security treaties with the Philippines, Japan, Korea, and other nations in the Pacific. These relationships provided an arc of protection spanning half of the Northern Hemisphere.

This new strategic focus on the Arctic region, and on the proximity of the Soviet menace to Canadian and American cities, was facilitated by a cartographic change: a shift from the Equator-based Mercator projection, mainly used for oceanic navigation, to various North Pole-centered azimuthal projections, which more clearly exhibited the direct relationship of the Eurasian land mass to the North American continent. An example of this new image is a chart, entitled "A Map to Show the Comparative Nearness of the U.S. to the U.S.S.R.," which was prepared in 1950 for the Senate Foreign Relations Committee and the Department of State.[9] The U.S. Defense Mapping Agency today produces many versions of these azimuthal maps. They are used for numerous military-related purposes including the construction of the new "North Warning" system in northern Canada and planning for the Strategic Defense Initiative, or "Star Wars" program. It is ironic that, for the general public, probably the best-known example of a North Pole-centered azimuthal projection is wholly irenic in purpose: the azimuthal equidistant map that is incorporated in the official emblem of the United Nations.[10] This was intended to be a symbol, as the two-hemisphere scheme could not be, of the peaceful ideal of One World.

The third phase in the evolution of Americans' cartographic imagination, as it is related to foreign policy, is associated with the current vogue of a map, a cylindrical projection like Mercator's, but, unlike it, equal-area or equivalent: the "Peters projection." Bearing the name of Arno Peters, a West German historian, this map has enthusiastically been taken up by church groups, development institutes, and even some governments as an alternative world-image to those conventionally employed in the design of world strategy and international diplomacy. Perhaps its most prominent usage so far is its appearance on the front cover of the report, *North-South: A Program for Survival* (1980), produced by the Independent Commission on International Development Issues headed by former West German Chancellor Willy Brandt.[11] As the title of the Brandt Commission report suggests, the Peters projection, like the view of the world the report represents, deliberately replaces the alleged "Western" or "Northern" bias of previous global cartography with a "Southern" focus. This effect is achieved not only by showing all areas in correct size relation to each other (at the cost of some distortion of shape), but also by the simple step of placing the Equator in the middle of the map, not below it.[12]

The huge continent of Africa emerges as central, if not actually predominant, in this world scheme. South America also looms larger and more significant that it ever has done cartographically. The general impact of the Peters map is to promote the Third World to prominence and, by implication, to demote the United States and Western Europe—the Atlantic region—to marginality. In a sense, what the developing countries and their proponents are trying to do is what the United States attempted to do when it was a young and growing country: to claim a hemisphere and make it the dominant one. Today this can only be done through diplomacy conducted on a global scale.

As the above discussion indicates, an understanding of maps and their role requires some knowledge of the basic principles of map construction, or projections. Because a spherical surface such as that of the earth cannot be transferred onto a plane without severe distortions or interruptions (consider what happens to an orange peel when it is flattened on a table top!), it is important for even a map viewer, as well as the map maker, to know what specific map qualities are lost as others are gained. Except for the globe, which enables us to see the world "round" though not "entire," no map is accurate in every respect. The usual choice that must be made is between conformality, or shape, and equivalence, or size commensurability.

Gaining a theoretical understanding of map projection is only a basic, preliminary stage in acquiring the detailed, concrete knowledge of the real world that maps can convey. Map learning—learning from, and with, maps—is a continuous process, and also a dynamic one. This is in part because the map itself, as a visual field, is dynamic. "Once the student sees the map, not as an assembly of shapes but as a configuration of forces," writes the psychologist of visual perception, Rudolf Arnheim, "the knowledge to be derived from them is appropriately transformed into a play of corresponding forces—physical, biological, economical, and political forces."[13]

Learning from and through maps, whether as a statesman or as a scholar, involves the constant subtraction and addition of particular facts, or the intelligent displacement of the irrelevant by the germane. It requires as well the constant reorganization of this flow of discrete data into new and more meaningful patterns. These schemata must exist in the mind. They do not exist on the map itself, however suggestive its forms, colors, and symbols. A systematic, sustained intellectual effort is required, an effort of world-framing.

"Watching the map," as the New Deal brain truster and diplomat Adolf A. Berle once advised, "is not a one-day affair. A good foreign affairs student will look at it while he scans the headlines in his daily newspaper or if he is in the State Department, while he is reading his daily grist of cablegrams. Or perhaps after he has read a book about any area or has listened to an impassioned campaign speech on foreign matters. He will do it a few minutes daily." The knowledge gained thereby will begin to accumulate. In a surprisingly short period of time, Berle attests, each scrap of information received "attaches itself" to a locale, a place on the changing map.

The benefit of such map viewing is to connect geography and history. As new information that is gathered forms around particular points on the map, the map begins almost to seem "a living thing."[14] The relationships that events in certain locales have to happenings in other places, among other peoples, become more vivid and meaningful.

The lines drawn on the map—sea lanes, aviation routes, or trade flows—turn into currents of active influence. As each new piece of news fits into this global picture, the story framed by a map comes to life.

Alan K. Henrikson
The Fletcher School of Law and Diplomacy
Tufts University
Medford, Massachusetts
(*Fellow, Woodrow Wilson International Center for Scholars, 1978–1979*)

Notes

[1] For an extraordinary example of the translation of satellite imagery into cartographic form, see *Images of the World: An Atlas of Satellite Imagery and Maps* (Chicago: Rand McNally and Company, 1983).

[2] Walter Lippmann, *Public Opinion* (New York: Harcourt, Brace and Company, 1922), pp.16, 29.

[3] For an explication of this concept, see Alan K. Henrikson, "The Geographical 'Mental Maps' of American Foreign Policy Makers," *International Political Science Review* 1, no. 4 (1980): 495–530.

[4] Yves Lacoste, "Geopolitics and Foreign Policy," *SAIS Review* 4, no. 2 (Summer-Fall 1984): 213.

[5] O.K.H. Spate, "Factors in the Development of Capital Cities," *The Geographical Review* 32, no. 4 (October 1942): 622–31.

[6] Quoted in Arthur P. Whitaker, *The Western Hemisphere Idea: Its Rise and Decline* (Ithaca, NY: Cornell University Press, 1954), p. 29.

[7] S. Whittemore Boggs, "This Hemisphere," *Department of State Bulletin* 12, no. 306 (May 6, 1945): 845–50. For further discussion of American hemispherism, see Alan K. Henrikson, "The Map as an 'Idea': The Role of Cartographic Imagery During the Second World War," *The American Cartographer* 2, no. 1 (1975): 19–53.

[8] (General of the Army) H. H. Arnold, "Air Power for Peace," *The National Geographic Magazine* 89, no. 2 (February 1946): 137–94.

[9] U.S. Congress, Senate, Committee on Foreign Relations, *A Decade of American Foreign Policy: Basic Documents* (Washington, D.C.: U.S. Government Printing Office, 1959), between pp. 906–7.

[10] On the genesis of this design, see Henrikson, "The Map as an 'Idea'": 45.

[11] *North-South: A Program for Survival* (Cambridge, MA: The MIT Press, 1980).

[12] See Arno Peters, *The Europe-centered Character of Our Geographical View of the World and its Correction,* trans. D.G. Smith (Frankfurt am Main: K. G. Lohse, Graphischer Grossbetrieb, 1979), and, for a critique, Arthur H. Robinson, "Arno Peters and His New Cartography," *The American Cartographer* 12, no. 2 (1985): 103–11.

[13] Rudolf Arnheim, "The Perception of Maps," *The American Cartographer* 3, no. 1 (1976): 5–10.

[14] Adolf A. Berle, Jr., *Tides of Crisis: A Primer of Foreign Relations* (New York: Reynal and Company, 1957), p. 129.

INTRODUCTION

Purpose. This *Guide* is intended to introduce researchers to the vast cartographic and remote sensing resources in Washington, D.C. and the surrounding metropolitan area. It contains descriptions of collections of cartographic and remote sensing materials as well as organizations that produce these materials or provide information and research concerning the broad field of spatial data resources. While written primarily for the serious researcher, it is hoped that this volume will stimulate use of these varied and rich resources by a broader audience.

The cartographic and remote sensing collections of the nation's capital are unmatched. The map collections contain more than 50,000 atlases and 9.2 million maps, while the remote sensing collections available to researchers hold more than 17 million aerial photographs and remote sensing images. The Library of Congress (A21) has custody of the largest and most comprehensive collection of atlases and maps in the world, while taken together, the National Archives and Records Administration (B19) and the Defense Intelligence Agency (G7) hold the greatest collections of aerial photographs. Another four million maps and five million aerial photographs, housed elsewhere in the country, are administered by government agencies located in Washington. There are also numerous federal libraries, military archives, university libraries and archives, and museums that maintain collections of maps, remote sensing images, and spatial data banks.

In addition to its role as the nation's major cartographic and remote sensing resource center, the Washington area serves as the production center of the cartographic and remote sensing industry in the United States. For example, the Geological Survey (G14) and the National Ocean Service (G20) produce and publish the basic topographic and geological maps and aeronautical and coastal charts of the United States, respectively, while the Defense Mapping Agency (G8) provides worldwide coverage of aeronautical, nautical and topographic charts and maps. The Washington area also can claim three major commercial publishers—Alexandria Drafting Company (Kl), American Automobile Association (K2), and Williams and Heintz Map Corporation (Kl8). In addition, the capital city boasts noteworthy academic cartographic laboratories and training facilities at George Mason University (F5), George Washington University (F7), and the University of Maryland (Fll). Major remote sensing agencies and corporations located in Washington are the National Aeronautics and Space Administration (G18), National Environmental Satellite, Data, and Information Service (D8), Earth Observation Satellite Company (E3) and SPOT Image Corporation (E8). Moreover, Washington is home to the leading professional societies for the mapping and remote sensing communities (J).

While most of the collections are open to serious researchers, the use of some collections is restricted or closed to the public due to national security classifications or donor restrictions. In some instances, materials classsified or restricted by Federal agencies may be petitioned for release through Freedom-of-Information procedures by directing FOI inquiries to FOI coordinators who are assigned to each agency. It should be noted, however, that the Freedom of Information Act does not apply to records of the legislative or judicial branches of government. Because of security sensitivity, several military collections have not been included in this *Guide*.

A special feature of this *Guide* is the inclusion of descriptions of collections of photographs and motion pictures that show past and current processes of preparing maps and aerial photographs. Also included are descriptions of surveying and map making tools and instruments for scholars interested in this aspect of cartography.

Scope and Content. This *Guide* contains descriptions of more than 200 collections, organizations, and agencies located in the Washington, D.C. area or administered by agencies whose headquarters are situated in the nation's capital. Entries provide names, addresses, telephone numbers, descriptions of collections, organizations, services, and publications. Because of the size and number of collections, the entries generally refer only to a sampling of representative maps, aerial photographs, or related materials.

The main body of this volume is divided into two parts. Part I lists and describes resource *collections* in libraries (government, academic, public, and special); archives and manuscript repositories, museums and galleries, and data banks. Each entry generally describes the size and contents of map and aerial photography holdings as well as related literature, primary sources, photographs, motion pictures concerning maps and aerial photographs and the processes associated with the production and use of these products. Related surveying and mapping instruments are also described. Part II examines *organizations* that produce maps and remote sensing images and provide pertinent information to researchers. Many of these institutions also maintain map and aerial photography collections. Organizations included are research centers and referral services, academic programs and departments, United States government agencies, state and local government agencies, embassies and international organizations, associations and societies, and publishers, publications, and media. Each entry generally describes the organization's functions, programs, and research activities, collections and reference facilities, and products as they relate to the mapping and remote sensing sciences.

A series of appendixes, bibliography, and indexes follow Part II. The appendixes include a list of map stores, map and remote sensing imagery collections ranked by size, information on housing, transportation and other services in the Washington, D.C. area, list of Federal government holidays, and standard entry formats. Indexes provide access to the entries by personal names, subject, geographic areas, and organizations and institutions.

This *Guide* covers traditional cartographic and remote sensing resources such as atlases, charts, globes, maps, and aerial photographs as well as digital cartographic databases, geographic information systems (GIS), satellite images and related literature and primary resources. Geographic coverage is world wide and includes the lunar and planetary surfaces and the celestial sphere. Topical coverage encompasses a wide range of mappable cultural, economic, geographical, physical, and social phenomena. Scale ranges from very large (a reduction ratio of one inch on the map equallying 100 feet on the ground) to small (1 unit on the map equalling 500,000 or more on the ground). The time frame extends from the beginning of recorded history to the present for maps, and from the 1880's to the present for remote sensing imagery. The heaviest concentration of cartographic and remote sensing resources, however, date from the World War II era.

Methodology. The author began by compiling a list of all map and remote sensing map holdings and organizations in the Washington area. The names of additional collections and organizations were provided during the course of the survey by the two project consultants and the curators and officials acknowleged below. From February through

November, 1985, each institution and organization was visited in person and/or contacted by telephone. Information was obtained during these visits from published and unpublished inventories, card catalogs, and printed literature and from discussions with staff members. In many instances, the collections were uncataloged and the author examined the holdings, item-by-item. Following the preparation of a preliminary draft in December, 1985, each entry was submitted to the respective organization for review. The survey was completed in March, 1986, and the data should be considered current through that date. To aid in the possible future revision of this *Guide*, the author would appreciate that additions, alterations, and suggested improvements be sent to the Librarian, Woodrow Wilson International Center for Scholars, Smithsonian Institution Building, 1000 Jefferson Drive, S.W. Washington, D.C.

Acknowledgments. The author is indebted to the United States Department of Education for financial support; Zdeněk V. David, editor of the Wilson Center's *Scholars Guide* series, who conceived the project and provided invaluable assistance and guidance; Joseph Wiedel and John A. Wolter for their services as consultants; and the Library of Congress for granting extended leave to work on this project.

Many other archivists, curators, librarians, information specialists, and officials have contributed to this *Guide* by generously sharing their indispensable knowledge of their collections and organizations. I am particularly grateful to Franklin Burch, George Chalou, John Dwyer, Janet Hargett, Robert Kvasnicka, Graham McCluggage, Robert Richardson, Charles South, Ronald Swerizek, and Charles Taylor of the National Archives staff; Paul Chestnut, Gary Fitzpatrick, James Flatness, Ronald Grim, John F. Hackett, Mary Ison, Charles Kelly, Gary Kohn, Andrew Modelski, Richard Stephenson and Mary Wolfskill of the Library of Congress; and Rosemary E. Aiello, Harold Ellis, Edward Johnson, Elizabeth Glenn, James R. Glenn, Elizabeth Kelly, Donald E. Kloster, Reidor Norby, Dan Stanton, Herman J. Viola, Debra Warner, Larry Wilson, and Helena Wright of the Smithsonian Institution. A special note of thanks is due William J. Heynen who carefully reviewed and updated the entire draft section on the National Archives and Records Administration. In addition, I wish to acknowledge the cooperation and assistance of the many staff members of the other institutions and organizations described in this *Guide*, particularly Margery Barkdull and Susan Fifer Canby, National Geographic Society; Cal Cavalcante, Naval Historical Center; Brenda G. Corbin, Naval Observatory Library; Frank H. Deter, Jr., National Capital Planning Commission; Martin Gordon and John Lane, Army Corps of Engineers; Steven Hardyman, Army Center of Military History; Nati Krivatsy, Folger Shakespeare Library; Joseph Langdon, Goddard Space Flight Center; Paul McDermott, Montgomery College; David Meier, Bureau of Land Management; Gary North, Bruce Ogilvie, and Donald Orth, Geological Survey; Richard Randall and Stephen Webb, Defense Mapping Agency; George Rohaley, Soil Conservation Service; Sandra Shaw, State Department; William A. Stanley, National Ocean Service; Silla Tomasi, Census Bureau; Thomas Welch, Organization of American States; and Charles Wood, Marine Corps Historical Society. Donna Watson was most diligent in preparing the final manuscript under a very tight schedule. Finally, I would like to thank my wife, Theresa, for her invaluable assistance and support, without which this volume would not have been published.

HOW TO USE THIS GUIDE

Format. The main body of this *Guide* is divided into eleven sections. The first four sections are devoted to research collections (A-D); the remaining seven pertain to organizations (E-K). Within each section, entries are arranged alphabetically by the name of the individual institution or organization. Entries describing United States government institutions and agencies have functional descriptors preceding the generic name (e.g., *Land Management Bureau* rather than *Bureau of Land Management*). In section I, embassies are arranged alphabetically according to geographic name under heading *Embassy of. . . .*

Standard Entry Format. Preceding each section and appendix I is a standard entry form which provides an outline of the categories of information contained within each entry. The sequence of information corresponds to the numerical arrangement of each entry. An omitted number indicates that that category of information was either not relevant or not available.

Personal Names, Addresses, and Telephone Numbers. All names, addresses, and telephone numbers are subject to frequent change, especially for government agencies, due to reorganizations and personnel changes. Telephone numbers include area codes, which are 202 for the District of Columbia, 301 for Maryland, and 703 for Virginia.

Place Names. Geographic place names appearing within collection descriptions follow the usage employed by the individual institutions or organizations. Therefore, the orthography of place names may differ from one entry to another (e.g., *Peking* and *Beijing*, China). In some instances where archaic or alternate place names are used, they have been cross referenced in the geographic index.

Map Scale. The scale of a map is expressed as a ratio relating a unit distance on the map to the same unit distance on the ground. Within the text, map scale is expressed either as a verbal statement (e.g., one inch to 1 mile) or as a representative fraction (e.g., 1:63,360).

Cross-Reference. Cartographic and remote sensing collections, archives, and data banks are cross referenced throughout the main body of this *Guide*, linking bodies of related materials that are dispersed or noting relevant materials and organizations that have more that one entry.

Indexes. Five indexes provide access to information in the text. The *Personal Names Index* includes the names of mapmakers, publishers, authors, and other individuals whose maps and collections are described in this volume. The *Subject Index* covers broad categories of subject headings. There are two separate *Geographic Indexes*, one devoted to aerial photographs and satellite images and the other to maps. The *Organizations and Institutions Index* contains the names of all organizations and institutions listed in the *Guide*, with those that refer to entry headings shown in italics.

Bibliographic Citations. References to publications cited within the text generally include standard bibliographic citations: author, title, imprint, and collation. In some instances, however, particularly with less common publications, the orthography and place of publication is given in the form cited on the publication rather than in the more common anglicized or vernacular form.

COLLECTIONS

A Libraries

Library Entry Format (A)

1. General Information
   a. address; telephone numbers
   b. hours of service
   c. conditions of access
   d. reproduction services
   e. name/title of director and heads of relevant divisions

2. Size of Holdings

3. Description of Holdings
   a. maps, atlases, and globes
   b. aerial photographs and remote sensing images
   c. literature, current and rare books
   d. manuscript collections
   e. photographs and motion pictures
   f. instruments

4. Bibliographic Aids Facilitating Use of Collection (cartobibliographies, catalog cards, computerized retrieval systems, inventories, special lists, catalog guides)

Agricultural Stabilization and Conservation Service (ASCS) (Agriculture Department)—Aerial Photography Field Office **See entry G1, Section 3**

A1 Air Transport Association of America—Library

1 a. *1709 New York Avenue, N.W.*
Washington, D.C. 20006
(202) 626–4184

b. 8:30 A.M.–5:00 P.M. Monday–Friday

c. Open to the public.

e. Marion Mistrik, Librarian

3. The Library's holdings include an incomplete set of the official Civil Aeronautics Board domestic airline route maps for each route and airline by year, 1961–1978 (17 volumes), published initially by the Air Transport Association of America and then by Airline Tariff Publishers Company (1965–1978).

A2 Alexandria Library—Lloyd House Branch

1 a. *Lloyd House*
220 North Washington Street
Alexandria, Virginia 22314

b. 9:00 A.M.–5:00 P.M. Monday–Saturday

c. Open to the public

d. Copying facilities available.

e. Allan Robbins, Librarian.

2. The Lloyd House Branch of the Alexandria Library has custody of the Virginiana Collection of 12,000 books and 4,500 papers, manuscripts, prints, and photographic materials relating to Virginia and local history up to 1936. Lloyd House was built in 1797 and is one of the finest examples of late Georgian Architecture in Alexandria.

3 a. This collection includes two manuscript plat books, *Plats of the Corporation Property of the Town of Alexandria* (1820s) and plats of town lots (1840s–1871), and a manuscript volume of *Surveyors Notes of Grades* showing the elevation of city streets by George Gilpin (1794) and an unidentified surveyor (1873–1874). The map collection contains 41 printed and reproduced maps relating to Alexandria, 1736–1962. The collection also contains Charles Magnus' lithographic bird's eye view of the City (1863).

3 b. The Vertical File Photographic Collection includes a set of twelve aerial photographs of the Alexandria Waterfront taken April 5, 1933, and two other views of the City dated 1920 and 1939.

A3 American Automobile Association Library

1 a. *8111 Gatehouse Road*
Falls Church, Virginia 22047
(703) 222–6466

b. 8:30 A.M.–5:00 P.M. Monday–Friday

c. Researchers must make appointments in advance. Maps do not circulate.

d. Photocopy service is available.

e. Sue Williams, Librarian

3 a. The map collection consists of an incomplete set of approximately 2000 American Automobile Association maps of North America dating from 1909 to the present. The earliest AAA map, for example, printed in 1905, is in the Geography and Map Division of the Library of Congress. Nevertheless, this collection is significant for it readily provides the researcher access to most of the maps produced by a commercial publisher. The library also maintains samples of early strip maps and *Trip-Tiks,* strip maps bound together. In addition, the geographic collection contains a small number of pre-World War II guide books of North America and Europe dating from the late nineteenth century, including the Official Automobile Blue Books, 1909.

4. The maps are not cataloged, but are arranged by year and thereunder alphabetically by title.

A4 Arlington County Library—Central Branch

1 a. *1015 North Quincy Street*
Arlington, Virginia 22201
(703) 527–4777

b. 9:00 A.M.–10:00 P.M. Monday–Thursday
9:00 A.M.–5:00 P.M. Friday–Saturday
1:00 P.M.–9:00 P.M. Sunday

c. The map collection may be examined in the Virginiana Room.

d. Photocopy facilities are available.

e. Lelia B. Saunders, Director
Sara Collins, Virginiana and Local History Librarian.

3 a. The map collection consists of some 600 current county government maps, trails and recreational maps, topographic quadrangles for Virginia, and special purpose maps relating to planning, regional studies, highway systems, zoning, historical sites, and land use, 1607 to the present. Many of the earlier maps are copies or facsimilies. In addition, the Library has a number of county and regional planning, highway, and real estate atlases including a real estate and fire insurance *Plat Book of Arlington County* by the Franklin Survey at a scale of 1 inch to 200 feet (1952) and an atlas, *Aerial/Map Volume of Arlington County, Virginia Including City of Alexandria* (REDI Corporation, 1980), which shows the streets and zoning codes with corresponding aerial photographs.

3 b. The Library has 108 aerial photographs of Arlington County dating from the 1920s to 1982, including a set of 94 aerial photographic negatives (each measuring 21 × 31¾ inches) taken on January 11, 1934 at a scale of 1 inch to 200 feet.

4. The map collection is cataloged. An exhibition brochure entitled *Arlington County in Maps 1608–1975,* describing 25 maps, is available on request.

Army Center of Military History (Army Department)—Library Branch **See entry B5**

Army Corps of Engineers (Defense Department)—Port Facilities Branch **See entry G3**

A5 Army Engineer School (Army Department)—Thayer Engineer Library

1 a. *Building 270*
Fort Belvoir, Virginia 22060
(703) 664-1140 (Reference)

b. 9:00 A.M.–9:00 P.M. Monday–Tuesday
9:00 A.M.–6:00 P.M. Wednesday–Thursday
9:00 A.M.–5:00 P.M. Friday

c. The Library is open to scholars by advance written permission. Interlibrary loan service is available. Some material is restricted to official use only.

d. Reproduction facilities are available (20 page limit).

e. William F. Tuceling, Supervisory Librarian

2. The Library, which serves the staff, faculty, and students of the U.S. Army Engineer School and the Defense Mapping Agency School (G8), focuses on engineering and military art and science. It includes 45,000 books, 110,000 technical manuals, 350 periodicals, a large number of mounted photographs relating to Corps of Engineer activities during World War II, and about 200 maps.

3 a. The map collection consists of general reference maps dating from the 1940s.

3 c. The general book collection contains a number of books and training manuals on the subjects of aerial photography (10), cartography (40), computer graphics (2), geodesy (18), mapping (8), maps (43), military topography (26), photogrammetry (30), surveying (80), and topographical drawing (9). Also of interest are a small collection of rare books containing French, British, and American works on engineering from the late 1700s, including Seth Eastman's *Treatise on Topographical Drawing* (1837); a set of unit histories of topographic companies and battalions for World Wars I and II; an extensive collection of technical reports, including studies prepared by the Army Engineer Topographic Laboratories (E5), the Army Engineer Geodesy, Intelligence and Mapping Unit Research and Development Agency, the Engineer School, the Fairchild Aerial Camera Corporation (1933), and the Defense Technical Information Center (K6); and a comprehensive set of military technical and field manuals issued by the Department of the Army, including manuals on map reproduction, photogrammetry, aerial photographic interpretation, map preparation, surveying, and color reproduction.

3 d. A collection of research papers prepared by students at the U.S. Army Engineer School includes several pertaining to cartography.

3 e. The photographic files contain some 200 prints showing surveying equipment,

military map compilation, production, and distribution during World War II, ground surveying, and aerial photography activities. Most of these photographs were taken by the U.S. Army Signal Corps.

4. A card catalog arranged by author, title, and subject provides access to the general and rare book collections, technical reports, and unit histories. A separate card catalog is available for the Staff Papers. The military and technical field manuals are indexed on microfiche by subject. A typescript subject index is available for the photographic file. A list of the current periodical collection is found in the Library's publication entitled *Periodicals 1985*. The Library maintains a very useful subject card file to all articles that appeared in *The Military Engineer* from 1920 to 1974 (K10). The following subjects are included: maps and mapping (266 titles), surveying (160 titles), and aerial photography (20 titles). *Engineer: The Magazine for Army Engineers*, produced at Fort Belvoir from 1971 to the present (K7), is also indexed. Subjects include: mapping (5 titles), surveying (2 titles), cartography (2 titles), and topography (5 titles). The Library publishes a list of new books on a quarterly basis.

A6 Association of American Railroads—Library, Economics, and Finance Department

1 a. *50 F Street, N.W.*
Washington, D.C. 20001
(202) 639-2334

b. 9:00 A.M.–4:00 P.M. Monday–Friday

c. Open to the public by appointment.

d. Reproduction facilities are available.

e. Joyce W. Koeneman, Supervisor

2–3. The Association of American Railroads Library was established in 1910 as the Bureau of Railway Economics Library. Once considered the finest library of railroad materials in the United States, and one of the largest such collections in the world, the Library has recently been reduced in size but still retains important collections covering all phases of railroading. The Library has more than 30,000 volumes and about 650 separate maps. Many more maps are found in railroad guides and corporate reports.

MAP FILES

Railroad Map File, ca. 1850's–1930's.—ca. 300 maps. Contains photoprocessed and printed maps of individual railroads loosely arranged alphabetically by name of railroad. Includes general railroad maps, promotional and complimentary maps issued by railroads, and maps prepared by the Reconstruction Finance Corporation showing corporate ownership of properties comprising or used by individual railroads.

State Railroad Map File, 1890's–1930's.—50 maps. Consists of state maps issued chiefly by state railroad commissions or the United States General Land Office.

Miscellaneous Map File, 1860's–1920's.—80 maps. Unorganized collection of railroad maps of the United States, including several military maps of United States railroads.

Federal Railroad Administration Map File, 1975–1977.—51 items. Set of printed state maps showing track ownership, principal stations, number of tracks, and county names and boundaries; and volume of printed United States Transportation Zone Maps showing rail systems and information on freight density for Class I railroads.

Railroad Travel and Guide Maps, 1840's–1940's.—140 maps. Contains printed maps of the United States, regions and individual states issued by nineteenth century commercial railroad map publishers (*American Railroad Journal,* Colton, Cram, Dinsmore, Ensign & Thayer, Mitchell, Rand-McNally, *Stiles Quarterly Railroad Register*), maps of individual railroad systems issued by railroad companies (American Railroad System, Union Pacific System, Pennsylvania Railroad System), and railroad maps of individual states issued by state railroad commissions. Also included are a set of large printed maps of North America by Henry F. Perley prepared to accompany Israel Andrews' report on trade and commerce of the British North American Colonies, 1853, and J.C. Fremont's map of the west, 1842.

OFFICIAL RAILROAD GUIDES

An extensive collection of rare railroad guides provides a unique source of nineteenth and twentieth century promotional and travelers page-size and fold-out maps of individual railroad lines and general railway systems at the national and state levels. The major guides include *The Rand-McNally Official Railway Guide and Handbook* (Chicago, 1878-84), 21 volumes; *Travelers Official Railway Guide* (Philadelphia, 1880–1985), 332 volumes; *Appleton's Railway and Stream Navigation Guide for the United States and the Canadas* (New York, 1856–1860), 35 volumes; and the *Great Trans-Continental Pacific Railroad Tourists Guide* (New York, 1870-1880), 12 volumes. Earlier general traveler's guides, often accompanied by large fold-out hand-colored maps, include *The Northern Traveler,* pertaining to New York and New England (New York, 1830-1831), 2 volumes; *Mitchell's Travel Guide Through the United States* (Philadelphia, 1832–1846), 4 volumes; *Tanner's American Traveller* (1834–1846), 5 volumes; *Colton's Traveler and Tourists Route Book* (New York, 1851, 1856), 2 volumes; and travelers' guides of America, the mid-Atlantic states, the Hudson River, and Western New York published by J. Disturnell, (New York, 1837–1864), 9 volumes.

ANNUAL REPORTS AND HISTORIES OF RAILROADS

The Library maintains the most complete file of corporate publications, state reports, and histories (375 linear feet) pertaining to the development of United States railroads, many of which are now defunct. Although not all railroad companies illustrated their reports and histories with maps, a surprisingly large number contain maps. A representative sample includes Charles Varle's *Complete View of Baltimore* (Baltimore, 1833), with a fold-out map of Baltimore; John H. Alexander's *Opinion on a Portion of the Location for the Baltimore and Ohio Railroad* (Baltimore, 1850), with a fold-out profile of the geological structure of southern Illinois and a map of the northern United States showing the routes of the B & O as far west as St. Louis, Missouri; and the Buffalo, Rochester and Pittsburgh Railroad Company's set of annual reports illustrated with fold-out and page-size maps of the railroad system, 1886–1930 (46 volumes).

4. The railroad travel and guide maps, official railroad guide books, and annual reports and histories are cataloged.

A7 Catholic University of America—Mullen Library

1 a. *620 Michigan Avenue, N.E.*
Washington, D.C. 20064
(202) 635-5070 (Reference)

b. General Reading Room
8:00 A.M.–11:45 P.M. Monday–Thursday
8:00 A.M.–8:00 P.M. Friday
9:00 A.M.–8:00 P.M. Saturday
12:00 Noon–11:45 P.M. Sunday

c. Open to the public. Use of the special collections requires permission in advance. Interlibrary loan is available.

d. Photoduplication services are available.

e. Eric L. Ormsby, Director

2–3. The library's general collection of over one million volumes includes about 150 reference atlases (general, historical, statistical, and ecclesiastical), and an equal number of books devoted to general cartographic subjects. The more significant cartographic materials are found among the special collections described below:

RARE BOOKS AND SPECIAL COLLECTIONS
Carolyn T. Lee, Curator (202) 635–5091

1:00 P.M.–5 P.M. Monday–Friday

The Division of Rare Books and Special Collections has custody of some 40,000 books dated prior to 1800, American books published before 1850, and Catholic Americana up to 1889. Less than one half of these books are listed in the library's main card catalog. Maps are found throughout the general rare book collection and two special collections.

The Rare Book Collection contains a small number of atlases as well as early works on geography, history, navigation, and travel that contain maps. Among the most noteworthy are Hartmann Schedel's *Liber Chronicarum* (Nuremberg, 1493), containing early hand-colored woodcut maps of Ptolemy's world view and northwestern Europe; Peter Heylyn's *Cosmographie in Four Books* (London, 1669); Ambrosius T. Macrobius' *In Somnium Scipionis* (Lugduni, 1560), with a world map; and John Ogilby's *Britannia . . . Description of the Principal Roads* (London, 1685). There are also atlases by Petrus Apianus (1584), Jean Chappé d'Auteroche (Paris, 1768), Mathew Carey (Philadelphia, 1801, 1809), Carey and Lea (Philadelphia, 1822), J.H. Colton (New York, 1862), Thomas Jefferys (1775), Gerard Mercator (London, 1635), Abraham Ortelius (1601), and Robert Wilkinson (London, 1817). An extensive collection of church histories contains maps of regions and church lands particularly in Italy, sixteenth to eighteenth centuries. The Rare Book Collection also includes the 1780 edition of the *Jesuit Relations* (23 volumes), which contains many printed maps of North America.

The Foster Stearns Collection on the Sovereign Military Order of St. John of Jerusalem (Knights of Malta) contains 282 items dating from the fifteenth century. A large number of the materials contain maps. These include, for example, statutes–Knights of Malta, *Statvta Hospitalis Hiervsalem* (Rome, 1588); general histories—Christian Von Osterhausen, *Eigentlicher vnd gründlicher Bericht dessen was zu einer volkommenen Erkantnuss vnd wissenschafft dess hochlöblichen ritterlichen Ordens S. Johannis von Jerusalem zu Malta vonnöthen* (Augsburg, 1650), Heinrich Pantaleon, *Militaris ordinis Iohannitarvm* (Basileae, 1581), and René Aubert de Vertot, *The History of the Knights of Malta* with maps by Delisle (London, 1728); general works on Rhodes—Vincenzo Coronelli, *Isola di Rodi geografica-storica, antica e moderna* (Venice, 1688); general works on Malta—Giovanni Francesco Abela, *Della descrittione di Malta (Malta, 1647), Malta Penny Magazine,* numbers 1–120 (1839–1841), and Jean Quintin, *Insvlae Melitae descriptio ex commentariis* (1536); and the siege of Malta, 1565—Giovanni Antonio Viperani, *De bello Militensi historia* (Perusiae, 1567). This collection is described in

Oliver L. Kapsner's *A Catalog of the Foster Stearns Collection* (Catholic University of America Library, 1955).

The Library of Pope Clement XI contains 10,000 books collected by the family of Gian Francesco Albani, a bibliophile who served as Pope Clement XI from 1700 to 1721. The books, which date from 1473 to 1800, and are still maintained in their original calfskin and goatskin bindings, beautifully tooled with gold leaf, relate chiefly to astronomy, law, science, and church histories. Of particular interest is Joannes de Sacrobosco's *Sphaera Opuscula* (Venice, 1485), an early treatise on the celestial sphere with colored woodcuts by Erhard Ratdolt. Maps are also found in some of the books, particularly church and parish histories. For example, three large fold-out topographic maps of the monastery of Farfa in Northern Italy, are found in *Synodus Dioecesana Insgnium Abbatiorum S. Mariae Farfensis, et S. Salvatoris Maioris ord. S. Benedicti* (Rome, 1685). The collection is currently being processed.

THE OLIVEIRA LIMA LIBRARY
Room 7 (202) 635-5059

9:00 A.M.-5:00 P.M. Monday-Friday

The Oliveira Lima Library is devoted to the history and culture of the Portuguese-speaking peoples. It began as the private library of Manoel de Oliveira Lima, a Brazilian diplomat and noted Portuguese historian, who donated his collection of some 16,000 items to The Catholic University of America in 1916. Today the library has more than 50,000 books and manuscripts, making it one of the most important resources for Portuguese-Brazilian material in the United States. The collection includes a small number of maps of the New World by Juan de la Cruz Cano y Olmedilla, printed during the eighteenth century. There is also a manuscript collection, which includes correspondence between Robert Stewart Londonderry, Lord Castlereagh, and Major General Brownriff concerning an ordnance map of the Tagus River, Iberia, 1808, and a letter from Manuel Vieira Tosta Muritiba concerning a survey of the Rio Granade do Sul prior to European settlement, 1855.

A major strength of the library is its collection of early travel books, many of which contain maps. These include voyages and travel to Brazil during the Portuguese period, 1507-1822, and other areas that came under Portuguese influence such as Africa, China, Japan, and India. Of particular interest are Balthazar Telles' *Historia Geral de Ethiopia* (Coimbra, 1660); *Relacion del Viaje que por Orden de Su Magd. y Acverdo del Real Consejo de Indias* (Madrid, 1621), with a rare reconnaissance chart of the Straits of Magellan, engraved by I. de Courbes; Gaspar Barlaeus' *Rerum Per Octennium in Brasilia* (Amsterdam, 1647), with illuminated maps and views of Brazil engraved by Joan Blaeu; and Antonio Francesco Cardim's *Elogios, e Ramalhete de Florres Borrifado com O Sanque dos Religiosos da Companhia de Iesu, a quem as tyrannos do Imperio de Iappao tirarao as vidas por odro de Fé Catholica* (Lisbon, 1650), with a map of Japan. The library also has the most important work on Portuguese discoveries, Manuel Francisco de Barros Santarem's *Essai sur l'histoire de la cosmographie et de la cartographie pendant le moyen-âge*, including the accompanying *Atlas, composé de Mappemondes et de Cartes Hydrographiques et Historiques depuis le XIe Jusqu'au XVIIe Siècle* (Paris, 1849-1852).

The Lima Library's card catalog has been published by G.K. Hall under the title *Catalog of the Oliveira Lima Library The Catholic University of America, Washington, D.C.* (2 volumes, Boston, 1970). An important guide to the early travel books is Ruth E.V. Holmes' *Bibliographical and Historical Description of the Rarest Books in the Oliveira Lima Collection at Catholic University of America* (Washington, 1926).

THE INSTITUTE OF CHRISTIAN ORIENTAL RESEARCH (ICOR) LIBRARY
Room 18
Monica J. Blanchard, Librarian (202) 635-5083

9:00 A.M.-5:00 P.M. Monday-Friday

The nucleus of the present ICOR collection is the private library of Msgr. Henry Hyvernat (1858-1941), which numbers some 20,000 volumes. He is best known for his work in the field of Coptic studies, the language and literature of Christian Egypt. He came to Washington in 1889 from his native France as part of the original faculty of The Catholic University of America. In 1895 he founded the Department of Semitic and Egyptian Languages and Literatures. In 1903, largely due to his efforts, the *Corpus Scriptorum Christianorum Orientalium (C.S.C.O.)* was established to make available to the scholarly world the works of the early Syriac, Arabic, Coptic, Ethiopic, Armenian and Georgian Christian writers. To date, the *C.S.C.O.* has published over 450 volumes of texts, translations and studies. In 1931 Hyvernat laid plans for what is now the Institute of Christian Oriental Research (ICOR). ICOR serves as an auxiliary to the Semitics department, and it supports the work of the *C.S.C.O.*, which today is jointly sponsored by The Catholic University in Washington and the Catholic University in Louvain. Hyvernat left his personal library to ICOR. This library, supplemented by later acquisitions, now includes some 32,000 volumes. The bulk of the collection deals with ancient Near Eastern philology and history, and with the languages, literature and history of the Christian Near East.

Of interest is a collection of some 1,000 travel books from the sixteenth to twentieth centuries (travel guides, memoirs, narratives of trips and expeditions), which are concerned with the Near East, Central Asia, and to a lesser extent, India and the Far East. They include many maps. The Holy Land is especially well represented.

There is a small uncataloged collection of some 50 topographical, geological and historical maps of Palestine, Jordan, Israel and the Levant prepared by the Department of Lands & Survey of Jordan (1948-1957); the Survey of Palestine (1942-1947); the Survey of Israel (1955); Institut géographique national, Paris (1945); Bureau topographique des troupes françaises du Levant (1935); and the National Geographic Society (1938-1956).

The collection also contains several atlases showing overseas missions, 1890-1915; a raised relief model of Jerusalem constructed by Charles Muret (Paris, 1885); and a topographic atlas issued as part of the 19-volume *Description de l'Egypte*, prepared at the request of Napoleon following the French Army expedition to Egypt, 1798-1799 (Paris, 1828).

4. A dictionary catalog, located on the second floor, provides access to the general collection and about half of the Rare Books Collection.

Census Bureau—Field Operations—Geography Division **See entry G5, Section 3**

A8 Census Bureau Library (Commerce Department)

1 a. *Room 2450*
Federal Office Building Nunber 3
Suitland, Maryland
Mailing Address: Washington, D.C. 20233
(301) 763-5040
(301) 763-5042 (Reference)

b. 8:00 A.M.–5:00 P.M. Monday–Friday

c. Open to qualified researchers. Interlibrary loan service is available.

d. Photocopy service is available.

e. Betty Baxtresser, Librarian.

2. The Bureau of the Census Library contains 250,000 volumes and 3,200 serials devoted chiefly to demography, economics, business, agriculture, foreign trade, and statistical and survey methodology, including 109 atlases. About 85 percent of the holdings are United States and foreign government documents (Federal, state, and local).

3 a. In addition to general world atlases dating from 1855, the library contains an incomplete set of statistical atlases of the United States published by the Census Bureau. The Census Collection includes a record set of most of the publications issued by the Census Bureau and its predecessor organization beginning in 1790. Many of the more recent publications contain maps.

3 c. About 400 titles relate directly to surveying and mapping. Reflecting a major interest of the Census Bureau, the Electronic Data Processing Collection contains publications on all aspects of computer processing, including computer graphics (88 titles).

3 d. A special collection of uncataloged papers presented by former Census staff members at professional conferences, many of which have never been published, include the works of several persons associated with the Bureau's Geography Division: Clarence Edmund Batschelet, various aspects of cartographic work in the Census Bureau, 1927–1960 (10 items); George Farnsworth, map encoding, 1967–1968 (2 items); William Thomas Fay, computer based geographic coding for the 1970 census, 1966–1971 (5 items); Robert C. Klove, thematic and statistical cartography, 1952–1973 (15 items); and Morton Allan Meyer, DIME Files and statistical mapping, 1958–1973 (9 items).

4. A card catalog provides access to the periodical and book collections by subject. *Library Notes* lists recent acquisitions on a monthly basis. The Library also has access to over 100 data bases including Lockheed's DIALOG Information Retrieval Service (D3) and Systems Development Corporations Orbit Search Service (D10), but service is limited to Census Bureau employees.

A9 Center for Defense Information Library

1 a. *1500 Massachusetts Avenue, N.W.*
Washington, D.C. 20005
(202) 862-0700

b. 9:00 A.M.–5:00 P.M. Monday–Friday

c. Open to the public.

e. Glenn Baker, Research Librarian

2. The Center's library includes some 300 recent maps of the world, published chiefly by the Central Intelligence Agency, and about 40 nautical charts relating to the Panama Canal Zone.

Defense Mapping Agency (DMA)—Scientific Data Department **See entry G8**

Engineer Topographic Laboratories (ETL) (Army Corps of Engineers)—Scientific and Technical Information Center **See entry E5, section 3**

A10 Fairfax City Regional Library—Virginiana Collection

1 a. *3915 Chain Bridge Road*
Fairfax, Virginia 22030
(703) 691-2123

b. 9:00 A.M.–9:00 P.M. Monday–Thursday
9:00 A.M.–6:00 P.M. Friday
9:00 A.M.–5:00 P.M. Saturday
1:00 P.M.–5:00 P.M. Sunday

c. Open to the public. Interlibrary loan service available.

d. Photocopies available.

e. Suzanne Levy, Virginiana Room Librarian

3 a. The Virginiana Collection at the Fairfax City Regional Library holds the largest collection of materials relating to Virginia in the Northern Virginia area. This collection includes some 2,800 maps and atlases organized in three collections: (1) a U.S. Geological Survey quadrangle collection covering primarily the northern half of the state and central southside Virginia, 1940s–1960s; (2) a general collection containing printed and photoprocessed historical maps, planning maps, census maps, land use maps, post office route maps, park and recreation maps and military maps pertaining to the Civil War, 1600–1985; and (3) a small number of recent county and state atlases relating to zoning, real property identification, water and sewer lines, and highways. Much of the focus of the general collection is on Fairfax County.

3 b. The Photographic Archives Collection contains about 230 aerial photographic prints. These include some 200 views of Route 66 taken for the Economic Development Authority of Fairfax County during the late 1960s and early 1970s. There are also miscellaneous oblique aerial views of major cities, shopping centers, airports, and business districts within Fairfax County, 1936–1977.

4. A subject card file provides access to the general map collection, which is classified and arranged chronologically. The Economic Development Authority aerial photographs are not identified; the remaining aerial photographs are described in a published catalog, *Photographic Archives of Fairfax County, Virginia* (1981).

A11 Folger Shakespeare Library

1 a. *201 East Capitol Street, S.E.*
Washington, D.C. 20003
(202) 544-4600

b. 8:45 A.M.–4:45 P.M. Monday–Friday
8:45 A.M.–Noon; 1:00 P.M.–4:30 P.M. Saturday

c. Open to serious researchers. Because staff time is limited, advance notice is strongly recommended. Readers must register. Materials are not loaned. Tea is served each afternoon at 3:00 P.M. in the Tea Room.

d. A coin-operated copier is available for copying modern works; copies of rare materials are subject to restrictions.

e. Werner Gundersheimer, Director
Nati Krivatsy, Reference Librarian
Laetitia Yeandle, Curator of Manuscripts

2. The Folger Shakespeare Library, established in 1932 as an independent research institution, has one of the world's most comprehensive collections for the study of Elizabethan England and the Renaissance, including some 550 cartographic items.

3 a. The map collection contains some 350 single-sheet printed maps principally of England and especially localities associated with Shakespeare, including Warwickshire, Stratford-Upon-Avon, and London, 1485–1969. Some of the maps are in the form of photographic copies and facsimilies. There are also a number of bird's eye views of London by Rudolf Agas, Claus J. Visscher, Antonie van der Wijngaerde, and others, dating from 1560.

Almost 40 printed atlases are found among the Rare Book Collection, which contains books printed before 1801. These include: Joan Blaeu, 1704; Willem Janszoon Blaeu, 1631–1663 (5 items); Braun and Hogenberg, 1606; Petrus Bertius, 1618–1619; Henri A. Chatelain, 1739; James Knapton, 1728; Herman Moll, 1701–1726 (3 items); Jonas Moore, 1681; Abraham Ortelius, 1584–1655 (8 items), including a 1606 edition from the former collection of Sir Thomas Phillipps; Claudius Ptolemy, 1546–1598 (7 items); Heinrich Scherer, 1702; John Seller, 1679, 1721; John Speed, 1614–1631 (5 items); Edward Wells, 1701; and Robert White, 1787. In addition, there are almost 30 historical, national, and nautical atlases printed during the nineteenth and twentieth centuries on the open shelves in the reading room.

3 c. The Rare Book Collection also contains pertinent map-related literature covering several fields. The following authors are represented.

Geography and Cosmography—Joannes Leo Africanus, 1600; Richard Arnold, 1535; Pierre d'Avity, 1638; Martin Borrhaus, 1551; Nathaniel Carpenter, 1635; Samuel Clarke, 1671; Abraham Farissol, 1691; Nicolas de Fer, 1714 ?; Georg Henisch, 1591; Peter Heylyn, 1652; Johannes Honter, 1578; al-Idrisi, 1619; Aubert LeMire, 1620; Sebastian Munster, 1628; Denis Petau, 1659; William Petty, 1720; Pope Pius II, 1501;

Jacques Robbe, 1688; Adrianus Romanus, 1595; Giuseppe Rosaccio, 1595; John Senex, 1721; Robert Stafford, 1634; Bernhard Varen, 1681; and Joachim von Watt, 1548.

Geographical Dictionaries—Giovanni Boccaccio, 1520; *Le dictionaire géographique*, 1694; Zacharias Lilius, 1551; Adam Littleton, 1678; Elio Antonio de Nebrija; Raffaello Savonarola; Stephanus of Byzantium, 1521; and John Thorie, 1601.

Globes—Willem J. Blaeu, 1663; Pierre Bourdin, 1661; Vincenzo Coronelli, 1693, 1701; Isaac Habrecht, 1666; John Harris, 1719; Richard Holland, 1684; Joseph Moxon, 1674; Albert Tanner, 1620; and Edward Wright, 1613.

Maps are also found among the rare voyage and travel books (over 300 items), military treatises, and history books. Only a few of these maps are cataloged, for example, William Alexander Stirling's *The Mapp and Description of New England* (1630).

3 d. Three special collections contain maps and related materials.

The Duke of Northumberland Map Collection includes an incomplete set of the first series, British Ordnance Survey maps, some hand-colored, 1805–1876 (51 sheets); and British Admiralty charts and commercial maps of England, Ireland, London, Scotland, and Wales, 1850–1880. A shelf list is available.

The Halliwell-Phillipps Collection consists of scrapbooks containing maps, guidebooks, and other materials relating to Shakespeare. The maps consist chiefly of hand-colored reproductions and printed maps of city plans, bird's eye views, and road maps of places associated with Shakespeare, 1593–1801 (96 maps). It includes a rare original manuscript map of Middlesex by John Norden, 1593. Part of this collection is described in Ernest E. Baker (ed.) *A Calendar of the Shakespearean Rarities, Drawings and Engravings Formerly Preserved at Hollingsburg Copse* (1891).

The Manuscript Collections include a receipt for Wenceslaus Hollar's map of London and Westminster, 1660; map of Goodman's Fields and its environs, London, ca. 1813; map of Stratford-Upon-Avon by Robert Treswell, 1599; map of Horsham, Norfolk, from the papers of the Hobart family, ca. 1550; and a manuscript fragment of a Spanish map relating to the Magellan Expedition.

4. Printed maps and atlases are accessed through the Catalog of Printed Books; manuscript maps through the Catalog of Manuscripts. Both are dictionary catalogs, with author, title, and subject entries interfiled in alphabetical order. A separate shelf-list catalog for printed single sheet maps is maintained by the Processing Department. Both catalogs have been published by G.K. Hall: *Catalog of Printed Books of the Folger Shakespeare Library*, 1970–1981 (28 volumes with 5 volume supplement) and *Catalog of Manuscripts of the Folger Shakespeare Library*, 1971 (3 volumes). The geographic literature and atlases printed in English prior to 1640 are listed in the *Short-Title Catalogue of Books Printed in England, Scotland, and Ireland and of English Books Printed Abroad 1475–1640*, compiled by A.W. Pollard and G.R. Redgrave, 2 volumes (London, 1926, revised 1976). A reader's guide, describing the collections, the catalog, reading room regulations, and reader services, is available from the Folger Library.

Forest Service (FS)—Aerial Photography Field Office **See entry G13, Section 3**

Forest Service (FS)—Maps and Atlas Branch **See entry G13, Section 3**

Geological Survey (USGS) (Interior Department)—Geographic Names Library See entry G14

A12 Geological Survey Library (Interior Department)

1 a. *National Center, Fourth Floor*
12201 Sunrise Valley Drive
Reston, Virginia 22092
(703) 860–6671 (Reference)

b. 7:45 A.M.–4:15 P.M. Monday–Friday

c. Open to public. Shuttle service is provided daily from the main Interior Department in Washington, D.C. for government employees only. Interlibrary loans available.

d. Photocopying facilities for books available in the Library. Reproductions of large maps, however, can be obtained only from local commercial firms for rather large fees.

e. Elizabeth Yeates, Chief Librarian
Carol Messick, Acting Chief, Reference

2. One of the premier earth science libraries in the world, the Geological Survey Library at Reston and its three branch libraries in Denver, Colorado; Menlo Park, California; and Flagstaff, Arizona contain 385,000 maps; more than one million monographs, serials, and government publications, including 6370 that deal directly with surveying and mapping; 15,600 geological field survey notebooks and manuscripts; and 250,000 photographic prints, transparencies, and negatives. Maps are maintained in Reston, Denver, and Menlo Park. About 10,000 new maps are added to the Reston map collection each year.

3 a. The map collection consists of special purpose maps dating from the 1840s. These include chiefly geological maps followed by tectonic maps, soil maps, mineral resource maps (including oil and gas), groundwater maps, and geophysical maps (gravity, magnetic). Coverage is comprehensive. Through its worldwide exchange programs with some 1800 official agencies, the Library attempts to collect all geoscience maps produced at national, state or province, and city levels. Maps produced by commercial publishers are purchased. For coverage of foreign areas, the researcher should consult the regional *Scholars Guides*.

The map collection also contains important USGS series including unpublished maps in the Open-File Reports, 1938 to date (5040 titles); Miscellaneous Investigations Series maps comprising a wide variety of formats and subject matter, including some 7.5 minute quadrangle photogeologic maps which show geology as interpreted from aerial photographs, 1954 to date (1399 titles); and very limited edition Miscellaneous Field Studies maps which show geology in relation to specific mining or mineral-deposit problems, general geology, environmental studies, and mineral resource potential, 1942 to date (1499 titles).

Maps of the United States, Canada, World, oceans, and solar systems are housed in the Reston Library by area, subject, scale, and date; maps of other areas are stored in the Survey's Herndon, Virginia warehouse. Scholars desiring maps of foreign areas, therefore, should request them in advance. Arrangements may also be made with a reference librarian to visit the map collection at Herndon on Tuesday and Thursday mornings. In addition to geoscience maps, the Library also maintains in Herndon a set of topographic quadrangle maps published by the Survey, which includes copies of all reprintings.

3 c. The book collection has important holdings relating to mapping and surveying. It is particularly strong in works pertaining to aerial photography and remote sensing imagery, reflecting the Surveys pioneering work in these areas. It also maintains nearly complete sets of the federal and state geological survey publications, which contain many topograhic and geological maps. These include rare works by noted nineteenth century geologists who made early contributions to geological mapping in the United States, such as David Dale Owen and William Barton Rogers. Some oversize maps, notably oil and gas maps, have been removed from their respective reports and journals and transferred to the map collection.

The subject distribution of surveying and mapping holdings are listed below.

Subject	*Number of Titles*
Aerial Photography	765
Aerial Surveys	205
Base Measuring	14
Cartography	965
Computer Graphics	78
Coordinates	20
Distance Measurements & Tables	23
Exploration	70
Gazetteers	20
Geodesy	960
Geographic Names	490
Geographic Positions	40
Geological Mapping/Surveying	210
Hydrographic Charting/Surveying	105
Latitude Determination	18
Leveling	100
Longitude	10
Maps & Mapping	700
Photogrammetry	225
Photographic Interpretation	200
Projections	11
Remote Sensing	910
Surveying	450
Topographic Mapping/Surveying	220
Triangulation	105

A small rare book collection includes early American national and state atlases by Jefferys (1776), Tanner (1823), F.W. Beers (Hudson River Valley, Indiana, 1876), O.W. Walker (Massachusetts, 1891), Walling (Massachusetts, 1871; Pennsylvania, 1872), Andreas (Minnesota, 1874), and Hurd (Connecticut, 1893). There is also a three-volume manuscript, *Map Record,* recording the engraving and printing history of individual early USGS quadrangle sheets.

The USGS Library also maintains an extensive translation file (55 cubic feet) of foreign technical reports, symposium papers, and journal articles translated into English. Although most of the translations relate to geochemistry, mineralogy, and paleontology, an incomplete perusal of the file (access is by author, no subject access is available) revealed a number of items relating to surveying and mapping. The following titles suggest the type of translations that are found in this file: Arne Bjerhammar, "Camel

Caravans and Satellites Mapped Out the Shape of the Earth" (Sweden, 1977); K. Felle and W. Rösel, "Automatic Plotting of Contours in the Course of Orthophoto Production" (Germany, 1969); A. Thomas, "Reflections on Geotechnical Mapping" (France, 1970); and V.A. Obruchev and A.P. Gerasimov, "Geological Map of the Lena Gold District - Description of Map-Sheets VI-1 and VI-2" (Russia, 1929).

3 d. The Field Records Library in Denver (Box 25046, Federal Center, Denver, CO 80225; telephone no. 303/236–1000) has custody of unpublished geologists' field notes which may contain field sketches and aerial photographs. These are not available through interlibrary loan and some are restricted due to proprietary information.

3 e. The Photographic Library is also in Denver (same address; telephone no. 303/236–1010). It contains photographs of the Hayden, King, Powell, and Wheeler surveys of the West, 1867–1879, the Canadian-Alaskan Boundary Survey, and other nineteenth century geological and geographical mapping expeditions. Also there are photographs of Survey personnel performing various surveying and mapping activities. A few oblique aerial photographs are included in this collection. The photographs are indexed by subject and geographic area. A selection of these photographs appears in *Images of the U.S. Geological Survey* (1983), available from the Survey's Publications Distribution Branch.

4. A card catalog provides access to the map collection by area and then subject for maps acquired prior to 1977, and by author, title, or subject for maps cataloged after 1977. A card catalog is also available for books and journals. One is arranged by author and title, the other by subject. The subject card file can be used to locate maps accompanying texts. These may be listed under the heading "Maps" or under the subject. For example, the subject heading "Geomorphology—Maps" includes sixteen titles for geomorphological maps as well as books devoted to the subject of geomorphological maps. The Library's card catalog has been printed by G.K. Hall in 46 volumes. Printed brochures describe the Library and the Photographic Library.

The Library's new online computerized catalog also contains the records of over 95,000 books and journals as well as maps cataloged since 1977. New acquisitions are being added on a regular basis. About 15 percent of the map collection is available through the Library's online computerized catalog.

The USGS Library maintains two major subject indexes which contain references to surveying, mapping and aerial photography. These are the American Geological Institute's *Bibliography and Index of Geology* (1919 to date), which is based on the collection of the USGS Library (J2), and *The Engineering Index* (1928 to date). Both indexes are also available as computerized data bases, known as GEOREF and COMPENDEX, respectively, through DIALOG Information Retrieval Service (D3). The Survey Library makes database searches for Survey employees only.

A13 George Mason University—Fenwick Library

1 a. *George Mason University*
4400 University Drive
Fairfax, Virginia 22030
(703) 323–2391 (Information)

b. 7:30 A.M.–12 Midnight — Monday–Thursday
7:30 A.M.–6:00 P.M. — Friday
9:00 A.M.–8:00 P.M. — Saturday
1:00 P.M.–12 Midnight — Sunday

Hours vary during the summer, intersessions, and holidays. The Special Collections are open 8:30 A.M.–5:00 P.M. Monday–Friday.

c. Open to the general public. Some materials may be borrowed through interlibrary loan.

d. Photocopy machines are located in the library's main lobby area and some departments.

e. Department heads are listed below.

3 a. Some 17,000 maps are found in the collection. They are mostly United States government maps of recent origin acquired through the Federal depository program.

SPECIAL COLLECTIONS AND ARCHIVES
Second Floor, Wing C
Ruth Kerns, Librarian
(703) 323–2251

8:30 A.M.–5:00 P.M. Monday–Friday

The Special Collections and Archives has custody of the C. Harrison Mann Map Collection which consists of 93 rare printed maps and atlases relating chiefly to Virginia but also including Washington, D.C., Maryland, North America, England, and various Caribbean islands. The maps date from 1585 to 1974. The collection also includes a manuscript map on vellum of the Darien Coast from a Scottish expedition dated about 1696. Typed shelf lists of both the map and atlas collections are available.

GOVERNMENT DOCUMENTS COLLECTION
Chris Kiser, Coordinator
(703) 323–2877
(703) 323–2392 (Service)

The Government Documents Collection has some 10,000 maps, most of which are United States Geological Survey quadrangles arranged by state, scale, and quadrangle name, dating from the 1950s to the present. The collection also contains a small number of recently printed maps arranged according to area or subject: counties, U.S. States, cities, countries, world regions, historical world, oceans, Antarctica, land use, aeronautical, historic ports, and transportation. The maps are not cataloged.

In addition, the Government Documents Collection contains 150 thematic maps of various countries throughout the world published by the Central Intelligence Agency (G6) and some 6,800 maps and atlases issued by the Census Bureau (G5). The latter includes atlases of United States urban areas compiled during the 1970s, thematic maps of the United States, an incomplete set of block statistics maps prepared for the 1980 census (6,400 sheets) and tract maps for the 1980 census (320 sheets). All of these maps are arranged numerically by Superintendent of Document's classification numbers.

A14 George Washington University Library—Gelman Library

1 a. *2130 H Street, N.W.*
Washington, D.C. 20052
(202) 676–6558

b. 8:30 A.M.–Midnight Monday–Friday
10:00 A.M.–Midnight Saturday and Sunday

Special Collections Division
9:00 A.M.–5:00 P.M. Monday–Friday
Noon–5:00 P.M. Saturday

These hours are for the Fall/Spring academic calendar only. Scholars planning to examine the collections at other times should contact the information office for a schedule of the hours.

c. Open to scholars but those not affiliated with a Washington Consortium library must present proper identification and register. Interlibrary loan services of maps and rare materials will be considered and evaluated in terms of their physical condition.

d. Coin-operated photocopiers are located on the first floor and in the basement.

e. Sharon Rogers, University Librarian

2. The Gelman Library houses some 900,000 volumes, including nearly 1,000 devoted to cartographic activities. The Library also maintains a map library, totaling about 15,600 maps and 100 atlases in support of the University's major programs in international relations and urban and regional planning. A small number of maps and related works are also found in the Special Collections Division.

3 a. The Reference Department atlas and map collection (Barbara Maxwell, Government Documents Section, Reference Librarian, 202/676–6047) is located on the main floor of the Library. The atlas collection, numbering about 100 volumes, dates from 1890. Census, historical, school, and world atlases predominate.

The map collection consists primarily of maps produced by Federal mapping agencies and deposited through the Federal government's depository map program. It contains about 15,600 maps, only a few of which were published before 1900. The collection includes the following series:

UNITED STATES GEOLOGICAL SURVEY (USGS) TOPOGRAPHIC QUADRANGLE MAPS (42 DRAWERS).—coverage for most of the northeastern, mid-Atlantic, and southeastern states as well as California, Puerto Rico, and the Virgin Islands.

DEFENSE MAPPING AGENCY AND ITS PREDECESSOR, THE ARMY MAP SERVICE (22 DRAWERS).—worldwide coverage with special emphasis on British Commonwealth countries and World War II strategic areas.

CENSUS BUREAU.—urban atlas tract data for standard metropolitan statistical areas (40 folios) and block statistics maps (70 linear feet).

NATIONAL GEOGRAPHIC (2 DRAWERS).—worldwide coverage, general reference maps.

MISCELLANEOUS (6 DRAWERS).—among the most interesting are a provisional malaria map of East Africa published by the East Africa Survey Group, British Directorate of Military Survey, 1943 (3 sheets); *Carta General de Archipielago Filipino* (Madrid, 1875), overprinted in English by the United States War Department's Military Intelligence Division, Adjutant General's Office, to show military telegraph lines, cable lines, and military departments, 1900; a map of the war in Turkey published by the United States Army Corps of Engineers, 1897; a series of topographic maps of Central America at 1:250,000 issued by the Geographic Branch, Military Intelligence Division, United States Army General Staff, 1933–1940 (27 sheets); a series of air navigation maps of South America at 1:500,000 published by the War Department Map Collection, Office of the Chief of Engineers, 1941–1942 (32 sheets); and mineral and gas maps (2 drawers).

The Special Collections Division map collection (William B. Keller, Head, Special Collections 202/676–7549) consists of approximately 250 printed maps pertaining chiefly to Washington, D.C. and the surrounding region, 1630 to the present. The collection also includes a large manuscript plat of the Port Royal tract, which now encompasses much of the George Washington University campus, superimposed on a plan of the City of Washington, June 8, 1796 by James R. Dermott. The locations of some lots acquired by George Washington University were added in pencil, probably during the 1950's. Among the most significant printed maps are Willem J. Blaeu's *Nova Virginiae Tabula,* 1630, Joshua Fry and Peter Jefferson's map of Virginia, 1775, several versions of Andrew Ellicott's plan of Washington, D.C. 1793, and J. Enthoffer's map of the City of Washington showing the progress of buildings up to 1873. The Division also has custody of several early atlases and geographical works containing maps, including Thomas Salmon, *The Modern Gazetteer* (London, 1782), Jedediah Morse, *The American Universal Geography* (Boston, 1819), S. Augustus Mitchell, *Ancient Atlas* (Philadelphia, 1856), and W. and R. Chambers, *Atlas to Accompany Chambers Encyclopaedia* (Philadelphia, 1862).

3 c. The following tabulation illustrates the general coverage of cartographic literature in the general collections:

Aerial Photography	60
Cartography	170
Computer Graphics	150
Exploration	80
Gazetteers	38
Geodesy	40
Latitude	3
Longitude	4
Maps and Mapping	110
Photogrammetry	14
Remote Sensing	60
Surveying	75

The Special Collections Division contains a few early works devoted to globe use by George Adams (London, 1790), John Harris (London, 1751), Robert Morton (London, 1702), and James Wallace (New York, 1812), and surveying, including César François Cassini de Thury's *La Méridienne de l'observatoire royal de Paris* (Paris, 1744).

3 d. The Lloyd Wright Collection in the Special Collections Division includes two manuscript items relating to the surveying and mapping work of Thomas Freeman in Virginia and the City of Washington, 1794.

The George Washington University collection of theses, which is also maintained by the Special Collections Division, includes the following relevant works listed by the name of the department that supervised the theses: American Studies–Anne Ellis, "James Cook and George Vancouver: A Comparative Study of Two Supplemental Cartographers" (M.A. Thesis, 1982); Business Administration–Dale D. Bajema, "Pricing Policy Considerations for Topographical Maps Produced by the Federal Government" (M.A. Thesis, 1978), and Thomas Joseph Vogel, "Development of a Management Information System for Maps and Chart Source Data Base Operations (M.B.A. Thesis, 1979); Geography and Regional Science–Richard A. West, "A Cartographic Guide for the Representation of International Boundaries in the Arabian Peninsula" (M.A. Thesis, 1969); Geology–Myrtle Thom, "Geomorphic and Structural Studies in Hispaniola Using Landsat, Skylab, and Low-Altitude Aerial Photography" (M.A. Thesis, 1976), Herbert W. Blodget, "Lithology Mapping of Crystalline Shield Test Sites in Western Saudi Arabia Using Computer-Manipulated Multispectral Satellite Data" (PhD. Thesis, 1977), and George A. Rabchevsky, "The Feasibility of Detecting Subsurface Coal Fires in Wyoming and Montana from the Ground, on Aerial Photography, and on Satellite Imagery" (PhD. Thesis, 1972).

4. Atlases are listed in the dictionary catalogs in the Reference Department and the Special Collections Division. The Reference Department map collection is not cataloged, but access to the collection, which is generally arranged by authority, series, and title, is furnished by the reference librarian. The Special Collections Division maintains a main catalog, organized by author, title, and subject, and separate catalogs for maps (incomplete), Washington, D.C., and theses.

A15 House of Representatives Library

1 a. *Cannon House Office Building, B-18*
New Jersey and Independence Avenue, S.E.
Washington, D.C. 20515
(202) 225–0462/0463

b. 9:00 A.M.–5:30 P.M. Monday–Friday

c. Open to the general public.

d. Photoreproduction services are not provided.

e. E. Raymond Lewis, Librarian.

2–3. The Library, which dates from 1792, serves as a legal and legislative reference resource to Congressional members and committees. It holds more than 100,000 volumes, consisting of complete sets of House and Senate Reports, the Congressional Record, published House and Joint Committee Hearings, and Statutes at Large. It also has custody of two rare bound volumes of maps, charts, and surveys published by Congress between 1820 and 1843. The volumes include national and state boundary maps, harbor and coastal charts, route maps, and cadastral plats of areas in the Eastern United States. Most of the maps were prepared under the direction of United States Army Corps of Topographical Engineers, the United States Board of Navy Commissioners, the United States Coast Survey, and the Surveyor General's Office.

4. The collections are not cataloged.

A16 Howard University—Architecture and Planning Library

1 a. *6th Street and Howard Place*
Washington, D.C. 20059
(202) 636–7773/7774

b. 8:30 A.M.–8:00 P.M. Monday–Thursday
8:30 A.M.–5:00 P.M. Friday
1:00 P.M.–5:00 P.M. Saturday

c. Open to the public.

d. Duplication processes available.

e. Mod Mekkawi, Librarian

3 a. The Architectural and Planning Library has a collection of master plans of Washington, D.C. and the metropolitan area (300 items), and a small number of separate maps and atlases relating to Washington, D.C.

A17 Howard University—Moorland-Spingarn Research Center

1 a. *Founders Library*
500 Howard Place, N.W.
Washington, D.C. 20059
(202) 636–7239/7240

b. Academic Year
7:00 A.M.–8:00 P.M. Monday–Thursday
9:00 A.M.–5:00 P.M. Friday and Saturday

Summer Hours
9:00 A.M.–5:00 P.M. Monday–Friday

c. Open to the public, but outside researchers must obtain a visitor research card.

e. Clifford L. Muse, Acting Director

2. The Moorland-Spingarn Research Center Library is the major world repository for the study of Afro-America, Pan-Africanism, and the African diaspora. It contains some 90,000 volumes, 400 collections of personal papers and organized archives, and approximately 100 maps.

3 a. The Library Division (James Johnson, Chief Librarian, 202/636–7260) contains some 60 printed and photocopy maps chiefly of Africa, Argentina, Brazil, the Caribbean, Mexico, and the United States. In addition to general location maps, there are maps showing "Americans of Negro Lineage" (1946), distribution of slaves in the southern states (n.d.), tribes of Africa, population of Kenya (1962), native population of Uganda and Kenya (1936), and historical maps of the Caribbean, 1823–1866 (1980).

The Manuscript Division (Thomas C. Battle, Curator, 202/636–7480) contains some 40 maps primarily of Africa, the West Indies, and the United States, 1635–1972. These include several early maps of the Congo, Ethiopia, and other parts of Africa by Pieter van der Aa, Blaeu, Hondius, and De L'Isle, 1635–1780; a map of the West Indies engraved by J. Cary, 1781; maps of the West Indies by J. Stockdale, 1794–1806; a folklore map of Norway, painted by Jorleif Uthaug with text by Pat Shaw Iverson (1962), a black woman who studied in Norway; a map of underground slave routes to Canada, drawn by W.H. Siebert, 1896; and geological maps of Africa, compiled by the Association of African Geological Surveys.

3 c. The book collection in the Library Division is also a good source of maps on Africa, the West Indies, South America, and the American South. Examples of the types of books containing significant maps include Jehudi Ashumn, *History of the American Colony in Liberia* (Washington City, 1826); James Bruce, *Travels to Discover the Source of the Nile* (Edinburgh, 1813); John Lewis Burckhardt, *Travels in Nubia* (London, 1822); John Campbell, *Travels in South Africa* (Andover, Massachusetts, 1816); Mathew Carey, *Letters on the Colonization Society* (Philadelphia, 1838); and *The Legion of Liberty! and the Force of Truth* (American Anti-Slavery Society, 1843).

4. A list of the maps in the Library and Manuscript Divisions is available on request. A card catalog provides access to the book collections. Published guides include *Dictionary Catalog of the Arthur B. Spingarn Collection of Negro Authors,* 2 volumes (Boston: G.K. Hall & Co., 1970), and *Dictionary Catalog of the Jesse E. Moorland Collection of Negro Life and History,* 9 volumes (Boston: G.K. Hall & Co., 1970), with a 3-volume supplement (1977).

A18 Inter-American Development Bank—Felipe Herrera Library

1 a. *1300 New York Avenue.*
Washington, D.C. 20577
(202) 634-8388

b. 9:00 A.M.–5:30 P.M. Monday–Friday

c. Open to the public.

e. Fernando Arbelaez, Chief of the Library

2–3. The Felipe Herrera Library has 75,000 volumes, periodicals, and newspapers pertaining chiefly to the finances and economics of Latin America and the Caribbean countries. There are also some 500 general, railroad, and thematic maps of Central America, the Caribbean, Argentina, Bolivia, Brazil, Chile, Columbia, Ecuador, Mexico, Paraguay, Uruguay, and Venezuela.

A19 Interior Department—Natural Resources Library

1 a. *18th and C Streets, N.W.*
Washington, D.C. 20240
(202) 343-5815 (Reference)
(202) 343-3896 (Computer Search Service)

b. 7:45 A.M.–5:00 P.M. Monday–Friday

c. Open to the public. Interlibrary loan service is available through OCLC and normal library channels.

d. Photocopies are provided free of charge for up to 20 pages. The researcher must provide his own paper for more than 20 pages.

e. Phillip M. Haymond, Chief

2. The Natural Resources Library contains more than 1,000,000 volumes (including 100 atlases), 21,000 serial titles, 250,000 microfiche and 8,000 microfilm reels. It serves the Fish and Wildlife Service, National Park Service, Bureau of Mines, Bureau of Indian Affairs, Bureau of Land Management, and the Bureau of Reclamation. The focus of the collection is on the scientific and engineering aspects of mining and minerals; oil, gas, and energy; land reclamation; preservation of scenic and historic sites; fish and wildlife management; and Indian lands of the United States and its territories.

3 a. The atlas collection contains a number of volumes relating to fishing grounds.

3 c. The Library maintains one copy of all publications issued by the Bureaus cited above. These should be requested in advance, however, since part of this collection is stored in another facility. Included are rare copies of map compilation manuals prepared by the Bureau of Indian Affairs, National Park Service, and the U.S. National Resources Committee (1936). A microfiche collection of more than 20,000 doctoral dissertations contains a number of dissertations relating to computer graphics and cartography. The Library also contains an incomplete set of U.S. Geological Survey Open-File Reports (G14) and selected technical reports from the National Technical Information Service (K12).

The subject distribution of surveying and mapping literature is listed below:

Subject	*Number of Titles*
Aerial Photography	200
Aerial Surveys	12
Cartography	114
Computer Graphics	50
Exploration	50
Gazetteers	30
Geodesy	40
Geological Mapping/Surveying	12
Maps & Mapping	277
Photogrammetry	60
Photographic Interpretation	55
Remote Sensing	400
Surveying	35

4. A card catalog file is arranged by author, title and subject, the latter according to Library of Congress classification headings. Access is also provided by the published *Dictionary Catalog of the Departmental Library*, 37 vols. (G.K. Hall, 1967), and 4 supplements (1969–1975).

A20 Library of Congress (LC)

1 a. *Thomas Jefferson Building*
10 First Street, S.E.

John Adams Building
110 Second Street, S.E.

James Madison Building
101 Independence Avenue, S.E.

Mail:
Washington, D.C. 20540

(202) 287-5000 Information

b. Hours for individual reading rooms and Divisions are listed below. They are closed on New Year's Day, Martin Luther King's Birthday, Memorial Day, the Fourth of July, Labor Day, Thanksgiving, and Christmas.

c. Open to researchers of college age and over. Loan service is available to other libraries, except for items that can easily be obtained from other sources, rare items, motion pictures, and items in poor physical condition. Photocopying machines are located in the general reading rooms and most division reading rooms. The Photoduplication Service, Room G-1009, John Adams Building (202/287–5640), provides microfilm and photocopies of rare items and those not available on interlibrary loan.

e. Daniel J. Boorstin, The Librarian of Congress
Division Chiefs and Section Heads are listed below.

2–3. The Library of Congress is the largest library in the world, with more than 80 million items in some 470 languages, including over 20 million books and pamphlets. It continues to grow at the rate of 7,000 items each working day. Established in 1800 to provide information for members of Congress, it has evolved into the nation's de facto national library. From its very beginning, LC has acquired maps and related cartographic materials. While the majority of these materials are found in the Geography and Map Division, other Divisions also maintain important holdings of maps, atlases, aerial photographs, and related literature.

Prior to visiting the Library, researchers should obtain a copy of *Guide to the Library of Congress,* which contains a description of the Library's services as well as a street map of the area. An 18-minute slide-sound presentation, "America's Library", is also recommended. It is shown hourly from 8:45 A.M. to 8:45 P.M., weekdays, and 8:45 A.M. to 5:45 P.M. weekends and holidays, in the Visitor Services Center, located at the 1st Street entrance of the ground floor of the Thomas Jefferson Building.

ASIAN DIVISION
Asian Reading Room
John Adams Building, Room LA 1024
(202) 287–5420/5426

Thomas Rimer, Chief (202) 287–5426
Chi Wang, Head, Chinese and Korean Section
(202) 287–5423/5425

Hisao Matsumoto, Head, Japanese Section
(202) 287–5430/5431

Louis Jacob, Head, Southern Asia Section
(202) 287–5600/5428

8:30 A.M.–4:30 P.M. Monday–Friday
8:30 A.M.–12:30 P.M. Saturday
Closed Sunday

This Division has custody of more than 1.4 million volumes in Chinese, Japanese, Korean, and Southern Asian languages. The Chinese, Japanese, and Korean collections are the largest collections of these materials outside of the Far East. The distribution of relevant titles is as follows:

Subject	*Chinese Titles*	*Indian Titles*	*Japanese Titles*	*Korean Titles*
Cartography	64	3	95	5
Hydrographic Surveying	5		62	
Remote Sensing	6		17	
Topographic Surveying	66	2	97	4
Toponymy	27		5	

There are also several special collections that contain unique maps. Chinese local histories (about 4,000 titles dating from the eighteenth to the twentieth centuries) often contain detailed, large-scale city plans and county or prefecture maps. Another rich source of rare maps is the collection of South Manchuria Railway Company publications (about 7,000 titles) on economics, natural sciences, and technology. These publications were based on systematic studies conducted by the Company in China, Manchuria, and Siberia from the 1920's to 1945. Most of the maps are found in the Company's geological studies, but there are also maps showing, for example, population density and distribution by prefecture in Shantung Province, 1940, irrigated areas of Korean farming villages in Manchuria, 1934, transportation and other thematic maps relating to a historical geographic study of Manchuria, 1940, and maps of railroad surveys. Among the Indian materials are a Jaina cosmographical map of the world painted on cotton cloth, sixteenth–nineteenth centuries; a set of World War II pictorial maps entitled *Map Review,* published in the Hindustani language by the Times of India, Bombay (9 items); a series of large-scale district and village maps of Pakistan showing administrative boundaries and land use, printed in the Urdu language (45 items); and geography school texts in Urdu and Bengali, with sections on map making and map reading, 1930–1951 (10 items).

COMPUTER CATALOG CENTER
Thomas Jefferson Building, Room LJ-154

8:30 A.M.–9:30 P.M. Monday–Friday
8:30 A.M.–5:00 P.M. Saturday
1:00 P.M.–5:00 P.M. Sunday

The CCC, located on the east end of the Main Reading Room, contains public computer terminals that provide access to LC's automated records, *LOCIS* (Library of Congress Information System). Since January, 1981, all current acquisitions have been cataloged in machine-readable form. The Library's current automated data base contains more than 7.5 million MARC (Machine Readable Cataloging) records, including 103,000 maps, and 4.4 million PREMARC records. The latter file consists of pre–1979 data derived from LC's shelflist. The books database is available on tape to some federal libraries, information centers, and national library networks such as OCLC (Online Computer Library Center), a shared cataloging service found in many university and research libraries.

LOCIS consists of two LC informational retrieval systems which provide online access to the MARC and PREMARC data bases: MUMS (Multiple-Use MARC System) and SCORPIO (Subject-Content-Oriented Retriever for Processing Information Online). The MUMS system contains most books and all maps cataloged since 1968, including book titles being processed, serials cataloged since 1973, visual materials, and music. Access is by subject, author, title, and component word. The SCORPIO book file, known as the Library of Congress Computerized Catalog (LCCC), contains all books cataloged since 1968. It can be accessed by subject, author, and title. SCORPIO also contains four other files:

BIBLIOGRAPHIC CITATION FILE (BIBL) includes selective titles and abstracts of articles from periodicals, pamphlets, and United States Government and United Nations publications published during the last four years. Access is by subject, names of persons, organizations, court cases, names of statutes, and treaties. The file is updated weekly.

LEGISLATIVE INFORMATION FILE provides an automated version of the *Digest of Public General Bills and Resolution,* which is prepared by LC's Congressional Research Service. This file can be searched by name or number of bill, subject, sponsor, committee, and public law number. It dates from 1975 and is updated each day.

National Referral Center Master File (NRCM) lists organizations willing to furnish information on science, technology, the social sciences and humanities to scholars and the general public. Each citation provides information on the organization's special collections, data bases, and publications. Retrieval is by name, subject, or location. It is updated weekly.

General Accounting Office Files contain citations and abstracts of reports pertaining to the evaluation of Federal programs, reports submitted by Federal agencies to Congress, and citations to fiscal, budgeting, and program information materials from Federal judicial, executive, and legislative agencies. These files are updated yearly.

Librarians on duty at the CCC will provide training and assistance in the use of the computer catalog. For researchers who are unable to visit the Center, a search of the database can be conducted on a fee basis and produced in printed form or on magnetic tape (Customer Services Section, Cataloging Distribution Service, Library of Congress, Washington, D.C. 20541). The automated program is described in *FIND: Automation at the Library of Congress: The First Twenty-Five Years and Beyond,* compiled by Peter T. Rohobach (1985). Two published brochures *Introducing LOCIS: MUMS* and *Introducing LOCIS: SCORPIO* are available on request.

COPYRIGHT OFFICE
Information and Reference Division, Room 453
James Madison Memorial Building
Winston Tabb, Chief (202) 287-6800

Reading Room for Record Books of Application, Room B-14
8:30–5:00 p.m. Monday–Friday

Copyright Card Catalog (CCC), Room 459
8:30–5:00 p.m. Monday–Friday

A major source of American commercial maps in the Library of Congress has been copyright deposit. Since the Copyright Act of 1870, the Library of Congress has acquired two copies of each map and atlas submitted to the Copyright Office for registration and deposit by commercial map publishers and private cartographers. Instructions and requirements for registering maps for copyright are available in circulars R40a, *Specifications for Visual Arts Identifying Material,* and R40b, *Deposit Requirements for Registration of Claims to Copyright in Visual Arts Material.*

Each year the Library receives about 2,000 recorded cartographic items, the majority of which are transferred to the Geography and Map Division (A21). Books, motion picture films, filmstrips, and computer software devoted to cartographic themes are transferred to other divisions within the Library, maintained by the Copyright Office, or disposed of. The disposition of individual items may be traced by consulting technicians in the Certification and Documents Section, Room 402 (202/287-6787).

The Reading Room for Record Books of Application maintains the original "Record Books for Maps and Charts, Record Books for Class E, 1901-1909" (16 volumes, 15,227 entries), "Class F, 1909–1945" (45 volumes, 61,771 entries), and "Class F Sanborn Maps, 1930-1940" (1 volume, 1,900 entries); and the original "Applications for Maps and Charts, Class F, 1946–1977" (134 volumes, 64,090 entries), and "Class VA", which includes other graphic arts as well as maps, 1977–1985 (200 volumes, 200,000 entries). The record books and application files provide the following information for each entry: name and address of the claimant, map title, name and address of the author, name of publisher, date, and, beginning in the 1950's, information on the nature of the new matter, compilation, editorial revision, and addition of the graphic or cartographic work. Registration information about maps copyrighted prior to 1898 is found in District Court Records, housed in the Rare Books and Special Collections Division of the Library of Congress, for the period 1790–1870 (A24), and in general registration record books maintained in the Copyright Records Maintainance Unit, Room B-14, for the period 1870–1897. Access to all registration books and applications files, which are arranged numerically by registration number, is through the Copyright Card Catalog (CCC) for the period 1790 to 1977 and thereafter through the Copyright Office History Monographs file (COHM), an online automated file. These files are described in circular R23, *The Copyright Card Catalog and the Online Files of the Copyright Office.* Catalog records are available in published book form as the *Catalog of Copyright Entries* (CCE) for the period 1891–1978 (660 volumes), with separate volumes for Class F, Maps, from 1950 to 1977 (27 volumes). The CCE, Fourth Series, Volume 2 part 6 Maps, was issued in microfiche, in 1985, with the first issuance covering the period January through June 1979. It is available from the United States Government Printing Office (K8).

GENERAL READING ROOM
Thomas Jefferson Building, Room 122 C
(202) 287–5530
Ellen Z. Hahn, Chief

Reading Room Hours
8:30 A.M.–9:30 P.M. Monday–Friday
8:30 A.M.–5:00 P.M. Saturday
1:00 P.M.–5:00 P.M. Sunday

This Division provides reference services for the Library's general collections through the Main Reading Room (202/287–5522) and the Local History and Genealogy Room (202/287–5537), both located in the Thomas Jefferson Building, the Microform Reading Room (described below), and the Social Science Reading Room (202/287–5539), located in the John Adams Building. The Division also assigns study facilities to readers undertaking extensive, long-term research through its Research Facilities Office (202/287–5211). Reference librarians in the Telephone Reference, Correspondence and Bibliography Section provide limited reference assistance by telephone or correspondence (202/287–5522).

Scholars using the reading room facilities of the Library of Congress for the first time should consult with the staff at the Research Guidance Office, located at the entrance to the Main Reading Room, for an introduction and orientation to the facilities. Reference librarians are also available for guidance at the Central Desk. The Main Reading Room maintains a reference collection of approximately 42,000 volumes in all subject areas but with emphasis on the humanities and bibliography. The Social Science Reading Room has more than 14,000 general and social science reference works and the Local History and Genealogy Room almost 9,000 volumes of reference materials relating to colonial families, census and military service records, passenger lists, land grants, birth, marriage, and death records, and the origin of names.

The general collections are organized by the Library of Congress Classification Schedule. In this classification scheme, maps and atlases have been assigned to class G along with the subjects of geography, anthropology, and recreation. In addition to the basic works relating to cartography and remote sensing imagery tabulated below, the general collections include many classes that contain maps such as C (archeology), D (travel and description), G (general geography), G159-163 (guidebooks and travel books, 1,172 titles), H (urban and regional planning), Q 115-116 (scientific voyages and expeditions, 1,688 titles), QE (geology), S 599 (soil surveys; 3,095 titles), SB 469-476 (landscape architecture), and VK 797-997 (sailing directions and pilot guides, 4,200 titles). Access to these collections is through the Main Card Catalog, an author, title, and subject catalog which lists all fully cataloged items through December 31, 1980 (25 million entries), with the exception of most music and recorded sound, pictorial images, maps, manuscripts, and braille and talking books, or through the Library of Congress Information System (see Computer Catalog Center).

The numerical distribution of cartographic-related titles in the general collections is indicated below.

Call Number	*Subject*	*Titles*
Archeology		
CC76.3	Surveying and Mapping	7
CC76.4	Aerial Photography	12
Geography		
G70.4	Remote Sensing Methodology	142
G100.5-108.5	Toponymy (Gazetteers, Geographic Names, Terms)	958
G109	Tables, Distances, Geographical Positions	26
Mathematical Geography		
GA1-2.9	Periodicals and Collected Works	17
GA4-23	Cartography General Works, Treatises, Textbooks, Fifteenth Century to Present	217
GA50-87	General Surveys	209
Cartography		
GA101-101.7	Periodicals, Collected Works	105
GA102-102.7	Dictionaries, Encyclopedias, Directories, Research	134
GA103-109.8	General Works, Treatises, and Advanced Textbooks	680
GA110-115	Projections	214
GA116-150.7	Compilation and Reproduction	356
GA151-155	Map Reading	229
GA190	Exhibitions	48
GA192-197.3	Collections and Map Libraries	88
GA198-246	History of Cartography	134
GA260-288	Globes	27
GA300	General Works	38
GA301-325	Ancient to Twentieth Century	106
GA351-357	Polar Regions	23
GA359-397	Marine Cartography	91
GA401-402	Western Hemisphere	28
GA405-460	United States	180
GA471-475	Canada	34
GA481-485	Mexico	22
GA491-555	Central America	21
GA561-635	West Indies	11
GA641-775	South America	50
GA781-1077	Europe	634
GA1081-1340	Asia	82
GA1341-1673	Africa	48
GA1681-1769	Australia and New Zealand	19
GA1771-1776	Pacific Islands	4
Social Sciences: Economics		
HE6183.M3	Maps: Topics on Postage Stamps	5
Science		
QB65	Celestial Atlases and Charts	167
QB66	Astronomical Globes	31
QB224-237	Latitude and Longitude	231
QB301-328	Geodetic Surveying	345
QB595-605	Lunar and Planetary Maps	91
QC822	Geometric Maps	8

QC878	Weather Maps	41
QE33.2A3	Aerial Photography	16
QE33.2R4	Remote Sensing Geology	40
QE36	Geological Maps	118
QK63	Vegetation Mapping	21
Agriculture		
S494	Agriculture Mapping	31
SD387	Forestry Mapping	44
Technology		
T385	Computer Graphics	277
TA501-555	Surveying (General and Historical)	1,302
TA562-614	Surveying Instruments and Methods	1,249
TA616	Topographic Drawing	74
TA622	Public Land Surveying	38
TL587	Aeronautical Charts	79
TN273	Mining Maps	191
TR693-696	Photogrammetry	91
TR713	Space Photography	16
TR810	Aerial Photography and Interpretation	177
Military Science		
UG470-474	Military Surveying, Topography, and Mapping	335
UG476	Photographic Interpretation	7
UG760-765	Aerial Reconnaissance	15
Naval Science		
VK588-597	Hydrographic Surveying	253
Bibliography, Library Science		
Z286.M3	Maps—Bookselling and Publishing	3
Z692.M3	Maps in Libraries	19
Z695.6	Cataloging of Maps	27
Z697.M17	Classification of Literature on Maps	10
Z7136.A3	Aerial Photography	5
Z6021-6027	Map and Cartography Bibliographies	839
Z6028	Map and Cartography Catalogs	227

GEOGRAPHY AND MAP DIVISION See entry A21

HISPANIC DIVISION
Thomas Jefferson Building, Room LJ 239
(202) 287-5397

8:30 A.M.-5:00 P.M. Monday-Friday

Sara Castro-Klarén, Chief
John Hébert, Assistant Chief
Georgette Dorn, Head of Reference

The Hispanic Division annually produces the *Handbook of Latin American Studies*, an annotated bibliography of selected works in the social sciences and the humanities. Each issue includes a chapter on cartography, compiled since 1975 by Andrew M. Modelski. The issue for 1985 contains bibliographic entries for 200 maps and atlases, which are housed in the Geography and Map Division (A21).

LAW LIBRARY
James Madison Memorial Building, Room 201
101 Independence Avenue, S.E.
Washington, D.C. 20540

Carleton W. Kenyon, Law Librarian (202) 287–5065
Reference Service (202) 287–5079

Law Library Reading Room
8:30 A.M.–9:30 P.M. Monday–Friday
8:30 A.M.–5:00 P.M. Saturday
1:00 P.M.–5:00 P.M. Sunday

The Law Library maintains a sequentially numbered bound volume set of Senate and House Reports and Documents, printed since 1817. Commonly known as the United States Congressional Serial Set, it contains many maps issued by Federal Agencies. A multivolume index to the reports and documents is also available. The earliest maps are cited in Martin P. Claussen and Herman R. Friis, *Descriptive Catalog of Maps Published by Congress, 1817–1843*. (Washington, D.C., 1941). Other Congressional indexes and documents maintained by the Law Library may include pertinent materials relating to Federal mapping and surveying programs. These provide access to information by way of subject, agency, and name of witness.

MANUSCRIPT DIVISION **See entry B15**

MICROFORM READING ROOM
Thomas Jefferson Building, Room 140-B
Alan C. Solomon, Section Head (202) 287–5471

8:30 A.M.–9:30 P.M. Monday–Friday
8:30 A.M.–5:00 P.M. Saturday
1:00 A.M.–5:00 P.M. Sunday

The Microform Reading Room has nearly 1.5 million titles. Many of these titles are not recorded in the Main Card Catalog or the computerized catalog. Major collections are listed in *Select Microform Collections in the Microform Reading Room.* There are also printed guides, card and online catalogs, and finding aids. Coin-operated reader-printers are available for both microfiche and microfilm. Interlibrary loan service is available. A brochure, *Microform Reading Room in the Library of Congress,* briefly describes services.

The following microform collections are particularly pertinent:

County and Regional Histories and Atlases Collection: Includes nineteenth and early twentieth century atlases for California, Michigan, New York, and Wisconsin. Microfilm reels.

Doctoral Dissertation Series: Contains about 90 percent of all dissertations prepared at United States universities from the late 1940s and some dissertations from European universities. This series is indexed by *The Comprehensive Dissertation Index, 1861–1983* (Xerox University Microfilms) which includes the following headings under the major categories of "geography" or "civil engineering": aerial (photography), cartography, map, map-area, mapping, maps, remote (sensing), and surveying.

Reports of Exploration Reported in the Documents of the United States Government: Based on Adelaide Hasse's bibliography (1899), this collection contains 554 reports on nineteenth century geography, cartography, surveying, and other topics related to exploration. 72 microfilm reels.

Inventories of Archives nationales (Paris): Includes inventories for the Archives de la Marine, Service Hydrographique, which served as the main repository for eighteenth century maps of North America. 16mm and 35mm microfilm.

History of Photography: Contains approximately 2100 rare monographs and 125 periodicals in English, French, and German relating to the development of photography as well as early photographs, including works by the United States Geological Survey and the geographical and geological surveys of the west, 1869–1879. 489 35mm reels.

Texas as Province and Republic, 1795–1845: Contains Spanish and American maps and other items listed in Thomas W. Streeter's *Bibliography of Texas, 1795–1845.*

Index to the Towns and Townlands of Ireland: Consists of the 1901 edition of this index, which locates each town or townland on Irish Ordnance Survey map sheets.

United States Serial Set: House and Senate reports and documents and annual reports of government agencies, including many mapping and surveying agencies, 1789–1969. A printed guide is available. Microfiche.

MOTION PICTURE, BROADCASTING, AND RECORDED SOUND DIVISION **See entry A22**

NATIONAL LIBRARY SERVICE FOR THE BLIND AND PHYSICALLY HANDICAPPED (NLS/BPH)
Taylor Street Annex
1291 Taylor Street, N.W.
Washington, D.C. 20542

Mailing Address:
Consumer Relations Section
National Library Service for the Blind and Physically Handicapped
Library of Congress
Washington, D.C. 20542

Frank Kurt Cylke, Director (202) 287–5104
Judith Dixon, Head Consumer Relations Section
(202) 287–6397

NLS/BPH distributes braille and recorded materials to some 526,000 visually handicapped users each year in the United States through a nationwide network of fifty-six regional and one hundred cooperating local libraries. The NLS/BPH map collection consists of 345 tactile maps. These include outline, physical, and political maps of most countries, general maps of each state in the United States, and historical maps. A checklist of the NLS Map Collection may be obtained from the Consumer Relations Section. Like the rest of the material distributed by NLS/BPH, tactile maps are not available to the general public as a whole, but only to eligible readers nationwide.

Two publications are available. *Maps and Graphics for Blind and Visually Handicapped Individuals: A Bibliography* (Washington: Library of Congress, 1984), compiled in response to the First International Symposium on Maps and Graphics for the Visually Handicapped, which was held in Washington, D.C., March 10-12, 1983, contains approximately 490 entries. The *International Directory of Tactile Map Collections* provides "a comprehensive list of tactile maps available for use, loan, or sale throughout the world".

NATIONAL REFERRAL CENTER (NRC)
John Adams Building, Room 5227
John A. Feulner, Head, Referral Services Section
(202) 287-5670

The purpose of the Referral Center is to direct researchers to appropriate information centers in response to specialized inquiries; it does not provide research or bibliographic assistance. To carry out its mission, the Center maintains a computerized file on 14,000 technical libraries, information and documentation centers, abstracting and indexing services, professional societies, university bureaus and institutes, Federal and state agencies, museums, and a variety of grass-roots organizations. This data is accessible by subject through LC's SCORPIO system (see Computer Catalog Center above) or nationwide through DOE/RECON or MEDLARS. A search of the data base revealed the following number of descriptions of pertinent information resources: aerial photography (30), cartography (28), mapping (46), maps (108), and remote sensing (85). Informal lists of resources, published by the Center under the title *Who Knows?,* includes two which contain references to organizations concerned with cartography and remote sensing: *Aeronautics and Astronautics* (1983. 60 p.) and *Land Use* (1983. 59 p.). NCR also compiles a formal series, *A Directory of Information Resources in the United States,* which is sold through the U.S. Government Printing Office. The most recent volume issued in this series is titled *Geoscience and Oceanography* (1981. 375 p.)

PRINTS AND PHOTOGRAPHS DIVISION **See entry A23**

RARE BOOKS AND SPECIAL COLLECTIONS DIVISION **See entry A24**

SCIENCE AND TECHNOLOGY DIVISION
Science Reading Room, 5th Floor, John Adams Building
(202) 287-5639 (General Reference)

Joseph W. Price, Chief
Karl R. Green, Head, Technical Reports Section
Constance Carter, Head, Science Reference Section

8:30 A.M.-9:30 P.M. Monday-Friday
8:30 A.M.-5:00 P.M. Saturday
1:00 P.M.-5:00 P.M. Sunday

The Science and Technology Division has custody of 3.3 million technical reports, which represent the most extensive collection of accessible civilian and military technical reports in the world. Dating from 1909, but chiefly from the 1940s, this collection contains technical reports from many Federal agencies as well as foreign sources. A brief guide, *How to Find Technical Reports in the Library of Congress,* is available from the Division.

The Technical Reports Section maintains over 250,000 unclassified current national standards. The following series contain pertinent cartographic materials: American National Standards Institute (ANSI)—complete set of some 39,000 items from 65 organizations; Captured German Research, World War II—15,000 microfilm reels; Department of Defense—unclassified, unlimited reports; Foreign Technical Reports—2,500 current series; National Aeronautics and Space Administration (NASA)—complete set from 1919; Office of Scientific Research and Development (OSRD)—complete for World War II related research, 1941–1946; National Technical Information Service (NTIS)—complete set, including unique series of 160,000 reports issued by the Publications Board, the predecessor to NTIS, 1946 to present (K12); Soviet State Standards (GOST)—unique set (23,000 items), including standards for geodesy and cartography, section R4; and Foreign Hardcopy Reports Collection—145,000 current reports from 56 countries.

The Technical Reports Section will assist the scholar in identifying and locating technical and scientific reports not held by the Library of Congress through appropriate online systems and microfilm reference files. Online systems include DROLS, DOE Recon, NASA Recon, DIALOG, SDC Orbit, BRS, MEDLARS, and OCLC, but these are not available to the general public. The Division, however, compiles a list of commercial vendors in the Washington, D.C. metropolitan area that will provide online bibliographic searches. The Technical Reports Section also maintains the National Technical Information Service (NTIS) Title File, a subject, author, and report microfiche index of some 700,000 technical reports dating from 1964.

The Science and Technology Division prepares the *Antarctic Bibliography* (Geza T. Thuronyi, Head, Cold Regions Bibliography Project, 202/287–5668), a continuing series of some 28,000 abstracts and indexes of current Antarctic literature which have appeared in print since 1962. Each issue, which covers approximately 18 months, has a section on "Cartography" devoted to maps, articles, and reports on mapping and remote sensing from American, English, German, Japanese, and Russian sources.

SERIAL AND GOVERNMENT PUBLICATIONS DIVISION
Newspaper and Current Periodical Room (N&CPR)
James Madison Building, Room LM 133
(202) 287–5690

Donald F. Wisdom, Chief

8:30 A.M.–9:30 P.M. Monday–Friday
8:30 A.M.–5:00 P.M. Saturday
1:00 P.M.–5:00 P.M. Sunday

This Division has custody of LC's newspaper collections, current periodicals, and government publications. For the researcher interested in journalistic cartography, LC receives some 1500 United States and foreign newspapers and maintains an extensive retrospective collection dating from the late seventeenth century. Current titles are listed in a pamphlet, *Newspapers Received Currently in the Library of Congress.*

Some 60,000 current, unbound foreign and domestic periodical titles are also retained by N&CPR for about two years, after which they are bound and added to the general collections. Among this number are more than 300 titles from 40 countries that relate directly to the field of cartography or occasionally include pertinent articles. Access to these articles is through the *Bibliography of Cartography,* which is compiled by the Geography and Map Division (A21). In addition, N&CPR services current serial publications of federal, state, municipal, and foreign governments. A brochure, *Newspaper and Current Periodical Room,* provides a list of publications describing selected series of newspapers, serials, and government publications. Also helpful is *A Guide to Accessing Major U.S. Government Publications in the Library of Congress* (1985. 15 p.). Both are available on request from N&CPR.

4. In addition to the reference aids and catalogs cited above, the following LC catalog publications should be consulted: *The Card Catalogs of the Library of Congress: A Brief Description,* compiled by Barbara Westby and William J. Sittig (1983. 50 p.); *The*

National Union Catalog, Pre–1956 Imprints (755 volumes), and its two predecessors, *A Catalog of Books Represented by Library of Congress Printed Cards Issued* with *Supplements* (1898–1942 209 volumes) and *The Library of Congress Author Catalog: A Cumulative List of Works Represented by Library of Congress Cards* (1948–1952, 24 volumes); *The National Union Catalog: A Cumulative Author List Representing Library of Congress Printed Cards and Titles Reported by Other American Libraries* (1953–1977); and *Library of Congress—Books: Subjects, A Cumulative List of Works Represented by Library of Congress Printed Cards* (1950–1974, 207 volumes).

In 1983, LC began offering the National Union Catalogs (NUC) in microfiche only. The following pertinent series are available: NUC Books, containing current United States and foreign publications, is issued monthly; NUC United States Books, consisting of books, pamphlets, and microforms published in the United States, is updated monthly; and NUC Cartographic Materials, containing the entire LC maps data base and currently cataloged maps, is issued quarterly. A brochure describing these microfiche catalogs is available from the NUC Desk, Customer Services Section, Cataloging Distribution Service, Library of Congress, Washington, D.C. 20541 (202/287–6171).

A general introduction to the resources of the Library of Congress is *Guide to the Library of Congress* (Washington, D.C.: Library of Congress, 1982. 119 p.) by Charles A. Goodrum and Helen W. Dalrymple. Goodrum's richly illustrated *Treasures of the Library of Congress* (New York: Abrams, 1980. 318 p.), includes pictures of rare atlases and maps. Special collections are described in Annette Melville's book, *Special Collections in the Library of Congress: A Selective Guide* (Washington: Library of Congress, 1980. 464 p.)

A21 Library of Congress—Geography and Map Division

1 a. *James Madison Memorial Building, Room B 01*
101 Independence Avenue, S.E.
Washington, D.C. 20540
(202) 287-6277 (Maps)

b. Reading Room:
8:30 A.M.–5:00 P.M. Monday–Friday
8:30 A.M.–12:30 P.M. Saturday

c. Open to the public; visitors must register. Interlibrary loan service is available on a limited basis.

d. Photocopying facilities are available. Scholars may also take pictures of maps with their own cameras.

e. John A. Wolter, Chief
Ralph E. Ehrenberg, Assistant Chief
Richard Stephenson, Head, Reference and Bibliography Section
David Carrington, Head, Technical Services Section

2. The Geography and Map Division has custody of the largest and most comprehensive cartographic collection in the world. It contains more than 4 million maps, 50,000 atlases, 78,000 microforms, 2.2 million aerial and remote sensing images, and 9,000 reference books and pamphlets. The collections date from the fourteenth century to the present and cover virtually every country on earth.

3. The Geography and Map Division was established as a distinct administrative unit in 1897, but maps, charts, and atlases were housed in the Library of Congress from the time of its establishment in 1800. About 60,000 cartographic items are added to its permanent collections each year. Current maps are received through copyright deposits, government deposits made by Federal and State map producing agencies, solicitation programs directed toward local government agencies and associations, and direct purchases and exchanges of foreign produced maps and charts through Library of Congress field offices or the United States Department of State. Retrospective maps are secured through government library transfers of outdated surplus maps, gifts, direct purchases, and duplicate exchanges with other research institutions and map dealers. New acquisitions are described in an annual publication, *Library of Congress Acquisitions Geography and Map Division,* which is available upon request.

The Division's resources are organized by format and/or area, subject, and date in six major groupings: maps, atlases, special collections, remote sensing imagery and aerial photography, microform collections, and cartographic literature.

MAPS

The Division maintains three general map collections: (1) the MARC Maps Collection; (2) the Title Collection; and (3) the Series Map Collection.

MARC Maps Collection. Consists of more than 100,000 (350,000 sheets) maps controlled by the LC computer-assisted map cataloging system (MARC). Approximately 8,000 new titles are added to the data base each year. Most of the cartographic items contained in the MARC Maps File have been acquired since 1968. Geographic coverage is worldwide. Examples of the types of maps comprising this collection can be found in the "Selected Acquisitions Current Maps" section of the annual acquisition publication cited above. The MARC Maps File is classified and filed according to the Library of Congress Classification Class G schedule, which is published under the title *Library of Congress Classification Class G Geography, Maps, Anthropology, Recreation* (1976. 435 p.). Access to the MARC Maps online data base is provided by computer terminals located in the Geography and Map Division and the Computer Catalog Center (A20) and through the On-Line Computer Library Center (OCLC), a national computer network which serves some 1,200 colleges, universities, and public libraries. The MARC Maps data base is also available to scholars through a Library of Congress microfiche publication, *National Union Catalog for Cartographic Materials,* which is revised quarterly.

In addition to current maps, the MARC map bibliographic data base includes some 2,000 maps relating to the American Revolution period, ca. 1750–1789, which were cataloged as part of the Library's Bicentennial Program. These consist of manuscript field sketches of land and sea battles and troop positions, as well as published topographic engravings by Joseph Des Barres and other noted eighteenth century American, English, French and German map engravers. Other earlier collections available through the MARC Maps data base include the Warner and Hummel collections of rare Oriental scroll maps, panoramic maps of North American cities, treasure maps, nautical charts on vellum collection, railroad maps, and celestial and terrestrial globes and globe gores. These collections are described below.

Title Collection. Consists of some one million small- and medium-scale single- and multi-sheet worldwide general purpose and thematic maps added to the permanent collections before 1969. Except for the states of Delaware, Maryland, Virginia, and the District of Columbia, the Title Collection is unclassified and uncataloged. The Title Collection is arranged geographically by regions, countries, provinces, and cities. Within these subdivisions, chronological and subject categories are maintained. The Title Collection represents the most comprehensive collection of single-sheet printed maps in the world. The earliest maps date from the seventeenth century. A few aerial photographs are also found in the collection such as a vertical view of Madrid, 1943.

Particularly noteworthy are thousands of photographic reproductions and facsimiles of manuscript maps from European archives and libraries, some of which were obtained before World War II. These include, for example, study collections of photographs, facsimiles and tracings of manuscript and printed maps of America in French, Spanish, and Portugese Archives brought together by noted historians of cartography and exploration such as Henry Harrisse (600 items) and Louis C. Karpinski (750 items); photocopies of manuscript maps from the papers and journals of Comte de Rochambeau in the Bibliotheque historique de la Marine, Paris, the papers of Generals Thomas Gage and Sir Henry Clinton in the William L. Clements Library at the University of Michigan, and the papers of Robert Erskine and Simeon DeWitt in the New York Historical Society; reproductions of manuscript maps and plans pertaining to Mexico and Florida from the Archivo General de Indias, Seville, Spain; photo reproductions of manuscript maps of Northern Virginia compiled by Confederate Major Albert V. Campbell during the Civil War and now in custody of the Virginia State Historical Society, Richmond, the United States Military Academy, West Point, and the College of William and Mary, Williamsburg, Virginia, (63 maps); copies of manuscript maps of North America from the British Library, eighteenth century (ca. 200 items); and photostatic reproductions of manuscript maps relating to Mexico and Texas collected by Henry R. Wagner, 1722–1838 (39 maps).

Selected maps of the Title Collection, which have high reference value, have been described in several published lists. These include *Ward Maps of the United States Cities* (1974), *Railroad Maps of the United States* (1984), *Treasure Maps and Charts* (1973), *Landownership Maps: A Checklist of Nineteenth Century United States County Maps* (1967), *Maps Showing Explorers Routes, Trails, and Early Roads in the United States* (1962), *Civil War Maps* (1961), *Aviation Cartography* (1960), *Selected Maps and Charts of Antarctica* (1959), *Marketing Maps of the United States* (1958), and *Detroit and Vicinity Before 1900* (1968).

For the general geographical distribution of maps in the MARC Map File and the Title Collection for a particular country, the scholar should consult the pertinent regional volume in the *Scholars' Guide* series. (See Bibliography for individual titles.)

Series Map Collection. Consists of approximately 2.1 million individual sheets of large- and medium-scale maps and charts dating from the eighteenth century. An individual series may range from two maps to several thousand maps. The predominant scales represented are 1:25,000, 1:50,000, 1:100,000, and 1:250,000, although coverage for most countries also includes some town plans at larger scales. Subject coverage is comprehensive. For most countries there are official geologic, land use, mineral, railroad and topographic map series as well as aeronautical and nautical chart series. Scholars may also find map series relating to forests, flood hazards, military activities, natural resources, population, recreation, roads, and weather. For example, this collection contains all editions of printed map series produced by some 40 federal agencies in the United States, including the Geological Survey (G14), the National Ocean Service and its predecessors, the Coast and Geodetic Survey and the Lake Survey (G20), the Soil Conservation Service (G25), the Federal Highway Administration (G11), and the Defense Mapping Agency and its predecessor agencies, the Army Map Service, the Aeronautical Chart and Information Center, and the Hydrographic Office (G8).

In terms of foreign coverage, most major European official surveying and mapping agencies are represented from the time of their establishment during the first half of the nineteenth century. Geographical coverage is particularly strong for Europe, Africa and East Asia in the twentieth century, areas that were systematically mapped by competing armies immediately before and during both World War I and World War II and between the wars for most colonial possessions.

A major strength of this collection is the nautical chart coverage. Current and retrospective editions of charts from hydrographic bureaus for the following countries are maintained: Argentina, Australia, Canada, Chile, China, Columbia, Cuba, Denmark, Ecuador, El Salvador, Estonia, Finland, France, Germany, Great Britain, Greece, Iceland, India, Italy, Japan, Latvia, Mexico, Netherlands, New Zealand, North Korea, Norway, Peru, Philippines, Poland, Portugal, Russia, South Africa, South Korea, Spain, Sweden, Thailand, Turkey, United States, Uruguay, Venezuala, and Yugoslavia.

Each series is classified and cataloged according to the Library's Classification Class G schedule. The Geography and Map Division Reading Room maintains an extensive file of map indexes (48 linear feet) which are annotated to show date and area coverage for most series. Often these indexes also show geographic coverage for individual map sheets within a series. A partial list of the map series is found in Philip Lee Phillip's *Check List of Large Scale Maps Published by Foreign Governments (Great Britain Excepted)* (Washington: Government Printing Office, 1905). The following list, organized according to the G schedule, provides an indication of the number of map series available for specific regions and countries, along with the earliest date and largest scale. The dates and scales provided are those indicated according to the card catalog.

Call Number	*Area*	*Number of Series*	*Earliest Date*	*Largest Scale*
G3190	Celestial & Lunar	30	1958	1:10,000
G3200	World	265	1912	1:250,000
G3290	Western Hemisphere	19	1753	1:250,000
G3300	North America	60	1778	1:10,000
G3380	Greenland	31	1932	1:2,000
G3400	Canada	240	1884	1:12,500
G3700	United States	123	1836	1:65,500
	Regions & States	1,175	1882	1:4,800
	Cities & Towns	252	1872	1:1,200
G4410	Mexico	130	1928	1:25,000
G4800	Central America	266	1871	1:1,056
G5200	South America	24	1895	1:250,000
G5250	Guyana	14	1949	1:50,000
G5260	Surinam	20	1930	1:10,000
G5270	French Guiana	11	1947	1:50,000
G5280	Venezuela	84	1946	1:5,000
G5290	Columbia	110	1936	1:2,000
G5300	Ecuador	70	1928	1:2,000
G5310	Peru	35	1880	1:2,000
G5320	Bolivia	15	1933	1:10,000
G5330	Chile	70	1873	1:2,000
G5350	Argentina	80	1900s	1:2,500
G5370	Uruguay	17	1920	1:5,000
G6380	Paraguay	8	1937	1:6,200
G5400	Brazil	180	1899	1:10,000
G5620	Eastern Hemisphere	26	1900	1:500,000
G5700	Europe	230	1844	1:10,000
G5740	Great Britain	462	1830s	1:1,250
	Counties	249	1752	1:2,500
	Cities	73	1728	1:2,500
G5830	France	208	1757	1:5,000
	Provinces	66	1879	1:2,000
	Cities & Towns	561	1885	1:5,000
G6000	Netherlands	110	1853	1:5,000
G6010	Belgium	90	1840s	1:10,000
G6020	Luxembourg	17	1904	1:5,000

Call Number	*Area*	*Number of Series*	*Earliest Date*	*Largest Scale*
G6030	Central Europe	55	1866	1:10,000
G6040	Switzerland	80	1833	1:5,000
G6080	Germany	80	1860s	1:10,000
G6090	East Germany	35	1830	1:15,000
G6295	West Germany	420	1791	1:5,000
G6480	Austria	125	1810	1:1,000
G6500	Hungary	31	1869	1:10,000
G6510	Czechoslovakia	49	1910	1:15,000
G6520	Poland	40	1807	1:10,000
G6540	Iberian Peninsula	27	1823	1:25,000
G6560	Spain	168	1875	1:500
G6690	Portugal	55	1862	1:1,000
G6700	Italy	230	1833	1:2,000
G6800	Balkan Peninsula	13	1877	1:50,000
G6810	Greece	125	1909	1:2,000
G6830	Albania	10	1910	1:5,000
G6840	Yugoslavia	43	1861	1:25,000
G6880	Romania	39	1890s	1:20,000
G6890	Bulgaria	18	1905	1:25,000
G6910	Scandinavia	15	1920	1:250,000
G6920	Denmark	78	1846	1:4,000
G6930	Iceland	26	1921	1:2,000
G6940	Norway	160	1861	1:5,000
G6950	Sweden	145	1858	1:10,000
G6960	Finland	85	1867	1:2,000
G6965	Eastern Europe	22	1912	1:25,000
G7000	USSR	185	1847	1:10,000
G7400	Asia	38	1894	1:500,000
G7420	Middle East	133	1890	1:10,000
G7500	Israel	67	1880	1:2,000
G7520	Arabian Peninsula	70	1916	1:2,000
G7610	Iraq	26	1918	1:7,200
G7620	Iran	148	1918	1:2,000
G7630	Afghanistan	5	1920s	1:50,000
G7640	Pakistan	16	1855	1:7,000
G7650	India	62	1860s	1:1,000
G7720	Burma	26	1904	1:3,960
G7750	Sri Lanka	62	1899	1:792
G7760	Nepal	8	1953	1:2,000
G7800	Far East	15	1894	1:63,360
G7810	China	222	1864	1:1,200
G7895	Mongolia	4	1927	1:250,000
G7900	Korea	59	1911	1:1,250
G7910	Taiwan	36	1895	1:1,250
G7940	Hongkong	19	1928	1:600
G7950	Japan	130	1877	1:10,000
	Islands	60	1894	1:10,000
	Prefectures	95	1936	1:1,200
G8000	Southeast Asia	9	1941	1:250,000
G8005	Indochina	44	1908	1:10,000
G8010	Kampuchea	4	1940s	1:20,000
G8015	Laos	5	1959	1:20,000
G8020	Vietnam	48	1904	1:5,000
G8025	Thailand	47	1897	1:4,000
G8030	Malaysia	57	1928	1:3,168
G8040	Singapore	8	1924	1:6,336
G8060	Philippines	95	1890s	1:2,000

Call Number	*Area*	*Number of Series*	*Earliest Date*	*Largest Scale*
G8070	Indonesia	190	1883	1:2,000
G8140	New Guinea	70	1925	1:20,000
G8200	Africa	75	1883	1:5,000
G8220	North Africa	13	1928	1:200,000
G8230	Morocco	50	1899	1:5,000
G8240	Algeria	42	1881	1:10,000
G8250	Tunisia	36	1881	1:2,000
G8260	Libya	44	1914	1:2,000
G8300	Egypt	136	1821	1:2,500
G8310	Sudan	45	1900	1:2,500
G8320	Eastern Africa	25	1904	1:25,000
G8330	Ethiopia	17	1881	1:25,000
G8350	Somalia	19	1908	1:25,000
G8410	Kenya	34	1895	1:2,500
G8420	Uganda	39	1908	1:2,500
G8425	Rwanda-Burundi	10	1925	1:25,000
G8440	Tanzania	47	1894	1:2,500
G8450	Mozambique	8	1896	1:20,000
G8460	Madagascar	45	1899	1:1,000
G8500	South Africa	60	1897	1:1,000
G8560	Zimbabwe	60	1909	1:5,000
G8570	Zambia	21	1933	1:5,000
G8580	Lesotho	4	1950s	1:2,500
G8590	Swaziland	6	1932	1:2,400
G8600	Botswana	26	1949	1:2,400
G8610	Malawi	12	1950	1:2,500
G8620	Namibia	8	1900s	1:50,000
G8630	Central Africa	10	1894	1:20,000
G8640	Angola	11	1905	1:1,000
G8650	Zaire	61	1910	1:2,000
G8660	Equatorial Guinea	3	1940s	1:100,000
G8680	French Equatorial Africa	20	1880s	1:50,000
G8690	Gabon	3	1952	1:2,000
G8710	Ubangi-Shari	3	1968	1:200,000
G8720	Chad	9	1951	1:2,000
G8730	Cameroon	14	1920s	1:5,000
G8735	West Africa	34	1886	1:10,000
G8750	Dahomy	9	1927	1:2,000
G8760	Togo	2	1902	1:200,000
G8770	Niger	7	1907	1:2,000
G8780	Ivory Coast	13	1895	1:2,000
G8800	Mali	2	1891	1:200,000
G8805	Upper Volta	2	1960s	1:2,000
G8810	Senegal	14	1941	1:5,000
G8820	Mauritania	5	1956	1:1,000
G8840	Nigeria	90	1886	1:2,400
G8850	Ghana	51	1907	1:1,250
G8860	Sierra Leone	21	1927	1:2,500
G8870	Gambia	8	1948	1:2,500
G8880	Liberia	6	1956	1:2,000
G8890	Guinea-Bissau	3	1950	1:50,000
G8900	Western Sahara	4	1958	1:1,000
G8960	Australia	270	1848	1:1,000
G9080	New Zealand	170	1900s	1:7,920
G9095	Oceans	9	1848	1:6M.
G9100	Atlantic Ocean	2	1868	1:22M.
G9110	North Atlantic	20	1859	1:50,000

Call Number	Area	Number of Series	Earliest Date	Largest Scale
G9120	Bermuda	3	1901	1:2,500
G9130	Azores	8	1940s	1:2,400
G9140	Madeira Islands	3	1967	1:25,000
G9150	Canary Islands	4	1954	1:12,500
G9160	Cape Verde Islands	4	1940	1:2,000
G9170	Saint Helena	9	1944	1:10,000
G9175	Falkland Islands	2	1971	varies
G9180	Indian Ocean	3	1942	varies
G9185	Mauritius	5	1952	1:2,500
G9190	Reunion	11	1964	1:2,000
G9195	British Indian Ocean Territory	2	1964	1:25,000
G9200	Seychelles	7	1963	1:1,250
G9210	Comoro Islands	1	1958	1:50,000
G9230	Pacific Ocean	7	1942	1:2M.
G9235	North Pacific	9	1942	1:1M.
G9250	South Pacific	10	1943	1:250,000
G9260	Melanesia	1	1942	1:500,000
G9280	Solomon Islands	29	1942	1:4,800
G9295	New Hebrides	4	1949	1:50,000
G9340	New Caledonia	9	1956	1:5,000
G9380	Fiji	13	1942	1:20,000
G9410	Mariana Islands	6	1921	1:20,000
G9415	Guam	4	1944	1:25,000
G9420	Caroline Islands	10	1921	1:12,500
G9460	Marshall Islands	3	1944	1:27,000
G9475	Gilbert Islands	5	1947	1:2,500
G9500	Polynesia	11	1927	1:2,500
G9780	Arctic Oceans	10	1925	1:10,000
G9800	Antarctica	26	1946	1:50,000
G9900	Theoretical Maps	4	1977	1:10,000

ATLASES

The atlas collection numbers about 42,000 titles (50,000 volumes) and increases yearly by about 1,000 volumes, representing the largest atlas collection in the world. If the average atlas contains about 150 maps, the atlas collection makes available another 7.2 million individual map sheets to the scholar. Atlases are also classified according to the G schedule and all have been cataloged, although all titles do not appear in the MARC data base. In addition to the catalog shelflist and MARC records, some 20,000 atlases acquired before 1973 are described in Clara Egli Legear's *United States Atlases* (Washington, 2 volumes, 1950–53) and Philip Lee Phillips and Legear's *A List of Geographical Atlases in the Library of Congress with Bibliographic Notes* (Washington, 8 volumes issued between 1909 and 1974).

The collection includes general geographical atlases of the world or individual regions, countries, states, and counties, as well as thematic or special purpose atlases that display aeronautic, climatic, ecclesiastic, economic, ethnographic, geologic, historic, linguistic, military, oceanographic, physical, and other data.

All periods and publishers are represented. An examination of the atlas shelf list reveals that 1246 atlases were published before 1799, including six atlases issued between 1475 and 1499, 133 during the sixteenth century, 325 during the seventeenth century, and 782 during the eighteenth century. For the period prior to 1599, the following cartographers and publishers are represented: Battista Agnese; Giulio Ballino; Benedetto Bordone (3); Giovanni Botero (6); Maurice Bouguereau; Georg Braun (2); Giovanni Camocio (2); Antoine Du Pinet; Hugo Favolius; Nicolaus Gerbel; Lodovico

Guicciardini (3); Pieter Heylyn (3); Gerard de Jode; Jacob de La Feuille; Antoine Lafrery (5); Barent Langenes; Conrad Low; Gerard Mercator (10); Abraham Ortelius (39); Tomaso Porcacchi (3); Claudius Ptolemaeus (34); Matthias Quad (3); Adrianus Romanus; Christopher Saxton (2); Francesco Valesio; Lucas J. Waghenaer (4); and Corneille Wytfliet (2).

Seventeenth century mapmakers include: Carolus Allard (2); Pierre d'Avity (2); Willem Barendsz; Sebastian Beaulieu (2); Anna Beek (4); William Berry (2); Petrus Bertius (7); Joan Blaeu (11); Willem Blaeu (11); Johann G. Bodenehr (2); Jean Boisseau (3); Hendrik Boom; Marco Boschini (2); Giovanni Botero; Braun; Jean Bremond; Antoine Bulifon; Giovanni M. Cassini (2); Philip Cluver (6); Jacob A. Colom (4); Vincenzo Coronelli (2); Pierre Duval (13); Nicolas de Fer (4); Pieter Goos (5); William Hacke; Wenceslaus Hollar (2); Jodocus Hondius; Georg Horn (3); Theunis Jacobsz (3); Alexis H. Jaillot (5); Jan Jansson (13); Thomas Jenner (3); Gerard de Jode; Jollain; Clement de Jonghe; Pieter van de Keere (2); Jacob de La Feuille; Langenes (3); Philip Lea; Jean LeClerc; Francesco Levanto; Augustin Lubin; Jan Luyts; Giovanni Magini; Alain Mallet; Martino Martini; Jean Matal; Mercator (41); Robert Morden; G.B. Nicolosi; John Ogilby (2); Ortelius (29); Geronimo M. Palacios; Jacques Peeters; William Petty; Porcacchi (6); Ptolemaeus (12); Quad (2); Romanus; Giovanni de Rossi (2); Nicolas Sanson; Marino Sanuto (4); John Seller (6); John Speed (9); Nicolas Tassin (8); Melchior Tavernier (2); João Teixeira (1); Francesco Villamena; Nicolas Visscher (9); Johannes Werdenhagen; Frederik de Wit (5); Abraham Wolfgang (1); and Martin Zeiller (2).

While the majority of atlases in the Geography and Map Division are printed, there are a small number in manuscript. Noteworthy examples include João Teixeira's secret maps of the Americas and the Indies from the Portuguese Archives, 1630; Agnese's atlas of portolan charts of the world on vellum, 1544; Joan Martines' nautical world atlas, ca. 1560; Giacomo Scotto's portolan atlas of Northwest Europe, ca. 1590; a Chinese atlas of the world, Ming Period (1368–1644); a Korean atlas of China, ca. 1721; an atlas of plans of military fortifications in Guadeloupe, 1768; Alexandre Gonzales' maritime atlas of the coast of Peru and Chile, 1787–1797; an atlas of maps of cities and ports made during the Portuguese occupation of Ceylon, ca. 1620; two atlases of "running charts" of the upper course of the Yukon River, 1913–1923; and a large-scale atlas of an English rural estate, 1767. The atlas collection also includes facsimiles and photocopies of rare atlases from other repositories. Some representative examples are: a photocopy of Ptolemaeus' *Geographie,* 1440, from the John Carter Brown Library; a collection of reproductions of 24 Agnese portolan atlases from various European repositories, 1563–1564; the English Pilot, 1689, from the Massachusetts Historical Society; photographs of manuscript maps prepared for Jean Baptiste Donation de Vimeur, Comte de Rochambeau during his American campaign, 1781, from the Rochambeau family and Princeton University; and a photocopy of a manuscript atlas of Brazil by João Teixeira, 1631, from the Mapoteca of the Ministerio das Relacoes Exteriores, Rio de Janeiro.

The following shelflist measurements reveal the relative strength of atlases, including facsimiles and photocopies, by geographical area.

Call Number	*Area*	*Titles*	*Earliest Date*
G1000	Celestial	16	1856
G1001	World Before 1570	31	1536
G1005	World Ptolemy	96	1440
G1006	World Ortelius	75	1570
G1007	World Mercator-Hondius	51	1585
G1015	World 1570–1800	950	1570
G1019	World 1801–1975	4,592	1801

Call Number	*Area*	*Titles*	*Earliest Date*
G1020	World School Atlases	132	1745
G1021	World 1976 +	650	1976
G1025	Facsimiles	140	1569
G1028	World Cities	50	1564
G1029	World Islands	20	1528
G1030	World History	580	1714
G1033	Ancient History	300	1628
G1034	Medieval History	35	1611
G1035	Modern History	70	1902
G1036	Discoveries, Travel, & Exploration	40	1665
G1037	World War I	130	1914
G1038	World War II	120	1939
G1046	World Other Subjects		
	Outline	90	1839
	Photomaps	8	1960
	Physical Science	90	1845
	Physiography	7	1960
	Geology	30	1872
	Oceanography	40	1884
	Climatology	40	1884
	Geophysics	2	1819
	Biogeography	22	1881
G1050	Northern Hemisphere	40	1864
G1052	Southern Hemisphere	3	1967
G1054	Polar Regions	6	1855
G1059	Maritime—Early to 1800	140	1656
G1060	Maritime—1801-	120	1804
G1100	Western Hemisphere America	160	1597
G1105	North America	340	1603
G1110	Greenland	4	1921
G1115	Canada	460	1734
G1200	United States	1,840	1792
	North Eastern States	720	
	Middle States	1,960	
	Southern States	1,360	
	South Central States	680	
	Mississippi Valley	280	
	Central States	5,240	
	West Central States	4,800	
	Pacific Mountain States	720	
	Southwestern States	440	
	California	760	
	Alaska	140	
G1535	Caribbean	260	1762
G1550	Central America	240	1754
G1700	South America	900	1647
G1780	Eastern Hemisphere	40	1745
G1787	Islamic World	22	1951
G1792	Europe by Period	840	1585
G1800	Western Europe	1,840	1567
G1880	Central Europe	1,480	1633
G1955	Southern Europe	1,200	1545
G2045	Northern Europe	900	1763
G2080	Eastern Europe	380	1704
G2180	Asia	80	1646
G2205	Middle East	480	166–

Call Number	Area	Titles	Earliest Date
G2265	Central Asia	360	162–
G2300	Far East	2,160	Ming Period
G2360	South East Asia	400	1777
G2245	Africa	800	1751
G2740	Australia	400	1811
G2800	Oceans & Islands	360	1716
G3100	Antarctica	55	1831

SPECIAL COLLECTIONS

The Division maintains a number of collections separately because they possess unique intrinsic, artistic, or historical significance. Some of these are described more thoroughly in Annette Melville's *Special Collections in the Library of Congress: A Selective Guide* (Library of Congress, 1980). The major special collections are listed below.

ACSM Award Maps Collection. Manuscript, printed, and photoprocessed maps that were submitted to the annual map design competition sponsored by the American Congress on Surveying and Mapping (entry J1) to promote map design and to recognize significant design advances in cartography, 1975–1983 (200 items). A selection of these maps is listed in a division exhibition brochure, *ACSM Award Winners Communication Through Map Design.*

American Map Collection. Rare printed maps of North America by Joshua Fry, Peter Jefferson, John Montresor, William Gerard DeBrahm, and others, 1750–1790 (167 items). These maps are cataloged in the MARC map data base.

Atlantic Neptune Collection. Printed navigational charts of American coastal waters and harbors based on hydrographic surveys directed by Joseph Frederick Wallet Des Barres, 1764–1775. This collection, the largest in the world, contains nineteen different sets of these charts. Among several nautical atlases complementing this collection is the *English Pilot, Fourth Book,* a marine atlas of American coastal regions preceding the *Atlantic Neptune,* 1689–1794. (17 editions).

Atlas Dust Covers. Representative sample of dust covers from atlases, 1834-the present (100 items).

Nathaniel Prentiss Banks Collection. Printed and photoprocessed maps relating chiefly to General Banks' Civil War military operations as commander of the Department of the Gulf (22 items).

John Barrett Collection. Printed maps of Latin America and Asia acquired by Barrett, an American diplomat and director of the Pan American Union, 1894–1920 (85 items). Includes a manuscript map of Manila compiled by Spanish Army engineers, 1894–1898.

Andrew H. Benton—Herschel V. Jones Collection. Printed title pages, indexes, introductory materials, time charts, royal genealogies, topographic profiles, and fortification plans from various atlases and geographical books, and one newspaper map, ca. 1700–1915 (ca. 250 items).

Braille Maps. Braille maps of Delaware, 1971 (36 items), the United States and individual states, 1982 (10 items), and Vietnam, 1972; braille map of Quebec prepared by Institut Louis-Braille; braille map of Southeastern United States with braille text, 1970; examples of maps for the blind devised by Joseph W. Wiedel with braille maps of the United States, North American cities and college campuses, Ethiopia, and East Africa, 1969–1971 (80 items); and a braille experimental map of St. Paul, Minnesota, designed by Mrs. Leslie R. Fellows, ca. 1936.

Canal Zone Library—Museum Collection. Manuscript, printed, and blueprint maps and photocopies of maps of the Panama Canal collected and maintained by the former Canal Zone Library—Museum, Balboa, Canal Zone, eighteenth century to 1967 (462 items). There are maps and plans of route surveys, land ownership, harbors, and towns. A number of these maps were prepared by the Panama Railroad Company, the French Compagnie Universelle de Canal Interoceanique de Panama, the United States Isthmian Canal Commission, and the United States Army Military Survey of Panama. These maps are described in *Subject Catalog of the Special Panama Collection of the Canal Zone Library—Museum* (Boston, Massachusetts: G.K. Hall, 1964).

Cartographic Artifacts. Circular chartograph drafting instrument, ca. 1925; circle flight calculator made in Paris, 1936; copper plate of a map of San Diego Province, New Spain, engraved in Mexico City, 1682; sixty-six foot Gunther chain and manuscript text illustrating land surveying with the chain, nineteenth century; wood block of a panoramic map of Fort Monroe, Virginia, engraved for the *Demorest's New York Illustrated News* during the Civil War; copper plates of New York Harbor, Hempsted Harbor, Long Island, engraved by the United States Coast Survey, 1840s–1850s; and two lithographic stones used by the Geological Survey.

Cartographic Miscellany. Manuscript maps and working papers compiled by J. Neilson Barry pertaining to his work on the Lewis and Clark expedition and John Colter (12 folders); manuscript maps drawn by Francis C. Pierce, age 12–13 years, 1837–1839; newspaper and magazine maps showing travels of political and cultural leaders such as Goethe's travels in Europe, 1749–1832, Charles De Gaulle's tour of Latin America in 1964, and Bishop Francis Ashbury's visits in South Carolina, 1785–1816 (15 maps); photocopies of John Filson's correspondence with George Washington, 1785; map material relating to the Thomas Jefferson Bicentennial Exhibition prepared by Lawrence Martin (4 folders); photocopies of geographical items relating to Abraham Lincoln (10 folders); photocopies of John Melish correspondence, 1816; photocopies of survey, correspondence, and other materials relating to George Washington, 1732–1954 (40 folders); proposals for publishing Thomas Hutchins' map of North America, 1770s; manuscript block diagrams drawn by William Morris Davis, ca. 1870–1930s (71 items); original surveying calculations by F.C. De Krafft, 1790s; Lawrence Vrooman's surveyor's field notebook pertaining to land patents along the Susquehanna River, 1810; autographed letter from Philippe Buache concerning a map, 1737; publishing proposals for a plan of Limerick by Christopher Colles, 1769; and manuscript and printed illustrations of cartographic techniques by C. Rau and J. Enthoffer, 1841–1854.

Classified Rare Map Collection. Manuscript and printed maps maintained separately from the Title and MARC map collections because of their unique intrinsic, artistic, or historical significance, sixteenth to twentieth centuries (3,000 items). Among the most significant are Pierre Charles L'Enfant's original manuscript plan of the City of Washington, 1791, and Andrew Ellicott's manuscript plan of the District of Columbia, 1793; John Mitchell's *Map of the British and French Dominions in North America,* 1755–1792 (20 English, Dutch, French, and Italian variants); a manuscript pictorial map of the Oztoticpac lands, an Aztec estate in the Valley of Mexico, 1540; John Melish's map of the United States, 1816–1823 (24 variants); Joseph Bouchette's manuscript report and map pertaining to the international boundary survey between Canada and the United States, 1818; Guillaume Le Vasseur de Beauplan's printed map of the Ukraine, engraved by Willem Hondius in Gdansk (Danzig), 1648; illuminated printed Dutch maps of Italy, the North Pole, and Switzerland that were painted with gold leaf, gold dust and silver by Dirck Jansz Van Santen to enhance geographical features, allegorical figures, and cartouches, 1630–1690 (3 items); Firmin Didot's demonstration copy of his map of France, one of the earliest examples of multiple color printing, 1823; and a wall map of Vienna by Joseph Daniel von Huber, 1777 (24 sheets, measuring more than 11 feet by 13 feet).

There are also a large number of manuscript maps. The following are representative: French railroad map of French Guinea, Africa, 1891; map of Chinese immigration in Inner Mongolia, 1908; map of the Defenses of Port Arthur, China, 1905; map in English of Nagasaki, Japan, 194-; map of south and east Africa showing H.L. Shantz's agricultural exploration trip, 1919–1920; intelligence map issued by G-2, Headquarters, French Army Morocco, showing tribal areas of North Morocco, 1925; map of the Mosel River, Germany, in seven sheets, 1841; set of statistical maps of Poland, 1930s; German ethnographic map of Romania, 1938; school map showing routes of Alexander the Great, eighteenth century; water resource and geology map of Saudi Arabia prepared by the United States Military Mission, 1944; outline map of China compiled by Erwin Raisz, 1938; map of Europe depicting language groups compiled by United States Office of War Information, 1943; map of the Isle of Man, England, 1785; intelligence map showing categories of main roads in southern France, 1943; plan of military fortifications of Cambrai, France, seventeenth century; German military panorama of Alsace-Lorraine battlefield found by a French observer, 1918; topographic maps of the French Alps, 1790; pictorial and cadastral maps of Shaker villages in the United States, 1807–1845 (5 maps); maps prepared for the Paris Peace Conference, 1921 (3 items); map of the northern frontier of Mexico by Nicolas de Lafora, 1769; reconnaissance map for a central railroad in Nicaragua, compiled by Corporal J.M. Bankler and Pfc. E.W. Bell, United States Marine Corps, 1930; map of a part of Haiti, with coastal soundings, 1780-1795; map of the Yapura River, Colombia, compiled by Francisco Requena, 1788; geological map of part of Peru made by Standard Oil of New Jersey; map of central Chile showing timberlands, 1944; and boundary survey maps of the Brazil-Uruguay frontier prepared by Josef Varela y Ulloa, Spanish commissioner following the Treaty of San Ildefonso, 1777 (6 items).

Copeland Railroad Surveys Collection. Printed maps and timetables for 79 railroads in the United States, 1921–1953 (3 cubic feet).

Copyright Map Titles Collection. Printed map titles or portions of maps with titles deposited by cartographers and map publishers with United States District Courts as evidence for their copyright claims, 1790–1896 (ca. 600 items).

East Asia Collection. Printed maps of China, Japan and Korea. Noteworthy examples include an engraved panoramic scroll map of the Tokaido Road between Tokyo and Kyoto, drawn by Yoshitora Utagawa, 1860s; manuscript map of Honan Province and the Grand Canal compiled by Tseng Kuo-Chuan, director general of the Yellow River and Grand Canal Water Conservancy, 1875–1877; manuscript atlas of China, ca. 1610; map of China drawn on a fan with index of place names on verso, Ching dynasty; manuscript map of Hainan Island, nineteenth century; map of Wu tai shan in Shansi province, China, one of four sacred mountains of Buddism, with place names in three languages, Chinese, Manchu, and Mongolian, 1845; manuscript atlas of Cholla province, Korea, eighteenth century; map of Yellow River (28 feet long); manuscript Chinese city plan of Foochow, China, with English annotations apparently by Thomas Dunn, American Counsul, 1850s; and a printed wall map of the world issued by the Ching Government, 1795.

Melville Eastham Collection. Rare atlases and printed maps from rare atlases, prepared by Blaeu, Hondius, Jansson, Lafreri, Mercator, Ortelius, Saxton, Visscher, and others, 1571–ca. 1850 (10 atlases and 434 maps).

Fabric Map Collection. Consists of maps printed or photoreproduced on silk, tissue, and other man-made fibers. These include a collection of World War II fabric maps produced for escape and evasion purposes by the British military intelligence organization designated as MI9 and the British Geographical Section, General Staff, 1939–1945 (94 items); maps of Palestine and Bible Lands by American Sunday School Union, 1874–1902 (5 items); escape and evasion maps of the Pacific Theater, prepared by the United States Army Map Service, 1943–1944 (21 items); military survey of Panama, 1926; British map of Anglo-Egyptian Sudan, 1924–1965 (13 items); map of mythical Fairyland, 1920; map of Detroit, Michigan, 1876; French road map, 1950; pictorial map of Frankfurt, Germany, 1962; map of Washington, D.C., 1792 (2 items); map of Turkey, 1978 (69x129 centimeters); tapestry map depicting the Dutch colony of New

Netherlands in 1626, woven by R. Page et Cie, France, 1970; and a sampler map of England and Wales embroidered by a young English woman, 1802.

William Faden Collection. A working collection of manuscript and annotated British military maps and plans pertaining to the French and Indian War and the American Revolution, which was assembled by Faden, geographer to the King of England and a noted British map publisher during the late eighteenth century (101 maps).

Ethel M. Fair Collection. Pictorial, historical, literary, and commercial maps derived from newspapers, magazines, and private publishers, road and city maps enhanced with illustrations, and decorative maps, twentieth century (879 items).

Millard Fillmore Collection. Printed maps of United States cities and states, European countries, and Civil War campaigns collected by President Fillmore. There is also a manuscript map of San Francisco by William Eddy, 1849 (2,247 items). For description, see Richard W. Stephenson's "The Millard Fillmore Map Collection", *The Map Collector* (1980).

Peter Force Collection. Manuscript and printed maps collected by Force concerning chiefly the French and Indian War, the American Revolution, and the District of Columbia, but also, cities, states, and some European countries. It includes maps by an American Indian, Thomas Hutchins, William Gerard DeBrahm, Charles Blaskowitz, John Montresor, Nicholas King, Benjamin Henry Latrobe, General John Cadwalader, and others, 1685–1842 (768 maps). Described by Richard W. Stephenson in *Quarterly Journal of the Library of Congress* (1973).

Games and Puzzles. A collection of maps, including nineteenthh century jigsaw puzzle maps manufactured in England, France, and the United States, that were designed to serve as games and educational aids, 1822–1976 (100 items).

Globe Collection. Original and facsimile terrestrial globes 1543–1980s (185 globes), celestial globes, 1816–1964 (25 globes), thematic globes, chiefly topographic, 1938–1976 (31 globes), and globe gores. Particularly noteworthy are Caspar Vopell's manuscript globe with armillary spheres depicting the Ptolemaic concept of the universe, 1543; a pair of celestial and terrestrial globes by John Cary, 1816, and James Wilson, the first American globe maker, 182-, 1834; inflatable and umbrella-like terrestrial globes designed by Elie Pocock, 1830, and John Betts, 1866, 1920; three-inch hemisphere globes which served as teaching aids during the nineteenth century; a fifty-inch terrestrial military globe designed and published by the United States Office of Strategic Services during World War II; and unmounted globe gores prepared by Vincenzo Maria Coronelli, 1688, and Jodocus Hondius, 1615.

Henry Harrisse Collection. Unique manuscript maps by Samuel de Champlain (now in Portolan Collection) and Johannes Vingboons of the exploration of the West Indies, Atlantic Coast and California, including a distinctive map of Manhattan Island, and an unidentified map of the Country of the Hurons, 1606–1650 (15 items); and a study collection of manuscript tracings, photographs, and facsimiles of sixteenth and seventeenth century maps relating to the exploration of America (600 items). For description, see Richard W. Stephenson's "The Henry Harrisse Collection of Publications, Papers, and Maps Pertaining to the Early Exploration of America", *Terrae Incognitae* (1986).

Karl M. Haushofer Collection. Printed topographic maps of Germany and Austria collected by Haushofer who was associated with the Geopolitical Institute in Munich during the 1930s (21 maps).

Hauslab-Liechtenstein Collection. Manuscript and printed maps assembled by Franz Ritter von Hauslab during the nineteenth century and later purchased by Prince Johann II of Liechtenstein. It includes topographic map series of European countries, a wide range of thematic maps, military maps, and city plans, sixteenth to nineteenth centuries. There are also several manuscript sketch maps drawn by Hauslab, Alexander von Humboldt, and Karl Ritter (10,000 items). A description is found in Walter W. Ristow's "The Hauslab-Liechtenstein Map Collection", *Library of Congress Quarterly* (April, 1978).

John Hills Collection. Manuscript maps prepared by Hill for Sir Henry Clinton concerning British military operations in New Jersey, 1778–1781 (20 maps).

General John L. Hines Collection. Printed and annotated maps concerning American military operations in France during World War I (187 maps).

Jedediah Hotchkiss Collection. Manuscript sketches and maps chiefly of Virginia and West Virginia prepared by Hotchkiss and Albert H. Campbell for Generals Robert E. Lee and T.J.(Stonewall) Jackson during the Civil War; and annotated and printed maps by Hotchkiss relating to the natural resources of Virginia, 1870s–1890s (600 items). Described in Clara Egli LeGear's *The Hotchkiss Map Collection* (Washington, 1951).

Richard Howe Collection. Manuscript maps and charts of coastal waters of North and South America, the West Indies, and the Philippine Islands that were acquired from the descendents of Admiral Lord Richard Howe, Commander in Chief of the British Fleet in North America during the American Revolution, 1750s–1770s (72 maps).

Arthur W. Hummel Collection. Manuscript and printed military, administrative, and general maps, charts, and atlases of China, Ming period (1368–1644)—nineteenth century (85 items), collected during the 1930s by Hummel, former head of the Orientalia Division of the Library of Congress. The following examples are representative: manuscript atlases of China compiled during the Ming Period; a printed Chinese atlas of the World, seventeenth century; a printed Chinese wall map of China, 1673; a scroll map of the World by Ferdinand Verbiest printed in Peking, 1674; a manuscript album of Chinese coastal defenses, 1705–1725 (51 feet long); manuscript mariner's scroll chart of Chinese coast, eighteenth century; manuscript wall map of Formosa, eighteenth century; manuscript flood control map of the Yellow River, eighteenth century; manuscript scroll road map of Southern Shensi, nineteenth century (60 feet long); manuscript wall map showing provincial forces attacking Taiping Rebels in Nanking, 1864; manuscript city plan of Hangchow, Chekiang, nineteenth century; and manuscript military map of Chinese and French fortifications on the Kuangsi-Indochina border, 1912.

Imaginary Maps. Printed maps of imaginary places such as Captain Kidd's Treasure Island, ca. 1745–1980 (29 items).

Andrew Jackson Collection. Manuscript maps relating to General Jackson's military operations in the south during the War of 1812 (11 items).

Thomas Jefferson Collection. Photostatic copies of maps and related correspondence from the Papers of Thomas Jefferson housed in the Manuscript Division of the Library of Congress (ca. 50 items).

John Johnson Maps and Notebooks. Manuscript maps and survey notebooks pertaining to the Northeastern International Boundary Survey in 1817 (4 items). They were compiled by Johnson, surveyor general of Vermont and United States representative for the Northeastern Boundary Survey.

Journalistic Art Map Collection. Original manuscript cartoon maps relating to politics and travel in the United States and to World War II, drawn by W.W. Shaw, Jr. for the *Chicago Tribune,* 1928 (16 items), Kenneth Stuart for the *Saturday Evening Post,* M. Chapin, Jr. for *Time,* Kenneth W. Thompson for *Liberty,* and James Cutter.

Johann Georg Kohl Collection. Unique series of manuscript maps and charts relating to the discovery and exploration of North America, which were copied or traced by Kohl during the 1850s from early printed geographical works or manuscripts in European public and private archives and libraries, eighth century–1836 (575 maps). Described by John A. Wolter, "Johann Georg Kohl and America", *Map Collector* (1981) and Justin Winsor, *The Kohl Collection of Maps Relating to America* (Washington: Library of Congress, 1904).

Waldo G. Leland Collection. Manuscript inventory of maps of the world, North America, and the West Indies located in the Section des Cartes et Plans, Bibliotheque Nationale and the archives of the Service Hydrographique de la Marine, Paris (formerly Dépôt des Cartes et Plans de la Marine). This inventory was prepared by Abel Doysie for Waldo G. Leland's *Guide to Materials for American History in the Libraries and Archives of Paris.* Most of the entries are not listed in Leland's published inventory (1 linear foot).

Lewis and Clark Collection. Manuscript maps of the Missouri River basin and the transmississippi west drawn or annotated by William Clark, George Drewyer (Drouillard), John Evans, Thomas Jefferson, Nicholas King, James Mackay, David Thompson, and others, 1796–1808. Also a manuscript sketch map of the Ojibway and Sioux boundary line, 1821; a manuscript map of the Illinois and Chicago Rivers relating to the Black Hawk War, 1832; and manuscript maps of Indian cessions in the midwest, 1825–1837. These maps were originally transferred to the Library of Congress from the Bureau of Indian Affairs (see National Archives and Records Administration, B19, RG 75).

Woodbury Lowery Collection. Study collection of printed maps and map reproductions relating to early Spanish exploration and settlement in North America (300 maps). Assembled by Lowery, a Washington lawyer and historian, these maps are described along with 450 other maps in his *The Lowery Collection: A Descriptive List of Maps of the Spanish Possessions Within the Present Limits of the United States, 1502–1820* (Washington: Government Printing Office, 1912).

Maggs Chart Collection. Manuscript hydrographic charts, chiefly of South America, compiled by students at the Naval Academy in Cadiz, Spain, as part of their naval training. Also charts of coasts along North America, the Caribbean Islands, Philippines, Indonesia, and China, 1729–1824 (ca. 400 charts).

George B. McClellan Collection. Unidentified manuscript cadastral plats showing land parcels (12 maps) and manuscript campaign sketch maps and fortification plans which were drawn or collected by McClellan while he was a cadet at the United States Military Academy at West Point, 1842–1846 (67 items).

Shannon McCune Collection. Manuscript and printed scrolls, atlases, and geographies of Korea, eighteenth to twentieth centuries (12 items). Some of these atlases are described and illustrated in Shannon McCune's "Old Korean Hand Atlases", *The Map Collector* (September, 1978).

John Melish Collection. Series of Melish's engraved wall maps of the United States, 1816–1823 (21 variants).

Mylon Merriam Collection. Manuscript and published relief maps, city plans, and panoramic views, chiefly of Switzerland, and related journals and monographs assembled by Merriam, a Federal government cartographer, to illustrate the development of relief representation on maps and related photographic and printing techniques (526 items).

Pierre Ozanne Collection. Manuscript maps and views of French naval engagements in the West Indies and North America drawn by Ozanne, a marine artist with the French Navy during the American Revolution (23 items).

Panoramic Map Collection. Manuscript, printed, and photoprocessed panoramic or bird's eye views of some 1,200 cities in the United States and Canada drawn by Albert Ruger, Thomas Mortimer Fowler, Lucien R. Burleigh, Henry Wellge, Oakley H. Bailey, Joseph J. Stoner, and other artist-cartographers, 1820–1930 (1,726 maps). Described in a published checklist by John Hébert and Patrick Dempsey, *Panoramic Maps of Cities in the United States and Canada* (Washington, Library of Congress, 1984).

Charles Oscar Paullin Collection. Manuscript maps on tracing paper showing yes-no votes by congressional districts for various bills such as the Bank Bill, 1791, bonus bill, 1817, tariff bill, 1883, and the results of presidential elections by congressional districts (62 portfolios).

Powder Horn Collection. Powder horns inscribed with maps and views of New York, Quebec, New York City, and Philadelphia by soldiers during the French and Indian War, American Revolution, and War of 1812 (8 items).

Walter W. Ristow Christmas Card Collection. Christmas cards illustated with maps, globes, and cartographic instruments printed by more than fifty commercial greeting card publishers, 1940s–1980s (ca. 500 items).

Rochambeau Collection. Manuscript and printed maps and plans of military fortifications and troop positions in North America prepared by French army engineers for Jean Baptiste Donatien de Vimeur, compte de Rochambeau, commander of French forces during the American Revolution, 1777–1783 (122 maps and plans).

Sanborn Fire Insurance Map Collection. Large scale printed maps of 12,000 American cities and towns prepared by the Sanborn Map Company that show the location and dimensions of individual residential, commercial, and industrial buildings as well as their construction material, height, and function, 1867–1970s (700,000 sheets). A printed checklist is available, *Fire Insurance Maps in the Library of Congress: Plans of North American Cities and Towns Produced by the Sanborn Map Company* (Washington: Library of Congress, 1980).

Hal Shelton Collection. Unique collection of 30 original colored zinc map plates, created by Shelton, one of America's foremost twentieth century cartographic artists, for the Jeppesen Company (later Times-Mirror Company). The plates are air-brushed in several colors directly on grained zinc plates which were first etched with cartographic base information. These maps are listed in an exhibition brochure.

William Tecumseh Sherman Collection. Manuscript reconnaissance and battle maps (202) and annotated atlases (3) relating to Sherman's Civil War Campaigns. These are described in Richard Stephenson's *Civil War Maps: An Annotated List of Maps and Atlases in the Map Collections of the Library of Congress* (Washington: Library of Congress, 1961).

Albert Speer Materials. Hand-colored printed and photoprocessed maps and plans of the redevelopment of Berlin prepared under the direction of Speer for Adolf Hitler, 1933–1942 (28 items). Originally housed in the official Nazi Party Archives. These materials are described in Stephen D. Helmer's *Hitler's Berlin: The Speer Plans for Reshaping the Central City* (Ann Arbor, Michigan: 1985. 370 p.).

Ephraim George Squier Collection. Detailed manuscript and printed annotated maps of Honduras, El Salvador, Nicaragua, and Peru relating chiefly to Squire's canal and railway interests, 1850s–1980s (38 maps). Described in John Hébert's "Maps by Ephraim George Squier Journalist, Scholar, and Diplomat", *Quarterly Journal of the Library of Congress* (January, 1972).

Herbert Thatcher Collection. Manuscript maps of North America traced from maps by Jedediah Morse and other British and American nineteenth century cartographers (20 items).

Gilbert Thompson Collection. Manuscript landscape sketches drawn by John E. Weyss during his work on the United States-Mexican Boundary Survey; original photographs of views and manuscript maps prepared for the Wheeler Survey, including photoprocessed proof sheets annotated with corrections, 1869; G.K. Warren's map of the West, 1854–1857; manuscript and photoprocessed map work sheets prepared during Thompson's service with the United States Geological Survey, 1895–1896 (130 items).

Three-Dimensional Relief Maps. Three-dimensional maps and terrain models printed or painted on plaster, paper-mache, vinyl plastic, and sponge rubber, 1879–1980 (500 items). Includes terrain models of Japan, the Philippines, and several Pacific Ocean islands prepared by the United States Office of Strategic Services (OSS) during World War II, a model of Cuba constructed during the Cuban missile crisis by the United States Naval Photographic Interpretation Center, 1960, and a set of raised relief maps of French cities and provinces prepared by the Institut geographique nationale, 1960–1969 (10 items). See Walter W. Ristow's, *Three Dimensional Maps, An Annotated List of Terrain Models* (Washington: Government Printing Office, 1964).

United States Congressional Serial Set Collection. Incomplete set of maps published by Congress as enclosures in Congressional publications, 1823–1906 (3,000 items).

Vellum Nautical Chart Collection. Manuscript portolan atlases and charts of the African, American, European, and Mediterranean coasts and the World Oceans by Dutch, English, Italian, Portuguese, and Spanish chartmakers, including Battista Agnese, Samuel de Champlain, Mateo Prunes, and Giacomo Scotto, ca. 1320–1770 (31 items). See Raleigh Skelton and Walter W. Ristow, *Nautical Charts on Vellum in the Library of Congress* (Washington: Library of Congress, 1977).

Langdon Warner Collection. Manuscript atlases and maps of Korea and China collected by Warner of the Fogg Art Museum, Harvard University. Includes chiefly maps of administrative units in Korea, nineteenth century, but there are also a map of Manchuria, eighteenth century, maps on fans, and two Korean atlases of China, one drawn during the Ming Period, the other in 1781 (26 maps, 4 atlases).

George Washington Collection. Manuscript maps compiled by Washington of Alexandria, Virginia, other areas in Virginia surveyed by him, and lands along the Ohio River patented by Washington and drawn by William Crawford, 1749-1780 (10 items); and photocopies of maps and plats compiled by Washington or his associates that were consulted by Lawrence Martin in the preparation of *The George Washington Atlas,* published in 1932 by the United States George Washington Bicentennial Commission. Also included are related memoranda and the printer's work-up for the *Atlas* (ca. 500 items).

Washington, D.C.—Virginia Boundary Commission Collection. Chiefly large scale blueline maps but also some manuscript and photographic copies of maps dating from the seventeenth century, annotated aerial photographic mosaics, and printed maps prepared or collected by the Commission, 1934–1935 (ca. 250 maps).

Mary J. Webb Collection. Manuscript tracings by Webb of nineteenth century maps of Texas relating to early land grants (39 maps).

Captain James M. Willis Collection. Manuscript charts of New Zealand, the South Atlantic, and the Northwest Coast of North America, 1852–1875 (6 charts). Also his drafting case with drawing and writing instruments, ca. 1850, and a chart case with 8 charts.

REMOTE SENSING IMAGERY AND AERIAL PHOTOGRAPHY COLLECTIONS

The Geography and Map Division has custody of an extensive browse file of remote sensing images and aerial photographs, as well as two aerial photographic print collections.

Remote Sensing Imagery and Aerial Photography Browse File. Provides access to nearly 7 million world wide photographic images taken by the National Aeronautics and Space Administration (NASA), the United States Geological Survey (USGS), the National Oceanic and Atmospheric Administration (NOAA), and the Department of Agriculture's Agricultural Stabilization and Conservation Service (ASCS). This file consists of film cassettes, microfiche indexes, and 105mm aerial photographic mosaics. The film cassettes contain 650,000 16mm black and white images of most countries taken by Landsat (Earth Resources Satellite) at an altitude of some 570 miles, 1972 to the present; 1.5 million 16mm conventional color and color infrared photographs of the United States, particularly metropolitan areas, taken by NASA aircraft or by aircraft associated with the National High Altitude Program (NHAP) at altitudes ranging from 3,000 to 60,000 feet, 1969 to the present; and 85,000 16mm experimental color images of large areas of the earth taken during Apollo, Gemini, Skylab, and Space Shuttle missions. About 15,000 microfiche indexes provide access to the cassettes in the form of geographic coordinates or map indexes. In addition, there are 8,500 105mm aerial photographic mosaic indexes that show the coverage of aerial photographic collections maintained by the ASCS (G1), USGS (E7), and NOS (G20).

Edgar Tobin Aerial Surveys Collection. Consists of large aerial photographic mosaic prints covering Florida, Louisiana, Mississippi, Texas, and parts of Alabama, Arkansas, Georgia, and Oklahoma at a scale of one inch to 6,000 feet, 1953–1954 (240 items).

NASA Print Collection. Consists of 630 8x10 inch color composite photographs made by Landsat Satellites 1, 2, and 3 launched in 1972, 1975, and 1978, respectively. The photographs were selected by NASA's Goddard Space Flight Center in Greenbelt, Maryland, to illustrate significant earth features and the value of Landsat images for scientific inquiry. Representative examples include views of the Dead Sea, the Gulf of Aqaba, Istanbul, Turkey, Peking, China, Juneau, Alaska, the Grand Canyon, Craters of the Moon, Idaho, the Island of Hawaii, Cape Hatteras, N.C., Washington, D.C., Lake Tahoe, San Francisco Bay, the Finger Lake region in New York, Philadelphia, western North Carolina, and the Chesapeake Bay. There are also images depicting the gypsy moth defoliation in the Harrisonburg, Pennsylvania, area in 1977, drought in the Sierra Nevada Mountains in 1977, frost damage to Brazilian coffee trees in 1975, the Soviet Union wheat drought in 1975, ice on the Chesapeake Bay in 1977, the South Dakota wheat drought in 1976, and flooding of the Mississippi River at St. Louis, Missouri, in 1973.

CARTOGRAPHIC MICROFORM COLLECTIONS

The Geography and Map Division maintains a small but rapidly growing collection of microforms acquired through accessions or its own preservation microfilm program. The latter includes 35mm microfilm of rare atlases (827 reels), Sanborn fire insurance maps (885 reels), and United States Geological Survey topographic map series, 1879–1983 (257 reels); and 105mm microfilm of United States city ward maps (250 fiche), nineteenth century United States county landownership maps (1,550 fiche), German 1:100,000 topographic map series, 1879–1944 (4,074 fiche), Polish 1:100,000 topographic map series, 1921–1938 (1,253 fiche), and *Carte de France,* 1757–1789 (208 fiche).

Accessioned microform collections include maps from a number of archives, libraries, and mapping agencies:

FRANCE.—Bibliothèque et Archives Inspection du Génie, Paris - manuscript and printed maps and charts relating to the American Revolution by Pierre Ozanne, Chevalier de Beaurain, Captaine de Chesnoy, Charles Blaskowitz, Claude Joseph Sauthier, Lt. Col. Thomas James, Philippe Buache, Desandrouins, Lt. Page, John Hills, and others, 1755–1782. (1 35mm reel).

GREAT BRITAIN.—Bodleian Library—selected maps (6 35mm reels). Corpus Christie College, Oxford—estate maps compiled by Thomas Langdon and Henry Wilcox, 1605–1615, (3 35mm reels). Public Record Office, London—manuscript maps relating to North America and the West Indies during the American Revolution (4 35mm reels). Royal Archives, Windsor Castle, Berkshire, England—campaign maps and papers from the Cumberland Collection, 1662–1849 (11 35mm reels).

ITALY.—Archivo di Stato, Florence—anonymous Portuguese atlas, sixteenth century. 1 35mm reel. Archivo di Stato, Turin—maps (1 35mm reel). Archivo di Stato, Venice—maps, charts, and atlases by Battista Agnese, Georgio Sideri, and others (6 35mm reels). Biblioteca Ambrosiana, Milan—maps by Battista Agnese, Vesconte Maggiolo, and Antonio Pigafetta, and various portolans, 1410 and later (4 35mm reels). Biblioteca Civica Quiriniana, Brescia—manuscript maps of America (1 35mm reel). Biblioteca Communale, Treviso—maps of the world by Vesconte Maggiolo, 1549 (1 35mm reel). Biblioteca Reale, Turin—portolans and charts, 1523 (1 35mm reel). Vatican Library, Rome—manuscript atlases by Johannes Vingboons and Barberini, sixteenth century (2 35mm reels).

NETHERLANDS.—Algemeen Rijksarchief, The Hague—inventory of maps (2 35mm reels).

PANAMA.—Panama Canal Zone Library and Biblioteca Nacional de Panama—maps relating to Panama, 1417–1925 (1 35mm reel).

SPAIN.—Archivo Historico Nacional, Madrid, and Archivo General de Indias, Seville—manuscript and printed maps of Spanish possessions in North America during the eighteenth century.

UNITED STATES.—American Geographical Society—maps of the East Indies (1 35mm reel). Cornell University Archives—correspondence and materials from Oliver J. Tillson Papers relating to cartography of Ulster County, New York, 1850–1897 (1 35mm reel). Clarke Historical Library, Central Michigan University—George A. Ogle Company's Chicago Record Book (1 35mm reel). Gilmer Map Collection, University of North Carolina—Civil War Maps (1 35mm reel). Historical Society of Pennsylvania, Philadelphia—Papers of Albert Newsam, concerning P.S. Duval and others, 1860-66 (1 35mm reel). Huntington Library—Petrus Bertius *La Geographie racourcie*, 1618 (1 35mm reel). Iowa Historical Society—twenty county atlases, 1884–1906 (3 35mm reels). Lilly Library, Indiana University—manuscript report of the General Survey in the Southern District of North America by William Gerard DeBrahm, 1773 (1 35mm reel). Michigan, Oakland County Planning Commission—county tax maps, 1973 (10 35mm reels). New Jersey State Library, Trenton—a plan of the Trenton and New Brunswick turnpike, 1805 (1 35mm reel). Ohio Historical Society—atlas of Muskingum County, Ohio, 1875 (1 35mm reel). Southern Historical Collection, University of North Carolina—Philip Lee Phillips Papers, 1857–1924 (1 35mm reel). Suffolk County, New York—maps, 1978 (18 35mm reels). United States Census Bureau—block statistics maps for 1980 census (42,000 105mm microfiche). University of Illinois, Urbana—Gorand's Street Map of Chicago, 1951 (1 35mm reel). Vermont, Office of the Secretary of State, State Papers Division—papers of the Surveyors-General of Vermont, 1749–1838 (9 35mm reels). West Virginia, Wood County—maps of magisterial districts, 1976 (3 35mm reels). William L. Clements Library, Michigan University—selected manuscript maps of the American Revolution (1 35mm reel). Wisconsin State Historical Society Library—atlas entries (1 35mm reel).

CARTOGRAPHIC LITERATURE

Some 9,000 books, serials, and pamphlets relating to cartography are available in the G&M division Reading Room. These are listed in the division card catalog and the *Bibliography of Cartography* (Boston, G.K. Hall, 1973–1980, 7 volumes). The latter is arranged by author, subject, and geographic heading. While many of the works cited in the *Bibliography* are found in the Library of Congress, it also includes references to works in other repositories. The *Bibliography* is maintained by the staff bibliographer (Ronald Grim 202/287–8532), who is available for consultation.

The Pamphlet File (51 linear feet) is a particularly important research source consisting of rare published and unpublished articles, bibliographies, brochures, dissertations, exhibition catalogs, monographs and papers presented at professional meetings. A few examples illustrate the wide variety of materials found in these files: copy of John Quincy Adams' letter to G.W. Erving, Madrid, concerning Aaron Arrowsmith's map of North America, 1816; copy of "List of Maps, Plans, etc. belonging to . . . Lord Commissioners for Trade and Plantations . . . 1780" in the Public Record Office, London; an unpublished report on "Topographical Mapping of Humid Tropical Asia" by Colonel Phoon Phon Asanachinta, Thailand, 1971; correspondence concerning Mongolian maps, 1977; a description of four Willem Janszoon Blaeu wall maps offered for sale in 1908 by Prince Ulrich von Schonburg; a Finnish-English glossary of map terms submitted as a thesis by Albert E. Palmerlee, University of Kansas, 1969; professional paper by Nakamura Hiroshi, "Old Chinese World Maps Preserved by the Koreans", 1966; a paper on transportation mapping in Israel, prepared for a professional meeting by Shalom Reichman; and assorted brochures on the regional remote-sensing facility in Nairobi, Kenya.

The Acquisition Unit (Andrew Modelski, Unit Head, 202/287-8533) maintains official and commercial map publication lists, sale catalogs, auction catalogs, and price lists (107 linear feet).

4. In addition to the finding aids cited above, there are a number of other card catalogs and published finding aids available to help the scholar. The Geography and Map Reading Room maintains a dictionary card catalog to the atlas collections (144 drawers), and author/title subject catalogs provide access to the MARC map collection, 1968–1980 (221 drawers).

A general introduction to the Division and its resources is Walter W. Ristow's *The Geography and Map Division: A Guide to its Collections and Services* (Washington: Library of Congress, 1975). A list of the Division's publications is available upon request. It describes almost seventy monographs, exhibit catalogs, checklists, short lists, article reprints, map facsimiles, microforms, and computer tapes available from the Division. Information regarding the Maps online data base is provided in *MARC Formats for Bibliographic Data,* which is available from the Cataloging Distribution Service, Library of Congress, Washington, D.C. 20541. A small booklet describing the National Union Catalog for Cartographic Materials may be obtained from the NUC Desk, Customer Services Section, Cataloging Distribution Service (202/287-6171).

A22 Library of Congress—Motion Picture, Broadcasting and Recorded Sound Division.

1 a. *James Madison Memorial Building*
Room 336
1st Street and Independence Ave. S.E.
Washington, D.C. 20540
(202) 287-1000

b. 8:30–4:30 P.M. Monday–Friday.

c. Opened to serious researchers for specialized individual research and viewing, but films are not available for public projection, rental, or loan. Since viewing facilities are limited, the scholar should contact the Division well in advance. Screening time is limited to three films a day. A handout, *Guidelines for Viewing Films and Videotapes* is available upon request.

d. Copies of film not protected by copyright or donor restriction may be ordered through the Division.

e. Robert Saudek, Chief
Patrick Sheehan, Head of Documentation and Reference Section

2. The Motion Picture, Broadcasting and Recorded Sound Division is one of the premier archives of commercially produced films in the world. The bulk of its collection, which numbers more than 75,000 motion pictures (200,000 reels) is derived from copyright deposits beginning in 1942, but the Division also contains several earlier collections dating from 1894 and some 5,000 titles of German, Italian, and Japanese films confiscated by the U.S. government following World War II. Both the copyright and captured film collections include educational, documentary, and scientific films. About sixty percent of all films submitted for copyright are retained.

3 e. The following films pertaining to cartography and surveying have been identified:

Aerial Photography. Part 1: Introduction to Aerial Camera Types. United States Army Air Forces, 1940. 9 min. Sound. b&w. 16mm.

Determining Direction in the Field. United States Army Signal Corps, 1941. 9 min. Sound. b&w. 16mm. Compass and map use.

Global Concepts in Maps. Coronet, 1947. 11 min. Sound. Color. 6mm. Collaborator: Erwin Raisz. Introduction to map projections.

Globes: An Introduction. Indiana University, 1964. 10 min. Sound. b&w. 16mm.

History of Maps. Doubleday Multimedia, 1970. Sound. Color. 16mm.

Introducing Globes. BFA Educational Media, 1978. Sound. Color. 16mm.

Language of Maps. Encyclopedia Britannica Films, 1964. Collaborator: Clarence W. Sorenson. 11 min. Sound. b&w. 16mm.

Map Projections in the Computer Age. Coronet, 1978. Sound. Color. 16mm. Consultant: Joel Morrison.

Map Reading and Trip Planning. American Automobile Association. 1967. 28 min. Sound. Color. 16mm. Use of road maps.

Maps: An Introduction. Indiana University, 1963. 12 min. Sound. Color. 16mm.

Maps and Their Meaning. Academy Films, 1969. Sound. Color. 16mm.

Maps and Their Uses. Coronet Instructional Films, 1951. 11 min. Sound. Color. 16mm. Collaborator: Erwin Raisz. Map symbols, scale, legends, special purpose maps.

Maps Are Fun. Coronet, 1946. 11 min. Sound. Color. 16mm. Fundamental map making and reading for junior high school students.

Maps for a Changing World. Encyclopedia Britannica Film, 1959. 11 min. Sound. b&w. 16mm. Collaborator: George T. Renner.

Maps—Land Symbols and Terms. Academy Films, 1956 and 1970. 14 min. Sound. Color. 16mm. Aerial views and photographs of representative areas of the United States are used to explain map symbols and terms.

Reconnaissance Pilot. U.S. Army Air Forces, 1945. 29 min. Sound. b&w. 16mm.

Weather Forecasting. Eastman Teaching Films, 1931. 16 min. Silent. b&w. 16mm. Preparation of a weather map.

4. A card catalog, arranged alphabetically by title, lists exact title, name of production company, release date, length and type of film, and sometimes a short synopsis. Useful published finding aids which serve as subject indexes to the card catalog include *1,000 and One: The Blue Book of Non-Theatrical Films* (incomplete set, 1920–35); *Educational Film Catalog* (H.W. Wilson Company, 1936–62); and *Library of Congress Catalogs - Film and Other Materials for Projection* (Washington, D.C.: U.S. Library of Congress, 1948 to present). Not all of the film titles relating to cartography are in the Library of Congress. The earliest relevant movie title listed in these published lists is "Elements of Map Reading", prepared by the University of Wisconsin in 1920.

Recent film acquisitions not yet added to the main card catalog may be found in the *Catalog of Copyright Entries* (Washington, D.C.: Copyright Office, The Library of Congress, various dates). The Main Card Catalog in the General Reading Room also contains a number of titles of motion pictures and film strips under the subject headings "Cartography", "Maps", and "Aerial Photography". These cards, prepared by the Descriptive Catalog Division, also describe films not held by the Library of Congress. The Library does not retain film strips.

A23 Library of Congress—Prints and Photographic Division.

1 a. *James Madison Memorial Building*
Room 339
First Street and Independence Ave.,S.E.
Washington, D.C. 20540
(202) 287-6394

b. 8:30 A.M.–5:00 P.M. Monday–Friday.

c. Open to the public. Loan service not available.

d. Photocopies of prints and photographs not protected by copyright or donor restrictions are available through the Library's Photoduplication Service.

e. Stephen E. Ostrow, Chief
Renata V. Shaw, Assistant Chief
Mary Ison, Head, Reference Section (202) 287–8867
George Hobart, Curator, Documentary Photography (202) 287–8938

Bernard Reilly, Curator, Popular, Applied and Graphic Arts (202) 287–8696

C. Ford Peatross, Curator, Architecture, Design and Engineering (202) 287–6344

2. The Prints and Photographs Division has custody of some 10 million photographic prints and negatives and 1 million architectural plans, posters, fine prints, cartoons, drawings, and commercial prints. The collections are international in scope but focus on the history and culture of the United States. The collections examined contain approximately 5900 aerial photographs, 160 photographs documenting surveying and mapping activities, and 750 maps.

3. The collections are grouped by common creator, source, donor, subject, or format, and are maintained in some 12,000 separate "lots". These lots are indexed by subject and the larger ones are subdivided geographically. However, not all collections containing aerial photographs are cross-referenced by subject. More than 200 lots were examined, but there are undoubtedly others that include materials relating to surveying and mapping.

MOUNTED PRINT FILES

A number of self-indexing files of copy prints and original file prints are maintained in open-file cabinets in the Prints and Photographic Reading Room.

Biographical File. Contains a large number of photographs and prints of individuals, including government officials associated with cartography such as John J. Abert, John Wesley Powell, and Gouverneur K. Warren (576 linear feet).

Civil War Drawings File. Includes copy photographs of a few topographic sketches, located under the subject heading "Views".

Geographical File. Includes some aerial photographs of cities and towns. The Foreign Geographical File (50,000 prints) is arranged alphabetically by name of country and thereunder by name of city and town; the United States Geographical File (40,000 prints) is arranged alphabetically by state, then city or town, and building or site.

Specific Subject File. Includes a few photographic prints with captions primarily relating to map printing at the National Geographic Society and the United States Geological Survey, 1930–1955.

United States Farm Security Administration/Office of War Information (FSA/OWI) Photoprint File. Contains numerous aerial photographs and documentary mounted photographs relating to surveying and mapping in the United States from 1935 to ca. 1945. These photographs were taken as part of a national effort to document life in America during the Great Depression and to record the domestic impact of World War II. Pertinent photographs are interfiled throughout regional subdivisions under the following classifications: aerial photography, agriculture, airfields, cities, industrial areas, land, military intelligence, military maps, photo interpretation, printing, railroad yards, seashore, and war. A few examples include aerial views of the development of the planned New Deal Communities of Greenbelt, Maryland, Radburn, New Jersey, and Greenhills, Ohio, 1935–1938; photographs of an army technician at Fort Belvoir, Virginia, working on a lithographic press used for map printing, January, 1943; and photographs of the preparation and analysis of weather maps at the United States Weather Bureau, 1943.

"Washingtoniana" File. Includes aerial and panoramic views of the nation's capital, 1863–1975 (81 prints).

COLLECTIONS

Aerial Photography Collections. A number of small collections, many of which were deposited for copyright, consist of aerial photographs. These include views of the Potomac River in flood, 1936 (5 prints); San Francisco bridges, 1937 (9 prints); Rotterdam, Netherlands, before and after the German blitz, 1940 and 1946 (6 prints); Miami Beach, Florida, following a hurricane, ca. 1926 (6 prints); Palestine, 1947; London and vicinity, 1949 (15 prints); industrial sites along the Seattle, Washington waterfront, 1922 (16 prints); San Diego and vicinity taken by H.A. Erickson, 1928–1935 (58 prints); Haines City, Winter Haven, and Auburndale, Florida, 1925 (40 prints); Electra and Wichita Falls, Texas, 1929–1930 (9 prints); Oakland, Berkeley, and San Jose, California, 1929–1930 (24 prints); Washington, D.C., 1930–1940 (30 prints); Lake Placid, New York, 1929 (5 prints); Jinsen and Keijo, Korea, 1945 (15 prints); dam sites, 1935 (23 prints); and Birmingham, Alabama, 1934 (10 prints). Also, photographic views taken from observation balloons of towns in Connecticut, ca. 1886 (13 prints), and New York City, 1906 (4 prints). (Lots 838, 2585, 3055, 4251, 4600, 5105, 5300, 5583, 5584, 6671, 7545, 7637, 11063).

American Battle Monuments Commission Collection. Contains original terrain photographs and maps of American World War I battlefields in Europe (69 volumes). (Lot 2556).

Lawrence Briggs Collection. Includes the original printer's maps compiled to illustrate his *The Ancient Kmer Empire*. The maps show Cambodia under different rulers from 500 to 1400 A.D. (17 maps). (Lot 5789).

La Documentation Photographique Collection. Consists of a series of portfolios, each relating to a different aspect of French life and history. Portfolios 121 and 122 are entitled "La Lecture de la Carte" (1954). (Lot 3901).

Ira Clarence Eaker Collection. Includes aerial photographs of oil refineries in Austria, Czechoslovakia, Germany, Hungary, Italy, Poland, Romania, and Yugoslavia, 1944 (ca. 200 items); aerial photographs of bombing attacks on airfields, bridges, convoys, and rail yards, and other targets by the Eighth and Ninth Air Forces in France and Germany, some during the German Ardennes offensive, 1944-1945 (ca. 750 prints); aerial photographs of bomb damage in cities and other areas in Burma, China, Formosa, Japan, Singapore, and Thailand, 1945 (142 prints and 2 maps); aerial photographic views of atomic bomb tests and photographs of the equipment and activities of Task Unit 1.52, Air Photo Unit, 58th Wing, United States Army Air Force, which recorded the atomic bomb tests over Bikini Atoll. (Lots 10407, 10410–10413).

German Aerial Photographic Collection. Comprises three separate collections of German aerial photographs of areas in Finland, France, and Italy, 1914–1918, originally collected by the Air Division of the German War Ministry or the Rehse Archives in Munich (ca. 200 prints). Also, a teaching set of aerial photographs and maps produced by the Reichsluftfahrtministerium for photo-interpretation instruction, 1943 (3 folders). (Lots 3146, 3638, 3656, 4641).

German Materials Confiscated by United States Military Intelligence Authorities Collection. Includes a set of photographs of pictorial propaganda maps relating to the Nazi repatriation of Germans from southern and southeastern Europe, ca. 1939 (40 items); German aerial photographic mosaics of Poland and Yugoslavia, 1943 (111 prints); and German aerial photographs of French towns and areas in Austria and northern Italy during World War I. (Lots 2674, 2838, 2893, 3679).

Greenough Collection. Contains aerial photographs of communication lines and trenches in France, some captioned, prepared by the French Army's Section de Photo Aérienne, 1915, and of Forts Domaumont and Fleury, and others, 1916 (ca. 75). (Lot 4028).

Historic American Buildings Survey (HABS) Collection. This collection of measured drawings and photographs, compiled under the direction of the National Park Service, provides a detailed record of early American architecture in all 50 states, the District of Columbia, Puerto Rico, and the Virgin Islands since 1933 (G21). It includes site maps for about half of the 5,700 structures in the collection documented by drawings. Also, a collection of some 300 glass plate (9x9 inch) aerial photographic stereopairs of towns and pueblos in New Mexico taken by the New Mexico State Highway Department at an altitude of 1,500 feet during the 1970s, as well as detailed maps derived photogrammetrically from these photographs. This collection is described in *Historic American Buildings, Structures, and Sites* (Washington: Library of Congress, 1983).

Historic American Engineering Record (HAER) Collection. Includes site plans, locational maps, and road maps for some 200 major engineering structures in the United States (G21).

Historic Print Collection. Includes nineteenth century lithographic panoramic views of cities and towns in 25 states, 1837–1902 (112 prints).

Adolf Hitler Collection. Includes an album of aerial photographs of 60 different German cities presented to Hitler by Lufthansa Airlines (65 prints). These photographs were made during travels on Hitler's private Lufthansa airplanes. Also, aerial photographs of Nuremberg by R. Pfretzschner during a Nazi party rally, 1933 (15 prints); aerial photographs of Olecko, Poland (formerly Treuberg) and the surrounding region, 1933; an album of photographs of German ethnic minorities in Eastern Europe, accompanied by eight pen-and-ink maps colored to show the distribution of these minorities; and a presentation album, including aerial photographs, documenting the role of the German Air Force in the Polish Campaign, including several photographs relating to aerial reconnaissance activities, September, 1939 (ca. 45 aerial photographs). (Lots 11368, 11407, 11414, 11422, 11432).

Herman Hoernes Collection. Contains Austrian aerial views of the Fichtelgebirge range, the Saale River, the towns of Helmbrechts and Munchberg, and other sites, ca. 1890 (12 prints), and the dock area in Vienna (7 prints), ca. 1888. (Lots 7561, 7605).

International News Photos Collection. Includes photographs showing United States Army Engineers using stereoscopic equipment, and military draftsmen, copyists, and others compiling maps, ca. 1945 (18 prints). (Lots 7065–7066).

Herbert Eugene Ives Collection. Contains aerial photographs of Washington, D.C., ca. 1935–1945 (19 prints). (Lot 12252).

Japanese Print Collection. Among the lots that have been described is a large sketchbook documenting the arrival of the first Americans to Japan, 1846–1855. It contains four printed maps showing the location of Japanese defense forces, Japanese clans and American ships. Also, a set of photographic reproductions of these maps, annotated with English translations. (Lot 10637).

Ernest L. Jones Collection. Includes an aerial photograph showing poisonous gas being used by French forces on the Western Front and other aerial photographs of cities taken or collected by Sergeant Robert Soubiran, later commander of the Lafayette Escadrille, 1917; and aerial photographs of cities in California, the Canal Zone, Germany, Italy, and New York, as well as prominent places including Annapolis, Jamestown, Mount Vernon, Richmond, Virginia, Washington, D.C., and West Point, 1917–1920 (ca. 150 prints). (Lot 11952).

George R. Lawrence Collection. Includes early aerial photographs taken from observation balloons or kites of Berkeley, California, Kansas City, Missouri, Lake Tahoe, California, Reno, Nevada, Rockford, Illinois, Waukegan, Illinois, Salinas, California, and Washington D.C. Also, aerial views of San Francisco, California, following the earthquake and fire, 1906–1908 (ca. 60 prints). (Lots 5784–5787, 9964).

Felix Locker Collection. Contains an educational film strip showing the use of maps, 1949 (150 frames). (Lot 3700).

Alfred Marie Collection. Consists of colored tracings by Marie of original architectural and landscape drawings in French archives and private collections, including large scale garden and estate plans, seventeenth to eighteenth centuries (2800 tracings).

Matson Photo Service Collection. Contains a large number of oblique aerial photographs of villages and landscapes in Egypt, Lebanon, Palestine, and Syria taken by G. Eric Matson, who photographed the Middle East for over a half century, 1931–1932, 1937 (ca. 500 negatives). Some of these aerial photographs are reproduced in Matson's *The Middle East* (Arno Press, 1980, 4 volumes).

William ("Billy") Mitchell Collection. Contains aerial photographs of Naples, Palermo, Pisa, Rome, Trieste, and Vesuvius, ca. 1930 (13 prints); aerial photographs of World War I battlefields and French and German landmarks, 1918–1921 (25 prints); aerial photographs of army installations in Arizona, Georgia, New Mexico, North Carolina, and Texas, 1920 (ca. 50 prints); aerial photographs of practice attacks on ex-German ships and submarines, 1920 (100 prints); aerial views of Texas cities, 1919–1920; aerial photographs of landmarks, geographical features, and cities in Thailand, 1924 (24 prints); and French aerial oblique views of battlefields and towns, 1916–1917 (ca. 30 prints). Also, an album compiled by the 91st Aero Squadron Photo Section contains photographs of the map intelligence room, aerial cameras, map drafting room, intelligence maps, maps showing reconnaissance flights, samples of aerial photographs, and aerial photographic mosaics, 1918 (ca. 120 prints). (Lots 6058–6059, 6067–6068, 6090–6092).

John J. Pershing Collection. Includes a series of fourteen albums relating to World War I combat activities, which contain many aerial photographs; large aerial photographic prints, aerial print mosaics, and aerial prints overprinted with intelligence and map information showing United States military installations, battlefields, and towns in France, 1918–1919 (56 prints); an album of aerial photographs of Washington D.C. taken from an observation balloon, 1919 (17 prints); and an album showing the facilities and work of the 29th Topographic Engineers (26 prints). (Lots 7707, 7712, 7715, 7729).

Polish Aerial Photograph Collection. Consists of composite German aerial photographs of Poland showing canals, rivers, roads, and towns, ca. 1943 (100 prints). (Lot 2893).

Scamahorn Air Photo Company Collection. Contains aerial panoramic views of mines and mining towns in Idaho, 1948 (93 prints). (Lot 3173).

Carl A. Spaatz Collection. Contains aerial photographic prints of airstrips, farms, and railroads in Alaska, including views of Mt. McKinley (75 prints); aerial views of bombing attacks by the Eighth Air Force in Germany, 1943–1944 (153 prints); aerial photographs of D-Day landing craft, Berlin, and other areas taken by the Royal Air Force 106 Photoreconnaissance Group and the United States Army Air Force 7th Photo Group, 1944 (56 prints); aerial views of urban areas and bombing targets in Japan, 1945 (ca. 150 prints); an album of captioned aerial photographs documenting the Allied invasion of Europe, 1944 (1 volume); annotated strike and reconnaissance aerial photography, some relating to the Normandy invasion on June 6, 1944 (ca. 50 prints); and a photographic history of the Ninth Air Force Tactical Operations during the German offensive in the Ardennes which contains about 100 aerial photographs, 1944–1945. (Lots 6116–6119, 7587).

Spence Air Photo Collection. Contains oblique aerial photographs of dams and scenes along the Colorado River, mountains and canyons in California, and cities and towns in Southern California, 1920–1939 (200 prints). (Lots 2287, 2296, 3175, 3181, 4922, 6208–6209, 6211).

Spencer and Wyckoff Collection. Contains aerial photographs of United States Army training camps in Louisiana and Mississippi, 1941 (13 prints). (Lot 6439).

Tissandier Collection. Includes aerial photographs collected by Gaston Tissandier (1843–1899), a prominent French balloonist. These consist of vertical and oblique aerial photographs of Rouen and vicinity taken at 1100 meters, 1880 (6 prints); panoramic views of Paris taken by Louis Triboulet, 1886 (12 prints); aerial photographs chiefly of Paris, but also French military forts and villages, some by the Service Géographique de l'Armée, 1885–1887 (23 prints); and aerial photographs of Paris, 1878. (Lots 7582–7583, 7586, 6000).

Nathan Farragut Twining Collection. Consists of aerial photographic prints documenting the reconnaissance and bombing operations of the United States Strategic Air Forces in Europe and the United States 15th Air Force in southeastern Europe, 1944–1945 (22 volumes); and two volumes of aerial photographs of Japanese cities and a photo album recording the activities of the Air Photo Unit of the 58th Wing of the Army Air Force "Operations Crossroads", which filmed the testing of the Atomic bomb, 1946.

Photocopy Collection of Miscellaneous Historical Lithographs of Washington, D.C. Contains file prints and photographic reproductions of proposed plans and bird's eye views of Washington, D.C. 1790–1900. (Lot 4386).

United States Agricultural Adjustment Administration Collection. Includes aerial photographs of United States farmlands displayed at the Pan-American Institute, 1938. (Lot 2236).

United States Air Force Collections. Composed of several lots, this collection includes aerial photographs of islands, shorelines, and landing fields in Costa Rica, Guatemala, Honduras, and Salvador, ca. 1932–1945 (74 prints); aerial photographs of the bombing of the United States battleship *Alabama,* 1921 (20 prints); aerial photographs of the ruined parts of Nagoya and Tokyo, Japan, following United States bombing raids, 1939–1945 (11 prints); photographs of photo reconnaissance equipment and photointerpreters during World War II (18 prints); and aerial views of the bombing of the Gilbert Islands and Ploesti, Romania, 1943. (Lots 838, 852, 2373–2375, 2399, 3541, 3894, 7735, 9779).

United States Army Collection. Contains aerial photographic prints of the Japanese occupied Aleutian Islands and the invasion of Sicily, 1943. Also, aerial photographs, interfiled among 4,500 captioned photographs prepared by the Photographic Branch of the United States Army's Persian Gulf Command, showing ports, railroads, and roads in Iran, ca. 1950. (Lots 803, 805).

United States Coast and Geodetic Survey Collection. Contains photographs showing activities relating to the establishment of triangulation stations, 1881–1938 (27 prints).

United States Coast Guard Collection. Contains captioned photographs of a special aerial mapping camera and its use, 1949 (6 prints). (Lot 4877).

United States Defense Department Collection. Contains aerial photographs of ballistic missile sites in Cuba, 1962 (14 copy photographs), and aerial photographs of airfields and seaplane landings in the Hawaiian Islands, ca. 1933 (62 prints). (Lot 6372).

United States Navy Collection. Contains a set of photographs showing the work of aerial photographers and photographic interpreters, 1944 (5 prints). (Lot 9780).

United States War Information Office Collection. Contains aerial photographic views of bombing raids in Europe and Japan, 1942–1945, and aerial views of the Bikini Atoll atomic bomb explosion, 1946 (3 prints). (Lots 836, 910).

George M. Wheeler Survey Collection. Contains photographic views of landscape scenes prepared by Timothy H. O'Sullivan and William Bell during Wheeler's mapping expedition, 1871–1874 (ca. 300 original and published prints). (Lots 3427, 4677).

4. The basic reference aid is the Division Card Catalog, arranged alphabetically by subject (119 drawers), which describes individual lots or collections. In addition, several indexes to individual items are available, including the Geographical Index (16 drawers), the Foreign and Historical Index (5 drawers), and the Specific Subject Index (63 drawers). An incomplete card index, listing illustrations in *Harper's Weekly,* contains 108 descriptions of maps for the period 1860–1866. A published brochure, *Prints and Photographs Division,* provides a short introduction to the Division.

A24 Library of Congress—Rare Book and Special Collections Division

1 a. *Thomas Jefferson Building, Room 256*
1st and Independence Avenue, S.E.
Washington, D.C.
(202) 287-5434

b. 8:30 A.M.–5:00 P.M. Monday–Friday

c. Open to scholars. Identification is required from first time readers. Because of the unique nature of the collection, no materials are available for loan.

d. No photocopy facilities. Depending upon physical condition of materials, reproduction may be furnished through the Library's Photoduplication Service.

e. William Matheson, Chief

2–3. The Rare Book and Special Collections Division has custody of some 300,000 volumes and 200,000 broadsides, pamphlets, title pages, prints, manuscripts, and posters. Among this number are a small but significant collection of atlases and early illustrated works containing maps of historical importance. The Division is particularly noted for its holdings of some 5,600 incunabula, the largest collection in the Western Hemisphere, for its fine collections of early illustrated books, and for its extensive holdings of early Americana, which began with the acquisition of Thomas Jefferson's library in 1815.

Several collections contain significant cartographic materials. The Hans P. and Hanni Kraus Collection of Sir Francis Drake materials includes an autograph letter from Gerard Mercator to Abraham Ortelius concerning Drake's voyage, 1580, engraved maps relating to Drake's circumnavigation of the earth, manuscript charts of Spanish harbors, 1589, and 2 silver commemorative medals engraved with world maps by Michael Mercator depicting Drake's circumnavigation, 1589. The Henry Harrisse Collection consists of personal copies of his publications (more than 200), many of which contain his marginal notes, and correspondence relating to research on the exploration and cartography of North America during the fifteenth and sixteenth centuries. The Lessing J. Rosenwald Collection contains 31 rare sixteenth century and 11 seventeenth century maps and atlases which are listed below. The John Boyd Thacher Collection has 34 early editions of Ptolemy's *Geographia.* Also useful for the historian of cartography are the Harrison Elliott Collection, containing 4,500 paper specimens and related research materials concerning the history of papermaking, and the Early Copyright Records Collection, which consists of 615 volumes of the district Court registers recording copyright registrations from 1790–1870.

About 95 percent of all the volumes in the Rare Book and Special Collections Division are listed in the Division's central card catalog of 650,000 cards, which provides access by author or subject.

The following subject headings, followed by names of authors and dates, provide a sample of the holdings.

Atlases. Pieter van der Aa, world, 1729; Rigobert Bonne, world, 1780; Mathew Carey, world, 1796; John Flamsteed, celestial, 1726, 1776; Joseph Griffen, world, 1833; Gerard Mercator, 1595; Arnoldus Montanus, China, 1671, Japan, 1670; John Pinkerton, world, 1804; Claudius Ptolemy, 1475–1695 (50 items); Johann Leonhard Rost, celestial, 1723; Thomas Tucker Smiley, world, 1834; Benjamin E. Smith, world, 1897; Robert White, celestial, 1751–1851 (various editions); Emma Hart Willard, world, 1826; Frederik de Wit, 1680; and Antonio Zatta, 1779–1785.

Cosmography. Petrus Apianus, 1482–1584 (18 items); Martin Borrhaus, 1551; Gilles Boileau de Bouillon, 1555; Vincenzo Coronelli, 1693; Giovanni Paolo Gallucci, 1588; Johannes Honter, 1554–1600 (5 items); Pomponius Mela, 1482,1502; Paulus Merula, 1605; Sebastian Münster, 1529–1752 (15 items); and Proclus, 1561, 1585.

Cartography. Nature, construction and use of maps. William Alingham, 1698, 1703; Jacques Nicolas Bellin, 1767; *Netherlands. Topographische Inrichting,* 1866; Jacque Ozanam, 1693, 1700; and Jacques Severt, 1598.

Description and Travel. The scholar must check this subject by geographical or political area. For example, under the subject heading "China—Description and Travel", the following works on exploration and travel contain maps: Clarke Abel, 1818; Roy Chapman Adams, 1918; Wystan Hugh Auden, 1939; Andreas Everard van Braam Houckgeest, 1798; Matthijs Cramer, 1670; Karl Friedrich August Gutzlaff, 1834, 1838; Athanasius Kircher, 1667, 1668, 1670; Arnoldus Montanus, 1671; Johan Nieuhof, 1665–1669 (5 items); George Smith, 1847; George Leonard Staunton, 1804–1805; Melchisedech Thevenot, 1681; and *Travels of the Jesuits,* 1743, 1762.

Geography. Limited to works on geography which contain maps, and sometimes, descriptions of the nature and use of maps. Giovanni Lorenzo d'Anania, 1582, 1596; Pierre d'Avity, 1646; Richard Blome, 1670; Giovanni Botero, 1617–1630 (4 items); Claude Buffier, 1773, 1775; Philip Cluver, 1652, 1661; Benjamin Davies, 1805; Hugo Favolius, 1585; Lorenz Fries, 1525; Simon Girault, 1592; Geronimo Girava, 1570; Patrick Gordon, 1693–1754 (4 items); Eberhard Werner Happel, 1688; Johann Hübner, 1742; Alain Menesson Mallet, 1683; William Frederick Martyn, 17–; Samuel Augustus Mitchell, 1840; Jedediah Morse, 1791–1798 (5 items); J.B. Nolin, 17–; John Payne, 1798–1800; Denis Petau, 1659; Giorgio Ponza, 1684; Matthias Quad, 1599, 1604; Johann Rauw, 1597; Blasius Vitalis Seywald, 1673; Charles Smith, 1795; Robert Stafford, 1607; André Thevet, 1575; Joachim Vadianus, 1534, 1548; and Jacob Ziegler, 1532, 1536;

Geography–Ancient. Limited to volumes containing maps. Christoph Cellarius, 1703–1731 (3 items); Periegetes Dionysius, 1688, 1704; Pomponius Mela, 1482–1582 (7 items); Giuseppe Rosaccio, 1594–1724 (8 items); Thomas Salmon, 1732; John Seller, 1694; C. Julius Solinus, 1520, 1538; John Speed, 1646; and Bernhard Varen, 1734 (3 items).

Geography–Dictionaries. Richard Brookes, 1762–1815 (3 items); Laurence Echard, 1704–06; Zaccaria Lilio, 1493, 152-; Sarah M. Lyon, 1848; John Malham, 1795, 1797; Abraham Ortelius, 1596; Thomas Salmon, 1769; Joseph Scott, 1799–1800; Ivan Ivanovich Stafengagen, 1753; and Peter Williamson, 1768.

Geography–Mathematical. Adam Aigenles, 1668; Giuseppe Biancani, 1653; Pierre Duval, 1672, 1680; Giovanni Paolo Gallucci, 1598; *Geographia generalis* (Nürnberg), 1696; *Globus Mundi* (Johannes Grueninger), 1509; Georg Wolfgang Krafft, 1739; Adriaan Adriaansz Metius, 1614; Jacques Michelet, 1615; Jose Vicente del Olmo, 1681; *Orbis in nuce* (Frankfurt and Leipzig), 1687; Wilhelm Schickard, 1669; Gines Rocamora y Torrano, 1599; and Cornelius Valerius, 1561.

Geography–Text Books. Claude Buffier, 1722; Jedediah Morse, 1796; and Benjamin Workman, 1796. For the period, 1800–1870, there are 83 titles, published chiefly in the United States, but also in Canada, France, Germany, Great Britain, Hawaii, Poland, and Russia.

Geology. Limited to volumes containing maps. Samuel Akerly, Hudson River, 1820; Frederick William Beechey, Oceania, 1839; Laurent Francois Dethier, 1803; Amos Eaton, 1824; George William Featherstonhaugh, United States, 1836; John Wells Foster, Lake Superior, 1850–1851; Ferdinand Vandeveer Hayden, 1859; Henry Youle Hind, 1860; Jacob Houghton, Lake Superior, 1846; Alexander Kircher, 1665, 1678; Charles Lyell, 1830–33; William Maclure, United States, 1817, 1832; Jules Marcou, North America, 1858; *Maryland Annual Report,* 1834, 1840; John Palliser, Canada, 1859, 1860; John Honeywood Steel, New York, 1819; *Transactions of the Geological Society of Pennsylvania,* 1835; Philip Thomas Tyson, California, 1851; and Charles Whittlesey, Ohio, 1856.

Globes. Description and use of globes. Simone Assemani, 1790; Willem Janszoon Blaeu, 1640–1701 (9 items); Roger Palmer Castlemaine, 1696; Daniel Fenning, 1792; Septimus Globus (pseudonym), 1824; Johann Ludwig Hocker, 1734; Robert Hues, 1639; Thomas Keith, 1811; William Leybourn, 1675; Joseph Moxon, 1665, 1686; Didier Robert de Vaugondy, 1745; R.T., 1647; and Edward Wright, 1613.

Map Catalogs. Pieter van der Aa, 1715; John Bowles, 1736; British Museum, 1829, 1844–61; Mathew Carey, 1795; Maggs Brothers, 1929; New York State Library, 1857; and Henry Overton, 1734.

Navigation. Limited to volumes with charts or maps. Rene Bougard, 1801; Greenville Collins, 1693; Martin Cortés, 1589, 1596; Bartolomeo Crescentio, 1607; Benjamin Franklin, 1786; Andreas Garcia de Cespedes, 1606; Charles Grant, 1808; Fedor Petrovich Litke, 1835; Pedro de Medina, 1545, 1569; Antonio Pigafetta, 1801; and Edward Wright, 1657.

Pilot Guides. Limited to volumes containing charts or maps. Blunt's *American Coast Pilot,* 1804, 1812 (3 items); Jacques Nicolas Bellin, West Indies, 1758; Rene Bougard, European Atlantic Coast, 1801; James Burney, China Sea, 1811; Greenville Collins, Great Britain, 1693; Edward Cooke, Pacific Coast, 1712; Georges-Boissaye DuBocage, France, 1761; Manuel de Figueiredo, 1614; George Gauld, Florida Strait, 1790, 1796; Domingo Gonzales Carranza, Caribbean Sea, 1740; Antoine Hyacinte Anne de Chastenet Puysegur, Haiti, 1787; Cadwalader Ringgold, Pacific Coast, 1851, 1852; Woodes Rogers, Pacific Coast, 1715, 1732; and Bernard Romans, Gulf of Mexico and Florida, 1775.

Lessing J. Rosenwald. Atlases and volumes illustrated with maps: Jean Poldo d'Albenas, 1559; Petrus Apianus, 1545, 1581; Rigobert Bonne, 1762, 1780; Benedetto Bordene, 1528; Giovanni Botero, 1596; Georg Braun, 1582; Hugh Broughton, 1590,1620; C. Julius Caesar, 1652; Diego Cisneros, 1618; Michael Drayton, 1622; Philippi Eckebrecht, 1627–1630; Jean Gaspard Gevaerts, 1642; Lodovico Guicciardini, 1567; Thomas Hariot, 1590; Sigmund Herberstein, 1556; Thomas Herbert, 1634; Hans Holbein, 1532; Cornelis de Houtman, 1598; Antoine de La Sale, 1527; Ambrosius Macrobius, 1515; Publius Vergilius Maro, 1648; Gerard Mercator, 1595; Claudius Ptolemaeus, 1482–1541 (5 items); Gregor Reisch, 1535; Christopher Saxton, 1579; John Seller, 1671–1672; Jacques Severt, 1598; John Speed, 1611; Joris van Spilbergen, 1619; Joachim Vadianus, 1534; Agustin de Zarate, 1564; and Antonio Zatta, 1779–

1785. Single maps include: Fernando Bertelli, America, 1562; Diego Gutierrez, America, 1562; Franz Hogenberg, America, 1589; Thomas Holme, Pennsylvania, ca. 1687; Gabriel Tatton, Pacific, 1600; and André Thevet, New World, 1581.

Surveying. Cosimo Bartoli, 1614; Silvio Belli, 1566; Richard Benese, 1562; Girolamo Cataneo, 1584; Miles W. Conway, 1807; *Corpus agrimesorum Romanorum,* 1554, 1614; Leonard Digges, 1591; Jonas Preston Fairlamb, 1818; Abel Flint, 1808, 1818; William Folkingham, 1610; Robert Gibson, 1789, 1803; John Gummere, 1817; Arthur Hopton, 1611; Levinus Hulsius, 1594; Zachariah Jess, 1799; Jakob Köbel, 1536, 1522; Valentine Leigh, 1577; William Leybourn, 1657; John Love, 1688–1796 (5 items); Giuseppe Malombra, 1630; Adam Martindale, 1702, 1711; Samuel Moore, 1796; New Jersey Surveyor General, 1746?; John Norden, 1610; Jacque Ozanam, 1693, 1700; Paul Pfinzing von Henfenfeld, 1598; Aaron Rathborne, 1616; Gaspar Schott, 1669; Stanislaw Solski, 1683; Samuel Sturmy, 1669; United States Surveyor General, 1833; H.W. Villee, 1824; Vincent Wing, 1664; Samuel Wyld, 1760; and Leonard Zubler, 1607.

Topography. Thomas Hutchins, Atlantic States, 1778; Gilbert Imlay, North America, 1793; and Martin Zeiller, separate countries and provinces in Europe, 1644–1680.

Voyages Around the World. Limited to volumes with maps. Faddei G. Bellingshausen, 1819; William Beresford, 1789; Louis Antoine de Bougainville, 1772; Théodor de Bry, 1619; Archibald Campbell, 1787; Ludovik Choris, 1822; James Cook, 1775–1796 (4 items); Edward Cooke, 1712; William Dampier, 1698–1703; Adolf Decker, 1629; Louis Isidore Duprerrey, 1825–1830; Charles Pierre Claret de Fleurieu, 1801; Johann Reinhold Forster, 1778; Vasili Mikhailovich Golovnin, 1822; William Hacke, 1699; John Hawkesworth, 1773–1785 (3 items); Antonio de Herrera y Tordesillas, 1622; Levinus Hulsius, 1616; Otto von Kotzebue, 1821, 1830; Ivan Fedorovich Kruzenstern, 1813; Georg Heinrich Langsdorf, 1813–1814, 1817; Jean Francois de Galaup Lapérouse, 1799, 1801; Iurii Fedorovich Lisianski, 1814; Fedor Petrovich Litke, 1835, 1836; John Marra, 1775; Olivier van Noort, 1602, 1610; Antonio Pigafetta, 1801; Nathaniel Portlock, 1789, 1795; Francis Pretty, 1598, 1742; Woodes Rogers, 1712–1726 (3 items); Camille de Roquefeuil, 1823; Willem Corneliszoon Schouten, 1618–1648 (4 items); Joris van Spilbergen, 1619, 1621; United States Exploring Expedition, 1838–42; George Vancouver, 1798; and Richard Walter, 1748–1767.

4. In addition to the Division catalog cited above, there are a number of published guides. The basic work is *The Rare Book Division A Guide To Its Collections and Services* (Washington: Library of Congress, 1965) which is supplemented by several recent publications pertaining to current acquisitions. Special publications include the *Lessing J. Rosenwald Collection* (Washington: Library of Congress, 1977); *Hans P. Kraus' Sir Francis Drake A Pictorial Biography* (Amsterdam: Nico Israel, 1970); and *Catalogue of the John Boyd Thacher Collection* (Washington: Library of Congress, 1915–31. 3 vols.). Two brochures, *Rare Books and Special Collections in the Library of Congress* and *Rare Book Reading Room,* provide general information on the services of the Division.

A25 Martin Luther King Memorial Library (District of Columbia Public Library)

1 a. *901 G Street, N.W.*
Washington, D.C. 20001
(202) 727-1126 (Information)

b. 9:00 A.M.–9:00 P.M. Monday–Thursday
9:00 A.M.–5:30 P.M. Friday–Saturday
1:00 P.M.–5:00 P.M. Sunday (except during the summer)

c. Open to the public. Interlibrary loan available, but most special collections do not circulate.

d. Coin-operated photocopy machines are available.

e. Kathleen Wood, Central Librarian

2. The library collection contains more than 12,000 maps, and 100 aerial photographs.

3 a. The History, Travel, and Geography Division has a collection of about 5,600 maps, including city plans, official state road maps, political maps of countries and areas of the world, and depository copies of United States Geological Survey topographical maps of Washington, D.C., Maryland, Delaware, New Jersey, Pennsylvania, Virginia, and West Virginia.

The Washingtoniana Division (Roxanna Deane, Chief 202/727–1213) maintains an important collection of 900 printed and photoprocessed maps that relate to Washington, D.C., 1612–1985. The collection contains plat and general maps prepared by early nineteenth century city surveyors, including a number of rare items such as F.C. De Krafft's map engraved by Mrs. William J. Stone, 1840, and Albert Boschke's topographical map, 1861, bird's eye views, historical maps, planning and zoning maps, real estate and subdivision maps, road maps, and special purpose maps relating to geology, inaugural ceremonies, and soils. The maps are organized chronologically. A card index provides access by date, subject, place names, and personal names. The latter index provides an unique index to names of individual land owners appearing on plat maps of the city.

The Washingtoniana Print Collection contains some 50 photographic prints of bird's eye views (1860s) and maps of Washington, D.C., 1791–1970s.

The Washington Star Collection, administered by the Washingtoniana Division, comprises the former working morgue and photo library of the *Washington Star* newspaper, which was published in Washington, D.C. from 1852 to 1981. The Photographic File includes a unique collection of approximately 5,700 news feature maps in the form of original compilation sheets, photographs, and newspaper clippings compiled by the *Star* or the wire services, United Press International and Associated Press. The collection, worldwide in scope, is arranged alphabetically by country, but is particularly strong for Washington, D.C., the Middle East, and Vietnam. The maps date from about 1939 to 1981. The Clippings File, numbering over 13 million items, contains several cartographic-related headings, such as aerial photography, Earth satellite mapping, maps and mapping, and photogrammetry and associations.

3 b. A small number of aerial photographic prints are found in the Washingtoniana Picture File under the heading "Description". These depict views chiefly of public buildings and areas in Washington, D.C. from about 1923–1979.

In the *Washington Star* photo morgue there are a number of categories where aerial photographs may be found. Some of the subject headings, both in the regular and oversized photographs, are: Washington, D.C.–Air Views, Washington, D.C.–Air and Night Views, Capitol, United States–Air Views, Highways & Roads, and Rivers - Potomac.

4. The History, Geography and Travel Division Map Collection, The Washingtoniana Print Collection, and the Washington Star Collection are not cataloged.

A26 The Middle East Institute (MEI)—George Camp Keiser Library

1 a. *1762 N Street, N.W.*
Washington, D.C. 20036
(202) 785–0182/0183

b. 10:00 A.M.–5:00 P.M. Monday–Friday. Open some Saturdays, call before visiting. Closed in August.

c. Open to the public. Borrowing privileges for MEI members only.

e. Ruth Baacke, Librarian

2. The George Camp Keiser Library, located in a renovated carriage house in the Institute's garden, maintains a collection of some 15,000 volumes, 300 periodicals, and 500 maps devoted chiefly to the history, politics, and economics of the Middle East.

3 a. The map collection consists chiefly of topographic maps issued by the United States Army Map Service of all Middle Eastern countries, and national and city tourist maps, some in Arabic or Turkish, prepared by tourist bureaus or information offices in Algeria, Egypt, Iraq, Israel, Saudi Arabia, Syria, and Turkey. While the earliest map, Gilles Robert de Vaugondy's *Asia Minor* is dated 1736, most of the maps date from World War II. Other maps of interest include an Arabic map of Israel, printed in Beruit in 1969 by the Fatah (Palestine Liberation Organization), showing Arab and Jewish villages prior to 1948 and Fatah military operations in 1964; a pilgrimage guide map to Mecca Mokarrama, published by the Kingdom of Saudi Arabia's Ministry of Petroleum and Mineral Resources; geographic, hydrographic, and topographic maps of oil regions issued by the Arabian American Oil Company, American Independent Oil Company, Kuwait, California Standard Oil Company, and the Oil Forum. The Library also has custody of six large wall maps of the Islamic World and the five continents published in Arabic by Denoyer-Geppert.

4. The map collection is uncataloged, but is generally arranged by country. Access to the Army Map Service topographic maps is provided by map indexes.

Metropolitan Washington Council of Governments (COG)—Information Center **See entry H5, Section 3**

Mine Map Repository (Interior Department—Surface Mining Office) **See entry G16**

A27 Montgomery County Department of Public Libraries—Rockville Library

1 a. *99 Maryland Avenue*
Rockville, Maryland 20850
(301) 279–1953 (Special Collections)

b. 9:00 A.M.–9:00 P.M. Monday–Thursday
9:00 A.M.–5:00 P.M. Friday–Saturday

c. Open to the public.

d. Agnes M. Griffen, Director

2–3. The Maryland Municipal Collection (Anne Bledsoe, Reference Librarian, 301/279–1953) contains photoprocessed and printed maps pertaining to Maryland with a special emphasis on Montgomery County.

A separate collection of 600 maps, dating from the eighteenth century to the present, consists of photostats of early maps from the Library of Congress, the National Archives and Records Administration, and other sources acquired for the county's bicentennial, including photostats of pen-and-ink maps showing the Maryland Civil War Campaign of 1862, compiled by R.E. Russell in 1932 (30 items). There are also maps printed by the United States Geological Survey and Corps of Engineers; general city zoning maps; an extensive number of maps issued by the Maryland-National Capital Park and Planning Commission; maps produced by county and state agencies for master plans; general county highway and city street maps; and county public school area maps.

A separate collection of recent master plans of the county are arranged by subject (agriculture, bikeways, highways, historic preservation, parks, and schools) and by communities (33 linear feet). In addition, the Maryland and Montgomery County Documents Files for the Maryland Department of Agriculture, the Maryland-National Capital Park and Planning Commission, the Maryland Department of Natural Resources, and the Highway Administration contain maps as part of master plans, zoning proposals, watershed studies, and environmental impact statements (13 linear feet).

4. A card file provides access to the map collection by acquisition number, author, subject, and date.

A28 Mount Vernon Ladies Association Research and Reference Library

1 a. *Ann Pamela Cunningham Building*
Mount Vernon, Virginia 22121
(703) 780-2000

b. 9:30 A.M.–5:00 P.M. Monday–Friday

c. Open to researchers by appointment only.

d. Copy facilities are available.

e. Ellen Clark, Librarian
Christine Meadows, Museum Curator

2. The Mount Vernon Ladies Association Research and Reference Library consists of a reference book collection numbering 10,000 volumes and a historical manuscript collection of 15,000 items, including 110 maps and 82 aerial photographs. The focus of the library and manuscript collection is the domestic life of George and Martha Washington with particular emphasis on Mount Vernon.

3 a. The library collection includes 3 cartographic items originally owned and signed by George Washington. These are Thomas Jefferys' *Map of New England* (1755), William Guthrie's *A New System of Modern Geography* (1795), and *Careys American Edition of Guthries Geography Improved* (1794–1795). The latter atlas contains 45 maps.

3 b. The aerial photography collection contains 82 oblique aerial photographic prints of Mount Vernon and vicinity, 1920–67. This includes a collection of 24 oblique views taken by Captain Herbert K. Baisley in 1938 to test the results of aerial views taken at different altitudes and time of day. These photographs were made at altitudes of 500 feet, 1,000 feet, 2,000 feet, 3,000 feet, 5,000 feet, and 10,000 feet.

3 d. The manuscript collection contains 53 survey plats and notes prepared by George Washington between 1749 and 1799, and 11 survey plats prepared by other surveyors, 1690–1831. Most of these plats relate to Mount Vernon or adjacent lands. Twelve are original pen-and-ink drawings, the rest are reproductions from other collections. The earliest original plat is George Brent's plat and memorandum of the land granted to Nicholas Spencer and John Washington (September 18, 1690). Manuscript plats drawn and signed by George Washington include maps of various land tracts in the vicinity of Mount Vernon (1770), plats of Ferry and French's Farm (1783), survey notes of his land (1759), plats of various tracts of land belonging to and adjoining those of Washington (1759–65), survey notes of Mount Vernon (1762), a survey plat for Capt. John Posey (1769), survey of the road from Ferry to Cameron (1788), and a survey of purchased land (1799).

4. Access to the maps and survey plats is provided by a card catalog file. The historical manuscript collection is arranged chronologically and cross-referenced by name of writer or recipient. The subject categories "Plats" and "Surveys" are listed under the names of George Washington and Mount Vernon.

National Aeronautics and Space Administration (NASA)—Headquarters Library **See entry G18, Section 3**

National Aeronautics and Space Administration (NASA)—Goddard Space Flight Center Library **See entry G18, Setion 3**

A29 National Agricultural Library (NAL) (Agriculture Department)

1 a. *Route 1*
Beltsville, Maryland 20705
(301) 344-4248
(301) 344-3755 (Reference Service)

b. 8:00 A.M.–4:30 P.M. Monday–Friday, except for legal holidays.

c. Open to all scholars with an interest in agricultural materials. Interlibrary loan service is available. Visiting scholars may have access to the bookstacks upon completion of a stack registration form at the circulation desk.

d. Self-operated copy machines are available for public use. Photocopy service is also available directly from the Photoduplication Laboratory.

e. Joseph Howard, Director

2. NAL attempts to acquire all substantive publications pertaining to agriculture in all major languages including related technical fields such as entomology, botany, biology, forestry, soil science, rural sociology, agricultural economics, natural history, and meteorology. This collection comprises 1.8 million volumes, about 13,000 maps, and 70,000 aerial photographs. In addition, NAL also maintains special collections of some 6,000 rare books, manuscript papers, and microforms.

3 a. Maps and atlases are scattered among the book and map collections. Some 5,000 individual and series maps are maintained as a separate map collection. The maps generally relate to soil classification, national forests, land use, vegetation, and erosion control but also include thematic topics such as the spread and distribution of certain insects and plant and animal diseases. The maps date from the 1870s but most were prepared during the twentieth century. Less than one-half are cataloged. A brief examination of the uncataloged maps revealed that about two-thirds were prepared by the Forest Service (G13), Soil Conservation Service (G25), State Agricultural Experimental Stations, and the Bureau of Public Roads (G11). Among the uncataloged materials is a series (166 sheets) of land use capability maps of Taiwan by the Government's Agriculture Research Institute, 1956–1960.

A series of county road maps prepared by the Bureau of Public Roads is arranged by state and county. It contains about 3,500 maps dated between 1937 and the 1960s.

Some 3,000 soil maps are found in the published soil surveys issued by the United States and many other countries. Most soil survey volumes contain large scale, fold-out maps. The NAL book collection includes a complete set of United States county soil survey reports issued by the Department of Agriculture, 1900 to the present (3,375 titles). Only in rare instances, however, are individual soil survey maps listed in the card catalog. The one exception is the 155 sheet soil map of Belgium (1954–1963), in which each map sheet is described. The following titles illustrate the variety of soil maps found among soil survey reports: "Soil Map for Administrative Area of Obihiro District", 1955, Japanese language, hand colored, scale 1:300,000; "The Soils of Southern Siberia", K.P. Gorshenin, 1953 (4 sheets); "Carta - Esboco dos Solos de Portugal", with accompanying typescript, "This sketch map was organized by J.T. Teles Grilo, postgraduate research student of the Chair of Pedology, Institute Superior de Agronomia, Lisbon, 1953; "Detailed Reconnaissance Soil Map of Thailand", Bangkok, 1974–1976 (25 folios, one for each province); and "Carte des Sols et de la Vegetation du Congo, du Rwanda et du Burundi," Brussels, 1954–1970 (100 sheets).

A small collection of some 100 atlases relate to agriculture, economics, natural resources, climate, and planning. They date from 1917 to the present.

3 b. NAL has a complete set of aerial photographic composite mosaic indexes prepared by the U.S. Department of Agriculture Stabilization and Conservation Service Aerial Photography Field Office, Salt Lake City (G1). This collection includes 70,000 prints (each 20 x 24 inches) for the period 1940–1975 (scales 1:20,000 to 1:40,000) and 3,400 105mm microfiche images for the period 1975 to 1984 (scales 1:40,000, 1:58,000). These indexes are arranged alphabetically by state and county, and thereunder by year. NAL also maintains an incomplete set of some 300 mosaic print indexes of the United States compiled from NASA imagery at a scale of 1:8,000,000.

3 c. The book collection is particularly strong with reference to aerial photography and photogrammetry (570 titles), remote sensing imagery (650 titles), soil mapping (65 titles), and forest mapping (50 titles). These include instructional manuals and explanations of soil and forest maps. The collection also contains 108 titles devoted to cartography. The library maintains a comprehensive collection of the reports issued by the

AgRISTARS (Agriculture and Resources Inventory Surveys Through Aerospace Remote Sensing) Program, a joint effort of the United States Department of Agriculture, National Aeronautical and Space Administration, National Oceanic and Atmospheric Administration, the Agency for International Development, and the United States Department of Interior to use satellite imagery as an aid in analyzing and forecasting agricultural production on a world-wide basis. Representative titles include *Taxonomic Classification of World Map Units in Crop Producing Areas of Argentina and Brazil* (1980); *Estimating Acreage by Double Sampling Using Landsat Data* (1982); and *Shuttle Imaging Radar (SIR-A) An Agricultural Analysis* (1982).

3 d. The library and papers of Charles E. Kellogg, former Chief of the United States Soil Survey (1934–1971), contains his personal collection of some 100 maps. Included are hand colored soil maps of the Danzig region (1928), the Lusitania-Iberia Peninsula, and a draft soil map of western Europe shown at the 7th Congress of the International Society of Soil Science. The legends of many of the foreign soil maps, particularly of the Soviet Union, have been transliterated. In addition to the map collection, there are six cubic feet of official papers relating to the Soil Survey including a folder marked "Soil Survey Cartography" and a working file of speeches and lectures. The latter contains three papers relating to cartography: "Cartographic Services, Soil Conservation Service, USDA" (1967); "National Cartographic Meeting, Fort Worth, Texas" (1969), and "The Principal Cartographic Requirements and Map Needs of the Soil Conservation Service, USDA" (1976).

4. A dictionary card catalog describes materials acquired between 1862 and 1965; separate subject and author card catalogs are available for materials obtained since 1965. Only about one-half of the maps are cataloged and these are listed by subject (agriculture, forest, soil) or area. Both card catalogs have been published: *Dictionary Catalog of the National Agricultural Library 1862–1965* (New York: Rowman and Littlefield, 1967–1970, 73 volumes) and *National Agricultural Library Catalog, 1966–* (Totowa, N.J.: Littlefield, Adams, & Company, 1972–). Also useful is the *Bibliography of Agriculture 1942–* (Various publishers, 1942–).

The primary data base is AGRICOLA (AGRICultural OnLine Access), a bibliographic data base consisting of literature citations to journal articles, monographs, theses, and technical reports from the comprehensive collection of NAL. The data base was begun in 1970 and now numbers over 2 million records. AGRICOLA is available for online retrieval through the Dialog Information Retrieval Systems (D3), Systems Development Corporation (D10), and Bibliographic Retrieval Service (D1). The following subject headings can be searched according to the *AGRICOLA Users Guide* (available from the National Technical Information Service (K12): remote sensing in agriculture, forest mapping, soil surveying and mapping, water surveying and mapping, climate and weather mapping, and geographical maps. The *Quick Bibliography* is a computerized online printed bibliography resulting from a NAL reference search in response to a customer request. This series includes *Remote Sensing: Applications for Agriculture.* It contains full bibliographic descriptions for 250 documents added to NAL's collection between 1979 and 1982. A list of current Quick Bibliographies can be obtained from the reference Section (301/344–3704).

National Air and Space Museum (NASM) (Smithsonian Institution)—Branch Library **See entry C5**

National Capital Planning Commission (NCPC)—Carto/Graphic Division See entry G19, Section 3

A30 National Geographic Society Library

1 a. *16th and M Streets N.W.*
Washington, D.C. 20036
(202) 857-7787
(202) 857-7783 (Reference Reading Room)
(202) 775-6173/6174 (Map Reading Room)

b. 8:30 A.M.–5:00 P.M. Monday–Friday.

c. Open to the public. Interlibrary loan service available.

d. A coin-operated photocopy machine is available in the Reference Reading Room.

e. Susan Fifer Canby, Director
Patricia Smith, Associate Director

2. The National Geographic Society Library, begun in the 1920s, supports the Society's interest in geography, travel, natural history, and general science. The Library Map Collection was added in the early 1940s to house cartographic source materials collected for use in map preparation by the Cartography Division (J7) and for geographic research. Today, the NGS Library has more than 78,000 books, 100,000 maps, and 850 atlases.

3 a. The Library Map Collection (Margery Barkdull 202/775-6131) contains a wide variety of published United States and foreign general reference maps, thematic maps, road maps, and city plans (1,560 titles). It is also a depository library for the United States Geological Survey (USGS) and the Defence Mapping Agency Hydrographic/Topographic Center (DMAHTC). It maintains the most recent published sets of USGS topographic quadrangle maps (1:24,000, 1:62,500), intermediate scale topographic series (1:100,000), state maps, and maps of the moon and planets; DMAHTC nautical and aeronautical charts, and some topographic sets; and Canadian topographic maps. The NGS Library also has an extensive collection of plastic raised relief maps of the United States (85 sheets) prepared by the Army Map Service and the Hubbard Scientific Company at a scale of 1:250,000.

The earliest map is Giuseppe Rosaccio's *Universale Descrittione di Tutto il Mondo* (Venice 1597, revised 1647), a large wall map on display in the Map Reading Room. Most of the maps, however, date from about 1900.

For a geographic distribution of single sheet general reference and thematic maps, see the regional *Scholars Guides*.

There are two atlas collections. The general atlas collection consists of some 800 recent geographical atlases (individual countries, States and provinces, cities), childrens atlases, historical atlases, and thematic atlases (roads, oceanography, population, economic, climatic, physical, archeology). A smaller collection of some 50 atlases published prior to 1900 is maintained in the Rare Book Room. This collection includes Claudius Ptolemy's *Cosmographie* (1486) and *Géographie* (1511, 1545, 1548, 1552, 1574) and world atlases by Gerard Mercator (1585, 1609), Abraham Ortelius (1595), Gerard de Jode (1593), and William Berry (1680–85). The collection also includes eleven world and national atlases produced during the eighteenth century by the Homann family (1799), John Senex (1708–1725), Antonio Zatta (1775), Matthäus Lotter (177–), Guillaume de L'Isle (1740–1750), John Seller (1700 ?), Herman Moll (1732–?), Guillaume Raynal (1780), and Tomás López de Vargas Machuca (1757), and the *Atlas Russicus* (1745, 1753).

3 c. The book collection (Carolyn Locke) contains a small collection of published works devoted to cartography (170 titles) and surveying (22 titles) as well as an extensive collection of gazetteers (260 titles) and guide books which contain city plans (1,140 titles). The latter includes the following series: Baedeker's *Handbooks, Blue Guides, Fieldings Travel Guides, Fodors Modern Guides, Michelin Guides,* and *Nagel Encyclopedia Guides.*

3 d. Two special collections contain cartographic materials.

The Library's Clipping Service, which was begun in the 1940s to collect newspaper and magazine clippings, press releases, travel brochures, and road maps, maintains a vertical file of some 1.5 million items arranged by subject (David Beveridge 202/857-7050). This file includes folders on the following subjects: maps and mapping, remote sensing imagery, exploration, surveying, aerial photography, space photography, geodetic satellites, Earth Resources Technology Satellite (ERTS), and biographies and obituaries of noted cartographers.

The Rare Book Collection (Marta Strada, Curator) contains the library of General Adolphus W. Greely, including 390 scrapbooks relating to his exploration of Alaska and the Arctic regions. There are several articles pertaining to the mapping of the Arctic region.

4. The Card Catalog in the Library Map Collection provides access to the single sheet map collection by geographical area and then subject. There are separate card catalogs for city plans (alphabetical by name of city), historical maps (geographic area), and atlases (author, area, subject, title). About one-fourth of the atlas collection has been converted to Library of Congress classification. The card catalog for the book collection (including rare atlases) is located in the Reference Reading Room and is arranged by author and subject. Map series are not cataloged.

The NGS Library issues subject guides to its services and resources under the title *Gateway to Information.* Among the guides in this series are "Atlases", "Clipping Service", "Gazetteers", "Guide Books", and "The Map Collection". A published *Visitors Guide to the National Geographic Society Library* briefly describes the Library.

A31 National Library of Medicine (NLM) (National Institute of Health)

1 a. *8600 Rockville Pike*
Bethesda, Maryland 20894
(301) 496-6095

b. Reading Room

Regular hours (Labor Day to Memorial Day)
8:30 A.M.–9:00 P.M. Monday–Thursday
8:30 A.M.–5:00 P.M. Friday–Saturday

Summer Hours (Memorial Day to Labor Day)
8:30 A.M.–5:00 P.M. Monday–Saturday

History of Medicine Collection
8:30 A.M.–5:00 P.M. Monday–Friday

c. The NLM collections are open to professionals, students in the health sciences and other serious scholars.

Interlibrary loans are also available.

d. Commercial coin-operated copy machines are available in the Main Reading Room.

e. Donald A.B. Lindberg, M.D., Director
Eve-Marie Lacroix, Chief, Reference Services Division
John L. Parascandola, Chief, History of Medicine Division

2–3. The NLM was originally established in 1836 as the library of the Army Surgeon Generals Office. Today it has the largest collection of biomedical materials in the world, numbering over three million items organized among four collections. These are the General Collection, which consists of monographs and serials published after 1870; the Documents Collection which includes health-related reports and vital statistics of United States, foreign, and international agencies published after 1870; the History of Medicine Division, which has the largest collection of medical history materials in the United States published prior to 1871; and the Reading Room Collection consisting of 200 English language journals, recent books and monograph serials, indexes, abstracts, bibliographies, reviews, dictionaries, directories, encyclopedias, and a limited collection of atlases.

A search of CATLINE (Catalog Online), a computerized catalog of 587,000 books and serials in NLM published since 1801, has 119 titles which contain the term "map" as a subject heading or text word. These titles include atlases, books on cartography, and books containing medical maps such as Howard C. Hopps', *Computerized Mapping of Disease and Environmental Data; a Report of the Mapping of Disease Project* (Washington, 1969); *Malaria Survey Maps* (Malaria Field Laboratory, 1943); Leonard Rogers and Ernest Muir, *Leprosy* (London, 1925), with a map showing the distribution of leprosy; *Skeleton Maps of Tropical Africa Showing the Distribution of Tsetse-Flies and Sleeping Sickness* (London, 1909); *Map of Soldiers Home Near Washington, D.C.* (1873); Alexander Williams, *Report on the Origin, Propagation, Nature, and Treatment of the Cattle Plague* (London, 1866), with maps showing the progress of the disease; Henry S. Tanner, *A Geographical and Statistical Account of the Epidemic Cholera from its Commencement in India to its Entrance into the United States, Comprehended with a Series of Maps and Tables, Exhibiting the Names and Places Visited by the Pestilence, the Time of its Commencement, the Number of Cases, and Deaths, and Duration at Each Place* (Philadelphia, 1832); *A Statement of the Occurances During a Malignant Yellow Fever in the City of New York... With a List of Cases and Names of the Sick Persons and a Map of Their Places of Residence* (New York, 1819).

The Prints and Photographs Collection (Lucinda Keister, 301/496–5961), which is located in the History of Medicine Division (Room 1 - N21), holds 75,000 items, including about 70 maps. These maps show the location and distribution of communicable diseases such as cholera, yellow fever, and smallpox; sanitation conditions; and the location of hospitals. The maps date from 1819 to 1967. Materials from the Prints and Photographs Collection are not available through interlibrary loan service. Slides and photographs of the maps, however, may be ordered.

4. The most comprehensive catalog to the holdings of NLM is CITE, a computerized catalog which is updated weekly. A microfilm catalog lists books and serial titles published since 1801. A printed *Current Catalog* has been published quarterly since 1965. For earlier works related to cartography, see the subject headings "Medical Geography" and "Medical Topography" in the *Index-Catalog of the Library of the Surgeon Generals Office, United States Army* (61 volumes in five series, 1880–1961).

NLM has developed a computerized system known as MEDLARS (Medical Literature Analysis and Retrieval System) which allows researchers access to some 6 million references to biomedical journal articles and books published since 1965. MEDLARS is a nationwide network of some 20 data bases available at more than 3,500 universities, medical schools, hospitals, government agencies, and commercial organizations. Most of these references appear in the printed *Index Medicus* a monthly subject/author guide. A brochure describing the system is available upon request. Three of the data bases contain references to cartographic literature. MEDLINE is the online data base used to access more than 800,000 articles from some 3,000 biomedical journals published in the United States and foreign countries during the last three years. About 4,000,000 article references are contained in the searchable backfiles which date from 1966. A search of the MEDLINE data base for the last three years revealed 2,535 citations containing the terms "map" or "maps". These include such titles as "Map analyses of psychiatric services: the application of a computerized psychiatric case register to geographical analysis (1984)", "Uses of computer-generated maps in occupational hazard and mortality surveillance (1984)", and "Temporal evolution of body surface map patterns following acute inferior myocardial infarction (1984)".

HISTLINE (History of Medicine Online) contains more than 50,000 citations to monographs, journal articles, symposia, and congresses. POPLINE (Population Information) has more than 100,000 citations and abstracts to published and unpublished literature on population and family planning, including 480 relating to cartography. Representative examples are "Mapping Cancer Mortality in England and Wales (1984)", "The Status of Census Cartography and Geography in the Sudan (Unpublished, 1982)", and "Cartography in Algeria in the Censuses of 1966 and 1977 (1982)".

National Museum of African Art Branch Library (Smithsonian Institution) **See entry C6**

A32 National Ocean Service (NOS) (Commerce Department—National Oceanic and Atmospheric Administration—Physical Sciences Services Section)

1 a. *6501 Lafayette Avenue*
Riverdale, Maryland 20737
(301) 436-5766

b. 8:30 A.M.–4:00 P.M. Monday–Friday

c. Open to the public. Interlibrary loan service is available.

d. Photocopies available for materials up to 40 x 80 inches.

e. Henry Carter, Chief

2–3. The section has custody of some 200,000 maps, charts, atlases, and aerial photographs assembled to support program activities of NOS.

Historical Map Collection, contains some 3,000 maps dating from the sixteenth century to the early twentieth century. Three major series are 800 Civil War manuscript and printed maps prepared by the United States Coast Survey, the Office of the Chief of Engineers, and the Office of Topographical Engineers, 1861–1904; 325 charts relating to the naval explorations and surveys of James Cook (1784), George Vancouver (1798), Charles Wilkes and the United States Exploring Expedition (1856–1923), John Rodgers and the United States North Pacific Exploring and Surveying Expedition (1849–1885), Robert E. Peary (1903), Edmund M. Blunt (1797–1862), Matthew F. Maury (1848–1860), James Imray (1849-69), and George Eldridge (1889–1911); and 1,200 plans of U.S. cities. The historical collection also contains a number of rare atlases, including Joseph F.W. Des Barres' *Atlantic Neptune* (1777), Louis Antoine de Bougainville's *Journal de la navigation autour de globe* (1824–1826), and Gavriil A. Sarychev's atlas displaying his exploration of the North Pacific for the Russian government in 1785–1793 (one of three known copies in the United States).

Present Day Source Materials Files, contain complete sets of recent United States Geological Survey quadrangles, including advance sheets; United States Army Corps of Engineers project books; Tennessee Valley Authority quadrangles; state and county highway maps made in cooperation with the Federal Highway Administration; and some 25,000 United States Department of Agriculture aerial photographic prints of coastal areas and major airports dating from the 1950s.

Record Set Collection, contains charts published by the Lake Survey (about 800 items) and NOS (80,000 items). The latter collection represents the most complete and comprehensive collection of NOS charts in the Washington D.C. area. It contains all editions issued by NOS and its predecessors (the Coast Survey and the Coast and Geodetic Survey) and all corrected copies of each edition, including hand corrections, 1841–1975.

Copper Engraved Plate Collection, contains 300 copper plates engraved by Survey personnel including a plate of a map showing General William T. Sherman's march through Georgia and the Carolinas in 1865 and 26 plates of charts from Charles Wilkes' Exploring Expedition of 1838–1842. Some of the plates were never printed; others were used only for limited printing in congressional documents or Survey reports.

4. Various published and unpublished finding aids are available. The Historical Map Collection has been cataloged and the cards are available for examination. A general description of this collection was prepared by William A. Stanley before part of it was transferred to the National Archives (Special Libraries Association Geography and Map Division *Bulletin,* vol. 91, March, 1973). Important segments of the collection have been described in cartobibliographies compiled and published by the Physical Science Services Branch: *National Ocean Survey Cartobibliography Civil War Collection* (1980) and *National Ocean Survey Historical Cartobibliography II: Age of Exploration* (1982). The Present Day Source Materials Files are accessed through unpublished color-coded map indexes known as the "New Materials Indexes." A microfiche index is maintained for the Record Set of NOS charts.

A33 National Oceanic and Atmospheric Administration (NOAA) (Commerce Department)—Library and Information Services Division

1 a. *Main Library*
6009 Executive Boulevard
Rockville, Maryland 20852
(301) 443–8330 (Reference)
(301) 443–8334 (Circulation)

b. 8:00 A.M.–4:30 P.M. Monday–Friday

c. Open to the public for on-site use. Interlibrary borrowing and lending services are available.

d. Photocopies, with no charge up to 20 pages.

e. Laurie Stackpole, Acting Chief

2. The NOAA Library is comprised of the libraries of the former Weather Bureau and Coast and Geodetic Survey, which were merged in 1967. Among the Library's 750,000 volumes and 9,000 current serial titles are approximately 2,780 volumes of bound weather maps received in exchange from countries throughout the world. While the strength of the library lies in its worldwide collections of current and classic climatological materials, it has a broad collection of more than 6,000 books and some papers relating to nautical and aeronautical cartography, geodetic and hydrographic surveying, photogrammetry, and geodesy.

3 a. The collection contains approximately one million sheets of daily weather charts covering most countries of the world. The earliest date from about 1859 (France), and some sets are incomplete or end about the time that the two libraries merged in 1967. Nevertheless, this collection is the most comprehensive collection of weather maps compiled by other countries available in Washington, D.C. The collection not only covers major countries but also many third-world areas, as well as smaller political entities.

The country and date distributions of daily weather maps are listed below. Other atlases include United States Pilot Charts, 1894–1945. Maps and charts are also scattered throughout the collections as enclosures in the annual reports of mapping and surveying agencies.

Country	*Date Range*	*Volumes*	*Map Sheets*
Algeria	1877–1938	61	21,350
Argentina	1902–1979	77	26,950
Australia	1887–1966	79	23,700
Austria	1873–1982	109	38,150
Bavaria	1873–1908	21	7,350
Belgium	1877–1969	92	32,200
Brazil	1928–1967	39	13,650
Canada	1895–1972	77	26,950
Catalonia	1934–1958	24	8,400
Chile	1907–1960	53	18,550
China	1906–1939	33	11,550
Czechoslovakia	1950–1982	32	11,200
Denmark	1880–1981	101	35,350
Egypt	1907–1957	50	17,500
Finland	1951–1982	31	10,850
France	1859–1982	123	43,050
Fr. W. Africa	1956–1968	12	4,200
Germany	1876–1983	107	37,450
Breslau	1926–1933	7	2,450
Hamburg	1930–1935	5	1,750
Saxony	1882–1950	68	23,800
Great Britain	1868–1979	111	38,880
Greece	1932–1980	48	16,800
Hungary	1937–1950	13	4,550
India	1878–1982	104	36,400

Country	*Date Range*	*Volumes*	*Map Sheets*
Italy	1879–1969	90	31,500
Venice	1931–1933	2	700
Japan	1883–1982	99	35,000
Latvia	1925–1939	14	4,900
Lithuania	1927–1939	12	4,200
Mexico	1900–1978	78	27,300
Morocco	1922–1978	56	19,600
Netherlands	1893–1977	84	29,400
Norway	1916–1955	39	13,650
Pakistan	1949–1970	21	7,350
Philippines	1927–1933	6	2,100
Poland	1920–1939	19	6,650
Portugal	1882–1982	100	35,000
Romania	1895–1938	43	15,050
South Africa	1937–1941	4	1,400
Spain	1893–1983	100	35,000
Sweden	1923–1977	54	18,900
Switzerland	1884–1982	98	34,300
Taiwan	1946–1947	2	400
Thailand	1950–1983	33	11,550
Trieste	1905–1924	19	6,550
USSR	1872–1981	118	42,300
Moscow	1933–1934	2	400
Vladivostok	1922–1930	8	1,000
United States	1871–1978	112	39,200
Uruguay	1943–1946	3	1,000
Venezuela	1950–1979	29	10,150
Vietnam	1953–1975	22	7,700
United Arab Republic	1958–1971	13	4,550

3 c. In addition to current books, the Dewey Decimal Classification Collection contains about 6,000 books, monographs, and serials devoted to cartography, surveying, and geodesy dated before 1971, and the "G" Collection contains extensive sets of the annual reports of Federal mapping agencies including the United States Army, Office of the Chief of Engineers, with the Pacific Railroads Survey, 1853–1857, and other western mapping expeditions; the Coast and Geodetic Survey; and foreign military surveys such as the Survey of India and the Topographical Survey of Austria.

A search of the card catalog through 1982 revealed the following subject distribution of titles:

Subject	*Titles*
Aerial Cameras	50
Aerial Photography and Interpretation	225
Aeronautical Charts	50
Base Measuring	130
Bathymetric Charts	25
Cartography	375
Charts	25
Conventional Signs and Symbols	65
Coordinates	110
Distances (Table Measurements)	105

Subject	*Titles*
Earth, Figure of the	135
Gazetteers	275
Geodesy	650
Geographic Names	250
Geographic Positions	120
Hydrographics Surveying	175
Latitude	310
Leveling	130
Longitude	300
Maps	450
Nautical Charts	130
Photogrammetry	475
Projections	225
Remote Sensing	15
Surveying	710
Topography	55
Triangulation	750

3 d. The Rare Book Collection focuses on historical meteorological texts dating from the seventeenth century, but it also contains many books and some manuscript papers devoted to surveying and charting. Among the several thousand volumes on surveying and charting are 77 typescript volumes in English of the annual reports of the Russian General Staff Military-Topographic Section, 1837–1934; a five-volume set of the professional and scientific papers of Dr. William Bowie, a Coast and Geodetic scientist, containing papers and articles respecting his work on the Federal Board of Surveys and Maps; a manuscript historical account of the plane table prepared by A.M. Harrison in 1865; Arnold Henry Guyot's manuscript report, *Mountain District of North Carolina, 1856–1860,* prepared for A.D. Bache; collections of typescript documents relating to Coast Survey activities during the Civil War, 1861–1865; a manuscript catalog of the Coast Survey Library; and annotated copies of Coast Survey reports.

4. A card file cross-referenced by author, corporate author, and subject is available in the Reading Room for the "G" Collection, Dewey Decimal Collection, and some of the Rare Book Collection. These cards have been published in G.K. Hall's *Catalog of the Atmospheric Sciences Collection,* comprising 24 volumes. Access to books acquired since 1971 is provided by the NOAA Automated Library Information System (NALIS), a fully searchable online catalog of approximately 50,000 titles in the main collection housed in Rockville and twelve other NOAA libraries located throughout the United States. In addition to being searched by author, title, and subject, appropriate materials in the NALIS system can also be searched by geographic coordinates. The NALIS catalog is available on COM (Computer Output Microfilm). An accession list is published regularly describing selected recent accessions.

National Park Service (NSP) (Interior Department)—Map Room **See entry G21, section 3**

National Philatelic Collection Library (Smithsonian Institution) **See entry C8**

A34 Naval Historical Center (Navy Department)—Navy Department Library

1 a. *Building 44*
Washington Navy Yard
Washington, D.C. 20374
(202) 433-4131/2

b. 9:00 A.M.–4:00 P.M. Monday–Friday

c. Open to the public.

d. Electrostatic copiers are located in the library.

e. Stanley Kalkus, Director

2. The Navy Department Library has 160,000 volumes, 10,000 rolls of microfilm, and a collection of some 1,000 maps and atlases.

3 a. The map collection consists of 28 portfolios of uncataloged manuscript, photoprocessed and printed maps and charts dating primarily from about the 1870s to 1920s.

These include chiefly British Admiralty charts, French nautical charts (1870s–1980s), Russian nautical charts, and some United States hydrographic charts. Some of these charts are annotated, including one of Dover and Calais that has been marked to show enemy submarine tracks and British sound bearings in 1915. A portfolio labeled "Miscellaneous" includes a manuscript United States Coast Survey map of Fort Jackson showing bombardment by United States Navy gunboats in 1862, manuscript and photoprocessed charts showing the tracks of British cruiser operations in the Pacific and in the vicinity of the Falkland Islands, 1914, and manuscript charts and maps of Cuba prepared for a publication, "Quasi War with France". Another portfolio, "Europe and World War I", contains a manuscript chart showing the war voyages of the *USS Siboney* between the United States and France, April–November, 1918; a large manuscript map of the defenses of Heligoland prepared by the Intelligence Section, United States Navy Headquarters, London, 1918; maps showing merchant steamship traffic and tonnage in the Mediterranean, 1918; and British Admiralty Coastal Air Charts showing prominent landmarks along the German coast.

The Library also has some 40 reference atlases, including the *English Pilot* (London, 1775), Robert Sayer's *American Military Pocket Atlas* (London, 1776), Rigobert Bonne's world atlas (1783), and the Naval History Division's own facsimile atlas, *The American Revolution 1775–1783 An Atlas of Eighteenth Century Maps and Charts Theatres of Operations* (1972). The latter was compiled by W. Bart Greenwood, former director of the Navy Department Library. It consists of a portfolio of 20 maps and charts and an accompanying volume (86 p.) with an essay on surveying and mapping at the time of the American Revolution by Louis DeVorsey, Jr., a list of the maps, and an index of some 10,000 names of places, features, Indian tribes, and landholders keyed to the maps.

3 d. The Library maintains some 300 unpublished narrative administrative histories of the naval establishment (headquarters offices, shore establishments, and operating forces) during World War II. This program was begun under the direction of Robert G. Albion in 1943. Most of the histories of operating forces in the Atlantic and Pacific Theaters and sea frontiers and operating bases in the Caribbean contain detailed maps and aerial photographs. In addition, there are histories of organizations that included

pertinent cartographic and aerial photographic functions. Administrative Histories of particular interest are:

"Naval Aviation Photography and Motion Pictures" (Washington, 1957. 128 p.). Describes the role of aerial photography and aerial photographic interpretation in naval aviation and the development and procurement of photographic equipment.

"Hydrographic Office" (326 p.). Describes the impact of World War II and the subsequent changes on the organization and function of the Hydrographic Office, 1939–1945.

"U.S. Naval Observatory" (Washington, 1948. 119 p.). A general history of the United States Naval Observatory from 1842 to 1945 by Commodore J.F. Hellweg, USN, who served as Superintendent of the Observatory from 1930 to 1946.

"U.S. Naval Gun Factory" (1945. 452 p.). Includes a chapter on the work of the Naval Photographic Intelligence Center, which was located within the Washington, D.C. Navy Yard during World War II.

"Administrative History, United States Naval Forces in Europe, 1940–1946" (London, n.d. 2,856 p.). Includes a description of the work of the hydrographic and intelligence activities of the command headquarters in London, particularly with respect to the Normandy invasion.

"Commander in Chief, United States Pacific Fleet and Pacific Ocean Areas" (1946. 419 p.). Includes a discussion of the photographic intelligence collection.

"History of Service Force, U.S. Pacific Fleet" (1946. 389 p.). Describes functions of the Service Force, which furnished a wide variety of support to the Pacific Fleet including photography and hydrographic surveying.

The manuscript collection maintained by the Library includes a letter from L.M. Goldsborough to Rear Admiral Charles H. Davis concerning charts for the *Colorado* and other vessels of the European Squadron, May 30, 1865.

4. The unpublished histories are described in *Guide to United States Naval Administrative Histories of World War II* (Naval History Division, 1976. 219 p.).

A35 Naval Observatory Library (Navy Department)

1 a. *Massachusetts Avenue and 34th Street, N.W.*
Washington, D.C. 20390
(202) 653-1499

b. 8:00 A.M.–4:30 P.M. Monday–Friday

c. Serious researchers from universities and other government agencies may use the library, but arrangements must be made in advance. The library will make interlibrary loans.

d. Photoduplication services are available.

e. Brenda G. Corbin, Librarian

2. The United States Naval Observatory Library is considered to have the best collection of astronomical materials in the United States. Originally established in 1830 as the Depot of Charts and Instruments, the United States Naval Observatory began assembling a library in 1842 when Congress sent Lieutenant James Gilliss, its first director, to Europe for that purpose. Some of the 80,000 volumes comprising the current collection still retain the original ownership stamp of the Depot of Charts and Instruments. While

the library does not have a large collection of cartographic materials, it contains an important collection of some 350 celestial atlases and star charts as well as related books.

3 a. The reference library collection contains about 100 celestial and lunar atlases, found on open shelves in the main reading room, and approximately 30 oversize atlases and 250 individual star charts, stored in 15 map drawers, in the stack area. This collection, dating from the 1830s to the present, includes the atlas of large sky overlap maps compiled for the National Geographic Society Palomar Observatory Sky Survey, 1981, and most of the significant atlases and charts prepared worldwide.

The Rare Book Collection, numbering over 800 pre–1830 volumes, has a number of early celestial atlases or astronomy books with star maps. Among the rarest early works are Johann Bayer's celestial atlas, the first to use Greek and Latin letters to designate stars in order of magnitude (1603, 1648, 1655, 1661, 1723); Johann Kepler's *De Stella Nova in Pede Serpentarii* (1606), which includes a star chart; and Johannes Hevelius' *Selenographia* (1647, 1690), the first atlas of moon maps. Other noted early authors include Johann Elert Bode, Johann Gabriel Doppelmayer, John Flamsteed (4 titles), Johann Kepler (1627), Eustachie Manfredi, and Giovanni Battista Riccioli (1651). Two other early important cartographic works are Petrus Apianus' *Cosmographie* (1540) and the *Atlas Maritimus* (London, 1728), the latter believed to have been compiled by J. Harris and J. Senex.

3 c. The Rare Book Collection includes early books on the construction of globes and maps, 1594–1826 (12 items), and on eighteenth century surveying (20 items), the latter chiefly devoted to the French effort to determine the measurements of the meridian for the triangulation of France. Of particular note are Thomas Blundeville's ...*cosmographie* (1594, 1636), with his description of globes and Petrus Plancius' map of 1592; the works of George Adams, Willem J. Blaeu, John Harris, and Isaac Watts on the construction and use of celestial and terrestrial globes; Johann Heinrich Lambert's treatise on map projections, 1765–1772; and Christopher Maire's report on his mapping survey of the Papal States, 1770. In addition to César Francois Cassini de Thury's *La méridienne de l'observataire royal de Paris (1774)* and his *Exposé de opérations faite en France en 1787 pour la junction des observataires de Paris et de Greenwich* (1792), there are eighteenth century treatises and reports on ascertaining longitude and the figure of the Earth by Jean Baptiste d'Anville, Ferdinand Berthaud, John Churchman, Alexis C. Clairaut, Johann Gerard W. De Brahm, Jean Baptiste J. Delambre, The Commissioner of Longitude, Great Britain, Nevil Maskelyne, and Pierre Louis Moreau de Maupertuis. Historians of cartography will also find early works on surveying instruments by Edmund Gunter, Jean Picard, Jesse Ramsden, and Franz Ritter, about 1616 to 1749.

The main library collection has additional works on geodesy (105 citations), geographic positions (45), latitude (135), and longitude (150), including Lieutenant James Gilliss' *On the Longitude of Washington* (1839).

4. The main dictionary catalog, located in the reading room, was published in 6 volumes by G.K. Hall in 1976. The contents of the map cases are listed in a typescript list and the rare books are described in a bound typescript compiled by Lettie S. Multhauf, *The Rare Book Collections of the U.S. Naval Observatory*. The latter contains useful bibliographic descriptions with biographical sketches of the authors.

A36 Organization of American States—Columbus Memorial Library

1 a. *Constitution Avenue and 17th Street, N.W.*
Washington, D.C. 20006
(202) 789-6038

b. 9:30 A.M.–4:30 P.M. Monday–Friday

c. Open to the public. Interlibrary loan service is available.

d. Photoduplication service is available.

e. Thomas L. Welch, Director

2. The Columbus Memorial Library has custody of more than 500,000 books and reports relating to the Caribbean and Latin America. The materials date from the eighteenth century to the present. The Library also maintains an uncataloged map collection of 2,500 maps.

3 a. The map collection provides the following number of maps for Latin American countries: Argentina (130), Bolivia (56), Brazil (250), Central America (100), Chile (200), Colombia (450), Costa Rica (50), Cuba (100), Dominican Republic (75), Ecuador (50), El Salvador (50), Guatemala (50), Guyana (50), Haiti (50), Honduras (50), Mexico (300), Nicaragua (75), Panama (100), Paraguay (50), Peru (200), South America (150), Uruguay (75), Venezuela (100), and the West Indies (25). Most of the maps date from 1880 to 1946. The collection includes cadastral maps, city plans, thematic maps, and topographic maps. It is particularly rich in large wall maps and railroad maps. Most of the maps are printed either in Spanish or Portuguese, and there are also a few manuscript maps. Particularly noteworthy are a manuscript map in Spanish of Bolivia showing proposed and constructed railroad lines; a large bound volume of agricultural maps of Brazil prepared by the National Society of Agriculture (Rio De Janeiro, 1910); a set of 18 medium scale maps (1:250,000) of Central America issued by the Geographic Branch, Military Intelligence Division, United States Army General Staff, 1933; a manuscript map of Cuba compiled for a Pan American Union exhibition showing agricultural production, 1943; a Spanish manuscript map displaying the 1824, 1882, and 1900 boundary lines between Guatemala and Mexico, copied by Jorge Contreras, 1900; and a manuscript map of the province of Bocas del Toro, Panama, showing the itinerary of the visit of Belisario Porras, Minister of the Republic of Panama and Costa Rica, 1909.

3 c. The general collection of the library includes a small number of titles relating to cartography (120), geodesy (60), geographic positions (35), and surveying (50). Several thousand maps and plans of towns and cities, international boundaries, and regions are found in works on city and town planning, boundary disputes, and description and travel.

The Rare Book Collection, numbering approximately 8000 volumes, consists chiefly of eighteenth and nineteenth century travel literature.

3 d. The collections of the Inter-American Specialized Organizations include documentation on the Pan American Institute of Geography and History (PAIGH), which was established in Mexico City in 1928 to coordinate and promote cartographic, geographic, and historic studies in the Americas (740 titles).

The library's collection of 9,700 information and technical reports issued by the OAS Secretariat include regional development reports that are often accompanied by maps. A finding aid to current reports is issued annually under the title *Catalog of OAS Technical Reports and Documents.*

The Library and Records Management Center Archives Collection includes some boundary maps and surveys relating to border disputes between member nations.

4. In addition to the finding aid described above, the general and special collections are accessed by a public authority/author and subject card catalog. A good introduction to the library is *Guide to the Columbus Memorial Library* (1982. 31 p.), available on request. Also useful is Thomas L. Welch's "The Organization of American States and Its Documentation Dissemination", *Revista Interamericana de Bibliografía,* vol. 32 (1982), p. 200–206.

A37 Prince George's County Memorial Library System

1 a. *Hyattsville Library*
6530 Adelphi Road
Hyattsville, Maryland 20782
(301) 779–9330

b. 9:00 A.M.–9:00 P.M. Monday–Thursday
1:00 P.M.–6 P.M. Friday
9:00 A.M.–5:00 P.M. Saturday
1:00 P.M.–5:00 P.M. Sunday
Hours vary during the summer.

c. Open to the public.

d. Reproduction services available.

e. Norman Jacob, Information Officer

3 a. The Hyattsville Library (Maralita Freeny, Branch Librarian) has a collection of some 200 printed maps and 28 general world atlases. Most of the maps relate to Prince George's County, the Washington metropolitan area, or Maryland. They consist chiefly of highway, census, and topographic maps, but there are also maps of congressional districts and the park system. The Maryland Room (located in the reference area, John Krivak, Librarian), includes large scale real estate atlases, atlases of recorded plats, and aerial photograph/map atlases of Prince George's County (5 volumes), and reference pamphlet files for Maryland (75 linear feet) and Prince George's County (45 linear feet) which contain several hundred topographic maps, city master plans, and city plans.

The Tugwell Room, Greenbelt Branch Library (11 Cresent Road, Greenbelt, Maryland 20770, telephone 301/345–5800) includes some 20 blueprint maps and a small number of aerial photographs of Greenbelt, Maryland, one of three communities planned by the Federal government during the 1930s.

Smithsonian Air and Space Museum (NASM) (Smithsonian Institution)—Branch Library **See entry C5**

Smithsonian Institution Libraries—Special Collections Branch—Dibner Library **See entry C8**

A38 Society of the Cincinnati—Harold Leonard Stuart Memorial Library

1 a. *2118 Massachusetts Avenue, N.W.*
Washington, D.C. 20008
(202) 785-0540

b. 10:00 A.M.–4:00 P.M. Monday–Friday

c. Open to the public.

e. John D. Kilbourne, Director

2. The Society of the Cincinnati is an organization composed of the lineal male descendants of commissioned officers who served in the Continental American Army or Navy or the French Forces under Rochambeau and de Grasse during the American Revolution, 1775–1783. The membership badge was designed by Pierre Charles L'Enfant, a French topographical engineer who later designed the plan for the City of Washington. The Harold Leonard Stuart Memorial Library maintains a 12,000-volume reference collection, including 37 atlases, and a map collection of some 300 items.

3 a. The map collection contains American, English, French, and German contemporary and retrospective maps and plans of military operations during the French and Indian War, the Revolution, and the War of 1812. There are also a small number of city plans and general state and regional maps. Although the maps range in date from 1657 to 1981, the large majority are dated between 1750 and 1813. A number of the maps originally appeared in eighteenth and early nineteenth century magazines and histories such as the *General Magazine of Arts and Sciences, Gentleman's Magazine, The London Magazine, The Scots Magazine,* John Marshall's *The Life of George Washington* (Philadelphia, 1807), and John H. Wynne's *A General History of the British Empire in America* (London, 1770). The collection includes a German manuscript map of North America by I.L. Hogreve showing French lands in about 1755. There is also a smaller version of this map by J. Lodge, which appeared in the *Gentleman's Magazine* (1755).

Other engravers and cartographers represented include D'Anville, W. Barker, J.N. Bellin, Joshua Fry, Samuel Hill, Peter Jefferson, Benjamin Jones, Thomas Kitchin, Samuel Lewis, John Montresor, Nicolas Sanson, Francis Shallus, and Tardier.

The atlas collection consists of historical and general reference atlases. Of particular interest is a fine copy of A.H. Brué's *Grand atlas universal* (Paris, 1816).

4. Maps are cataloged by subject, author, title, area, and engraver. There is also a map catalog arranged chronologically.

A39 University of Maryland Libraries (College Park Campus)—General Collection

1 a. *Theodore R. McKeldin Library*
College Park, Maryland 20742
(301) 454-5704 (Reference)
(301) 454-3032 (Periodicals/Microforms Reading Room)

b. 8:00 A.M.—11:00 P.M. Monday-Thursday
8:00 A.M.-6:00 P.M. Friday
11:00 A.M.-6:00 P.M. Saturday
12:00 Noon—11:00 P.M. Sunday

c. Open to the public. Books are available through interlibrary loan.

d. Coin-operated copy machines are located throughout the building. A photocopy service, located in the basement, provides enlargements, reductions, two-sided copies, transparencies, and other copying services.

e. H. Joanne Harrar, Director

2. The current holdings of the University of Maryland Libraries numbers nearly 1,700,000 volumes and over 2,300,000 microform items, making it the largest academic library system in the Washington, D.C. metropolitan area.

3 a. The library's general collection has approximately 225 world and special purpose atlases, including a number of early, rare atlases in microform or facsimile formats. Other map collections are described in entries A40 and B23.

3 c. The tabulation of cartographic reference books is given below. Many of the earliest works are in a microform format, for example, Robert Hues' treatise on the use of globes (1659).

Subject	*Number*
Aerial Photography	100
Cartography	330
Computer Graphics	140
Gazetteers	15
Geodesy	110
Globes	25
Latitude	18
Longitude	30
Maps and Mapping	275
Photogrammetry	34
Photographic Interpretation	45
Remote Sensing	160
Surveying	225
Triangulation	10

4. Access to the general book collection is through the card catalog, located in the Bibliography Area on the second floor. It is divided into an author/title section and a subject section.

A40 University of Maryland Libraries (College Park Campus)—Government Documents/Maps Room

1 a. *Theodore R. McKeldin Library, Third Floor*
College Park, Maryland
(301) 454-3034

b. 8:00 A.M.-11:00 P.M. Monday-Thursday
8:00 A.M.-6:00 P.M. Friday
10:00 A.M.-6:00 P.M. Saturday
12:00 P.M.-11:00 P.M. Sunday

c. Open to the public.

d. Photoduplication services are available.

e. Robert Staley, Map Librarian

3 a. The map collection numbers approximately 100,000 sheets. It consists chiefly of United States government depository maps, but also includes several other collections. The maps are not cataloged but since they are generally arranged by geographic area, access is not difficult.

Foreign Area Map Collection. Consists of printed general maps and national topographic series arranged by country. The distribution is as follows: Canada (1 drawer), South America (5 drawers), Africa (20 drawers), Europe (40 drawers), Asia (21 drawers), and Australia and New Zealand (6 drawers). The Asian section contains an excellent set of Japanese 1:25,000 topographic maps (12 drawers).

Geographical Section, General Staff (GSGS) Collection. Consists of topographic map series of foreign areas prepared by the British Directorate of Military Survey, World War II-1970s (4 drawers).

Miscellaneous Map Collections. Includes two drawers of maps printed by the National Geographic Society and the American Geographical Society; a 35-folio set of the *Deutsches Sprachatlas auf Grund des von Georg Wenker begründeten Sprachatlas des Deutschen Reiches* (Marburg, 1931-1956); and three drawers of nineteenth century and early twentieth century maps including a fine hand-colored example of G. Bradshaw's large *Map of Canals, Navigable Rivers, Railroads, etc. in the Midland Counties of England* (Manchester, 1820), Camille Calliere's *Carte de la Syrie Méridionale et de la Palestine,* (Paris, 1840), a nineteenth century map of Constantinople, printed in Arabic, and J.J. Hellert's *Nouvel Atlas physique politique et historique de L'Empire Ottoman* (Paris, 1844).

Raised Relief Map Collection. Consists of United States Army Map Service raised relief quadrangle maps of mountainous areas in the United States (130 items).

Roadmap Collection. Consists of recent road maps covering most states and foreign countries.

UNESCO Collection. Consists chiefly of large geological, soil, and vegetation maps of the world or Europe issued by UNESCO, 1970s-1980s (115 items).

United States Depository Maps Collection. This collection consists of map series deposited by Federal mapmaking agencies. It includes Army Map Service and the Defense Mapping Agency topographic maps, ca. 1941 to the present (91 drawers); Hydrographic Office nautical charts, chiefly of Japan during World War II; Air Force Aeronautical Chart and Information Center aeronautical charts, 1940s-1950s (10 drawers); Coast and Geodetic Survey nautical charts, 1904-1970 (8 drawers); Geological Survey quadrangles maps (100 drawers) and land use maps pertaining to the United

States, 1970s (3 drawers); Census Bureau state, congressional district, and statistical maps (2 drawers); Central Intelligence Agency large-scale plans of foreign regions and cities, including Beijing, Guangzhou, Leningrad, Moscow, and Shanghai, 1970s–1980s (3 drawers); National Forest Service maps of forest areas in the United States, 1940s–1970s (4 drawers), Department of Transportation state highway maps, 1920s–1950s (3 drawers); and Fish and Wildlife Service maps of wetlands, 1965–1975 (1 drawer).

United States Office of Strategic Services (OSS) Collection. This unique collection consists of a series of 1300 printed provisional map editions prepared by the OSS Branch of Research and Analysis and printed by the OSS Reproduction Division during World War II. Some of the maps were compiled by the Board of Economic Warfare, United Nations Division, and the Foreign Economic Administration, Enemy Branch. The series include a wide variety of general and thematic maps covering countries in which hostilities were taking place or which contained strategic resources. Examples of the types of maps that may be found include: population density map of Sardinia (1942), location map of minor nonferrous metal produced in South America (1942), map depicting original vegetation formation in Southern Nigeria (1943),series of maps of Brittany showing terrain, vegetation, roads, beaches, and military objectives (1943), map showing distribution of Japanese in Peru in 1940 (1943), map of the ecclesiastical provinces of the Roman Catholic Church in Italy (1944), map of the net of precision leveling of Eastern Germany measured and compiled by the trigonometrical division of the Reichsamt für Landesaufnahme in 1941 (1945), map of caves and cave regions of "Greater Germany", (1945), and a series of five maps of Java and Madoera showing major regions of estate products (rubber, cinchona, sugar, tea, coffee, and tobacco), population distribution, ethnic groups, Christian missions, elementary education, major native food crops, and telecommunications (1945).

A41 The World Bank (International Bank for Reconstruction and Development) Sectoral Library

1 a. *Room N–145*
801 19th Street, N.W.
Washington, D.C. 20433
(202) 676–0153

b. 9:00 A.M.–5:00 P.M. Monday–Friday

c. The Sectoral Library is closed to the general public but scholars are occasionally permitted access to examine materials not available in other libraries. Visitors must formally apply for admission at least seven working days prior to the day they wish to visit the library. Visitors who are granted permission to visit the library must present a photo identification card and proof of affiliation with the organization they are representing.

d. Photocopy facilities are available. Some of the materials are restricted.

e. Sue Dyer, Managing Librarian
Christine Windheuser, Map Librarian

3 a. The Sectoral Library map collection includes 15,000 maps, about 300 atlases, and 125 geographic names gazetteers. The map collection consists of printed and photoprocessed maps of some 170 developing countries, many acquired by World Bank staff members during visits to these countries. Coverage is particularly strong for Africa,

Brazil, China, Colombia, India, Indonesia, Mexico, Nigeria, Peru, and Venezuela. The maps generally date from 1975.

The atlas collection is comprised of national and thematic atlases (census, climate, economic), a large number of which were published in third world countries. They date from 1960. Examples include Sahab Geographic and Drafting Institute's *General Atlas of Afghanistan* (Tehran, 1973), with text in English, French, and Persian; Marcel Leroux's *Le Climat de l'Afrique Tropicale* (Paris, 1983); a tourist atlas of China (Beijing, 1984); Instituto Geográfico's *Atlas de Colombia* (Bogota, 1967); Ministère du Plan et du Développment's *Cartes pour servir a l'Amenagement du Territoire* (Dakar, Senegal, 1965); and the Census of India's *Census Atlas* (New Delhi, 1964).

4. An online card catalog provides access to the collection.

B Archives and Manuscript Repositories

Archives and Manuscript Repositories Entry Format (B)

1. General Information
   a. address; telephone numbers
   b. hours of service
   c. conditions of access
   d. reproduction services
   e. name/title of director and heads of relevant divisions
2. Size of Holdings
3. Description of Holdings
   a. maps, atlases, and globes
   b. aerial photographs and remote sensing images
   c. literature
   d. manuscript collections
   e. photographs and motion pictures
   f. instruments
4. Bibliographic Aids Facilitating Use of Collection (cartobibliographies, catalog cards, computerized retrieval systems, inventories, special lists, catalog guides)

B1 Air Force History Office (Air Force Department)

1 a. *Bolling Air Force Base, Building 5681*
Washington, D.C. 20332–6089
(202) 767–5764

b. 9:00 A.M.–5:00 P.M. Monday–Friday

c. Open to the public. Visitors must have prior visitation clearance, which can be arranged by phone.

d. Copier service is available.

e. Richard H. Kohn, Chief of Air Force History
William C. Heimdahl, Chief of Reference Services Branch

2–3. The Office of Air Force History possesses microfilm copies of archival materials in the United States Air Force Historical Research Center (Maxwell Air Force Base, Alabama 36112–6678), which number some 500,000 documents relating to the history of United States military aviation from the time of the Civil War.

About one-half of these holdings consist of unit histories with supporting maps, charts, and aerial photographs prepared and assembled by field historians serving with commands, air forces, wings, groups and squadrons. Of particular note are the unit histories for the 1st Mapping Group (later the 1st Photographic Charting Group which charted and mapped parts of the United States, Alaska, Canada, Africa, the Middle East, India, and Central and South America (1941–1943); the 2nd Photographic Reconnaissance and Mapping Group, which trained other crews and units for photographic reconnaissance and mapping, 1942–1943; the 3rd Photographic Reconnaissance and Mapping Group, which provided photographic intelligence in Tunisia, Sicily, and Italy and mapped areas in France and the Balkans, 1942–1945; the 4th Photographic Reconnaissance and Mapping Group, which was active in New Caledonia, Guadalcanal, Morotai, Mindanao, and Borneo, 1942–1945; the 5th Photographic Reconnaissance and Mapping Group, which mapped coastal areas of Southern France, 1944; the 6th Reconnaissance and Mapping Group, which engaged in mapping activities in Luzon and Mindanao and photographed Japanese strategic areas in New Guinea, the Bismarcks, Formosa, China, and Kyushu, 1943–1946; and the 7th Photographic and Reconnaissance Group which provided mapping support for allied troops in France, the Low Countries, and Germany, 1943–1945.

Also of interest are the records of the Air Photographic and Charting Service and the Army Air Force Charting Service, which form part of the Major Global Services of the Army Air Force and United States Air Force Collection, 1935– (838 linear feet), and the records of the Aeronautical Chart Service, located in the Zone of Interior Commands and Organization Collection, 1926– (3392 linear feet). The historical records of the Aerospace Cartographic and Geodetic Service, which was established in 1954, are maintained by the Office of Air Force History (Forbes Air Force Base, Kansas 66620).

Personal papers include the following pertinent collections. The Papers of Joseph L. Albright, Chief of the Photographic Records and Services Division, Aeronautical Chart and Information Center, contain manuals, catalogs, memoranda, regulations, and personnel rosters, 1919–1943. The Papers of General Charles P. Cahill include material on British aerial photography during World War II. The Papers of Walter D. Edmonds include source maps collected for his book, *They Fought With What They Had* (1941–1942), a story of the Army Air Force during the first years of the war in the Pacific. The Papers of General Thomas D. White contain maps relating to China, 1927–1930.

Among the oral history records is Geoffrey Linnell's description of the use of navigational aids and maps used during bombing runs as a pilot with the Royal Flying Corps during World War II.

4. A microfilm catalog provides access to the microfilm collection by subject and country. Published guides include the *Air Force Historical Archives Document Classification Guide* (1971. 173 p.); *Personal Papers in the USAF Historical Research Center,* compiled by Richard E. Morse and Thomas C. Lobenstein (1980. 74 p.); *U.S. Air Force Oral History Catalog* (1982. 762 p.); and a *United States Air Force History: A Guide to Documentary Sources,* compiled by Lawrence J. Paszek (1973. 245 p.). Also useful is *Air Force Combat Units of World War II,* edited by Maurer Maurer (1983), which provides a chronological listing of the activities of each unit.

B2 City of Alexandria—Clerk of the Court

1 a. *Room 307*
Court House
520 King Street
Alexandria, Virginia
(703) 838–4044 (Information)

b. 9:00 A.M.–5:00 P.M. Monday–Friday

c. Open to the public

d. Copy facilities are available.

e. Edward Semonian, Clerk of the Court

2–3. The Clerk of the Court has custody of some 1,000 Deed Books for the City of Alexandria which date from 1785 to the present. These provide descriptions of individual property boundaries. Except for George Gilpin's original 1797 plan of Alexandria (Deed Book H, Folio 332), the earlier Deed Books do not include survey plats. Some of the more recent books, however, contain copies of plats. A few nineteenth century plat books relating to Alexandria are now in the Alexandria Library (A2).

The Deed Books are arranged chronologically. A facsimile of George Gilpin's map of 1797 is available from the Office of Planning and Community Development (H1).

B3 The American University—Archives and Special Collections

1 a. *University Library, Room 316*
4400 Massachusetts Ave., N.W.
Washington, D.C. 20016
(202) 885–3255

b. 9:00 A.M.–4:30 P.M. Monday–Friday

c. Open to the public. Materials do not circulate.

d. Because of the rarity and condition of the materials, photocopying is restricted.

e. William E. Ross, University Archivist and Special Collections Librarian.

3 a. The Manrakudo Library of Charles Nelson Spinks contains approximately 2,000 volumes of Japanese and East Asian manuscript and printed books, prints, and maps collected by Spinks during the 1930s and 1940s. This includes some 240 separate manuscript and printed maps and about 30 books, mostly travel guides, with fold-out maps. The maps and books date from 1666 to the 1940s, with more than half drawn or printed during the nineteenth century or earlier. Among the earliest are two road maps, 1667 and 1672, and a general bird's eye view map of Japan, dated 1666. There is also a beautifully hand-colored two-hemisphere world map by Sokichi Hashimoto. Other early Japanese cartographers represented are Ryo Fujita, Takeshiro Matsura, Sekisui Nagakubo, Ken Onodera, Wasuke Suzuki, Ranzan Takai, and Tadashi Tamanushi. The collection also includes 3 published works on Japanese land surveying, one of which has been translated and printed in English, dated between 1917 and 1932. A printed classified list of the collection is available.

3 c. The Artemus Martin Mathematics Library, a collection of early books devoted to the broad field of mathematics, and the Rare Book Collection include some 20 handbooks, manuals, and treatises relating to surveying and globe construction. Most of the surveying books were printed in the United States during the nineteenth century. Among the earliest authors are Valentine Leigh, 1562, Thomas Digges, 1591, John Love, 1715, George Adams, 1772, and Samuel Moore, 1796. The main card catalog on the first floor of the library provides subject and author access to these works.

B4 Arlington Historical Society

1 a. *The Arlington Historical Museum*
1805 South Arlington Ridge Road
Arlington, Virginia 22210

b. 11:00 A.M.–3:00 P.M. Friday and Saturday
2:00 P.M.–5:00 P.M. Sunday; other times by appointment.

c. Open to the public.

3 a. Housed in the former Hume School, the oldest school building in Arlington County, the Arlington Historical Society maintains a collection of 600 printed and photoprocessed maps of the county dating from 1608 to 1975. These include cadastral plats and maps of boundaries, topography, streets, zoning districts, school districts, fire department districts, voting precincts, and proposed water projects.

3 d. The Mason Family Papers include a manuscript survey plat of lands in Stafford County, Virginia, drawn by Thomas Hooper, 1712, and a portion of a land survey of Mount Hybla.

4. A typed shelf list of the map collection is available.

B5 Army Center of Military History (Army Department)

1 a. *20 Massachusetts Avenue, N.W.*
Washington, D.C. 20314
(202) 272-0291

b. 8:00 A.M.–4:30 P.M. Monday–Friday

c. Researchers should contact the Center in advance. Foreign nationals are required to apply for permission to visit through the military attaché at their embassy in Washington, D.C.

d. Limited photoduplication services are available.

e. David F. Trask, Chief Historian

2–3. The Army Center of Military History operates the Army Historical Program which collects and edits basic records relating to the Department of the Army and prepares and publishes original works, including books, monographs, and special reports. A unique function of this publication program is the design and publication of maps by the Center's cartographic staff (G2). A considerable number of these maps are found in the Center's basic series on World War II, the Korean War, and the Vietnam War. Of particular interest to the historian of military cartography are *The Corps of Engineers: The War Against Germany* (Reprint, 1984), *The Corps of Engineers: The War Against Japan* (Reprint, 1982, 759 p.); and *The Corps of Engineers: Troops and Equipment* (Reprint, 1974. 622 p.).

To support its publication program, the Center maintains extensive published and unpublished materials, including maps and related documents.

HISTORICAL RECORDS BRANCH
Room 4128
Hannah M. Zeidlik, Chief (202) 272-0317

This Branch maintains an extensive collection of reference materials (600 linear feet) relating to United States Army history. The following subject files contain pertinent cartographic material:

Misc. 060-061. Maps and Mapping, 1944–1950.—4 inches. Correspondence relating to military mapping; photographs of a set of maps in "Report by the Supreme Commander to the Combined Chiefs of Staff on the Operations in Europe of the Allied Expeditionary Force 6 June 1944–8 May 1945" (54 photographs); "Mapping and Charting Directive Western Hemisphere July 15, 1947", with map enclosures showing areas of mapping projects in North and South America and specifications for postwar photography for multiplex mapping; and specifications for map drafting prepared for the Historical Branch by Lieutenant Coalridge, with 5 map examples, n.d.

Misc. 314.8. World War I Maps.—54 maps. Photoprocessed maps relating to the documentary history of World War I prepared by the Army Center of Military History.

Geography, ca. 1940–1967.—102 feet. Maps are scattered throughout the reports and documents of this file, which relates chiefly to World War II but also contains some material on Korea and Vietnam. Examples include topographic maps and manuscript overlays of the German counteroffensive in the Ardennes and Bastogne area, December 23, 1944–January 16, 1945; small atlas showing trans-Pacific routes of the Army Air Force Air Transport Command by time and type of aircraft from California to the Pacific Theater, 1943–1945; and a set of topographic maps and overlays showing battle situations of II Corps in Tunisia, North Africa, 1943.

ORGANIZATIONAL HISTORY BRANCH
Room 4236
John Wilson, Chief (202) 272-0306

This Branch serves as a repository for some 5,000 unpublished United States Army organizational history files ranging from Army group to detachment unit level, including topographical units such as the 29th Engineer Topographical Battalion, 1917–1980 (1.5 inches); 30th Engineer Base Topographical Battalion, 1939–1982 (1.5 inches); 64th Engineer Topographic Battalion, 1940–1970 (3/4 inch); and the 34th Engineer Base Photomapping Company, 1954–1972 (.5 inch). Each unit history file normally includes a chronological listing of posts and activities, brief administrative history, list of lineage and honors of unit commendations, and, sometimes, yearly operations reports.

LIBRARY BRANCH
Room 4124-C
Mary Sawyer, Library Technician (202) 272-0321

The Library holds 37,000 volumes relating to the United States Army from 1776 to the present, including a number of pertinent series. Unique situation maps illustrate a 26 volume set of Southwest Pacific Area (SWPA) Intelligence Reports prepared by the General Staff, Military Intelligence Section and other SWPA intelligence sections, General Headquarters Far East Command, Tokyo. The maps pertain to the military situation in China, 1947–1948, guerrilla resistance in the Philippines, 1942–1945, and operations in Korea during World War II and the Korean War. Additional SWPA material includes an atlas of the disposition and movement of Japanese Ground Forces, 1941–1945, and an incomplete set of the *Monthly Summary of Operations,* with fold-out situation maps, April, 1944–October, 1945 (18 volumes). The Library also has a mimeographed set of the reports of the General Board, United States Forces, European Theater, which analyzes the strategy, tactics, and administration employed by United States Forces in Europe during World War II. Pertinent reports include "The Utilization of Tactical Air Force Reconnaissance Units of the Army Air Force to Secure Information for Ground Forces in the European Theater" (1945. 21 p.), which reviews the role of aerial photography; "Engineer Technical Policies" (1945. 28 p.), which examines map production and distribution; and "The Information and Education Program in the European Theater of Operations" (1945. 24 p.) which analyzes the value of *Newsmap* as an informational and educational medium for troops. Other sources of information relating to the mapping activities of the Army can be found in the official Secretary of War Annual Reports, 1943–1960 (ca. 600 volumes); United States Army General Orders and Circulars, 1838–1984 (ca. 300 volumes); United States Army Regulations, 1861 to the present (222 feet); Army Field manuals (198 feet); Army Technical Reports (108 feet); and published unit histories (108 feet).

4. The reference collection of the Historical Records Branch is accessible through an extensive card file. The Library's holdings are cataloged by author/title and subject. Current activities of the Center are described in *The Army Historian,* a quarterly publication.

B6 Army Corps of Engineers—Office, Chief of Engineers—Historical Division

1 a. *Kingman Building*
Fort Belvoir, Virginia 22060
(703) 355-2543

b. 8:00 A.M.–4:00 P.M. Monday–Friday.

c. Scholars must call in advance to make arrangements to see the collection.

d. Photocopy services are available.

e. Dr. John T. Greenwood, Chief
Dr. Martin K. Gordon, Historian/Curator

2–3. Established in 1942, the Historical Division prepares historical monographs and bibliographies chronicling the past activities of the Corps of Engineers, provides reference service related to engineering history, and maintains an extensive research collection. The latter is divided into nine record groups and one miscellaneous collection (biography). The following record groups contain information related to cartography:

RG 2: General Files.—Published and unpublished histories, historical outlines, lectures, newspaper clippings, movie scripts, and articles relating to the Corps of Engineers (67 file folders) and the Corps of Topographical Engineers (1 folder). The latter contains historical and operational reports for the 64th Engineer Battalion (Base Topographic).

RG 3: Military Files.—Memoranda, correspondence and reports prepared by officers of the Corps of Engineers and other government agencies; published and unpublished articles and monographs prepared by historians of the History Division; and other materials (including some maps) relating to the military activities of the Corps. The file is arranged chronologically according to major military epochs. An examination of the file revealed the following useful topics: western exploration and surveying, 1845–1971 (45 file folders); aerial photography and equipment, 1922–1937 (53 file folders); mapping the Southwest Pacific Area, 1942–1945 (27 file folders); and topographic engineer units, 1941–1972 (5 folders). Among the files are David A. Lilley's unpublished "Mapping in North America, 1775–1865, Emphasizing Union Military Topography in the Civil War"; a list of manuscript maps of the War of 1812 in the Lilly Library, Indiana University; a brief interview with Paul Alexander concerning the early history of the Army Map Service; a three-volume typescript relating to photomapping, map reproduction, and surveying by the Historical Staff of the Engineer Board at Fort Belvoir, 1946–1947; and action reports, quarterly reports, and unit histories for several Engineer Topographic Battalions and Companies, 1941–1972. Particularly rich is the material relating to the development of aerial photographic mapping. This includes correspondence, early test results of equipment and techniques by military officers, photographs of equipment, sales catalogs, and military reports.

RG 7: Iconographic Collections.—Photographic prints relating to the Southwest Pacific Area (SWPA) during World War II including an undetermined number of aerial photographs and photographs of the activities of the 1603rd Engineer Map Detachment in New Guinea, 1944 (8 boxes). The photographic collection of Major General Kenneth David Nichols includes aerial photographic prints of the construction of Oak Ridge, Tennessee and Richland, Washington for the Manhattan Project, 1943–1944.

RG 8: Cartographic Collection.—Several hundred maps, many of which are photostatic copies of maps in the National Archives and Records Administration (NARA) (B19).

4. The General Files and Military Files have been inventoried and paper copies are available. They can also be searched by key words on the History Division's data base. The Iconographic Collection is currently being inventoried. The Cartographic Collection is partially arranged and cataloged.

B7 Army Military History Institute (Army Department)

1 a. *Upton Hall*
Carlisle Barracks, Pennsylvania 17013-5008
(717) 245-3611

b. 8:00 A.M.–4:30 P.M. Monday–Friday, except for Federal holidays and during the second week of July.

c. Open to the public. Books published after 1879 may be borrowed through interlibrary loan, but manuscripts, maps, oral histories, and photographs do not circulate. Some of the material is accessible only to researchers with appropriate security clearances specified by current Army regulations.

d. Photocopying facilities are available but are limited due to security classifications, demands upon staff and equipment, copyright restrictions, and fragility of material.

e. John Slonaker, Chief, Reference and Circulation Branch (717) 245-3611
Richard J. Sommers, Archivist-Historian (717) 245-3601
Nancy Gilbert, Librarian (717) 245-4139
Michael Winey, Curator, Special Collections (717) 245-3434

2. The Military History Institute houses the largest collection of materials in the world relating exclusively to American military history. It has custody of more than 211,000 volumes, 11,400 bound periodicals, 500,000 photographs, 40,000 audiovisual items, 25,000 military artifacts, 11,000 boxes of personal manuscripts, diaries, and letters, 67,000 documents, 6,000 maps, and several thousand aerial photographs.

3 a. An unorganized collection of maps (60 map drawers) relates chiefly to World Wars I and II, but there are also a few maps pertaining to nineteenth century wars and the Vietnam War.

3 b. Aerial photographs are interspersed among donated collections of photographs. Particularly noteworthy are the Hatlaem Collection, consisting of aerial photographs of most cities in Belgium, France, Germany, and Italy filmed by Captain Hatlaem, an Army historian, immediately after World War II, 1945–1947 (24 linear feet); the Charles W. Gardner Collection of aerial photographs of Europe filmed following World War I (1.5 feet); and the United States Army Signal Corps Collection, which includes aerial photographs taken during both World Wars.

3 c. An extensive collection of United States Army Unit Histories includes unit histories for Engineer Topographic Companies, Engineer Base Reproduction Companies, Engineer Base Photomapping Companies, Engineer Topographic Battalions (649th-660th, 942nd), and the 29th Engineer Regiment Base Printing Plant, American Expeditionary Force (1918).

3 d. The following manuscript collections of the Military History Institute include maps:

ARMOR–UNITED STATES–66TH REGIMENT COLLECTION.—Papers of the 66th United States Armored Regiment and its successors include combat maps, World War II–1953.

CHARLES L. BOLTE COLLECTION.—Contain numerous battle maps relating to Bolte's World War I service and a map of Peking, China, ca. 1932–1936.

S.L.A. MARSHALL COLLECTION.—Includes maps accumulated by Marshall, noted military historian, relating to World War II, the Korean War, the Vietnam War, and the Arab-Israeli Wars of 1956 and 1967. There are also sketches of battlefields compiled by Marshall.

STANHOPE B. MASON COLLECTION.—Includes maps showing troop locations of the 1st Infantry Division in North Africa, Sicily, and France during World War II.

GARRISON MCCASKEY COLLECTION.—Includes maps used by McCaskey in service school exercises and during service in the Philippines, the United States, and Western Europe, 1901–1920.

WARREN NCNAUGHT COLLECTION.—Includes maps relating to the trial of General Masaharu Homma for alleged crimes in the Philippines during World War II and a map of Thailand showing the disposition of Thai troops, 1950–1951.

WILLIAM M. MILEY COLLECTION.—Contains battle maps acquired by General Miley pertaining chiefly to actions of the 17th Airborne Division in Europe during World War II.

JOSEPH G.K. MILLER COLLECTION.—Includes battle maps of the 8th Infantry Division during World War II.

CHARLES COUDERT NAST COLLECTION.—Includes battle maps of combat operations of the 27th Division on Saipan, June–July, 1944, collected by Nast, former Judge Advocate of the 27th Division.

4. Pertinent published bibliographies include *United States Army Unit Histories* (Special Bibliographic Series Number 4) and *Manuscript Holdings of the Military History Research Collection* (Special Bibliographic Series Number 6). A brochure describing access to the holdings and facilities is available on request.

B8 B'nai B'rith International Archives

1 a. *1640 Rhode Island Avenue, N.W.*
Washington, D.C. 20036
(202) 857-6588

b. Tuesday and Thursday. Call in advance.

c. Open to the public.

e. Hannah R. Sinauer, Archival Consultant

3 d. The Archives has a brochure describing an exhibition of maps and engravings by Julius Bien, a noted nineteenth century lithographer and map engraver who served as President of B'nai B'rith, 1854–1957 and 1868–1900. In addition, there are a small number of reports and letters, some prepared by Bien, relating to his work with B'nai B'rith, 1867–1900.

Census Bureau—Field Operations—Field Division—Geography Branch **See entry G5, section 4**

B9 The Columbia Historical Society

1 a. *1307 New Hampshire Avenue, N.W.*
Washington, D.C. 20036
(202) 785-2068

b. 10:00 A.M.–4:00 P.M. Wednesday, Friday, and Saturday

c. Open to the public. Nonmember fee of $2.00. Scholars must register.

d. Photocopying facilities available to 11 x 17 inches.

e. Lawrence Baume, Curator of Collections

2. The Columbia Historical Society was organized in 1894 to collect, preserve, and disseminate information about the history of the nation's capital. The collections, housed in the Christian Heurich Mansion, a late Victorian museum and city landmark, include some 350 maps and atlases, 1,100 aerial photographs, and related textual materials.

3 a. Cartographic materials are found among three collections:

Map Collection, contains 250 maps of the city dating from the late eighteenth century, including map engravings of Washington, D.C. by Samuel Hill (1792), Thackara and Vallance (1792), William Bussard (1830), and Albert Boschke (1857); rare plat maps of subdivisions such as the Palisades of the Potomac (1890) and Columbia Heights (1885); topographic maps; Civil War military maps; and statistical and special purpose maps recording the location of public water pumps and sewers, and the distribution of typhoid fever (1895), segregated schools, and other social and economic conditions of the city. A few manuscript maps are included. Of special interest is a hand-drawn map on tracing paper of "Jackson City–Opposite the City of Washington at South End of Potomac Free Bridge (ca. 1836)".

Baist's Real Estate Atlas Collection, contains 31 volumes of detailed city plats for the years 1903, 1907, 1909–1911, 1913–1915, 1919–1921, 1924–1928, 1931–1936, 1937–1943, and 1945–1950.

Machen Collection, consists of 536 engravings, lithographs, and wood cuts collected by Thomas G. Machen of which 76 are general and panoramic views of the city by prominent artists and publishers such as Robert P. Smith (1850), E. Saches (1857–1871), and P. Haas (1840). Also included are 13 nineteenth century maps and a balloon view of Washington from *Harpers Weekly,* 1861. Several of the views are on display in the Reception Room of the Heurich Mansion.

3 b. A collection of 1100 aerial photographs show significant landmarks of the city lying within the Capital Beltway. The photographs were taken by the Winged Camera Service Company in the late 1950s from an altitude of 5,000 feet.

3 d. The Manuscript Collection contains some early land records, including plats and related correspondence by Robert King who was City Surveyor from 1797–1802. The Unpublished Papers Collections, comprising lectures presented at Columbia Historical Society meetings, include papers relating to Isaac Roberdeau, the Office of the Surveyor of the District of Columbia, and Potomac River Place Names. A complete set of city directories (1822–1967) provides a list of city surveyors and map engravers.

4. A general published introduction to the collection is the Society's *Guide to Research Collections* (June 1984). An unpublished inventory of the Map Collection and a catalog *The Machen Collection* are available in the reading room. Since 1897 the Society has annually published the *Records of the Columbia Historical Society,* which contains a number of papers devoted to the surveying and mapping of Washington, D.C., and local Washington history.

B10 Defense Department Still Media Depository

1 a. *Anacostia Naval Air Station, Building 168*
Washington, D.C. 20374
(202) 433–2166

Mail inquiries:
DOD Still Media Depository (Code LGP-R)
Washington, D.C. 20374–1681

b. 8:30 A.M.–4:30 P.M. Monday–Friday

c. Open to the public by appointment only. Scholars are requested to make arrangements for a visit at least three days prior to their arrival to insure that materials are available. Requests by mail should include specific information on unit, place, event, equipment, etc. Original negatives or prints do not circulate.

d. Copies of unclassified, official photographs may be purchased. A price list with ordering instructions is available on request.

e. Robert Waller, Customer Services Supervisor

2. The Department of Defense Still Media Depository maintains the official Armed Forces photographic collections that were formerly housed separately in the Army Audiovisual Center at the Pentagon and the United States Naval Photographic Center. The approximate coverage for each specific service is as follows: Army, 1941 to the present (885,604 photographs); Air Force, 1954 to the present (347,047); Navy, 1958 to the

present (399,648); and Marine Corps, 1941 to the present (347,181). Still picture records predating the Army and Marine collections and the Navy collection covering the period 1920–1958 have been transferred to the National Archives and Records Administration, Still Pictures Branch (B19). The pre-1954 Air Force photographic files are on extended loan to the National Air and Space Museum, Records Management Division (C5). Navy photographic materials for the period prior to 1920, as well as some later coverage, are in the Naval Historical Center Photographic Section (B20). An estimate of the number of pertinent photographs is as follows: about 150 maps, more than 5,000 aerial photographs, and approximately 1,675 photographs of mapping and aerial reconnaissance activities.

3 a. The Navy Collection includes about 100 photographs of unique maps and photomosaics prepared for planning or administrative purposes, 1957–1983. Of particular note are the large wall-size plotting board used by General Dwight Eisenhower for the Normandy Invasion, displayed in the room used by Eisenhower at the Royal Navy's Anti-Air Warfare and Navigation School, 1957; a series of uncontrolled mosaics of naval air facilities in the Far East, a map of Vietnam used during the first pre-flight briefing of Attack Squadron Four's reconnaissance flight to Binh Thuy, 1969; a chart of the coastline of Korea prepared for use by the Court of Inquiry on the capture of the Environmental Ship U.S.S. Pueblo, 1969; a chart showing Soviet Task Group Caribbean deployment, 1982–1983; and a map of Grenada with Cuban bases identified, 1983.

The Marine Corps Collection includes only a few photographic maps, one of which is a Japanese map of supply routes in Southeast Asia that was found in a Japanese barracks in Tientsin, China, October 8, 1945.

3 b. The Army Black and White Picture Collection includes 2,200 aerial photographs of airports, troop movements, training operations, military posts, military targets, engineering and construction sites, and gun emplacements, chiefly for the World War II and Korean period. Coverage is worldwide, with the following countries predominating: France (75), Germany (100), Italy (75), Japan (100), Korea (175), New Guinea (100), Okinawa (50), Philippines (300), South Pacific (30), United States (353), and Vietnam (50). Another 630 aerial photographs in color provide more recent coverage of the United States (350), Southeast Asia (100), and Latin and South America.

The Air Force Collection contains an undetermined number of black and white aerial photographs of Air Force facilities and some 1,200 color aerial photograhs of military posts and target areas in Vietnam during the 1960s.

The Marine Corps Collection contains about 300 black and white reconnaissance combat and post-strike aerial photographic prints of towns, cities, harbors, and airports in Alaska, China, and the Pacific Islands taken during World War II campaigns; about 150 color aerial photographs of Marine Corps bases in the United States during the 1970s; and approximately 300 color aerial photographs of airports, outposts, villages, and strategic Marine positions in Vietnam during the 1960s and 1970s.

3 e. These collections provide unique photographs documenting the use, preparation, and analysis of military maps and aerial photographs, many of which contain captions describing these activities. The Army Collection is the most extensive, with some 1,500 photographs dated from 1941–1978. Some examples include pictures of a photointerpretation team annotating aerial photographic mosaics for use by the 29th Infantry Division of the 9th United States Army in Europe during World War II, photogrammetrists operating multiplex machines in the Philippines, 1947, work of the United States 8th Army Aerial Photo School in Korea, 1952, surveying work in South America being carried out by teams of the Inter-American Geodetic Survey (IAGS), 1970s, and the operation of a computer-assisted map maneuver system at military exercises, 1978. There are also pictures of the activities of the various Engineer Base Topographical

Battalions and Companies, Engineer Photomapping Companies, and Engineer Aerial Photointerpretation Companies, 1943–1969. The Air Force Collection contains color and black and white photographs related chiefly to cartographic activities of the Aeronautical Chart and Information Center, 1950s–1970s (ca. 100 items), and survey work of the Aerospace Cartographic and Geodetic Service, chiefly in Brazil and Panama, 1959–1970 (75 items). There are only a few pertinent Navy photographs relating chiefly to map use, such as the work of a photointerpreter aboard the U.S.S. Oklahoma City in the South China Sea, 1965. The Marine Corps Collection contains an excellent series of photographs showing combat mapping units preparing situation maps and relief models on Bougainville, Guadalcanal, Iwo Jima, and Saipan during World War II.

4. There are separate card indexes for each of the collections, which are arranged by one or more of the following headings: geographic area, organization, activity, subject, and personality. Many of the cards contain extensive descriptions of the photographs. Pertinent cartographic materials are usually listed under the subheadings "Aerial Photographs", "Aerial Views", "Engineer Units", and "Map".

District of Columbia—Office of the Surveyor **See entry H2, section 3**

B11 Dominican House of Studies—Provincial Archives

1 a. *487 Michigan Avenue, N.W.*
Washington, D.C. 20017
(202) 529-5300

b. 10:00 A.M.–4:00 P.M. Monday–Friday

c. Open by appointment.

e. Rev. Adrian M. Wade O.P., Archivist

3 a. The archives contains a small number of maps, including two overlays annotated to show mission stations of the American Dominican Order in Fukien Province, China, 1922–1946, and the R.C. Diocese of Multan, Pakistan.

3 b. There are also a few aerial photographs of Dominican establishments in the United States.

B12 Fairfax County—Archives of the Circuit Court

1 a. *Archives Room, Room 38*
Judicial Center
4110 Chain Bridge Road
Fairfax, Virginia 22030
(703) 385-5379

b. 8:00 A.M.–4:30 P.M. Monday–Friday. Closed Election Day and holidays.

c. Open to the public.

d. Reproduction services are available.

e. Constance Ring, Librarian

2–3. The Archives has custody of the official manuscript records of Fairfax County, an historic county established in 1742. It was home to George Washington and George Mason and now comprises the western portion of the Washington D.C. metropolitan region. The following series contain survey plats or references to plats.

Minute Books of the County Court, contain references to plats prepared between 1666 and 1858. A card index lists about 60 such references.

Deed Books, contain the records of land transactions and occasionally hand-colored plats of land surveys, 1742–1867. The 1832 volume, for instance, contains 5 plats including James M. Brown's "A Map of Mount Vernon". The Deed Books dated from 1866 to the present are in the Land Records Section, Room 336.

Record of Surveys, contain land surveys and plats made between 1742 and 1856.

Record of Roads, contain surveys and maps of roads, 1860–1903. Related correspondence files, 1850–1920, also contain a few maps.

Papers Accompanying Court Sessions, contain some original plats dating from as early as 1787 but most date from 1830–1904.

Chancery Papers, occasionally contain plats submitted in support of litigation, 1810–1917.

In addition to these early manuscript records, the Archives also has a number of County real estate atlases, 1965–1978; tax map atlases, 1960–1984; property identification map atlases, 1966–1980; a property atlas of Arlington County published by Franklin Survey Company, 1935; G.M. Hopkins' *Atlas of Fairfax and Alexandria*, 1879; and 10 volumes of plat books of subdivisions, 1892–1943.

4. The plats and atlases are not cataloged or indexed. A useful introduction to the county records is *Official Records of the Colonial Period in Fairfax County, Virginia*, which is available in the Archives. A study of the patents and land grants of the original owners has been compiled by Beth Mitchell under the title *Beginning at a White Oak... Patents and Northern Neck Grants of Fairfax County, Virginia* (1977). This book and a large separate cadastral map depicting the boundaries of the patents are available from the Fairfax County Publications Center, 4100 Chain Bridge Road, Fairfax, Virginia 22030 (703/691–2974).

B13 Gallaudet College Archives

1 a. *800 Florida Avenue, N.E.*
Washington, D.C. 20002
(202) 651–5582

b. 8:00 A.M.–5:00 P.M. Monday–Friday

c. Open to people researching the education of the deaf and the hearing-impaired, deafness and the history of deaf education, and deaf organizations.

d. Photographic services available.

e. David de Lorenzo, Archivist and Special Collections Librarian

2–3. The Gallaudet College Archives collects and preserves the records of the College, materials from other schools and organizations devoted to working with the hearing-impaired, and papers of the hearing-impaired. A small map collection includes a plan of

Ivy City by J.C. Lang, 1873, a map of Trinidad, D.C., 1888, and maps of city highways, 1928–1930. There are also manuscript site plans, 1845–1965, and approximately 10 aerial photographs of the campus, 1865–1984.

4. A list of blueprints and plans of Gallaudet College is available.

Geological Survey (USGS) (Interior Department) **See entry G14, section 3**

B14 Georgetown University Library—Special Collection Division

1 a. *Lauinger Library, Fifth Floor*
37th and O Streets, N.W.
Washington, D.C. 20057
(202) 625-3230
(202) 625-4160

b. 9:00 A.M.–7:00 P.M. Monday–Thursday
9:00 A.M.–5:00 P.M. Friday

c. Open to scholars.

d. Photocopying facilities available.

e. George M. Barringer, Special Collections Librarian
Jon K. Reynolds, University Archivist
Nicholas B. Scheetz, Manuscript Librarian

2. The Special Collections, which house the library's archives, manuscripts, and rare books materials, contain more than 850 maps and about 120 aerial photographs.

3 a. The general cartographic collection includes several early maps of Maryland, 1671–1814, most notably Dennis Griffith's *Map of the State of Maryland* (1794) and John Ogilby's *Noua Terra-Mariae* (1671).

The Eric F. Menke Map Collection contains maps of Washington, D.C., maps and city views of Europe, 1650–1850, particularly the Rhineland region, and also a few maps of Asia. Notable items are a complete set of Braun and Hogenberg's *Civitates orbis theatrum,* two made-up atlases, one German, 1740s, and one American, 1820s, a Blaue atlas, 1640s, and John Speed's atlas of England, 1611–1612. The collection totals 800 items.

The Archives of the Maryland Province of the Society of Jesus contains extensive files pertaining to Jesuit estates in Maryland, including a large number of manuscript plats, 1770s–1890s.

The Brother Joseph Mobberly, S.J. Papers include a manuscript map of the Jesuit estate at St. Inigoes, Maryland, ca. 1814.

3 b. The Archives has approximately 30 aerial photographic prints of Georgetown University, dating from 1918 to the present.

The Ernest Larue Jones Collection has aerial photographic views of San Diego, California and College Park, Maryland, dated 1911.

The Guatemala-Honduras Boundary Survey Collection contains three volumes of official aerial photographic mosaics, annotated to show the territorial boundary between these two countries in 1932.

3 c. The Russell J. Bowen Collection consists of a large collection of articles and books on spying and covert activities, including 26 titles on aerial photographic reconnaissance, 1922–1981. The first 5,300 titles of this collection are described in *Scholar's Guide to Intelligence Literature: Bibliography of the Russell J. Bowen Collection* (Washington, D.C.: National Intelligence Study Center, 1983), compiled by Marjorie W. Cline, Carla E. Christianson, and Judith M. Fontaine.

The Reverend Henry Neale, S.J. Papers include manuscripts on geometry and geography, ca. 1730.

4. The holdings of the Special Collections Division are described in *Special Collections at Georgetown: A Descriptive Catalog* (Washington, D.C.: Georgetown University Library, 1985).

Land Management Bureau (BLM) (Interior Department)—Cadastral Survey Branch **See entry G17**

B15 Library of Congress—Manuscript Division

1 a. *James Madison Memorial Building*
Room 101
First Street and Independence Ave., S.E.
Washinton, D.C. 20540
(202) 287-5387

b. 8:30 A.M.–5:00 P.M. Monday–Saturday

c. Open to serious researchers with proper identification. Researchers must register. Examination of some collections is limited by donor or national security restrictions. Researchers are not allowed to take personal papers into the Reading Room; the Division will provide note paper or note cards. Original documents are not available for loan, but reproductions and microfilms, when available, may be requested through interlibrary loan.

d. Two coin-operated copiers are located in the Manuscript Reading Room. Unbound manuscripts may be copied providing there are no preservation or copyright restrictions.

e. James H. Hutson, Chief
Paul T. Chestnut, Head Reference and Reader Service.

2–3. The Manuscript Division's earliest papers were acquired when Thomas Jefferson sold his book and manuscript collection to the Library following the War of 1812. Today the Division has custody of over 40 million individual items in the form of letters, diaries, memoranda, scrapbooks, photographs, and maps, many of which are one-of-a-kind documents. These items are assembled or organized in some 10,000 collections representing the writings and work of American and World leaders in politics, science, technology, military affairs, literature, labor, and civil rights. Research areas for which the Division is particularly noted are American political history, uniquely represented by the papers of 23 United States Presidents from Washington to Coolidge and 900 members of Congress, the American Revolution and Civil War periods, naval history, American colonial history, cultural and scientific history, and Hispanic history.

Manuscript maps, aerial photographs, survey notes, and related correspondence and reports are found among a number of personal papers and other collections, some of which are described below. This compilation is based on a fairly systematic survey of existing indexes and finding aids as well as inspections of some 200 individual collections. Additional cartographic materials, however, are undoubtedly found in other collections which have not been fully processed. The collections described below contain approximately 2,000 maps and 1,000 aerial photographs.

FOREIGN COPYING PROGRAM

The Manuscript Division has augmented its collections by systematically microfilming or photocopying pertinent collections found in foreign libraries and archives. This program, which began in 1905, originally included only documents relating to American history but more recently entire series have been copied thereby expanding considerably the geographic range of the materials collected. Among the 4,000,000 documents copied, a small but significant number relate to mapping and surveying.

AUSTRIA.—Reproductions of the Vienna Military Archives include manuscript maps of Santo Domingo, 1756–1763 (185 glass negatives).

FRANCE.—Reproductions of the Archives nationale include maps of Montreal and French missions in the Upper Mississippi and Missouri valleys and Illinois country, seventeenth to eighteen centuries; Father Leonard's account on the geography of Northwest American with respect to Cook and surveys of the coast and harbors from Brest to Dunkirk, seventeenth century; annual orders and dispatches of the Navy with references to the preparation of charts and maps relating chiefly to the exploration and discovery of North America and Louisiana but also French activities in Latin America, 1680–1798; maps of Normandy ports, 1778–1785; and maps of Louisiana, the Mississippi River, New Orleans, Mobile, the Isle Dauphine and Biloxi prepared by the Depot of Fortifications for the Colonies, 1698–1802 (85 negatives); memoirs relating to the French discovery and exploration of the Mississippi River and Louisiana by La Salle, Tonti, and Bernard de la Harpe, 1681–1723; calculations of longitude and latitude for Louisiana and New Orleans, 1729; geographical report by Jacque N. Bellin and Philippe Buache's memoir concerning the latter's map of the Gulf of Mexico, 1710–1724; and numerous logs and journals with charts relating to voyages and hydrographic expenditions along the Gulf Coast and Caribbean Islands, 1684–1789.

GREAT BRITAIN.—Colonial Office records include correspondence concerning maps of Ohio, Mississippi, and Missouri Rivers, 1773, and warrant to John Henry allowing him to engrave a map of Virginia, 1768; Foreign Office records contain letters concerning John Mitchell's map of North America, in relation to the Northeast Boundary Survey, 1838–1839, maps and plans relating to defenses of Halifax, 1778, and the French advance on Lake Erie, 1754; British Museum Manuscript collections include a projection by John Dee, 1580, chart of James River, Virginia, 1608, maps from the library of George III relating to military campaigns in America, 1751–1787, map of Russian discoveries on northwest coast of America, 1761, map of Barbados, 1684, map of the Madeira River, Brazil, 1749, charts of bays in the West Indies, 1762, Spanish maps of religious estates in Manila, 1699, journals relating to military expeditions in North America with maps, including a map of Lake Ontario, 1760, and the Quabache River by Thomas Hutchins, 1768 (7 items); and the Royal Society Papers containing a description of Pedro Maldonado's map of South America, about 1750.

NETHERLANDS.—Holland Land Company Archives consists of numerous plats and maps of lots, towns, villages, districts, and reservations in New York and Pennsylvania, 1785–1838, including maps drawn by Benjamin Ellicott.

RUSSIA.—Photocopies of the records of the Academy of Sciences contain two harbor charts from the journal of St. Peter. The Ministry of Marine Records includes maps of

Vitus Bering's Route to Okhotsk and a plan of Okhotsk, 1737, transcript of instructions to Bering, Martin Spanberg, and Joseph Nicholas Delisle relating to the expedition of 1738 (71 pp), views of Alaskan headlands from logbook of the *Neva,* 1803–1806, chart of harbor of Petropavlovsk by Ivan Elagin, 1740, sketches of headlands from atlas of Captain Joseph Billings, ca. 1770; transcript (in French) of charting and other instructions chiefly relating to the Bering Expedition by the Academy of Sciences, 1732–1733.

SPAIN.—Spanish and Spanish American Reproduction Collection contains a variety of pertinent microfilms and photostats collected from various sources. A few examples include a map of the Yucatan peninsula by Torres Lanzos, 1785; the voyage of discovery by Sebastian Vizcaino, 1602 (21 feet); file relating to the boundaries of Louisiana and West Florida, 1804–1805 (1,122 sheets); and file concerning land grants in the Floridas (163 sheets).

MISCELLANEOUS MANUSCRIPT COLLECTIONS

The miscellaneous manuscript collections comprise a large number of small collections which have been brought together for convenience. Some of these collections relate to surveying and mapping.

ANONYMOUS.—journal with five accompanying hand drawn strip maps recording the Mississippi River from Maryville, Ohio, to New Orleans, Louisiana, 1811.

ANONYMOUS.—large manuscript mileage chart for cities and towns along the eastern seaboard, undated.

ANONYMOUS.—manuscript treatise in Spanish on navigation and astronomy with diagrams, eighteenth century.

ANDRES BALEATO.—published plan of Peru with manuscript description in Spanish, 1792.

DAVID BARRY.—hand-drawn topographic map in color of the Rio de San Juan, Nicaragua, 1745.

JOHN A. CLARKE.—surveying notes pertaining to the Sioux-Chippewa boundary line in Minnesota, 1835.

JAMES COOK.—photocopy of journal of his first voyage, 1768–1771.

CAROLINE DANA.—penmanship book in the form of a beautifully hand-drawn and colored world atlas prepared by a young schoolgirl, 1819 (26 maps).

WILLIAM DARBY.—letter inscribed on title page of his *Universal Geographical Dictionary* regarding the publication and sale of the dictionary, 1843.

DISTRICT OF COLUMBIA LANDS.—original instructions and certification of Andrew Ellicott's plat of the District of Columbia, 1793, and several other plats relating to individual squares, 1796–1852.

LEWIS EVANS.—letter concerning his map, 1756.

GEOMETRY EXERCISE BOOK.—book containing problems in geometry and surveying with illustrations, 1867–1868.

THEOPHILUS HANSON.—plat and related notes of land in Charles County, Maryland, 1770.

JOHN L.K. HOLZENDORFF.—plat of his land in Camden County, Georgia, surveyed by William Niblack, County Surveyor, 1818.

JOSE INFANTE.—four manuscript sketch maps and a topographic map of the province of Cajamarca, Peru, 1776.

JOSEPH INGRAHAM.—logbook containing thirteen manuscript charts relating to the voyage of the Brigantine *Hope* in the South Atlantic and Pacific Oceans, 1790–1792.

HEINRICH KELLER.—letters to Christian Gotlieb Reichard and Adolf Stieler concerning the cartography of Switzerland, 1818.

CHARLES LUKENS.—almanac containing notes relating to surveying in Carlisle, Pennsylvania, 1783.

MARCLE AUDLEYS MANOR.—tracing of original map and terrier of the manor in Herefordshire, England, 1741.

MICHAEL MCDERMOTT.—volume of recollections concerning his activities as city surveyor of Chicago, 1862–1863.

EPHRAIM MITCHELL.—plat of lot and wharf, Charleston, South Carolina, 1785.

DAVID BANISTER MORGAN.—three manuscript campaign maps relating to the Battle of New Orleans, 1812.

JEDEDIAH MORSE.—letter concerning maps, 1793.

NICARAGUAN CANAL CONSTRUCTION COMPANY.—field survey books and soundings, 1887–1913 (95 volumes).

THOMAS PARKER.—a survey by Alexander Allen of part of the Isle of Wright County, Virginia, 1678.

TITIAN RAMSAY PEALE.—map of Tahiti, 1839.

RECUERDOS DE FILIPINAS.—manuscript maps of coastal areas, provinces, and the Manila region; maps of Cadiz and Madrid; and a map of the Battle of Waterloo drawn by Juan Novella, an artillery officer in Cebu, 1842 (24 maps).

JAMES THOMAS.—field notes of his survey of the north branch of the Rappahannock River, 1736.

WILLIAM WILTON.—plat of his land in West Florida, 1774.

ANGELO WISER.—set of his sketch maps prepared during the Civil War Stoneman Expedition through Tennessee, Virginia, North Carolina, South Carolina, Georgia, and Alabama, 1865.

PERSONAL PAPERS

Papers of Cleveland Abbe, meteorologist, include diaries, general correspondence with Benjamin A. Gould relating to their work on telegraphic longitude for the United States Coast Survey, 1860–1864, meteorological maps of the United States which he compiled in 1870, lecture notebooks, and biographical material.

Papers of Edward Porter Alexander, Confederate General, include part of a map of the lower James River carried by Robert E. Lee during the Civil War.

Papers of William Allen, politician, include materials relating to land surveys in Ohio, nineteenth century.

Diaries of William A.H. Allen, United States Navy engineer, contain maps of the Mexican frontier, 1863–1864.

Papers of the Allen Family include 6 manuscript and printed maps by Charles J. Allen, United States Army engineer, showing the approaches and Confederate defenses of Mobile Bay, 1865.

Records of the American Colonization Society contain maps of Liberia and plans of West African towns, 1823–1889.

Archives of the American Institute of Aeronautics and Astronautics include sketches, newspaper clippings, correspondence, and photos pertaining to the aerial reconnaissance work of Thaddeus Lowe, 1859–1943. Maps are also found among the biographical information files, 1784–1962 (130 boxes); Airplane Company files (43 boxes); and scrapbooks, 1805–1947 (82 volumes).

Records of the American Peace Commission to Versailles contain about 40 photoprocessed maps chiefly of the Middle East and Africa prepared by or for the Committee of Reference and Council of the Foreign Missions Conference of North America in 1919.

Papers of John C. Babcock, a Civil War intelligence agent, contain correspondence relating to intelligence gathering and mapping during the Peninsular, Antietam, and Petersburg campaigns, 1863–1864.

Papers of Alexander Dallas Bache, director of United States Coast Survey, consist chiefly of his general correspondence, 1826–1863 (2000 items).

Papers of Nathaniel P. Banks, United States Army Officer, contain manuscript and annotated photoprocessed Civil War campaign and topographic maps of areas in Northern Virginia, Louisiana, and Texas, 1862–1864; and a manuscript map of the defenses of Mexico, 1847 (28 items).

Microfilm of the Papers of John Russell Bartlett in the John Carter Brown Library contain correspondence and the official journal relating to the Mexican Boundary Commission, 1850–1853.

Papers of George F. Becker, mining engineer and geologist, include a photoprocessed map prepared during his service as a geologist with the United States Army in the Philippines, 1898, a map of the Manila region issued by the *Manila Times,* 1899, five incomplete manuscript sketch maps, annotated USGS maps, and various German and Mexican maps (20 items).

Papers of Henry W. Beecher, clergyman and theologian, include several maps collected by him including a hand-colored map of Dakota Territory published by B.M. Smith and Alfred J. Hill, 1863.

Papers of the Blair Family include a copy of the route of General Braddock's Army by Christopher Gist, 1755, and 4 manuscript plats of Falkland Manor, Montgomery County, Maryland, 1854–1882.

Papers of Samuel Whittemore Boggs, former chief geographer, United States State Department, contain correspondence files, rough map compilations, 1927–1954, and subject files relating to his work on boundaries, the *Atlas of Ignorance,* the national atlas, and map projections, 1914–1954 (4,500 items).

Papers of Isaac Briggs, early American surveyor, include correspondence with William C.C. Claiborne, Thomas Jefferson, Albert Gallatin, and others relating to his work as Surveyor General of the Mississippi Territory and other matters, 1787- 1825, and plats of lands in Georgia, 1786–1787 (220 items).

Papers of Benjamin Franklin Butler contain a contemporary photoprocessed map of eastern South Carolina issued by the Army of the James "in the field" and annotated to show routes, December 4, 1864.

Papers of Charles Butler, businessman, contain published maps of Indiana, 1846–1847 and 1856–1857, and a map depicting a proposed canal route from Toledo to St. Louis and Chicago, 1873.

Papers of John Lansing Callan, pioneer naval aviator, include a manuscript map by Ensign I.R. Metcalf showing daily progress of the Allied Forces, July 18 to November 11, 1918; an aerial photograph of Rome and aerial photographic mosaics of the Dalmatian Coast, and the ports of Pola and Trieste, Italy, 1918; a set of three maps of Italy showing the location of bases for sea-planes, dirigibles, and airplanes, 1918; and a blueprint map of aerial routes in the United States.

Captured German Material Collection includes an Air Force Intelligence map of allied bombing attacks, May, 1944; Publication Board files containing plans for geographical research and military mapping programs, the latter directed by Dr. Schulz-Kampfhenkel, Feb. 1943–Dec. 1944; report on geological mapping in southern Syria, July 1944; miscellaneous correspondence of Karl Haushofer, 1935–1941; and the Deutsches Auslands-Institute Collection, containing a register of maps received, 1943–1945.

Papers of Caleb H. Carlton contain sketch maps and annotated maps of Civil War battle areas in the Southeast, 1862–1890 (11 items).

Papers of Ezra Carman, Civil War officer, contain working copies of manuscript, annotated, and printed maps used in the preparation of his unfinished history of the Civil War. Most of the maps relate to campaigns in Maryland and Virginia (80 maps).

Papers of Daniel Carroll of Duddington include manuscript plats of various squares in Washington, D.C. drawn by James Dermott, 1796, and William Elliot, 1853 (3 items).

Papers of Joshua Lawrence Chamberlain, Civil War officer, contain manuscript and printed maps relating to Gettysburg, Pennsylvania, and Yorktown, Petersburg, and Five Forks, Virginia (13 items).

Papers of John A. Cook, naval officer, include Jedediah Morse and Sidney E. Morse's *A New Universal Atlas of the World* (New Haven: Howe and Spalding), 1822.

Papers of Felipe Maria de la Corte Y Ruano Calderon include an English translation with five blueprint charts of his memoir and history of the Mariana Islands, originally compiled in 1870.

Records of Criminal Proceedings Instituted in the Courts of Puebla, Mexico, include 24 large colored plats and maps of the towns Ocotlan, Teposantitlan, San Matias Tepetomatitla and others that were prepared in the 1860s but fraudulently dated between 1578 and 1768.

Papers of C.G. Vial d' Alais, French Army Officer, contain a large manuscript map of the City of Cayenne, French Guiana, and its surroundings, ca. 1787.

Papers of James H. Doolittle, military aviator, include correspondence concerning photographic interpretation and photographic reproduction by the Eighth Air Force; maps of strategic bombing sites in North Africa, 1941–1942; a series of annotated and printed maps relating to his bombing raid on Japan, April 18, 1942; and maps of the northern hemisphere prepared for the Task Force on Air Inspection showing systems to detect Soviet missile tests, 1957.

Papers of the Dunlop Family include examples of cadastral survey plats, apparently prepared by Dunlop; and survey plats of Dunlop lands in Virginia, Maryland, and Washington D.C. prepared by various surveyors including Nicholas King, 1770–1834 (9 plats).

Papers of William West Durant include a printed map of the property of Forest Park and Land Company in Hamilton County, New York, 1902, and a printed map showing the location of the New Orleans Pacific Railway in Arkansas, Louisiana, and Texas, 1877.

East Florida Papers, comprising the Archives of the Spanish government of East Florida, 1783–1821, contain surveys and correspondence relating to surveys, 1791–1816.

The Papers of Melville Eastham, book and map collector, contain correspondence and catalogs relating to maps and atlases, 1939–1955; five manuscript and typescript notebooks devoted to mapmakers, atlases, and Ptolemy; and pamphlets and printed material pertaining to maps and atlases.

Papers of Andrew Ellicott, surveyor, consist of correspondence, maps, and reports relating to his surveys of Federal and State boundaries and the city of Washington, 1795–1815 (925 items).

Journal of John Evans, geologist and explorer, includes geological and topographical sketches of his journey from Fort St. Pierre, South Dakota to the Salmon River, 1853.

Diary of Pedro Font contains a manuscript map of the harbor of San Francisco, 1776.

Papers of Peter Force, nineteenth century antiquarian, include a list of maps and plans acquired by him; autobiography of Ira Allen relating to his surveys in New Hampshire, 1769–1773; journals and reports relating to the northeastern boundary survey of the United States, 1796–1798 (90 items); surveying journal of Walter Bryant relating to the New Hampshire-Massachusetts boundary settlement, 1741; manuscript map showing the routes of Spanish Conquistadores in the United States, 1536–1540, made by or for Buckingham Smith during his study of the history of Florida; Nicholas King's manuscript copy of Zebulon Montgomery Pike's voyage up the Mississippi River, 1805–1806; George Washington's Commission to Thomas Freeman to survey the boundary of Florida, 1796; journal relating to Thomas Freeman and Peter Custis' exploration of the Red River, 1806; Manning Ferguson Force's collection of letters and maps pertaining to French exploration of the Mississippi River, 1678–1846; maps and report of Nicolas Joseph Thierry de Menonville's voyage to the interior of Mexico during the eighteenth century; list of maps for a proposed publication by Ebenezer Hazard, 1772–1774; surveyor's notes and correspondence concerning maps prepared by John Fitch, 1783–1789; surveying notebook compiled by John Bull during the United States-Mexican

Boundary Commission survey, 1850; and nautical journal by James Henderson concerning United States Navy voyage from Callao, Peru, 1831. Among his miscellaneous manuscript series are charts, maps, plats, and surveys and related reports and correspondence by F.C. De Krafft, William Elliot, Robert King, and others pertaining to Washington, D.C., 1790– ca. 1830.

Papers of Edward Frost contain a manuscript map of part of St. Andrews Parish, South Carolina, showing the location of the proposed public road, n.d.

Joseph Gales and William W. Seaton Collection includes a letter by Benjamin Henry Latrobe and Robert King concerning their activities as surveyors in the Nation's Capital, 1815, and a manuscript plan of the proposed basin south of the President's Square, Washington, D.C., compiled by Benjamin Wright and Nathan S. Roberts, Engineers for the Chesapeake and Ohio Canal, 1829.

Papers of Thomas F. Galwey, include a memoir containing a number of manuscript maps of Civil War battle sites in Northern Virginia, 1863.

Papers of Harry Garfield, lawyer and educator, include three manuscript tracings from the Hopkins' City Atlas of Cleveland, Ohio, with names of residences added.

Papers of George Sabin Gibbs, United States Signal Corps Officer, contain maps of the German order of battle and the daily positions for the Meuse-Argonne Offensive, 1918–1919 (3 items), and a collection of maps relating chiefly to California, Fort Leavenworth, Kansas, Fort Sam Houston, Texas, Cuba, and Alaska, some of which show telegraph and cable systems, 1904–1910 (20 items). There is also a blueprint map showing the courses of balloons during the 1907 international race, compiled by William Welch of the United States Signal Corps.

Papers of Anselme-Michel de Gisors, French soldier, consist of a manuscript topographical description and map of Puerto-Cabello, Venezuela, 1816.

Papers of George W. Goddard, pioneer military aerial photographer, consist of unarranged aerial photographs, audio tapes, photographs, newspaper clippings, and glass negatives pertaining to the development of aerial photography in the United States Army and Air Force, 1917–1976 (10,000 items).

Papers of William C. Gorgas, United States Army medical pioneer in tropical medicine, contain among the subject files, a map of Vladivostok, Siberia, annotated to show the location of United States troops and hospital of the American Expeditionary Forces, 1918, and a large annotated map of the Panama Canal Zone, 1909.

The Papers of Adolphus Greely, leader of the Lady Franklin Bay Expedition of 1881–1884 and Chief Signal Officer of the United States Army, include manuscript and annotated maps of the Coast of North Greenland, 1882, and San Francisco following the earthquake in 1906. The papers also contain an extensive collection of his manuscript and published articles, speeches and lectures, a number of which are devoted to the geographical work of the Lady Franklin Bay Expedition, geographical knowledge during the nineteenth century, Thomas Jefferson's work as a geographer, and the cartography of Bering's first voyage.

Papers of Joseph F. Green contain manuscript maps accompanying instructions for attack on Morrill's Inlet, South Carolina, 1863 (2 maps).

Papers of John Wills Greenslade, naval officer, contain aerial oblique photographic prints and manuscript maps of areas selected for proposed naval air bases in Antigua, the Bahamas, Bermuda, British Guiana, Jamaica, Martinique, Newfoundland, St. Lucia, and Trinidad, 1940 (49 maps, 131 aerial prints).

Papers of William F. Halsey, naval commander, include several hydrographic and aeronautical charts of the Pacific, one containing annotations in the vicinity of the Philippine Islands, 1945.

Papers of James Guthrie Harbord, Chief of Staff, American Expeditionary Force in France, include operations maps of the Second Division, 1917–1918 (2 volumes), and maps of the Black Sea and Eastern Mediterranean region, 1914-1920.

Papers of Samuel Peter Heintzelman, Civil War Army General, include journals of his survey of Lake Huron, 1832–1834, and maps of the south and west relating to his participation in the Seminole and Creek Indian Wars in Florida, the Mexican War, and the Civil War, 1839–1865.

Papers of John L. Hines, United States Army officer, contain manuscript maps, plans, and drawing exercises prepared by Hines while he was a cadet at West Point, 1889–1891 (37 items), and annotated photoprocessed intelligence maps showing operations of General John J. Pershing's Punitive Expedition in Mexico, 1916 (3 maps). There are also numerous annotated and printed maps attached to the orders and intelligence summaries of the 3rd Corps, which he commanded during World War I (3 linear feet).

Papers of Ethen Allen Hitchcock include a captured confederate letter with sketch maps of defenses of New Orleans, 1862 (2 maps).

Notebook of Washington Hood, United States Army officer and engineer, contains manuscript notes and instructions for field surveying with illustrations of techniques for sketching terrain features.

Papers of Jedediah Hotchkiss, Confederate topographical engineer and cartographer, contain his diaries, 1845–1899; correspondence, 1846–1899; contracts and copyrights pertaining to maps; and lecture notes and writings including "History of Mapmaking", ca. 1873 (20,000 items). There are also copies of William Barton Rogers' notebooks and correspondence concerning geological surveying of Virginia, 1835–1841. In addition, a microfilm of the Hotchkiss-McCullough Papers from the University of Virginia Library contains personal and business papers, account books, and maps 1846–1912 (700 items and 52 volumes).

Papers of Richard L. Hoxie, United States Army Corps of Engineers, include a manuscript sketch map of the Civil War battle at Chattanooga, a United States Coast Survey map of Northern Alabama and Georgia purportedly carried by General William Sherman on his march through Georgia, and notebooks compiled by Hoxie during the Wheeler Expedition, 1872–1873.

Papers of Emil Hurja contain pencil sketch maps of roads in Northern Virginia and Gettysburg during the Civil War (3 maps).

Papers of Frederic Ives, an American pioneer in the development of aerial photography during World War I, contain his general correspondence, articles, notebooks, daily journals, and book entitled "Illustrations to Accompany Notes on the Interpretation of Aeroplane Photographs (1918)".

Papers of John S. Jackman, confederate soldier, include his journal with manuscript maps of troop positions at Murfreesboro, Pine Mountain and other engagements of the 9th Kentucky Volunteers (7 maps).

Papers of Alonzo C. Jackson contain James Armstrong's journal of the cruise of the Frigate *Savannah* to the Peruvian coast, Chile, Hawaii, Mexico, and California, which includes 14 maps and charts, soundings, and other geographical and hydrographical data, 1844–1845.

Papers of John Franklin Jameson, historian, contain the records of the Department of Historical Research of the Carnegie Institution of Washington, 1905–1928, which include correspondence and subject files concerning the *Atlas of Historical Geography of the United States* (3 folders), geography and history, 1901–1908, Jedediah Hotchkiss, 1895–1897, Lawrence Martin, 1926, the National Geographic Society, 1907–1922, Charles O. Paullin, 1904–1926, and Zebulon Pike.

Papers of Thomas Jefferson include correspondence with the Commissioners of the City of Washington concerning the surveying and platting of the nation's capital, and with a number of early surveyors and mapmakers: Abraham Bradley, Isaac Briggs, Mathew Carey, William Clark, Andrew Ellicott, Ferdinand Hassler, Thomas Hutchins, Nicholas King, Robert King, Benjamin Henry Latrobe, Pierre Charles L'Enfant, John Melish, Jedediah Morse, William Tatham, and Alexander von Humboldt. There are also several map enclosures, including at least two drawn or copied by Jefferson.

Journal of Andrew Johnson, surveyor, relates to surveys in western Virginia during the eighteenth century.

Papers of Charles Dehaven Jones, Union Army Officer, include a map of the southern states issued by *The Sun,* January 4, 1862, showing the blockade.

Papers of MacKinlay Kantor, author and war correspondent, include a hand-drawn map recreating the Andersonville military prison and vicinity at the time of the Civil War, maps relating to Spirit Lake, Iowa, and a pictorial map showing the bombing record of the 364th Squadron in Germany and France during World War II.

Papers of George Kennan, explorer and journalist, contain several maps relating to Siberia and the Arctic including a manuscript Russian sketch map of the Nerchinsk mining district, 1885.

Papers of Nicholas King, include journals and letterbooks relating to his work and that of his father, Robert King, as surveyors for the City of Washington, 1792–1798.

Logbook of Louis Albert Kingsley, naval officer on the *U.S.S. Lackawanna,* Pacific Squadron, includes a manuscript map of the Strait of Magellan, 1866–1868.

Papers of Herbert Bain Knowles, naval officer, contain manuscript and annotated maps and aerial photographs relating to the invasions of the Solomon Islands, Tarawa, and Saipan, and aerial photographic prints of the 2nd Marine Division field training activities near Wellington, New Zealand, 1942–1943 (35 maps and 6 aerial photographs).

Papers of Johann Georg Kohl, nineteenth century geographer, consist of three manuscript histories and a catalog relating to the exploration and charting of the East and Gulf Coasts of the United States, 1854–1858.

Hans P. Kraus Collection of Latin American Documents contains an historical treatise on the rights of Spain to the British claims in Georgia compiled by Antonio de Arredondo which includes a map of the present southeastern United States, 1742.

Papers of George F. Kunz, geologist, include several Russian geological and mineral maps of the Ural Mountains, 1890s.

Microfiche of the Papers of Benjamin Henry Latrobe, architect and engineer, contains material relating to his surveying work for the City of Washington, 1815; Newcastle, Delaware, 1804–1805; the Potomac River, 1802–1804; and the Susquehanna River, 1801.

Papers of Samuel Phillips Lee, contain manuscript sketch map of the road network in the vicinity of Wilmington, North Carolina, and manuscript maps and charts of the North Carolina coast showing the capture of the schooners *Ceres* and *St. George* and the English steamer *Pet* during the Civil War, 1863–1886 (8 maps).

Papers of Curtis LeMay, United States Air Force Chief of Staff, include notebooks with maps of Africa, United States Air Force target complex maps, maps and aerial photographs of Kirun Harbor, and bombing missions reports, with aerial photographs, 1943–1945. The use of these papers is restricted.

Papers of Pierre Charles L'Enfant, collected by James Dudley Morgan, include correspondence with George Washington, Thomas Jefferson, Andrew Ellicott, Isaac Roberdeau, James Dermott, and others, 1778–1814, notes and printed materials, and maps relating to the District of Columbia, 1792–1809 (600 items).

Papers of Charles A. Lindbergh, pioneer aviator, include a manuscript map with editorial notes of his transatlantic flight prepared for his book, *Spirit of St. Louis,* several aeronautical charts annotated and signed by Lindbergh, 1939–1945 photographic print of his original transatlantic flight chart, 1927, is in the Harold Bixby Papers.

John Logan Family Papers include a volume of 29 manuscript military campaign and intelligence maps prepared during the Civil War, chiefly of areas in Alabama, 1862–1864.

Collection of Louisiana Miscellany includes surveyor's notebooks, 1795–1797, and Chevalier de Beaurain's manuscript copy of Jean Baptiste Bénard de La Harpe's *Journal*

Historique with six manuscript maps relating to La Harpe's discoveries and exploration in the lower Mississippi River Valley, 1766.

Papers of James Morrison MacKaye, nineteenth century abolitionist, include two lists of maps furnished to the American Freedmen's Inquiry Commission by the Coast Survey and the Corps of Engineers, 1862–1863.

Papers of President James Madison contain surveys, plats, and maps relating to lands in Kentucky, Louisiana, and New York, 1786–1804, and correspondence with surveyors and map makers including Isaac Briggs, Matthew Carey, Andrew Ellicott, Ferdinand Hassler, Alexander von Humboldt, Nicholas King, Benjamin Henry Latrobe, John Melish, Jedediah Morse, and William Tatham.

Papers of Matthew Fontaine Maury, United States Naval officer and pioneer oceanographer, comprise letterbooks, correspondence, diaries, notebooks, journals, charts, and copies of speeches and articles relating to his oceanographic and other scientific activities (14,000 items).

Papers of William John McGee, United States geologist and ethnologist, include correspondence with Julius Bien, William Morris Davis, G.K. Gilbert, James Hall, Jedediah Hotchkiss, William Henry Holmes, Jules Marcou, Emmanuel de Margerie, John Wesley Powell, Raphael Pumpelly, and Roland D. Salisbury and other noted cartographers and surveyors relating to the mapping activities of the United States Geological Survey, 1885–1907; correspondence relating to the International Geographical Meeting, 1903–1904; and field notebooks and sketchbooks compiled during geological surveys, 1878–1896, including a survey of the South Potomac River, 1885 (7,000 items).

Papers of Montgomery C. Meigs, United States Army engineer, include numerous manuscript and annotated maps relating to the Civil War and to his activities as supervisor of Federal buildings in Washington, D.C., 1872–1892; his West Point common place book containing notes from Conrad Malte-Brun's *Geography* on measuring meridians, notes on drawing, coloring, and drawing instruments, and field notes and maps of a reconnaissance in Washington City, 1831–1844; and a hand-drawn map by John Rogers Meigs accompanying his account of the Battle of Bull Run, 1864.

Papers of Mercy-Argenteau Family include manuscript maps and plans of the estates of Mercy Argenteau in Belgium, ca. 1741–1811, but several may be much earlier (16 items), and printed maps of European countries and Vienna, 1805–1811 (9 items). One of the estate maps is sewn with colored threads to distinguish estate boundaries.

Papers of C. Hart Merriam, naturalist and ethnologist, contain correspondence and congressional testimony relating to the Mount Rainier name controversy during his chairmanship of the United States Board on Geographic Names, 1924–1926; and manuscript and annotated linguistic maps showing American Indian language groups, chiefly in California during the 1920s.

Papers of George Perkins Merrill, geologist, contain correspondence from Jules Marcou, G.K. Gilbert, Matthew Fontaine Maury, William Henry Holmes, Gouverneur K. Warren, Henry R. Schoolcraft and other geologists to Ferdinand V. Hayden and Merrill, much of which relates to geological maps and mapping.

Papers of William Mitchell, United States Army aviator, contain an undated annotated map showing the locations of United States Army Air Force bombing and pursuit wings in the United States; an operations map annotated to show army, corps and divisional limits of the 3rd American Army's plan of occupation and a series of assumed German order of battle maps prepared by G-2 3rd United States Army, Nov.19-24, 1918 (6 sheets); a set of aerial photographic prints and maps prepared by the aerial photographic section of the IV French Army relating to German airfields, defenses, military camps and transportation networks, Sept. 1917 (60 prints and 4 maps); a map of all air service units assigned to the 1st Army in France during the Meuse-Argonne Operation, prepared under Mitchell's direction, 1919; unpublished French Army intelligence reports and aerial photographic prints of towns and transportation networks whose locations are shown on accompanying map sections, 1917–1918 (ca. 300 prints and 220 maps); a set of small manuscript maps prepared to illustrate a book on World War I; a railroad strip map from Epernay to Vitry-de-Francois during World War I; reduced copies of a series of maps prepared under Mitchell's direction for his world flight in 1923–1924 showing his route and strategic information for various areas in the world; and typescript notes on the interpretation of aerial photographs, prepared by the Training Section of the Air Service, AEF, during World War I.

Papers of Marc Mitscher, naval aviator, contain manuscript, annotated, and printed maps relating to the Truk Islands and the New Georgia Group, 1943 (7 maps); and a set of photographs of daily enemy situation maps showing the South Pacific region, Jan. 20 to March 27, 1943 (42 prints).

Microfilm records of Moravian Missions among the Indians of North America contain sketch maps of Indian missions in Georgia, Kansas, North Carolina, Ohio, Ontario, and Pennsylvania drawn by John Heckewelder, David Zeisberger and other Moravian missionaries, 1753–1868.

Papers of Samuel Finley Breese Morse, artist and inventor, contain correspondence with Jedediah Morse, Charles Wilkes, and Sidney Edwards Morse, the latter concerning his cerographic atlas, 1842–1844, and 5 printed and annotated maps showing telegraph lines throughout the world, 1850s.

Papers of Kirk Munroe, author, include descriptions of his experience with a survey team for the Union Pacific Railroad and the Atchison, Topeka and Santa Fe Railway, 1867–1870s.

Papers of Joseph Nicolas Nicollet, mapmaker and explorer, includes correspondence, manuscript reports and journals, field notes, astronomical observations and maps relating to his exploration and mapping of the upper Mississippi Valley and upper Missouri River, 1837–1841 (97 maps).

Diaries of William Owner contain 19 small-scale manuscript maps and two newspaper maps of the major campaigns of the Civil War.

Papers of Francis Le Jau Parker, United States Army officer and government official, contain printed and annotated Russian and Romanian maps of the Eastern Front collected by Parker during his service as a military observer and attaché in Romania and Russia during World War I (8 items); annotated maps accompanying World War I battle histories, and printed artillery, operational, and situation maps of the Western Front, 1918; manuscript maps relating to the Tacna-Arica boundary dispute between Chile and Peru compiled by Major P.D. Glassford, Army War College, 1926 (51 items); and a photoprocessed wall map of Nicaragua, reproduced by the Military Intelligence Division, United States Army General Staff, 1920s.

Papers of George S. Patton, United States Army officer, include a blueprint map showing positions of United States troops along the Rio Grande, Texas, 1913; a printed map of the Battle of Mukden, Manchuria, prepared by Major Charles Lynch, United States Army Surgeon, showing the locations of Medical Departments of the Japanese Army and lines of evacuation of wounded soldiers, 1906; a battle map carried and annotated by Patton, when he led the 1st Brigade Tank Corps in St. Michiel Campaign, July 1918; and oblique aerial photographic prints of military sites in France apparently annotated for intelligence purposes during World War I (21 prints). There are also maps relating to his World War II campaigns, including a map of Europe annotated by Patton in 1944 to show his proposed route for the Third Army in France and Germany (4 folders). Examination of materials dated after 1940 requires permission of the donors.

Papers of Aurestus S. Perham contain correspondence and one map relating chiefly to General Gouverneur K. Warren and the Battle of Five Forks.

Papers of John J. Pershing, former General of the Armies of the United States, contain annotated and photoprocessed maps relating to the Tacna-Arica boundary dispute in 1926 between Chile and Peru, including a rough sketch of railroad, telegraph, and telephone lines of Tacna Province by the American Consul in Arica, Chile (4 items); and manuscript maps by Charles E. Riddiford with page proofs of these maps prepared for Pershing's book, *My Experiences in the World War* (1931) (200 items).

Papers of Philip Lee Phillips, first chief, Library of Congress Map Division, holds correspondence, newspaper clippings, and notes concerning the establishment of the Map Division and the surveying career of Bernard Romans, 1887–1917 (2 linear feet).

Collection of Sir Thomas Phillipps, private collector, includes Giuseppe Pujati's manuscript book, *Elementi di Geografia Antica e Moderna*, with a description of the history of geography and early maps, 1766; manuscript journals and maps from the papers of Jean Louis Berlandier, French botanist, relating to the city of Matamoros, Mexico, and the Battle of Palo Alto during the United States-Mexican War, 1823–1846 (related material is in B22); notes and journals prepared by the Mexican Boundary Commission which surveyed the United States-Mexican boundary as defined by the Adams-Onis Treaty of 1819, 1826–1834 (8 volumes); and an undated Dutch journal containing nautical charts and geographical descriptions of the islands in the West Indies.

Papers of Vicente Sebastian Pintado, Surveyor General of Spanish West Florida, contain general correspondence with his land surveyors in Louisiana and Florida, Ira C. Kneeland, Patrick Tegart, Joseph Collins, and Pedro Reggio, 1799–1817, and with Carlos Trudeau, Spanish surveyor in Louisiana; surveys and field notebooks; and maps and plats of the United States West Florida, and regions, towns, plantations, and land districts within Spanish West Florida (Florida, Alabama, Mississippi, and Louisiana), 1783–1830 (62 maps).

Papers of Orlando Metcalfe Poe, Civil War military engineer, include a notebook recording the distribution of maps of the Atlanta Campaign and siege of Savannah by name and address of recipient, 1878–1907 (120 pages).

Papers of Fitz-John Porter, Civil War Army officer, contain annotated and printed maps relating to the 2nd Manassas battle in Virginia, August 28-30, 1862, prepared to accompany the proceedings of a Board of Army Officers convened in 1886 to review his court martial for the Union defeat at Manassas. Many of the maps were compiled under the direction of Gouverneur K. Warren (53 maps).

Portugese Manuscripts Collection includes a manuscript entitled *Porto de S. Murtinho* with three colored maps of the Portuguese coastal town by Luis d'Alencourt, 1794; Francois Nicolas Baudot's *Geographie Universelle* (1689), containing printed maps and several manuscript maps; and Felix da Costa's manuscript *Liber Unicus* (1687) with maps of the Turkish realms.

Microfilm of Papers of Preston Family of Virginia includes survey notebooks prepared by William Preston, James Trimble, John Taylor, and other land surveyors in Virginia, 1740–1780s (ca. 1,400 surveys).

Diaries of Georg Carl Preuss, surveyor and cartographer, relate to John C. Fremont's western exploring and mapping expeditions, 1842–1849 (7 volumes).

Papers of Elwood R. Quesada, World War II Air Force Commander, include aerial photographs and related materials, including a typescript "History of the Photographic Section IX Tactical Air Command"; intelligence reports based on aerial photographs; photographs of photographic technical support activities, with suggested captions for press releases (3 folders); and an operations report for the 9th Tactical Air Command on air support for the 1st and 9th United States Armies, November 16, 1944, which contains 29 aerial photographic prints and indexes covering targets in Germany.

Journal of Charles Whitesides Rae, naval officer, concerns the survey of the Isthmus of Tehuantepec, Mexico, 1870–1871.

Papers of Charles W. Reed, topographical engineer with the Army of the Potomac during the Civil War, contain manuscript and printed maps by Reed in 1884 showing the Battle of Gettysburg (12 maps).

Papers of Arthur Stanley Riggs, naval officer and author, include printed and photo-processed maps collected by Riggs for his unpublished book, *Drake of the Seven Seas*, 1582–1948 (7 maps).

Papers of William Edward Riley, United States Marine Corps officer, contain a series of maps relating to Pacific campaigns, including intelligence maps of Pacific Islands derived from aerial photographs and printed on the *USS Mt. Olympus*, annotated maps showing tentative operations of the Third Fleet and enemy defenses relating to Peleliu Island, a target map of Manila annotated to show United States POW or civilian internment camps, hospitals, churches, and Japanese installations suitable for bombing, and maps showing operational airfields in Japan and bombing sites in Burma, China, and Formosa, 1944 (30 maps); and an incomplete set of the journal, *Weekly Intelligence*, which contains maps and aerial photographs, 1944–1945 (18 issues).

Papers of Walter William Ristow, map librarian and cartographic historian, contain correspondence files; articles relating to maps; papers relating to the American Congress on Surveying and Mapping Publications Committee, 1951–1969, International Geographic Union, and the Seventh International Conference on the History of Cartography, 1977; and his study concerning Christopher Colles (2 linear feet).

Papers of Rodgers Family contain the personal correspondence of John N. Macomb, United States Army topographical engineer, pertaining to his duties in the Territory of New Mexico, 1850s, and a manuscript topographical memoir by Charles Dimmock, Macomb's assistant, concerning the San Juan River exploring and mapping expedition.

Papers of Elihu Root, diplomat, include some correspondence and five portfolios of maps and charts relating to the Alaskan Boundary Commission, 1903, and a photoprocessed map showing the route of the *USS Buffalo* during Root's diplomatic mission to Russia, 1917.

Papers of Rufus Harvey Sargent, geologist and cartographer, include his topographic survey notes prepared during the Carnegie Institution of Washington's expedition to northeastern China, 1903–1904.

Papers of John M. Schofield, soldier and public official, contain a manuscript instructional manual prepared by Lieutenant John P. Finley for the Post School at Madison Barracks, New York, and a collection of 22 manuscript maps prepared by student soldiers for the map drawing class, 1893–1894. There are also annotated blueprint maps of the Military Department of Arizona, ca. 1880s; a map of Colorado Territory, 1862; an annotated map of Korea, East China and Japan issued by the Military Information Division; a collection of manuscript and printed Civil War maps of the Atlanta, Franklin, and Nashville Campaigns, and Manassas, Virginia, the latter relating to Major General Fitz-John Porter's court martial (8 maps); Gouverneur K. Warren's map of the west showing military departments and districts; and a collection of United States Coast Survey charts of the Pleiades annotated to show occultations at West Point, 1860.

Papers of Henry Rowe Schoolcraft, Indian agent, explorer, geologist, and author, include the 1836 expedition journal of Joseph N. Nicollet to the source of the Mississippi; Jean Baptiste Perrault's journal of his travels to the upper Mississippi and the west, with eleven maps, 1783–1820; various printed and manuscript maps relating to the Old Northwest; articles and clippings relating to the development of American geography and the spread of geographical knowledge; and an extensive correspondence file (25,000 items).

Notebooks of Charles Anthony Schott, meteorologist, include calculations and correspondence with Joseph Henry, Adolph and Henry Lindenkohl, Julius Bien and Francis Amasa Walker relating to the preparation of a weather map of the United States, 1870–1880.

Papers of Thomas Oliver Selfridge, Jr., naval officer and explorer, include materials on the Amazon and Madeira River Survey in South America, 1875–1878, and correspondence and maps relating to the survey of the Isthmus of Darien for a proposed interoceanic canal, 1869–1874.

Papers of John Sessford contain a printed plat book of Washington, D.C. with manuscript annotations, plats, and newspaper clippings relating to surveying by Nicholas

King, Robert King, and Benjamin Henry Latrobe, 1785–1850. Also included are enumerations of buildings, 1801–1860s.

Papers of William Short, diplomat and landowner, include printed and manuscript maps of townships and land patents in New York and Ohio, 1803–1804.

Papers of Robert Wilson Shufeldt, naval officer and explorer, contain correspondence and manuscript and printed maps pertaining to his survey expedition to Tehuantepec, Mexico, in search of a transisthmus canal, 1870–1871 (22 maps); maps and charts associated with the round-the-world cruise of the *USS Ticonderoga,* commanded by Shufeldt, 1878–1880, including manuscripts of a meteorological chart of the Japan and Yellow Seas showing the typhoon of August 4-6, 1880; plans and maps of railways in South Africa and steamship routes in Indonesia (14 maps). The papers of his son, Mason, contain a manuscript map of the Congo showing centers of slavery and a proposed route through slave districts and a German manuscript map of the Congo, 1883.

Microfilm of Papers of Philipp Franz von Siebold, German explorer and geographer, from originals in Ruhr-Universitat Bochum, Germany, contains maps relating to his work on the flora, fauna, and physical geography of Japan during the nineteenth century.

Papers of Carl Andrew Spaatz, Army and Air Force officer, contain aerial photographic prints of Auschwitz and target areas in Hungary and Yugoslavia, 1945 (80 prints); photographs of Eighth Air Force Operations maps of Europe and maps of areas bombed by the Fifteenth Air Force, April, 1945; reference file relating to the development of photographic reconnaissance aircraft in Europe, 1944; aerial photographic prints and maps comprising part of bombing assessment and target analysis files, 1944–1945 (4.5 linear feet); and material relating to the preparation of tactical maps of Europe using aerial photography, 1942–1944 (.5 linear foot).

Papers of Ephraim George Squier, archaeologist and diplomat, contain a volume of maps and drawings made by Squier during an expedition in Central America, 1853.

Papers of George Hay Stuart contain a manuscript map of the battle of Gettysburg sketched by a reporter for the Pittsburgh *Gazette,* 1863.

Collection of Hugh Taggart contains papers concerning the surveying of lots and squares in the District of Columbia, including survey notes by Robert King, 1793–1795; and papers relating to Pierre Charles L'Enfant.

Papers of Herbert Thatcher, English historian, contain correspondence with American libraries and journal editors relating to his research on John Mitchell, 1928–1932; page-size manuscript sketch maps of North America accompanying a typescript entitled "The Cause (Not the Pretext) of the American Revolution" (24 maps); and a typescript concerning "John Mitchell, Cartographer".

Papers of Ambrose W. Thompson, railroad, canal, and land entrepreneur, include manuscript maps relating to his activities in the vicinity of Coney Island and Jamaica Bay, New York, 1878, Chiriqui Province, Panama, and Central America, ca. 1854 (7 maps); and annotated maps showing the proposed New York and Northwest Railway, 1870s, and coal and ore deposits in Virginia.

Journal of Gilbert Thompson, recording the activities of the United States Topographical Engineer Battalion of the Army of the Potomac, 1861–1864, is interleaved with pencil sketches of West Point, Harper's Ferry, and campaign camp sites and battlefields in Virginia, photographs and sketches of officers and men including Thompson, and maps, 1861–1903. For related maps by Thompson, see the Library of Congress Geography and Map Division (A21).

Tissandier Collection, comprising materials on the history of aeronautics acquired by Albert and Gaston Tissandier, includes manuscript and printed French strip maps showing routes of balloonists and an undated aerial photograph taken from a balloon, 1875–1884 (10 items); and an article on aerial photography with illustrations from *La Nature* magazine, ca. 1880.

Papers of John Toland, author, include photostatic maps with hand-drawn overlays prepared by Toland during research for his book, *Battle of the Bulge* (1955, 1961) (12 sheets), and maps collected or prepared for *The Last Hundred Days* (1966).

Papers of Joseph M. Toner, physician, biographer, and collector, include manuscript cadastral plats relating to land parcels in Washington, D.C. by Robert King, George Fenwick, and other surveyors, 1801–1871 (15 items); copies of George Washington's surveys and related notes and memoranda, 1749–1799 (.5 linear foot); correspondence and lists of elevations, with a few railroad maps, submitted by railroad companies for his *Dictionary of Elevations and Climatic Register of the United States,* 1873–1874 (1 linear foot); and an extensive biographical file (155 linear feet) that contains obituaries and notices of a number of nineteenth century topographers and surveyors.

Records of the United States Army Utah Expedition comprise the printer's manuscript copy of the report of the exploration and mapping of the Great Basin by Capt. James H. Simpson, 1859, including Philip Harry's English translation of Silvestre Vélez de Escalante's journey from Santa Fe to Lake Utah, 1776, from the Spanish manuscript in the Peter Force Collection, and Edward H. Kern's journal of the exploration of the Humboldt River in 1845. For the related manuscript maps, see National Archives and Records Administration, B19, RG 77.

Records of the United States Naval Observatory include correspondence, accounts, and receipts by Matthew F. Maury and his wind and current chart agents, concerning the sale and production of these charts, 1848–1859 (2 linear feet).

Records of the United States Work Projects Administration include two relevant series. The Federal Writers Project contains research notes and sketch maps relating to the various routes of the "Underground Railroad" before the Civil War (3 folders). The Historical Records Survey contains descriptions of the holdings of the District of Columbia's Surveyor's Office (3 folders).

Papers of George Washington contain correspondence with a number of surveyors and mapmakers including Christopher Colles, James Dermott, Simeon DeWitt, Andrew and Benjamin Ellicott, Robert Erskine, George Fairfax, Thomas Hutchins, Pierre L'Enfant, Jedediah Morse, and Isaac Roberdeau, 1750–1794. There are also surveys and plats prepared by Washington, 1749–1752, a survey of Mount Vernon, 1784, and maps scattered throughout his correspondence including several associated with Anthony Wayne, 1780, a map of Lexington, Virginia, 1798, and a map of Valley Forge sent by Louis Le Beque Du Portail, 1777. A published finding aid is available.

Journals of George P. Welsh, naval officer, contain manuscript charts of islands and harbors in the Pacific, the coast of Peru, and a world map showing the tracks of the voyages on which Welsh served: *USS Brandywine,* 1841–1842, *USS Independence,* 1843, and *USS Levant,* 1843–1845.

Papers of Charles Wilkes, naval officer, include journals and notebooks relating to his surveying and charting of Antarctica and the Pacific basin, associated computation tables, charts, and maps, and correspondence with Joseph Drayton, Frederick D. Stuart and others concerning the publication of his charts, 1838–1865. Also maps relating to the Dauphine and Susquehanna Coal Company, 1853–1870, and a map of his property in Washington D.C. (6,500 items).

Papers of John David Woelpper, surveyor, consist of one volume of correspondence and invoices relating to the surveying of the Virginia military lands in the Ohio Valley, 1763–1810 by Thomas Bullitt, Surveyor of the District of Ohio in Virginia, and Woelpper.

Papers of Leonard Wood, United States Army officer, include a manuscript map by Oskar Huber of the pursuit of the Chiricahua Indians based on information from Wood, 1886, maps of Fort Leavenworth and Gettysburg used for map training, and a large printed Spanish map of Mexico, 1910.

4. No comprehensive card catalog or index to individual items is available, but the Division has compiled a number of unpublished and published finding aids to assist the scholar. These are described in a brochure, *Reference Aids to Manuscript Collections in*

the Library of Congress. A two-part computer print-out, known as the Master Record of Manuscript Collections, serves as the basic guide to all collections. Master Record I provides a checklist of all collections arranged alphabetically by name of individual or organization. Master Record II contains summary descriptions of collections. It is augmented by a name and key word index. In addition, some 52,000 collections are described in the *National Union Catalog of Manuscript Collections* (NUCMC), a national summary listing of individual collections in manuscript repositories and archives from 1959 to 1983. It should be available in most large public and research libraries. Still useful, also, is the *Handbook of Manuscripts in the Library of Congress* (1918, and supplements to 1931 and 1938).

More thorough descriptions of individual collections are found in some 1,500 published and unpublished registers maintained alphabetically by name of collection in vertical file cabinets in the Manuscript Reading Room; card catalog indexes to selected collections; and name indexes to the Presidential Papers collections. Other pertinent finding aids include the general catalog and indexes pertaining to the foreign copying project; guide to Civil War collections in the Manuscript Division, which is scheduled for publication shortly; the *Naval Historical Foundation Manuscript Collection: A Catalog* (1974); *Manuscript Sources in the Library of Congress for Research on the American Revolution* (1975); guide to Hispanic manuscript collections; and guide to collections relating to Asia, the Far East, and Pacific Regions.

B15a Maryland State Archives

1 a. *Hall of Records*
350 Rowe Boulevard
Annapolis, Maryland 21404
(301) 269-3914/3916

b. 8:30 A.M.–4:30 P.M. Monday–Saturday. Closed on state holidays. Closed on Saturday if a holiday falls on Friday.

c. Open to the public.

d. Copy facilities are available. All major maps of Maryland are available in color transparencies for rental or purchase.

e. Edward C. Papenfuse, State Archivist and Commissioner of Land Patents

2–3. The holdings of the Maryland State Archives contain 3000 original and reference facsimile maps of Maryland, concentrated in three principal special collections: Md HR G1213, consisting of 35mm slides of Pre–1908 Maryland maps held in the Library of Congress, Enoch Pratt Free Library, the Peabody Collection, the John Work Garrett Library, and private collections (600 maps); Md HR 1427; and Md HR G1399, consisting of photographic facsimiles of the Huntington Collection of maps relating to the Chesapeake region. In addition to printed maps, the Archives has extensive holdings of manuscript maps as well as copies of all cadastral (tax) maps of the state dating from the 1960s.

4. The special collections are described in unpublished finding aids. Special Collections Md HR G1213 and Md HR G1399 are described and illustrated respectively in *The Hammond-Harwood House Atlas of Historical Maps of Maryland, 1608–1908* (Baltimore: The Johns Hopkins University Press, 1982. 128 p.), compiled by Edward C. Papenfuse and Joseph M. Coale III, and *On the Map. An Exhibit and Catalogue of Maps Relating to Maryland and the Chesapeake Bay...February 21 - March 6, 1983* (Chester-

town, Maryland: Washington College, 1983. 102 p.), compiled by Russell Morrison, Edward C. Papenfuse, Nancy M. Bramucci, and Robert J.H. Janson-La Palme.

B16 Marine Corps Historical Center (Navy Department)

1 a. *Washington Navy Yard, Building 58*
9th and M Streets, S.E.
Washington, D.C. 20374
(202) 433-3396 (Personal Papers Collection)
(202) 433-3439 (Archives Section)

b. 8:00 A.M.–4:30 P.M. Monday–Friday

c. Open to researchers, but scholars must sign in at the Security Section or the Information Desk near the main entrance and obtain individual visitors passes.

d. Photoreproduction facilities are available.

e. Edwin H. Simmons (Brigadier General, Retired), Director
Joyce E. Bonnett, Head, Archives Section
Charles A. Wood, Chief, Museum Curator
Michael Miller, Personal Papers Curator

2–3. The Center serves as an archives and museum for the Marine Corps. In addition to a small map and aerial photography collection, maps and aerial photographs are found scattered throughout the records and papers of the Archives Section and Personal Papers Collection. The Museum has a number of printed and manuscript maps on permanent display relating to Marine Corps actions in World War II, Korea, Vietnam, and the Middle East.

MAP COLLECTION

The Map Collection numbers about 2000 items. It is unclassified and uncataloged, but the materials are generally grouped by names of regions or islands associated with Marine Corps military actions. These include France; Nicaragua, Dominican Republic, and Haiti; Guadalcanal (2 map drawers); Iwo Jima; Okinawa; Marshall Islands; Saipan/Tinian; Guam, Korea (2 map drawers); Peleliu Island; Tarawa; Solomon Islands; Bougainville; New Britain; Philippines; Vietnam; and Marine training camps in California, Hawaii Islands, Samoa, Australia, and New Zealand. While some of the materials are duplicated in the National Archives and Library of Congress, the collection also includes unique manuscript sketch maps, action overlays from battle reports, printed and manuscript Japanese maps, some 200-300 aerial photographic prints and mosaics (some of which are annotated), and air targets. The materials on the Guadalcanal action, for example, contain cadastral plats of local plantations, British and Japanese navigation charts, and aerial photographs which provided the data for compiling the basic 12 sheet topographic map of the battle site.

ARCHIVES SECTION

The Archives Section serves as the official repository for combat operational reports, plans, after-action reports, and related documents for World War II and later. The Section also maintains a few pre-World War II materials. In general, however, pre-World War II Marine Corps Records have been transferred to the National Archives and Records Administration (B19, RG 127), and records continue to be transferred on a regular basis. Vietnam era records (1500 cubic feet) are housed in the Archives Section, while the remaining records (3500 cubic feet) are stored temporarily in the Washington National Records Center, Suitland, Maryland. The latter may be recalled to the Archives Section when required for research.

The operation reports and related files are generally organized by Marine Corps unit, activity, or subject, and loosely indexed by accession lists. Cartographic materials are found throughout the files. Some of the more significant materials are listed below:

World War I Collection, 1917–1919–maps and aerial photographs of battle sites, operations, training areas, and military sectors.

Marine Corps Units in Nicaragua, 1927–1933–maps, sketches, intelligence reports, and air mission reports.

1st Provisional Brigade in Haiti, 1933–1934–maps of Santo Domingo, 1919–1922.

Marine Corps Air Force Units Historical Reports and Diaries–reports and histories of ComFleet Air Photographic Group Two, 1940s, and Marine Corps Photographic Squadrons VMD and VMP 154, 254, 354, and 954, 1943–1946.

United States Marine Corps Geographic Files, 1940–1945– divisional, regimental, and battalion operational plans and action reports contain cartographic data relating to all campaigns in which the Marine Corps participated. For example, the file on Okinawa contains documents on aerial photo support, May–June, 1945, and stereographic study, 1st Marine Division photo interpretation reports, and maps and overlays prepared for various battalions of the 1st and 7th Marines.

Marine Corps Aviation History Reference Notes–photo intelligence and interpretation reports based on aerial photographic reconnaissance sorties carried out by Navy and Marine Corps photo interpretation squadrons, 1943–1944 (7 cubic feet).

Terrain Studies, S.W. Pacific, 1942–1945–studies of islands, capes, bays, and peninsulas in the Southwest Pacific area and Japan (115 items).

1st Provisional Brigade, Korea, July–September, 1950– overlays and plans for Inchon-Seoul, Korea, and Wonson- Hanhung, Manchuria.

PERSONAL PAPERS COLLECTION

The Personal Papers Collection (PC) contains the papers of some 2,000 Marines, many of which include maps and aerial photographs. The following sample is representative of the collection.

PC 2: Clayton B. Vogel Papers contain maps found among his official papers, including two blueprint maps of Veracruz, one annotated to show the location of public buildings, hospitals, churches, and military and police facilities, 1913; and Fort Benning maneuver area maps, prepared by the Infantry School, Fort Benning, Georgia, 1942 (5 items).

PC 72: Robert L. Ghormley Papers contain photostat copies of Admiral Ghormley's 98-page personal log of the Guadalcanal-Tulagi Campaign (August 1–November 13, 1942), which includes many charts and maps.

PC 112: James Roosevelt Papers include a manuscript sketch map of Makin Island prepared from aerial photographs and his typescript operational order for a raid on the island, August, 1942.

PC 174: Frank D. Weir Papers contain aerial photographic prints of towns, villages, and airfields in Nicaragua taken about 1927–1928 by Marine Observation Squadron Seven (91 prints), related correspondence, and air patrol reports. Weir served as photographic officer for the squadron. The collection also contains manuscript and annotated blueprint maps of various Nicaraguan provinces and districts, 1924–1928 (9 items).

PC 224: Littleton W.T. Waller, Jr. Papers contain French situation maps of Verdun and St. Etienne (8 items) and annotated aerial photographic prints of Sivry-Lez (3 items), World War I.

PC 248: William P.T. Hill Papers contain miscellaneous printed and blueprint maps, including war game and terrain exercise maps, blueprint maps of Marine Corps facilities at Quantico, Virginia (1924) and New River, North Carolina (1942), a printed map of Culebra Island, West Indies, compiled by the Intelligence Section Fleet Marine Force, 1936, and topographic and geological maps relating to Navy coal resources and land leases in Alaska (80 items).

PC 316: Victor J. Croizat Papers consist of maps pertaining to military actions on Guadalcanal, August 18, 1942.

PC 349: Edward W. Snedecker Papers contain a series of aerial photographs of the Chateau-Thierry sector in France dated July, 1918, and working maps (some with annotations) used during campaigns on Guadalcanal (1942), Empress Augusta Bay, Bougainville, (194 –), and Nanyi-Ri, Korea (1950).

PC 496: Alpha L. Bowser Papers contain maps with overlays relating to the withdrawal from the Chosin Reservoir during the Korean War.

PC 521: Norman C. Bates Papers include pictures of student officers attending USMC School of Application at Gettysburg College, which involved plane table mapping of areas of the Gettysburg Battlefield, 1913; and aerial photographs of Veracruz and Fort San Juan Ulvoa, taken from a seaplane with the United States Expeditionary Forces, Vera Cruz, Mexico, 1914.

PC 526: John R. Blandford Papers include various map overlays pertaining to military actions on Guadalcanal and Cape Gloucester during World War II.

4. A brochure, *Guide to the Marine Corps Historical Center* (1979, 30 pages) provides general information on the facility. The Personal Papers Collection is described in a catalog compiled by Charles A. Wood (1974, rev. 1980, 56 pages). The researcher should also consult *An Annotated Bibliography of the United States Marine Corps in the Second World War,* by Michael O'Quinlivan and Jack B. Hilliard (1970, 42 pages).

B17 Montgomery County Historical Society

1 a. *1891 Courthouse*
50 Courthouse Square
Rockville, Maryland 20850
(301) 762–1492

b. 12:00 Noon–4:00 P.M. Tuesday–Saturday

c. Open to the public; research fee for nonmembers.

e. Jane Sween, Librarian

2–3. The Society maintains a collection of some 500 maps and plats, the latter used for litigation in land cases. The collection dates from the 1790s and is indexed by tract name, names of individuals appearing on the maps, and by location.

National Aeronautics and Space Administration (NASA)—History Office **See entry G18**

National Air and Space Museum (NASM) (Smithsonian Institution)—Records Management Division **See entry C5**

B18 National Anthropological Archives (NAA) (Smithsonian Institution)

1 a. *National Museum of Natural History*
10th Street and Constitution Avenue, N.W.
Washington, D.C. 20560
(202) 357-1976

b. 9:00 A.M.–5:00 P.M. Monday–Friday. Requests for materials are not accepted from noon–2:00 P.M.

c. Open to the public; visitors must register. Since some of the materials are restricted, it is suggested that readers contact NAA well in advance of their visit.

d. Photcopying facilities are available; prints can be purchased at the office.

e. Herman J. Viola, Director
James R. Glenn, Deputy Director

2–3. The National Anthropological Archives was formerly the Bureau of American Ethnology (BAE), a Smithsonian agency established in 1879 to study native Americans. In addition to the records of the BAE, the Archives has custody of the records of the Smithsonian Institution's Anthropology Department. It also collects papers of prominent anthropologists and records of several regional and national anthropological organizations. Its collections relate primarily to the linguistics, ethnology, archeology, history, and physical anthropology of native North Americans. Scattered among the official records, private papers, and photographic collections are some 5,000 maps and 3,000 aerial photographs.

SMITHSONIAN OFFICIAL RECORDS

Bureau of American Ethnology Map Collection, contains 532 photocopy, printed, manuscript, and annotated maps dating from 1665–1965. These maps are limited primarily to North America but include some maps of South America. They depict American Indian tribes, linguistic boundaries, Indian mounds, and archeological sites. A number of the maps were prepared or annotated by noted American cartographers and geographers associated with the BAE, including John Wesley Powell (its first director from 1879–1902); Henry W. Henshaw, and William Henry Holmes. Several maps were drawn by native Americans. A computer print-out describing this collection is available in the Reading Room; it is cross-referenced by geographic area, subject, and author.

Division of Archeology Map Collection, contains about 500 printed, annotated, and manuscript maps dating from the nineteenth century. The collection, relating primarily to North America, is loosely arranged by region, county, and state. Some of the manuscript and annotated maps show archeological sites. Also included is a set of four original thematic maps of the United States compiled under the direction of Henry Gannett, probably for the 1890 or 1900 statistical atlas of the United States.

River Basin Surveys Records, contain about 2,400 maps of archeological sites now located in reservoir areas. The RBS records consist of studies by Smithsonian staff of archeological sites threatened by the construction of dams and reservoirs following World War II. This survey was carried out under the auspices of the Inter-Agency Salvage Program, a cooperative effort among public and private organizations to promote salvage archeological work throughout the United States. RBS work focused on the Missouri River Basin, the West Coast, Texas, and the southeastern states. An unpublished preliminary inventory briefly describes four series of cartographic materials dating from 1909–1963, with some copies of maps dating from the 18th century. Examples of the types of maps found in this collection are a set of maps of the John H. Kerr Reservoir area in Virginia showing archeological sites, 1940s; the Alabama Anthropological Society's map of East Central Alabama showing aboriginal mounds, townsites and villages of the Upper and Lower Creeks prior to 1832, 1921; and the North Carolina Department of Archives and History archeological base map of the site of the Moravian Community, Bethabara, Forsythe County, North Carolina, 1965.

There are also pioneer aerial photographs of archeological sites along the Missouri River collected by Waldo R. Wedel and Paul L. Cooper. Some of these photographs were taken by Thomas E. Huddleston (1930s), Ralph S. Solecki, and Nathaniel L. Dewell (1952). This aerial photography collection is described in *Remote Sensing: The American Great Plains* (National Park Service, Supplement No. 9 to *Remote Sensing: A Handbook for Archeologists and Cultural Resource Managers,* 1984), compiled by W. Raymond Wood, Robert K. Nickel, and David E. Griffin.

Numbered Manuscript Collection, contains several hundred maps among the research materials originally prepared or collected by the BAE between 1879 and 1965. Some of the major subjects represented are archeological sites, native place names, military battles, exploration, and East Asia. A number of the maps were prepared by George Gibbs, James Mooney, and J.R. Swanton. The following examples suggest the wide range of materials: map of the Sun Dance camp circle of the Kiowa and Apache Indians during the Medicine Lodge Treaty of 1867, drawn by Mooney, 1896; printed maps annotated by Swanton to show Hernando DeSoto's route in the Southeast; several manuscript maps drawn by native Americans including maps of Baffin Island, Canada, by Eskimos with related notes by Franz Boas, 1883–1884, and a map showing the battle between General Alfred Sully's company and the Dakota Sioux at Heart River by one of Sully's Winnebago scouts, 1864; manuscript map of Nebraska with stream names given in Dhegiha by James Owen Dorsey; copies of Lewis and Clarks maps annotated by J. Neilson Barry to show current place names; a manuscript map of Paraguay by Joao Pedro Gay showing the location of Jesuit missions, 1881; and a letter to William Henry Holmes from W. Hallet Phillips concerning early maps of Virginia and Maryland, 1892.

In addition to these maps of North America, there are 16 manuscript and woodblock prints of pictorial maps of cities by Japanese and Chinese artists and mapmakers. These include Nagasaki (1750–1778), Shimoda (1786), Tokyo (1849–1934), Yokohama (1859–1870), Yokosuka (1888), and Peking (1891). There are also maps of the Tokaido road from Tokyo to Kyoto (1820–1824), and Uragoa, showing Commodore Matthew Perry's arrival in 1853.

A subject-author index, published by G.K. Hall in four volumes, is available in the Reading Room. Since only a small number of the maps are listed under the subject heading "maps", the researcher must also check other headings such as geography, drawings, archeology, and exploration.

PRIVATE PAPERS

Papers of Homer G. Barnett contain a language map of the territory of Papua and New Guinea by S.A. Wurm of the Australian National University, 1958–1959.

Papers of Robert LeMoyne Barrett contain field notes, map sketches, and some correspondence and photographic terrain views relating to his geographical expeditions to Norway, Siberia, Baja Peninsula, Inner Asia, Abyssinia, Morocco, Canadian Rockies, Arizona-New Mexico-Colorado, and Himalayas, 1892–1909 and 1923. A typescript finding aid is available.

Papers of Henry Bascom Collins contain twelve reference and research maps of Alaska and Canada dated from 1795–1940, including a map of Nunivak Island by an Eskimo (1927) and a map of Siberian Eskimo village sites by James A. Ford, c. 1930.

Papers of James Alfred Ford contain a small number of sketch maps and aerial photographs of archeological sites relating to his work in South America and Alaska, 1930s–1950s.

Papers of Robert W. Grant contain aerial photographs and maps of the Central Pacific islands and China used for military intelligence during his work as a photographic interpreter with the 9th Photographic Intelligence Detachment, United States Airforce, 1940s. A typescript finding aid is available.

Papers of John Peabody Harrington contain sketch maps scattered among his field notes recording native place names primarily in California, Oregon, Washington, and Alaska but also Mexico and South America, 1907–1957. These maps were made with the help of native and local linguistic informants to show the specific location of each place that names were recorded. A portion of the 750,000 pages of these documents has been described in the *Papers of John Peabody Harrington in the Smithsonian Institution 1907–1957 Volume One A Guide to Field Notes: Native American History, Language, and Culture of Alaska/Northwest Coast,* edited by Elaine L. Mills (Kraus International Publications, 1981). The field notes described in this guide are available on microfilm from Kraus International Publications, Route 100, Millwood, New York 10546.

Papers of Robert King Harris contain almost 100 manuscript, published, and photocopy copies of archeology, historical, geological, and county maps related to Texas, some of which are annotated to show archeological sites, 1960–1967. A typescript inventory is available.

Papers of Robert F. Heizer contain some 167 sketch maps, tracings, and printed maps relating to his expeditions to La Venta, Mexico, 1955–1968.

Papers of Neil Merton Judd contain some 200 original cartographic items relating to his archeological investigations at Chaco Canyon, New Mexico during the 1920s, including plans of numerous Pueblos; eight aerial photographs of Pueblo Bonito by Charles A. Lindberg, 1929; and a manuscript map of explorations and surveys in New Mexico and Utah by geologist John S. Newberry during the Captain John Macomb expedition in the 1850s.

Papers of the Pan American Institute of Geography and History contain the unofficial papers of Arch C. Gerlach, former Chief of the Geography and Map Division of the Library of Congress and United States Representative to the Directing Council of the PAIGH, and Richard Randall, President of the Institute, 1950–1955. These papers include correspondence, reports, and speeches relating to the Institute's Commission of Cartography, 1943–1961, as well as some maps and aerial photographs.

Papers of Dache McClain Reeves contain notes and aerial photographs by an early specialist in balloon reconnaissance and aerial photography. Included in the collection are over 1,500 aerial photographic negatives with prints primarily of earth mounds in Ohio, but also views of archeological sites in California, Louisiana, Georgia, Illinois, and Colorado (1911–1946). Some aerial photographs pertain to his activities with the Army Air Service in France during World War I, land forms in the Philippine Islands and Kitty Hawk, North Carolina. The collection also contains a set of lantern slides used during his lectures on photographic intelligence at the United States Military Academy at West Point. Also included is a number of archeological maps of Indian mounds studied by Reeves; correspondence and notes related to aerial photography and its application to archeology and history; a report summarizing the cartographic work of balloon observers in the AEF Air Service, Oct. 9, 1918; and material relating to stereoscopic procedures and equipment. A typescript register is available.

Papers of Saul H. Reisenberg contain two hand-drawn maps recording land ownership along the Samoan coast, ca. 1950s.

Papers of Harold Hanna Roberts, Jr. contain manuscript plans, profiles, and field maps of archeological sites at Chaco Canyon, New Mexico, 1924–1927; Shiloh Mound, Tennessee, 1933–1934; Lindenmeier sites, Colorado, 1935–1940; and San Jon, New Mexico, 1941; maps of prehistoric sites in Arizona; and a few aerial photographic views of Lindenmeier, Colorado, 1934–1940 and San Jon, New Mexico, 1941.

Papers of Frank Maryl Setzler contain maps of Australia and aerial photographs and related flight logs pertaining to Markville, Louisiana, ca. 1940s.

Papers of William Duncan Strong contain many maps of Central America and Labrador compiled or annotated by Strong to show locations of Indian tribes, including an Indian sketch map of northeastern Labrador, 1930s.

Papers of A.F. Whiting contain 56 manuscript maps relating to land ownership in Micronesia, 1952–1953.

PHOTOGRAPHIC COLLECTIONS

Aerial Photographs of Hohokam Canals in Salt River and Gila River Valleys, Arizona (Photographic Lot 3) consist of seven rolls of film, 139 annotated mosaic prints and 68 maps. The oblique and vertical aerial photographs were made by the War Department in the 1930s at the urging of Senator Carl Hayden in an effort to record these ancient canals that were then being destroyed by agricultural development. The mosaic prints were annotated by subsequent studies carried out by the Smithsonian.

4. There is no single inventory to the maps and aerial photographs. A typescript *Preliminary Guide to the Smithsonian Institution National Archives* provides a general introduction to most of the official records, private papers, and photographic collections. It is supplemented by expanded published and unpublished shelf lists and inventories for selected collections, which have been cited above.

B19 National Archives and Records Administration (NARA)—Office of the National Archives

1 a. *8th and Pennsylvania Avenue, N.W.*
Washington, D.C. 20408
(202) 523-3218 (General Information)
(202) 523-3232 (Central Research Room)
(202) 523-3285 (Microfilm Reading Room)

b. Central Research Room and Microfilm Reading Room:
8:45 A.M.–10:00 P.M. Monday–Friday
8:45 A.M.–5:00 P.M. Saturday

Cartographic and Architectural Branch
841 South Pickett Street
Alexandria, Virginia
8:00 A.M.–4:30 P.M. Monday–Friday

Other Research Rooms:
Hours vary, but generally 8:45 A.M.–5:00 P.M. Monday–Friday.

c. Open to all serious researchers. The researcher must obtain a National Archives researcher identification card from the Central Reference Division, Room 200-B. These cards are also available at Pickett Street and Suitland. The use of some materials is restricted due to national security classifications.

d. Photocopying and microfilming services are available. The Cartographic and Architectural Branch has an oversize photocopier which can accommodate maps up to 42 inches wide by any length.

e. Frank Burke, Acting Archivist

2. The National Archives and Records Administration (NARA) is the official repository for noncurrent permanently valuable records produced by the federal government since 1774. With holdings of more than one million cubic feet of primary source material, including 1.8 million maps and 7 million aerial photographs, it is one of the world's major research centers for nineteenth and twentieth century history.

Most of the materials in NARA were originally created or acquired by legislative, judicial, or executive agencies of the federal government in pursuance of their official activities and maintained by them to document these activities or for their informational value. They are organized among some 400 record groups (RG). A record group is defined by NARA as "a body of organizationally and functionally related records established with particular regard for the administrative history, complexity, and volume of the records and archives of an agency". A typical record group consists of the documents produced by a government administrative unit at the department, bureau, or agency level. Within a record group, the filing arrangement generally follows the system employed by the government body that generated or acquired the records.

Access to the holdings is provided through general guides, inventories (INV.), preliminary inventories (PI), unpublished preliminary inventories (NC, NM), and microfilm publications. The basic printed research aid to the general holdings is the *Guide to the National Archives of the United States* (1974. 884 pages), which should be available in most large libraries. A loose leaf *Guide* (1977) is available in the Central Research Room. The *Guide to Cartographic Records in the National Archives* (1971. 444 pages) serves as a general introduction to cartographic materials acquired prior to July 1, 1966.

In addition to the holdings described below, which are maintained in the Washington, D.C. area, NARA administers a nationwide system of Federal Records Centers (David Peterson, Assistant Archivist 202/724–1614), National Archives Field Branches (202/523–4887), and Presidential Libraries (James E. O'Neill, Assistant Archivist 202/523–3212). Federal Records Centers and Archives Field Branches maintain government records that relate primarily to the states or regions in which they were created or accumulated. The Federal Records Centers and Archives Field Branches are located in Atlanta, Boston, Chicago, Denver, Fort Worth, Kansas City, Laguna Niguel, California, New York, Philadelphia, San Francisco, and Seattle metropolitan areas. Federal Records Centers without Archives Field Branches are found in Dayton, Los Angeles, and St. Louis.

3. The collections of NARA are immense. The map collection is surpassed in size in North America only by that of the Library of Congress. The maps in NARA differ from those in the Library of Congress, however, in two ways. First, since these records were at one time closely associated with government agency programs, their scope reflects the activities of the United States government. The majority of those maps dated prior to World War I relate to the mapping and surveying of the United States, particularly the Western United States, and to military mapping. Those dated during or after World War I provide more worldwide coverage as a result of the increased role that the United States has played in world affairs. There are also significant thematic or special purpose maps associated with New Deal agencies. Second, almost one-half of the maps are manuscript or printed maps containing manuscript annotations, making it one of the largest collections of its kind in the world. The aerial photographic collection, numbering more than 7 million photographs, is probably the largest accessible collection of historical aerial photographs in the world. It provides unique coverage for most of the United States in the 1930s, prior to the many changes that took place in the urban and rural landscape during and after World War II. There is also extensive worldwide coverage documenting military activities from 1918 to the 1960s.

Since cartographic records in NARA are often closely related to documents maintained by other branches within NARA, the cartographic and related textual record groups are described together. Within each record group description, the records of the

Cartographic and Architectural Branch are listed first, followed by related textual, pictorial, and motion picture records. The inclusive dates and item counts following the record group title refer only to the items maintained by the Cartographic and Architectural Branch. The location of related materials is noted by the appropriate custodial branch symbol designation. A list of all custodial branches, with their branch symbols noted in parentheses, is given below.

Diplomatic Branch (NNFD)
Room 5-E (202) 523–3174
Milton O. Gustafson, Chief

Judicial, Fiscal, and Social Branch (NNFJ)
Room 5-W (202) 523–3089
Clarence F. Lyons, Chief

General Branch (NNFG)
Room 103
Washington National Records Center (WNRC) Building
Suitland, Maryland
Mailing Address: Washington, D.C. 20408
(301) 763–7410
Janet L. Hargett, Chief

Scientific, Economic, and Natural Resources Branch (NNFN)
Room 13-E (202) 523–3238
Franklin W. Burch, Chief

Legislative Reference Branch (NNLR)
Room 307 (202) 523–4185
David R. Kepley, Chief

Military Reference Branch (NNMR)
Room 13-W (202) 523–3340
Robert Wolfe, Chief
George Chalou, Assistant Chief

Military Field Branch (NNMF)
Washington National Records Center Building Room 117
Suitland, Maryland
Mailing Address: Washington, D.C. 20408
(301) 763–1710
Elaine E. Everly, Chief
Richard Boylan, Assistant Chief for Reference

Cartographic and Architectural Branch (NNSC)
Mailing Address: Washington, D.C. 20408
(703) 756–6700
John Dwyer, Chief
Robert Richardson, Assistant Chief for Reference

Motion Picture, Sound and Video Branch (NNSM)
Motion Picture Reference Room G-13 (202) 523–3063
William T. Murphy, Chief

Still Pictures Branch (NNSP)
Room 18-N (202) 523–3010
Joe D. Thomas, Chief

Machine—Readable Branch (NNSR)
Room 20-E (202) 523-3267
Richard F. Myers, Chief

RG 7: Records of the Bureau of Entomology and Plant Quarantine, 1930–1950.—1,640 maps. State, county and township maps of Florida relating to the Mediterranean fruit fly eradication campaign, 1930–1933. Maps prepared by the Division of Disease and Insect Control relating to the distribution and control of a variety of plant diseases and insect infestations in the United States, 1930–1947.

RG 8: Records of the Bureau of Agricultural Engineering, 1931–1939.—300 maps. Maps of individual farms depicting soil types and crop production.

RG 9: Records of the National Recovery Administration, 1933–1935.—238 maps. Administrative maps showing boundaries of NRA operating codes for various industries. Statistical and economic maps relating to trade areas, transportation facilities, and individual industries in the United States prepared by the Division of Research and Planning, 1933–1935.

RG 11: General Records of the United States Government, 1818–1867.—4 maps. Published and manuscript maps associated with international treaties: the John Melish map of the United States, 1818, J. Disturnell's map of Mexico, 1847, a chart of Shimoda Harbor, Japan, 1854, and a plan of Sitka, Alaska, 1867. The records of presidential proclamations in NNFD include a set of Geological Survey Alaskan topographic quadrangles (1:250,000), annotated to show the boundaries of national monuments, which accompany original proclamations signed by President Jimmy Carter, 1979. Among the records of ratified Indian treaties are at least two treaties which contain maps by Rene Paul, one showing the lands of the Illinois Indians and the other the lands of the Quapaw Indians, 1818.

RG 16: Records of the Office of the Secretary of Agriculture, 1889, 1914–1947.—2,081 maps. An incomplete set of statistical atlases published by the Department, including the *Album of Agricultural Statistics of the United States* (1889). Published and annotated maps and atlases prepared by postwar regional planning committees showing soil types, crop and animal distribution, natural vegetation, climate, population and settlement patterns, and marketing areas for the Southwest, Far West, Appalachia, Southeast, and Northern Great Plains. Maps showing the status of aerial photography conducted by the Department, 1939–1944.

RG 18: Records of the Army Air Force, 1917–1947.—6,650 maps. Maps and plans relating to early airfields, 1917–1929. Airstrip charts prepared by the Army Air Service, 1918–1936. Flak and target maps prepared by the Assistant Chief of Air Staff for Intelligence showing towns and areas in Japan, Formosa, Manchuria, and North Africa, 1942–1944. Climatic weather plotting charts for Italy, France, the Balkans and other parts of the world. Incomplete series of the World Aeronautical Charts (1:1,000,000), World Pilotage Charts (1:500,000), and World Approach Charts (1:250,000) issued by the Aeronautical Chart Service, 1939–1947.

World War II combat operation and intelligence reports in NNMF contain numerous aerial photographic prints recording bombing runs and other operational activities, and "Captains of Aircraft Maps" annotated to show flight lines, 1941–1946.

Aerial photographs in NNSP provide coverage of terrain features, cities, historic areas, flood disaster areas, and airfields worldwide made by the Aeronautical Division of the Signal Corps, the Air Service, the Air Corps, and the Army Air Forces 1923–1945 (4,750 photographs). Also, aerial photographs of airports, landing fields, cities and towns, and prominent natural features taken along flight routes over North and South America, the Middle East, Africa, Asia, and the South Pacific by the Air Transport Command to help orient pilots, 1943–1945 (26,000 photographs); a lantern slide collection relating to aviation history contains aerial photographs of United States and foreign cities, 1903–1927 (ca. 2,200 items); oblique aerial photographs of towns, cities, and battlefields in France and Germany made by the Photographic Section, Air Service, American Expeditionary Forces, 1918–1919 (6,335 photographs); oblique and vertical aerial views of military airfields and some cities and historic sites made by United States Army Reconnaissance Squadrons along the east and west coasts, 1925–1947 (430 photographs); aerial photographs of United States Army Air Service balloon and airship convoys, camps, and Scofield Barracks, Hawaii, 1908–1920 (250 photographs); and oblique and vertical photographs taken by the 15th and 21st Photo Squadrons of terrain features, urban areas, military bases, and flood damage in Florida, Illinois, Indiana, Kentucky, Michigan, Missouri, and Wisconsin 1923–1939 (1,500 photographs).

Motion picture films in NNSM include films showing the preparation of combat maps in the South Pacific based on aerial photographs by the 8th Photographic Reconnaissance Squadron, 1943 (2 reels); the preparation of photo maps of Burma and India by the 9th Photo Reconnaissance Squadron and the 17th Photo Intelligence Detachment of the 10th Army Air Force, 1941 (3 reels); and the printing and distribution of maps at Cheltenham, England, 1944 (1 reel).

RG 19: Records of the Bureau of Ships, 1820–1910.—100 items. Plans of major Navy bases in the United States filed among a larger series of ship plans.

RG 22: Records of the Fish and Wildlife Service, 1888–1941.—281 maps. Annotated maps of fur seal rookeries in the Pribilof Islands, Alaska. Maps of Alaskan coasts annotated to show fisheries, canneries, and packing plants. Maps prepared by the United States Biological Survey showing routes of the Death Valley Expedition, 1891; and maps of Federal bird refuges and game preserves.

RG 23: Records of the Coast and Geodetic Survey, 1839–1965.—67,353 maps and drawings. Manuscript and annotated maps and charts of the northeast coast, associated with Henry L. Whiting. A set of 31,000 published air navigation charts issued by the Aeronautical Division, 1926–1965. A set of 17,000 published charts issued by the Nautical Division, which includes a few manuscript compilations, 1839–1965. Special maps published by the Nautical Division including a large-scale topographic set of maps of Washington, D.C., 1887, and maps and charts of the southeast during the Civil War. Published shoreline, planimetric, and topographic maps of coastal areas of the United States prepared by the Division of Photogrammetry from aerial photographs, 1927–1961. An atlas of the Philippines prepared in 1899 from Jesuit surveys supervised by Jose Algue, S.J., and large-scale topographic maps of the Philippines prepared by the Survey, 1913–1934.

Drawings of surveying and photogrammetric instruments and equipment prepared by the Instruments Division, 1922–1959 (3,100 items). Charts illustrating compilation and printing techniques employed by the C&GS (40 items).

The textual records of the Office of the Director, which are maintained in NNFN, include the correspondence and working papers of Alexander Dallas Bache, 1843–1865 (Microfilm M642) and other superintendents, 1866–1940; the records of the Division of Geodesy, containing reports and correspondence relating to surveys and geodetic field work, 1844–1914; the records of the Charts Division, relating to the compilation, production and distribution of charts, 1844–1916; and log books of survey vessels, 1846–1947 (2,125 items). NNFG maintains scientific records prepared by survey field parties, consisting of astronomical observations, baseline measurements, topographic reconnaissance journals with maps and sketches, triangulation and traverse measurements, spirit level observations, and hydrographic survey soundings, 1834–1939. A detailed description of these records is found in *Preliminary Inventory* 105 (1958).

RG 24: Records of the Bureau of Naval Personnel, 1898–1935.—15 maps. Manuscript maps relating to naval activities off Cuba during the Spanish American War. Economic and strategic maps of the world produced by the Naval War College, 1905–1932.

Correspondence files in NNMR include copies of letters relating to the Depot of Charts and Instruments, the Naval Observatory, the Nautical Almanac Office, and Navigation Offices concerning the procurement and distribution of navigational and surveying instruments, technical books, and charts; hydrographic instructions for field parties; and the preparation and distribution of the *American Ephermeris and Nautical Almanac,* 1862–1884, 1910–1911 (172 volumes). Logs of United States naval vessels contain hydrographic data, 1801–1946 (72,500 volumes).

RG 26: Records of the United States Coast Guard, 1915–1941.—393 maps and charts. Manuscript and annotated maps showing harbor and Coast Guard facilities along the North Atlantic Coast. Charts prepared by Coast Guard cutters in Alaskan waters (1933–1934). Mississippi River Commission charts annotated to show the location of lighthouses.

RG 27: Records of the United States Weather Bureau, 1870–1965.—7,751 maps and charts. Daily surface weather condition maps, including some drawn by Cleveland Abbe, Sr. and Increase Lapham, pioneer developers of the weather map, 1870–1875. Maps relating to studies of storms and floods in specific regions or time periods. Charts of the Great Lakes depicting the locations of wrecks, 1886–1894. Charts of the oceans and Great Lakes showing storm tracks, fog, currents, and temperature in reference to shipping lanes, 1892–1914. Crop weather maps showing climate and weather conditions during the planting, growing, and harvesting seasons as aids to farmers, 1891–1914. Manual relating to the preparation and use of weather maps.

Related records in NNFN include correspondence files of the Meteorological Division of the Smithsonian Institution, 1847–1867 (4 feet), of the Signal Corps, 1870–1895 (495 feet), and of the Weather Bureau, 1894–1965 (877 feet); records of surface land observation, 1819–1941 (671 feet); records of marine observations begun by Lieutenant Matthew Fontaine Maury, Depot of Charts and Instruments, 1842–1930 (342 feet); and the diaries and journals of Cleveland Abbe and other early meteorologists, 1792–1946 (93 feet). These records are described in *Preliminary Inventory* 38 (1952).

RG 28: Records of the United States Postal Service, 1839, 1867–1970.—3,163 maps. Atlas of postal maps of the United States and individual states by David Burr, 1839. Post route maps of regions, states and territories, including manuscript maps, showing postal routes, mail-carrying railroads, and frequency of postal service, 1867–1970. Special map series of postal zones, 1913, navigable waters, 1917, rural-delivery routes, 1927–1928, and congressional districts, 1935–1940. Published and manuscript city maps showing delivery routes and locations of postal facilities, business sections, and mail boxes, 1912–1935. Maps and plans of airmail routes and landing fields, including the first airmail routes connecting New York and Washington, D.C. and Cleveland and Chicago, 1920–1935, air mail feeder lines at St. Louis, Missouri, 1946, and helicopter air mail service at Chicago, Illinois, 1946.

Textual records of the Division of Topography, maintained in NNFJ, include press copies of letters and reports relating to the reproduction and distribution of post route maps, 1910–1911, and site location reports with map diagrams submitted by postmasters for use in the preparation of postal maps, 1865–1946 (292 feet). The journal of Hugh Finlay, Surveyor of Post Roads for North Carolina, contains surveys and sketches of potential mail routes, 1773–1774 (microfilm). Letters sent by the Dispersing Clerk relate to orders for post route maps, 1862–1887.

RG 29: Records of the Bureau of the Census, 1850–1970.—95,000 maps. Published sets of decennial census maps and statistical atlases, 1860–1945, including a map showing the distribution of slaves in the south; and base and outline maps of the United States and individual states and territories portraying minor civil divisions, 1930–1950. Manuscript and annotated statistical maps displaying a wide range of census data relating to employment, trade, industry, population, religion, agricultural production, and farm labor, 1930–1960. A large series (90,000 maps) of manuscript, photocopied, and published maps of cities and counties annotated to show census enumeration districts for each of the decennial censuses, 1880–1970. Bound volumes describing the geographical bounds of the enumeration districts, 1880–1970. Descriptions of these maps are found in *Preliminary Inventory* 103 (1958).

Related textual records in NNFN contain the Geography Division's subject file of correspondence, reports, special studies, working papers and maps, 1889–1950. This file is further described in *Preliminary Inventory* 161 (1964). The preparation of enumeration district maps is shown in a motion picture film in NNSM entitled "Roll Call—U.S.A.", 1960 (29 minutes).

RG 30: Records of the Bureau of Public Roads, 1920–1982.—58,139 maps and 4,900 aerial photographs. Maps relating to defense and interstate highways, including maps signed or annotated by General John J. Pershing, Army Chief of Staff, 1922, and President Franklin Roosevelt, 1938. Traffic flow maps of the United States, 1937–1952. A large series of state and county "Log Maps", annotated to show progress of federally aided highway systems, 1922–1935. State transportation maps showing highways, railroads, canals, air lanes, and dredged channels, 1936–1947. Detailed county transportation maps showing towns and villages, farm units, major dwellings and public buildings, township and section lines, railroad lines, and industrial facilities, 1940–1982 (50,000 items). An incomplete series of aerial photographic prints and negatives documenting the planning and construction of the Mississippi River Parkway, the Inter-American Highway, the Alaska Highway, and several interstate and forest highways in the United States, 1936–1959.

Maps also are found among the general correspondence files in NNFG, 1912–1950, and a series of reports based on the economic impact of road improvement for selected counties, 1910–1918. Both cartographic and textual records are described in *Preliminary Inventory* 134 (1962).

RG 31: Records of the Federal Housing Administration, 1934–1942.—3,972 maps. Administrative and statistical maps of 362 American cities based on real property surveys and housing market analysis studies of housing conditions include large scale city maps annotated to show detailed economic and social data in relation to housing by block; analytical maps showing age, structural condition, sanitation, and occupancy information of houses and households by block; and maps showing land use, spread of built-up areas and transportation systems, population distribution and characteristics, average rent of dwellings by block, and blighted areas. A description of these maps is found in *Preliminary Inventory* 45 (1952).

RG 32: Records of the United States Shipping Board, 1914–1934.—900 maps. Maps depicting American shipping routes, 1914–1931, and plans of shipyards involved in World War I merchant ship construction, c. 1918–1928.

RG 37: Records of the Hydrographic Office, 1754–1984.—118,721 maps and 8,840 aerial photographs. Large-scale manuscript plotting sheets (boat sheets) prepared aboard survey ships; revised plotting sheets (smooth sheets) prepared in the Hydrographic Office from boat sheets, field notes, and other sources; and published charts annotated to show corrections and revisions, 1839–1945. Some 2,000 of these charts dated prior to 1908 are listed and described in *Special List* 43, 1978.

Manuscript and published maps and charts of the Philippines prepared for Spanish naval commanders and apparently obtained during the Spanish-American War, 1754–1901. An incomplete set of Matthew F. Maury's wind and current charts, 1849–1952. A series of 19 mounted charts selected to show copper plate engraving, hand drafting and lettering, the application of certain symbols, and the use of plastic mediums, 1882–1943. Published nautical charts issued by the Hydrographic Office, including some manuscripts, 1867–1972 (92,000 items). Reproductions of foreign nautical charts from 23 countries photolithographed by the Division of Chart Construction for regions not yet surveyed by the Hydrographic Office, 1939–1968. Published aeronautical charts prepared by the Division of Air Navigation, 1923–1972. An incomplete set of provisional nautical charts prepared aboard combat ships for invasion forces in the Southwest Pacific during World War II. Vertical and oblique aerial photographs of the Naval Oceanographic Office at Suitland, Maryland, portions of the gulf coast of Florida, San Clemente Island, California, the Aleutian Islands, and islands in the Pacific Ocean, 1923–1950.

Textual records in NNMR contain correspondence files of Matthew F. Maury and James M. Gilliss relating to hydrographic surveying and charting, 1842–1863; general correspondence files of the Hydrographic Office, 1863–1945, including correspondence with the United States Coast and Geodetic Survey, the British Admiralty, and the Bureau of Longitudes in Paris; journals and logs kept by Charles Wilkes and other members of his United States Exploring Expedition, 1838–1842 (Microfilm M 75); and the records of the Division of Chart Construction concerning the publication and correction of charts, 1903–1908. Correspondence and reports in NNMF relate to plans for hydrographic surveys and hydrographic survey field notes (980 linear feet), 1837–1946. These records are further described in *Inventory* 4 (1971).

Audiovisual records in NNSP include photographs and drawings of navigational aids and hydrographic instruments, 1889–1922 (37 photographs).

RG 38: Records of the Office of the Chief of Naval Operations, 1884–1955.—280 items. Manuscript, printed, and annotated maps collected by naval attaches or prepared by the Office of Naval Intelligence showing naval, transportation and communication facilities, naval engagements, population, wealth, political boundaries, and trade routes chiefly for Latin America but also China, Japan, France, Germany, the British Empire, and the Middle East. Harbor and port charts used during the Navy's Around-the-World Cruise, 1907–1912. A large-scale aerial photographic mosaic of Nanking, China, 1929. Plans of major United States Navy yards, 1917–1918. Described in *Preliminary Inventory* 85 (1955).

Related textual records of the Office of Naval Intelligence in NNMR contain general correspondence files and the correspondence files and intelligence reports of naval attaches.

RG 42: Records of the Office of Public Buildings and Grounds, 1771–1925.—120 maps. Maps relating to the planning and development of Washington, D.C., including plats of towns in existence prior to the establishment of the City of Washington in 1792; maps prepared at the direction of the City Commissioners by Nicholas King, 1793–1803; plats of squares near the Capitol and White House prepared by F.C. De Krafft, 1799–1836; and maps showing public reservations, wards, and street patterns. A published set of statistical maps of the District of Columbia relating to real property, public utilities, and transportation and communication systems.

Related textual records in NNFN include the minutes and correspondence of the Commissioners relating to the original planning and surveying of the City of Washington, and the division sheets relating to the surveying of city blocks and government reservations. The records of the United States Surveyor and Custodian of Records include platbooks and surveyors' reports for Washington, D.C. and Georgetown, 1882-97. Records, 1882–1897.

RG 43: Records of United States Participation in International Conferences, Commissions, and Expositions, 1890–1947.—1,240 maps. Chiefly large-scale manuscript survey maps of the Intercontinental Railway Commission showing cities, towns, and existing and proposed railroad routes in Central America and Columbia, Ecuador, and Peru, 1890–1898. Maps from peace conferences at the end of World War II relating to boundary questions in Eastern Europe, Italy, and France.

RG 45: Naval Records Collection of the Office of Naval Records and Library, 1775–1946.—516 maps. Manuscript, printed, and annotated maps, charts, and harbor plans separated from the Subject File, relating to naval operations from the Revolutionary War to World War I, including a few maps pertaining to the Siberian intervention, 1920–

1921. A set of photoprocessed charts relating to the Mediterranean, 1780–1816 (8 items).

Textual records of the Bureau of Ordnance and Hydrography, maintained in NNMR, include letters and journals of officers commanding hydrographic expeditions, notably the Charles Wilkes Exploring Expedition, 1838–1842; the Cadwalader Ringgold and John Rodgers North Pacific Ocean Expedition, 1852–1863 (microfilm M88); and the Matthew C. Perry Expedition to the China Sea, 1852–1854 (microfilm T1097).

RG 46: Records of the United States Senate, 1800–1966.—1,427 maps. Miscellaneous manuscript and annotated maps prepared for the Senate by Federal agencies relate to Indian land cessions, river, harbor, and road surveys, public domain, international boundaries, private land claims, battlefields of the Civil War, Washington, D.C., geology, Alaska, and exploring expeditions. A set of manuscript maps showing river and road improvements, 1825–1840. An incomplete set of maps published by the Senate. Maps relating to the Alaskan Boundary Tribunal; the United States Nicaragua Ship Canal Commission, 1886; Latin America, 1892–1894; the Venezuela-British Guiana boundary, 1898; and Puerto Rico, 1908. A volume of United States weather maps prepared by James P. Espy, 1851.

Messages and reports in NNLR, which were sent to the Senate from executive departments and agencies, sometimes include manuscript maps. A few representative examples are E.P. Kendrick's survey of the northern boundary line of Indiana, 1827; a plat of part of Milwaukee, 1839; Joseph Shriver's map of the National Road through Indiana, Illinois, and Ohio, 1828; Seth Eastman's map of Indian tribes in Iowa, Minnesota, and Dakota Territory, 1854; and a sketch map of the lands ceded by the Walla Walla and Wasco Indians in Oregon Territory, 1855.

RG 48: Records of the Office of the Secretary of the Interior, 1849–1953.—616 maps. Maps of western states and territories showing national parks and forests, Indian tribes and reservations, and mineral lands, 1875–1907. Manuscript and annotated maps and plats of Washington, D.C. relating to public reservations, government hospitals, parks, and the highway systems, 1887–1919. Maps of cities that were located in more than one congressional district in 1903. Manuscript maps of railroad lines, rights-of-way, and land grants in western states, 1865–1891. Maps, graphs, cross sections, and profiles relating to the lower part of the Colorado River, 1906–1912. Manuscript topographic and geological maps, sketches, and profiles of four trans-Mississippi railroad routes prepared by the War Department's Pacific Railroad Surveys and the Office of Exploration and Surveys, 1849–1858. These maps are described in *Preliminary Inventory* 81 (1955).

Among the textual records of the Patents and Miscellaneous Division, maintained in NNFN, are the correspondence files and field notes of the Office of Exploration and Surveys pertaining to western exploration and the Isaac Stevens survey of a Northern route for the Pacific Railroad (microfilm M126), 1852–1865. The records of the Lands and Railroads Division contain correspondence with map enclosures and field notes relating to the Pacific Railroad Surveys, surveys of land grant railroads throughout the United States, the United States-Mexican Boundary Survey, Territorial and State boundary surveys in the southwest, 1849–1907, and surveys of wagon roads (microfilm M95). The Central Classified Files contain miscellaneous maps and plats, 1907–1953.

Pictures of the original boundary markers of the District of Columbia (1 composite photograph) and drawings relating to the Pacific Railroad Survey, 1858 (14 items), are found in NNSP.

RG 49: Records of the Bureau of Land Management, 1785–1975.—120,417 maps. Manuscript and annotated maps and plats comprising the "Old Map File" show the development and disposition of the public lands of the United States and individual states and territories, beginning with surveys in Ohio directed by Thomas Hutchins and Rufus Putnam, 1790–1946; manuscript survey maps, diagrams and related field notes of the boundaries of public land States, Territories and Indian lands, 1790–1944; and maps and plats of the United States, and smaller areas published by the General Land Office, 1827–1846. These cartographic records are described in more detail in *Special List* 19 (1964).

Manuscript township plats and field notes for Alabama, Illinois, Indiana, Iowa, Kansas, Mississippi, Missouri, Ohio, and Wisconsin, and parts of Oklahoma and Washington, 1785–1930 (Microfilm T 1234 and T 1240). Manuscript plats of Indian land grants and reserves in Indiana, Michigan and Ohio (1807–1849), Kansas 1857–1865, Nebraska, and Indian Territory, 1856–1892. Plats of 582 townsites in public land states, 1817–1967. Plats of private land claims originally granted by French and Spanish authorities in Arizona, California, Colorado, Florida, Illinois, Louisiana, Missouri, and New Mexico, 1852–1915. Township plats of lands on Indian Reservations, 1904–1931.

Maps and diagrams showing land grants and rights-of-way for railroads, military roads, highways, canals and irrigation ditches, and transmission lines in public land states, 1851–1939 (10,776 items). Plats of mineral claims in western States and Alaska, 1872–1908 (45,367 items). Maps showing land use and grazing districts in western States and Alaska, 1934–1945.

Extensive textual records in NNFN (pre-1908 records) and NNFG (post-1908 records) relate to the land surveys of the public domain, particularly the records of the Division of Surveys (Division "E") which include correspondence and reports of the surveyors general of public land States, 1797–1901 (Microfilm M 25, 27, 478, 477, 479); surveyors contracts with special instructions and diagrams, 1817–1913; records relating to boundary, townsite, and public land surveys, 1860–1940; group survey records containing special instructions to surveyors, progress reports, and plats, 1910–1962; records, including plats and field notes, pertaining to rejected or abandoned surveys, 1847–1965; records pertaining to surveys in Alaska, 1918–1953. Records relating to the disposal of public land include docket files for private land claims in California, Florida, Louisiana and Mississippi containing survey notes and plats, 1803–1908; case files for townsites in western states but chiefly Oklahoma, Colorado, North and South Dakota, Arizona, Montana, and Idaho contain plats and diagrams, some duplicating those described above, 1855-1925; files for abandoned military reservations have plats and maps, 1822–1937; and papers pertaining to mineral claims contain field notes, plats, and reports on surveys. A typescript finding aid is available in NNFN.

RG 51: Records of the Office of Management and Budget, 1920–1942.—2,000 items. General correspondence files, reports, and minutes of the Federal Board of Surveys and Maps relating to the coordination and standardization of mapping activities of Federal agencies.

RG 54: Records of the Bureau of Plant Industry, Soils, and Agricultural Engineering, 1898–1953.—27,317 maps. Manuscript soil survey field maps of counties in the United States, 1898–1953 (25,000 items), and maps of the United States and regions showing soil types, land classification, surface geology, and soil regions. Related records in NNFN include extensive reports and correspondence of the Soil Survey Division pertaining to the surveying and classifying of soils, 1899–1927.

RG 56: General Records of the Department of the Treasury, 1851–1883.—19 items. Manuscript and annotated maps of captured and abandoned plantations along the Mississippi River and government farms for freedmen in the First and Second Districts, Negro Affairs, Department of Virginia and North Carolina, 1860–1874.

Correspondence files in NNFJ concern surveys of the North Carolina coast, 1806–1839, and other coastal waters; expenses for surveying public roads, lands, and State and Territorial boundaries; and the preparation of Land Office plats and field notes, 1804–1845. Land Office plats and field notes, 1804–1845.

RG 57: Records of the Geological Survey, 1869–1984.—85,995 maps and 34,845 aerial photographs. Manuscript, published and proof copies relating to the United States Geological and Geographical Survey of the Territories (Ferdinand V. Hayden Survey) and the United States Geographical and Geological Survey of the Rocky Mountain Region (John Wesley Powell Survey), 1869–1879. Post route maps of Mississippi, Louisiana, Missouri, and Alabama annotated to show race, crop yields, and livestock by county during the Civil War. Maps, cross sections, graphs and diagrams prepared by the Illustrations Section for annual reports, professional papers, and water supply papers. A set of topographic quadrangle maps of the United States, including original manuscript plane-table drawings, and other topographic maps of the United States and its Territories published by the Topographic Division, 1879–1984 (55,000 items). Manuscript and annotated maps prepared by Arnold Hague relating chiefly to Yellowstone Park, 1880–1916. A set of folios comprising the *Geological Atlas of the United States* and other geological maps published by the Geological Division, 1879–1966 (4,500 items). Aerial photographic negatives of project areas throughout the United States but chiefly New England, used in the preparation of topographic maps, ca. 1935–1945, and aerial mosaics of southern coastal areas, 1934. Computation field note books (35mm microfilm), 1867–1939.

Related textual records in NNFN contain the early files of the Hayden Survey (Microfilm M623), Powell Survey (Microfilm M156), United States Geographical Surveys West of the One Hundredth Meridian (George M. Wheeler Survey), and the Geological Exploration of the Fortieth Parallel (Clarence King Survey), 1853–81 (Microfilm M622). There are also correspondence files of the director of the Geological Survey (1879–1948; Microfilm M590, M152); monthly field reports, some of which contain geological maps and sketches (1882–1890, M590); maps and other records relating to the geological survey of the Dominican Republic, 1917–1923; maps and other reports pertaining to Naval Oil Reserves, 1922–1927; records relating to the Office of the Chief Geographer and working papers of Arch Gerlach, 1950–1972, including records pertaining to the *National Atlas of the United States,* 1957–1971; correspondence files concerning the preparation, editing, and engraving of maps and other illustrations, 1891–1938; records relating to the production of the *Geological Atlas of the United States,* 1893–1899, 1907–1919; correspondence and minutes relating to the survey's participation on the Federal Board of Surveys and Maps (1934–1936) and the American Society of Photogrammetry, 1938–1940; copies of patents relating to map making and aerial photography, 1887–1936; correspondence files of the Geologic Division concerning geologic and topographic field work, 1879–1952; manuscript geological field notes, sketches, and maps compiled by S.F. Emmons, Clarence King, Henry Gannett, G.K. Gilbert, Arnold Hague, William Henry Holmes, and other Survey geologists, 1861–1949, (975 volumes); correspondence pertaining to the 1944 and 1962 editions of the *Tectonic Map of the United States,* 1934–1946, 1955–1965; maps and other records relating to mineral deposits, 1910–1953; correspondence reports and maps prepared by the Base Map Unit of the Geologic Division, 1941–1960; maps, sketches, and reports from geological surveys in the United States, 1923–1955 (21 feet); photostatic copies of geological maps of East Asia compiled by Japanese geologists from the records of the Military Geology Branch, 1947–1960; correspondence files documenting mapping programs of the Topographic Division, 1890–1959 (196 feet); correspondence and reports pertaining to aerial photographic mapping, 1927–1948 (6 feet); records concerning cooperative State and Federal agency mapping programs, 1927–1947 (6 feet); triangulation record books, 1882–1906 (17 volumes); correspondence of Captain William O. Tufts relating to his service with the 29th Topographic Engineers, American Expeditionary Forces, in France, particularly with respect to aerial photography, 1917–1919; reports and maps pertaining to the topographic requirements of the Water Resources Division, 1950–1956; field notebooks and accompanying maps of drainage areas in the Eastern United States prepared by the Water Resources Division, 1908–1944 (30 volumes); and maps, field notes, and other records relating to mapping activities from the

Central Files of the Alaskan Branch, 1899–1947 (2.5 feet). A typescript author index to the geologists' field notebooks and a draft inventory for RG 57 are available in NNFN.

Audiovisual records in NNSP include photographs relating to the Hayden and Powell Surveys, 1869–1878, (ca. 2,500 photographs).

RG 58: Records of the Internal Revenue Service, 1862–1912.—100 items. Original and survey field books and maps of areas in the parishes of St. Helena and St. Luke and the cities of Port Royal and Beaufort, South Carolina, relating to property ownership and school farms.

RG 59: General Records of the Department of State, 1844–1974.—3,171 maps. Maps of foreign cities annotated to show the locations of American embassies and consulates, 1906–1939 (259 maps). Economic maps accompanying consular trade reports, 1943–1949 (220 maps). Records of the Office of the Geographer include the correspondence, research reports, and notebooks of Lawrence Martin, 1921–1924, and Samuel Whittemore Boggs, 1924–1954, most of which pertain to special mapping projects carried out during World War II; thematic maps of Europe, the Middle East, and Asia prepared under the direction of Leo Pasvolsky in preparation for a peace conference following World War II, 1943–1944 (620 maps); thematic and boundary maps of the world prepared by the Division of Geography and Cartography; and a report analyzing cartographic and map collecting agencies in Germany, 1946–1947.

Among the textual records in NNFD are the original journals of Charles Mason and Jeremiah Dixon relating to the Pennsylvania and Maryland boundary survey, 1763–1768; lists of appointments for surveyors general of public lands and land surveyors, 1789–1909; expense accounts for maps, salaries and supplies for the Northeastern Boundary Survey; maps from Joseph Bouchette's *A Topographical Description of the Province of Lower Canada,* 1815; maps accompanying correspondence of General W.S. Rosecrans with Mexican officials regarding an interoceanic railroad across Mexico, 1871–1873; maps and reports relating to explorations and surveys filed for a canal across the Central American Isthmus, 1875; memoranda concerning the transfer of the Johann Kohl map collection to the Library of Congress; and a large manuscript map of the Wachita River and vicinity with accompanying letter (1799) obtained from the Spanish Archives of Florida and Louisiana in 1835. These records are described in -Preliminary Inventory 157 (1963).

RG 60: Records of the Department of Justice, 1851–1949.—5,110 maps. Map enclosures from the general correspondence files pertaining to particular cases such as maps of Spanish land grants in the Southwest, 1890s; maps of land adjacent to the Colorado, San Juan, and Green River, Utah 1928–1938; maps showing beach erosion at Galveston Bay, Texas, 1891-1994; *News Maps of the Week* relating to World War II; and maps of the United States showing the film exchange districts and tribunal cities of major Hollywood movie studios, 1940–1946.

Textual records in NNFJ contain indexes to maps used by the Commission to Investigate the Title of the United States to Lands (19 inches); maps from the records relating to California land claims, 1851–1856; and maps from the records relating to the Pueblo Lands Board, 1924–1930. The cartographic records are described in *Preliminary Inventory* 194 (1981).

RG 64: Records of the National Archives and Records Service, 1937–54.—125 items. Daily journals of W.L.G. Joerg and Herman Friis, 1937–1954, and accession records of cartographic materials, 1943–1951.

RG 66: Records of the Commission of Fine Arts, 1748–1953.—147 maps. Published and photoprocessed maps of Washington, D.C., Virginia and Maryland.

RG 69: Records of the Work Projects Administration, 1933–1941.—34,824 maps. Real property survey maps of cities in Georgia showing housing conditions, average rents, and sanitary conditions by block, 1935–1941 (also see RG 31). Manuscript maps and related worksheets prepared in the 1930s for the proposed *Atlas of Congressional Roll Calls* that show the geographic distribution of yea-nay roll call votes by congressmen and senators, boundaries of congressional districts, county boundaries, and some city wards for most congresses from 1789–1941 (34,772 items).

RG 70: Records of the Bureau of Mines, 1908–1970.—1,241 maps. Manuscript and annotated maps of the United States and individual States showing petroleum, mineral and coal deposits and number of men employed in coal industry, 1908–1944. Maps and plans of mines and geological features compiled by the Eastern Field Operation Center at Pittsburgh, 1942–1970.

RG 71: Records of the Bureau of Yards and Docks, 1876–1941.—300 items. Manuscript plans of Navy bases in the United States and foreign countries, filed among a larger body of architectural engineering plans of those bases.

RG 72: Records of the Bureau of Aeronautics, 1916–1946.—Audiovisual records in NNSP contain training slides of aerial charts and maps; and pictures of Navy aerial photography trainees, 1917–1918.

RG 74: Records of the Bureau of Ordnance, 1842–1923.—18 items. Manuscript and annotated maps showing land ownership in the District of Columbia along the Potomac River, 1842–1868; and a manuscript map showing the track of the *U.S.S. Constitution* along the coast of Massachusetts, 1876.

RG 75: Records of the Bureau of Indian Affairs, 1794–1968.—38,427 maps and 700 aerial photographs. Manuscript and annotated maps comprising the Central Map File of the BIA show early western exploration, tribal cessions, reservations, boundaries, private land claims and other information concerning Indian lands, 1800–1968 (14,000 items). Manuscript and printed township plats and maps relating to surveys and allotments on Indian reservations prepared by the Land Division, 1832–1940. Manuscript and printed maps relating to Indian irrigation projects and programs, 1900–1948, and forestry and grazing activities on Indian lands, 1908–1956; maps prepared by the Education Division showing locations of native schools, 1928–1941; and maps of roads on Indian reservations, 1917–1943. These maps are further described in *Special List* 13 (1977).

Maps, plats, and related land and boundary survey records are also found in NNFN, interspersed among the general correspondence files and the textual records of the Irrigation, Forestry, and Land Divisions. The Land Division includes field notes of cadastral surveys of Indian lands and reservations, 1797–1919 (290 volumes) and maps, plats, and other documents relating to lands reserved for individual Indians, 1825–1907 (13 feet). The records of the Finance Division include financial accounts relating to survey work, 1866–1936. These records are described in *Preliminary Inventory* 163 (1965). Filed separately in NNSP are 10,000 aerial photographic prints of Fort Apache, Navajo, Hopi, and Zuni Reservations, 1934–1936.

RG 76: Records of Boundary and Claims Commissions and Arbitrations, 1794–1952.—20,241 maps, charts and topographical sketches. Cartographic records relating to the international boundaries of the United States contain original treaty, exploratory and survey maps delimiting the boundary of the United States with Great Britain, Canada, Spain, Texas, and Mexico (4,000 maps), including the printed edition of John Mitchell's map of the British Colonies which was used by the negotiators for the treaty with Great Britain in 1783, and another copy annotated by Benjamin Franklin. Textual records in NNFD contain extensive correspondence files and reports relating to surveying and mapping, field books and journals, surveyors' reports, and astronomical observations and computations. Audiovisual records in NNSP include 50 volumes of photographs showing terrestrial photogrammetric views made by the British Section of the Alaskan Boundary Commission for use in the preparation of their maps (1893–1894), activities of Commission survey teams, and the placement of boundary monuments along the Alaskan boundary, 1893–1913, 1926. These records are described in *Preliminary Inventory* 170 (1968).

Cartographic records relating to international claims by individuals or groups settled by treaties or other conventions contain manuscript, printed and annotated maps pertaining to fishing rights in coastal waters of the northeastern United States and Canada, 1854–1871. There are also charts of the Straits of Georgia and San Juan de Fuca relating to the sockeye salmon treaty with Canada, 1930, and maps pertaining to various conventions with Mexico respecting Sonora and the Mexican Revolution, 1868–1923. Related textual records in NNFD concern the map claim of Joseph H. Colton with Bolivia in 1878. There are also map enclosures of Stevens County, Washington, showing crop damage from sulfur pollution submitted as evidence in arbitration with Canada, 1935; maps relating to Oregon Territory prepared by the Hudsons Bay and Pugets Sound Agricultural Companies as part of their claims, 1863; maps depicting guano deposits submitted as evidence in claims against Peru, 1875–1896; and a plat of the Tennessee Company land grant from the records of the Yazoo Land Claims, 1795–1816. These records are described in *Preliminary Inventory* 177 (1974).

Cartographic records relating to international arbitrations include maps and charts relating to disputes between the United States and Great Britain concerning fur seals in the Bering Sea and fishing rights in the Atlantic, 1892–1909. Also, manuscript and printed maps submitted as evidence by several Latin American countries concerning boundary disputes with their neighbors where the United States served as arbitrator, some of which were copied from originals in the British Museum, the Archives of the Minister of Foreign Affairs in Paris, the Portuguese Archives in Lisbon, and the Archives of the Indies in Madrid, 1630–1945 (15,000 items). Some aerial photographs record the disputed boundary between Peru and Ecuador, 1945.

RG 77: Records of the Office of the Chief of Engineers, 1790–1982.—249,874 maps; 59,000 aerial photographs. Manuscript and annotated maps (Headquarters Map File) prepared by the Bureau of Topographical Engineers, 1812–1839, the Corps of Topographical Engineers, 1839–1863, and other topographical and engineering units pertaining to western exploration, military surveys of roads and canals, military campaigns, and the administration of army commands and districts (32,500 items). Manuscript maps and plans (Fortification Map File) of United States military forts, camps and reservations, (57,000 items). Manuscript and published maps and plans by the Corps of Engineers district field offices, including charts published by the United States Lake Survey, 1829–1958 (14,300 items). Manuscript and annotated maps collected or issued by the Military Intelligence Division of the General Staff (War Department Map Collection) cover a wide range of subjects including the Seminole Indian campaigns in Florida, 1836–1837, but the majority of maps pertain to military activities in Mexico and Central America, Cuba, Eastern Europe, Africa, China, Japan, and the Philippines, 1890–1940 (3,000 items). A set of Japanese Imperial Land Survey maps overprinted with English place names, 1925–1935. Tactical and Training maps issued by the Engineer Reproduction Plant, 1917–1942. Large-scale topographic map series published by the Army Map Service of most areas of the world, including a number of manuscript and annotated maps transferred from the former Army Map Service Library, 1942–1982 (140,000 items). Maps and charts prepared by District Engineer Offices relate to the development of the intra-coastal waterway through New Jersey and Delaware, 1870–1930, and property surveys along the Allegheny and Ohio Rivers, 1935–1942. Photographs of photogrammetric and mapmaking equipment used by German mapping units during World War II. Field survey notebooks prepared by the United States Board of Engineers on Deep Waterways; 1897–1899, by the United States Lake Survey and the Mississippi River Commission pertaining to surveys of the Mississippi River and its tributaries, 1876–1928 (440 volumes); and by the United States Lake Survey relating to surveys of the Great Lakes, 1826, 1839, 1841–1881, and 1892–1930 (6,000 volumes). Aerial photographic series include views of military fortifications and trenches in France during World War I; film negatives of the lower Mississippi River and its tributaries taken as part of a series of alluvial, low-water and flood surveys, 1929–1939; coverage of Corps of Engineer reclamation projects along the Missouri River, 1926–1940; and prints of the Inter-American Highway Survey in Central America, 1932.

General correspondence files in NNMR (pre-1923) and NNMF (post-1923) contain letters and reports relating to military exploration, surveying and mapping, 1789–1942. Other important series include topographical field notes and observations, 1793–1916; materials relating to the planning and surveying of the Cumberland Road and other internal improvements, 1810–1840 (Microfilm M65); quarterly returns of books, maps, and instruments, 1816-1850; correspondence, reports, and instructions relating to the Coast Survey, 1816–1841; correspondence files of the Topographical Bureau and the Corps of Topographical Engineers, 1824–1870 (Microfilm M66, M505, M506); monthly returns of topographical engineers, 1831–1863; correspondence files, account books, and chart catalogs of the United States Lake Survey, 1839–1913; materials relating to the Office of Exploration and Surveys, 1857–1861; extensive files pertaining to the Office of the United States Geographical Surveys West of the 100th Meridian, directed by Captain George M. Wheeler, 1869–1883; and field notebooks of military surveys in the South, 1863–1865.

Textual records of Engineer Divisions and Districts, also maintained in NNMR and NNMF, contain materials relating to river and harbor improvements that were undertaken by the Corps of Engineers after the Civil War. These records include quite an extensive collection (207 ft.) of field survey notebooks containing information on topography, triangulation, soundings, and borings as well as some maps and charts prepared by the following district offices: Newport (1870–1919); New London (1866–1915); Providence (1870–1922); New York (1909–1933); Philadelphia (1880,1884); Wilmington (1903–1934); Jacksonville (1896–1897); Tampa Bay (1876–1902); Cleveland (1914); Detroit (1873–1896); St. Paul (1898–1941); Vicksburg (1871–1883); Seattle (1858–1942); and Portland (1919–1935). The textual records are described in two unpublished inventories, NM-19 and NM-45.

Audiovisual records in NNSP include portraits and photographs of engineering officers, 1789–1884, 1927–1939 (75 items); photographs relating to the activities of United States-Mexican Boundary Commission, 1892–1894 (550 photographs); and photographs relating to western exploration and surveys, 1867–1872 (ca. 575 photographs).

RG 78: Records of the Naval Observatory, 1842–1861.—Records in NNMR concern Matthew F. Maury and his work on the production and distribution of wind and current charts; the purchase, inspection, and issuance of nautical instruments and charts, 1840–1865; the United States Naval Astronomical Expedition to the Southern Hemisphere, 1848–1861 (Microfilm T54); and the Nautical Almanac Office, 1849–1911.

RG 79: Records of the National Park Service, 1791–1977.—8,235 maps and 61 aerial photographs. Manuscript maps and plats relating to the Chesapeake and Ohio Canal, 1826–1937. Manuscript and published maps relating to Washington, D.C. showing highways, public reservations, parkways, and recreational areas. Maps and plans of the Capitol and White House grounds (the latter is restricted and may only be examined with permission of the Assistant General Superintendent, White House Liaison, National Capital Parks). Master plans of the national parks prepared by the Branch of Plans and Design, 1931–1941 (3,000 items). Maps of Civil War battlefields and parks, 1896–1972, and national parks, 1905–1977. Area study maps of state parks, parkway and recreational areas in North Carolina, Mississippi, Louisiana, and Tennessee, 1937–1939. Aerial photographic prints of Northwest Washington, D.C., 1937.

Related textual records in NNFN include field notebooks of surveys in the District of Columbia for 1878, 1905–1933, and 1937; and correspondence, land surveys, and field notebooks of the engineers who worked for the Potomac Company and the Chesapeake and Ohio Canal Company, 1828–1873.

Audiovisual records in NNSP contain photographs of the Hayden Geological Survey of the Territories, 1871–1872 (71 photographs).

RG 80: General Records of the Department of the Navy, 1798–1947. Still picture collection in NNSP made or acquired by the United States Naval Photographic Center contains many aerial photographs and pictures relating to the training of aerial photographers and photographic interpreters at the Naval School of Photography, Pensacola, Florida, 1918–1961 (785,672 pictures).

RG 83: Records of the Bureau of Agricultural Economics, 1897–1950.—4,361 maps. Manuscript thematic maps showing crop and animal distribution prepared under the direction of W.J. Spillman, Henry C. Taylor, Oliver E. Baker, and the Division of Agricultural History and Geography, 1898–1922. Manuscript maps and work sheets prepared by Francis J. Marschner and R.G. Hainsworth for the *Atlas of American Agriculture* (1918–1936) and V.C. Finch and Baker's *Geography of the Worlds Agriculture* (1917). Other important series include land use classification maps compiled by state and county planning committees, 1938–1941, and maps and graphs relating to studies of migration to the Pacific Coast based on data gathered from recently arrived school children, 1930–1939. A description of BAE maps is given in *Special List* 28 (1971).

Among the textual records maintained in NNFN are extensive files accumulated by Charles E. Gage relating to the use of aerial photography as a tool for estimating crop acreage, 1923–1925; personal correspondence of Baker relating to the publication of economic wall maps and various research projects, 1915–1928; and maps accompanying the project files of the Division of Farm Management, 1906–1921. Many printed and manuscript maps and aerial photographs are also found in the records of the Division of Land Economics relating to land settlement studies in the cut-over areas of Minnesota, Michigan, and Wisconsin, 1925–1930; land use planning, 1936–1938; studies of the Great Plains drought area, 1936–1937; and flood control and water utilization studies, 1931–1943. These records are described in *Preliminary Inventory* 104 (1958).

RG 84: Records of the Foreign Service Posts of the Department of State, 1914–1944.—12 maps. A map of Smyrna (Izmir), Turkey, and a mineral atlas of Turkey. Maps of bombed areas of Chungking and roads in China prepared by a United States military attaché, 1939–1944.

RG 92: Records of the Office of the Quartermaster General, 1820–1952.—1,694 maps. Manuscript and annotated maps of plans of military installations, routes of exploration, and Indian lands in the United States, 1820–1905. A series of landform and climatic zone maps prepared by Erwin Raisz and Harry Hoy for thr Military Planning Division relating to clothing requirements worldwide, 1943–1952. Among textual records in NNMR are maps of harbors and military posts in the United States, Alaska, and the Philippine Islands, 1904–1905; a report by James Gadsden relating to his survey of the route from St. Augustine to Cape Florida, 1825; maps relating to National Battlefield parks of the Civil War including Antietam, Chickamauga, Chattanooga, and Vicksburg, 1893–1923; maps relating to historical sketches of military reservations, 1888–1889; maps of United States military railroads operated from 1861–1866; maps relating to the Quartermaster General's Office of the American Expeditionary Force, 1919–1923; and files pertaining to equipment purchased for balloon aerial reconnaissance during the Civil War and the work of aeronauts, T.S. Lowe and John La Mountain. Textual records in NNMF contain a few manuscript maps accompanying missing air crewmen reports showing the location of downed aircraft during World War II.

RG 94: Records of the Adjutant General's Office, 1780s–1917.—3,121 maps. Among the more significant series are General George B. McClellan's portfolio of printed maps relating to the Pacific Railroad Surveys, 1853–1855; manuscript and annotated maps used in the preparation of the *Atlas to Accompany the Official Records of the Union and Confederate Armies* (Washington, 1891–1895), 1861–1895 (1051 items); manuscript maps prepared by the Military Information Division pertaining to military operations in Africa, Greece, Korea, China, Cuba, Puerto Rico, and the Philippines, 1897–1902;

manuscript maps relating to the Seminole Indian War in Florida and to the western frontier, 1812–1855; and maps prepared during the Mexican Punitive Expedition, 1916.

Textual records in NNMR contain the monthly returns of the Topographical Engineers, 1831–1863 (Microfilm M852), the Corps of Engineers, 1832–1916 (Microfilm M851), and the Regular Army Engineer Battalions, 1846–1916 (Microfilm M691); map enclosures and accounts of military explorations and surveys in the American West among the general correspondence files, 1805–1889 (851 linear feet); maps, notebooks, and traverse table taken from Lieutenant Zebulon M. Pike by Spanish authorities, 1806 (Microfilm T36); correspondence pertaining to the preparation of the *Atlas to Accompany the Official Records of the Union and Confederate Armies,* 1892–1895 (2 volumes); and letters and reports relating to Civil War battles, some of which contain map enclosures, 1861–1865 (87 linear feet).

RG 95: Records of the Forest Service, 1897–1962.—15,858 maps and 43,084 aerial photographs. Published maps of national forests, 1911–1960 (2,050 maps); photoprocessed maps annotated to show transportation systems in national forests, grassland areas, and land-use areas, 1962 (592 maps); printed maps showing authorized timber sale areas in national forests, 1913–1916 (800 maps); manuscript and published thematic maps comprising the project files of the Drafting and Atlas Section, 1916–1959 (1,192 maps); manuscript maps of rangelands in national forests, 1922–1927 (208 maps); maps accompanying presidential proclamations and executive orders establishing national forests, 1891–1935 (1,350 maps). Also, a wide variety of manuscript historical and thematic maps relating to rangelands and forests; published atlases containing maps of individual national forests, 1908–1925 (173 atlases); specimen maps and instructions for preparing Forest Service Maps, 1907–1935. Vertical and oblique aerial photographs of national forest areas in the Western United States at a scale of 1:20,000 to 1:24,000, 1932–1942. These records are described in *Preliminary Inventory* 167 (1967).

Textual records of the Division of Engineering in NNFN contain general correspondence files which include references to mapping and survey projects of forest areas, 1932–1952 (95 feet); correspondence relating to the preparation and compilation of the *Forest Atlas,* 1906–1908 (9 inches); and correspondence between the Office of Geography and field officials concerning mapping and other technical matters, 1906–1909 (3 feet). For maps scattered throughout other textual series, see *Preliminary Inventory* 18 (1969).

RG 97: Records of the Bureau of Agricultural and Industrial Chemistry, 1928–1930. Among the textual records in NNFN are a small series of maps showing damage in Stevens County, Washington, from sulphur dioxide fumes emitted by a lead and zinc smelter located at Trail, British Columbia.

RG 109: War Department Collection of Confederate Records, 1861–1865.—112 maps. Manuscript maps and drawings of campaigns and fortifications in the South and border states. Textual records of the Engineer Department in NNMR include correspondence files (Microfilm M628) and a collection of bound topographical sketches prepared by Captain B.L. Blackford and W.R. Martin, 1862–1864. A map register prepared by the Union Department of Virginia and North Carolina, 1865 (1 volume).

RG 111: Records of the Chief Signal Officer, 1900–1945.—12 maps. Maps showing progress of the establishment of Signal Corps telegraph lines in Alaska, Cuba, and the Philippines, 1900-1911, and in France, 1944-1945. The general correspondence files in NNMR contain some materials relating to aerial photography, 1914–1917. The Photographic and Print Negative "Historical File" in NNSP contains aerial photographs of terrain features, military bases, military trenches, and towns in France as well as pictures of aerial photographic cameras and airplanes during World War I. Training films in NNSM made or acquired by the Signal Corps during World War II from the various military services include "Map Reading", 1934 (43 minutes) (TF 12); "Aerial Navigation - Maps and Compass", 1942 (12 minutes) (TF 245); "Aerial Photography - An

Introduction to Aerial Cameras", 1941 (9 minutes); "Aerial Photography—The K-12 Camera", ca. 1941 (10 minutes); and "Photographic Interpretation Technique", 1943 (21 minutes). Also, there is a training film using an animated map to show battles and maneuvers in the vicinity of Gettysburg, Pennsylvania, 1929 (67 minutes).

RG 114: Records of the Soil Conservation Service, 1898–1974.—195,763 maps and 428,900 aerial photographs. Major series include manuscript and published maps of states, counties, and project areas showing soils, erosion, irrigation, drainage, and agricultural lands, 1934–1974; manuscript soil survey field maps of counties in the United States, 1954–1960 (RG 54); manuscript maps and field notebooks from sedimentation surveys of lakes, streams, and reservoirs in the United States, 1934–1947; climatological charts of the world, Italy, Mexico, and parts of the United States prepared by C. Warren Thornthwaite, 1900–1939; manuscript and printed climatological charts of experimental project areas prepared by the Climatological and Physiographic Division, 1934–1942 (168,161 items); maps relating to drainage patterns and irrigation work, 1901–1940; and maps relating to various aspects of forestry and recreational and agricultural land use, 1930–1952. Aerial photographic negatives provide coverage of watersheds and soil erosion districts in the southwestern United States at scales between 1:15,840 and 1:31,680, 1933–1939.

Among related records in NNFN, the general correspondence files of the SCS Central Office include files relating to maps and aerial surveys, 1933–1941 (10 linear feet). The Office of Research includes related research information files, 1929–1940. The Climatic and Physiographic Division contains meteorological charts for New Philadelphia and Zanesville, Ohio, 1936–1943. Records of regional and State Office records also include correspondence and reports pertaining to mapping programs and soil surveys, 1934–1944.

RG 115: Records of the Bureau of Reclamation, 1904–1963.—1,924 maps and 19,642 aerial photographs. Maps relating to reclamation activities chiefly in the west, showing river basins, transmission lines, reservoirs, dam sites, and irrigation, 1904–1951. Plats of townships located in Federal irrigation project areas showing farm units, private lands, reserved land, and canals, 1907–1963. Aerial photographs of the Colorado River and other river basins in Arizona, Idaho, Oregon, Utah, and Washington at a scale of 1:20,000, 1938–1942. Maps are also found among the general administrative and projects records in NNFN, 1902–1945; records relating to Civilian Conservation Corps activities, 1935–1943; progress maps of the Kendrick project, 1939–1941; and maps enclosed with reports prepared by project engineers or managers, 1902–1945 (63 feet). See *Preliminary Inventory* 109 (1958).

RG 117: Records of the American Battle Monuments Commission, 1923–1944.—456 maps. Manuscript and annotated maps summarizing the military operations of the American Expeditionary Forces in Europe during World War I, many of which later appeared at reduced scales in the 28 volume *A Guide to the American Battlefields in Europe in 1927.* Plans and maps relating to American cemetaries and monuments in Europe.

The correspondence files in NNMF contain printed maps annotated or verified by former division officers of the AEF showing small-unit action information not found elsewhere.

RG 120: Records of the American Expeditionary Forces (World War I), 1917–1923.—24,000 maps and 4,000 aerial photographs. Maps prepared or collected chiefly by the Intelligence (G-2) and Operations (G-3) Sections of the General Staff showing German troop movements and other enemy information, bombing targets, the location and activities of Bolshevist forces, the situation of Allied and German forces on the Western Front on a daily or weekly basis, 1914–1919, and details of troop dispositions on specific dates. Maps prepared or annotated by American armies, corps, and divisions showing the locations and activities of artillery batteries, and troop and unit disposition movements. Maps relating to American military activities in Italy and Siberia, including maps of Russia and Siberia based on a Russian General Staff map. Maps prepared or collected after the war by the Historical Branch of the War Plans Division of the General Staff pertaining to troop operations during the war and the following occupation in Germany. Maps produced by military mapping services in Belgium, 1911–1919 (479 items), Great Britain, 1909–1919 (1,720 items), France, 1871–1920 (5,742 items), Italy, 1895–1919 (531 items), Austria-Hungary, 1894–1917 (134 items), and Germany, 1848–1920 (3,325 items).

Aerial photographs include a small number of aerial photo mosaics and maps of cities in France, Belgium, Luxembourg, Alsace-Lorraine and Germany prepared or acquired by AEF Air Intelligence Section and by the French Army Ground Survey Groups, 1917–1918. Also printed aerial views of Giogo dell Stelvio and Spondinig Prad by the Italian Seventh Army in 1918, and battle sites in northern France by the German, French, and American Air Forces.

Among the textual records of the Intelligence Section of the General Staff in NNMR are course syllabuses in map problems prepared by the Army General Staff College of the AEF; French maps showing daily allied submarine activity; and correspondence files of the Topographical, Map Supply, and Sound and Flash Ranging Division relating to maps, 1917–1919. The records of the Army Engineer School contain notes and illustrations pertaining to the interpretation of aerial photographs, 1918. Textual records of G-3 Section, General Headquarters, and of tactical divisions, corps, and armies include numerous operational maps.

RG 122: Records of the Federal Trade Commission, 1914–1936.—293 maps. Manuscript and annotated maps showing transmission lines and pipelines, areas served by public utility companies, and principal oil and gas fields in the United States.

RG 123: Records of the United States Court of Claims, 1940–1947.—194 items. Aerial mosaic photographs and manuscript exhibit maps of Ute tribal lands in Western Colorado submitted by the Confederated Bands of the Ute Indians and the United States showing land use, land ownership, topography, and precipitation.

RG 126: Records of the Office of Territories, 1878–1942.—123 maps and 12,256 aerial photographs. Maps prepared by the Alaska Railroad and the Alaska Road Commission; topographic maps of the Hawaiian Islands compiled from surveys directed by the Hawaiian Government or the Secretary of the Interior, 1878–1906; manuscript and annotated maps relating to the Antarctic expedition of 1939–1941, and oblique aerial photographic negatives and prints of Antarctica taken during this expedition.

Maps and geological and topographic surveys are found among the central classified files in NNFN relating to the territorial administration of Alaska, Canton Island, Guam, Hawaii, Puerto Rico, and the District of Columbia, 1919–1951. A description of these records is found in *Preliminary Inventory* 154 (1963). The textual records of the United States Antarctic Service (USAS), headed by Richard E. Byrd, include correspondence concerning the compilation, editing, and publishing of USAS maps, 1941–1943; ground survey field notes; and progress reports. These records are described in *Preliminary Inventory* 90 (1955).

RG 127: Records of the United States Marine Corps, 1885–1943.—999 maps. Maps and plans of Marine Corps installations in the United States, 1910–1939; manuscript maps prepared by the Marine Intelligence Section of the Headquarters Division of Operations and Training, intelligence sections of individual Brigades, and the Mapping Section of the Marine Corps School pertaining to Aruba, the Azores, Barbados, China, Costa Rica, Cuba, Culebra, Curacao, Dominican Republic, El Salvador, Grenada, Guadeloupe, Guatemala, Haiti, Honduras, Ireland, Jamaica, Korea, Martinique, Mexico, Nicaragua, Panama, and Venezuela, 1918–1940; and maps relating to the activities of the 4th Marine Brigade in France during World War I. These maps are described in *Preliminary Inventory* 73 (1954).

An unknown number of maps in NNMR and NNMF are interfiled among the general correspondence files (1913–1950) and security-classified correspondence files related to Central American countries, Brazil, and China, (1915–1937). There are also 44 oblique aerial photographic prints of landing fields in the Dominican Republic and Haiti, 1923, and maps relating to the Marine Corps Battalion at the Louisiana Purchase Exposition, St. Louis, 1903–1904. The textual records are described in *Inventory* 2 (1970).

RG 134: Records of the Interstate Commerce Commission, 1900–1941.—683 maps. Manuscript and published maps showing existing and proposed railroad lines and rights-of-way, associated industries and facilities, railroad properties, and ownership.

RG 138: Records of the Federal Energy Regulatory Commission, 1924–1954.—879 maps. Manuscript maps and profiles of river basins, watersheds, dam facilities, flood damage, and transmission lines in the United States and other countries prepared by the Drafting and Duplication Section of the former Federal Power Commission.

RG 140: Records of the Military Government of Cuba, 1898–1902.—50 maps. Maps and plans of engineer surveys and military sites. Similar maps are also found in the correspondence files in NNFN, including a map showing yellow fever distribution by districts and correspondence relating to surveys for maps and charts. See *Preliminary Inventory* 145 (1962).

RG 142: Records of the Tennessee Valley Authority, 1934–1957.—1,754 maps. Published topographic and planimetric quadrangles prepared by the Maps and Surveys Division; county maps showing forest types, 1939-1941; a set of thematic maps showing social and economic data by county, 1937; and aerial photographs made in the 1930s (45,000 photographs).

RG 145: Records of the Agricultural Stabilization and Conservation Service, 1935–1942.—2,241,000 aerial photographs. Aerial photographic negative and photoindexes made by the Agricultural Adjustment Administration showing most of the agricultural areas of the United States on a county basis at a scale of 1:20,000. Related subject correspondence files are in NNFN, 1933–1938.

RG 151: Records of the Bureau of Foreign and Domestic Commerce and Successor Agencies, 1905–1950.—53 maps. An incomplete set of *Geographic News,* a monthly publication of the Geographic Section containing information about foreign map publishers, 1931–1933. Published maps of district offices, consumer trading areas, steel furnaces, economic development, and major ports in the United States, a map of transportation routes in South America, and a map of oil fields in the Dutch East Indies.

RG 153: Records of the Office of the Judge Advocate General (Army), 1838–1947.—352 maps. Manuscript and published maps of military reservations in the United States and their hay and timber reserves. Maps relating to the Battle of Five Forks, Virginia (1865) prepared for the Gouverneur K. Warren Court of Inquiry. Among the textual records in NNMR, the military reservation files contain maps and plats of land formerly owned by the War Department.

RG 160: Records of the Headquarters Army Service Forces, 1942–1946.—98 items. An incomplete series of *Newsmap,* a publication issued by the Army Information Branch to inform soldiers of military events during World War II. Among the textual records in NNMR are several series which contain maps, including the records of the Commanding General relating to trips overseas, 1942–1945; reports and maps of the Atlantic Section pertaining to the Caribbean Defense Command, 1942–1943; and maps showing sources of raw materials, War Department Procurement Districts, and facilities for production, 1921–1942.

RG 165: Records of the War Department General and Special Staffs, 1904–1946.—12,873 maps, 1,100 aerial photographs. Maps prepared or collected by the Military Intelligence Division include maps of Cuba, the Philippines, Central America and Panama; maps relating to the Russo-Japanese War, 1904–1905, and the Russian Civil War; maps of Mexico, 1916–1922; maps relating to areas of strategic interest throughout the world, 1927–1946. Cartographic records of the Army War College and the Command

and General Staff Schools contain topographic and strategic maps of Central American countries, including a 70-sheet map of Cuba prepared by the Army of Cuban Pacification 1906–1909, with corrections in 1913; maps relating to World War I, including a set of "Colonel Prices Lecture Maps: Mineral Resources of the German Defense System"; manuscript maps of Revolutionary War battles prepared for the George Washington Bicentennial Atlas; and topographic and strategic maps of Civil War campaigns prepared for use in war games.

Aerial photographic prints relating to combat activities in France and bombing targets in Germany during World War I. Also, French, English, and German publications describing the military use of aerial photographs. Color photographs of relief models annotated to show troop locations for specific periods during World War II (11,300 photographs). Aerial photographic prints in NNSP collected by the Military Intelligence Division show airfields in Mexico, 1930–1935 (26 photographs), allied and German positions on the Belgian Coast, 1917 (859 photographs), and military maneuvers in the Philippine Islands, 1925 (69 photographs).

The textual records of the Office of the Director of Intelligence (G-2) in NNMF include intelligence reference publications known as "Regional Files", collected from United States military attachés and other sources containing numerous general and thematic maps covering many countries and regions, 1933–1944; and Intelligence Library ("P" Publication File) field monographs with maps relating to South America, Asia, and Europe, 1940–1945. There are also maps and aerial photographs among the First Special Service Collection in NNMR relating to the vital areas and industries in foreign countries, 1941–1943 (7 feet).

RG 167: Records of the National Bureau of Standards. The records of the Office of Standard Weights and Measures in NNFN include some correspondence and reports of Ferdinand R. Hassler concerning the survey of the United States coasts.

RG 169: Records of the Foreign Economic Administration, 1942–1945.—2,992 maps. Published thematic maps of the world regions and countries relating to transportation, resources, and industry. Maps and plans of terrain intelligence prepared for strategic engineering studies, chiefly for beaches and waterways in France and, to a lesser degree, in East Asia.

RG 171: Records of the Office of Civilian Defense, 1941–1945.—533 maps. Maps of the United States, the Ninth Civilian Defense Region (Washington, Oregon, and California), and urban areas annotated to show distribution of civilian defense supplies and facilities, population, target areas, and industrial and military installations.

RG 177: Records of the Chiefs of Arms, 1880–1926.—45 maps. Manuscript and annotated published maps prepared by military students at the Coast Artillery, Infantry, and Mounted Service Schools, 1908–1913. Charts prepared for joint Army and Navy coast defense exercises in Georgia and New York, 1910–1913.

RG 185: Records of the Panama Canal, 1870–1957.—9,844 maps. Maps, plans of cities and harbors, survey sheets and profiles compiled by the Compagnie Universelle Canal Interoceanique, 1881–1900 (6,774 items), the Compagnie Nouvelle du Canal du Panama, 1889–1899 (730 items), the Nicaragua Canal Commission, 1895–1899 (417 items), and the Isthmian Canal Commissions, 1899–1913 (1,284 items). Also microfilm copies of maps and engineering plans from the Special Panama Collection of the Canal Zone Library—Museum (A21). Related field notebooks and correspondence files are in NNFG. For a further description of these records see *Preliminary Inventory* 153 (1963).

RG 187: Records of the National Planning Board, 1933–1943.—3,876 maps. Manuscript and annotated maps of the United States, regions, states, and counties (including Puerto Rico and the Virgin Islands) relating to climate, land use, population, public works, transportation, water and mineral resources, regional and urban planning, forestry, defense, recreation, trade, and economics. These maps are described in *Special List* 41.

RG 189: Records of the National Academy of Sciences, 1918–1958.—101 maps. Maps used by the National Research Council to study World War I mapping; thematic agricultural maps compiled and submitted by Vernor C. Finch to the National Resources Committee for his study of isopleth symbols, 1934; an incomplete series of printed thematic maps prepared for the *National Atlas of the United States* (74 sheets), 1954–1958. Textual records in NNFN include correspondence and reports prepared by The Special Committee on International Geophysical Year (IGY) Geographic Names in Antarctica, 1956–1964.

RG 196: Records of the Public Housing Administration, 1933–1950.—30 items. Maps of the experimental greentowns of the New Deal period, including Greenbelt, Maryland, Greenhills, Ohio, and Greendale, Wisconsin, filed among a larger series of construction drawings of these towns.

RG 199: Records of the Provisional Government of Cuba, 1906–1909.—Correspondence files of the Provisional Governor in NNFN contain letters pertaining to the preparation of a topographical map of Cuba by A.A. Aguirre, and correspondence with the War Department relating to a survey of Havana Harbor, 1907.

RG 200: National Archives Gift Collection, 1822–1947.—321 maps. Maps relating to Indian campaigns in the west and other military maps from the Papers of General W.C. Brown, 1865–1927; Civil War maps of Virginia, Maryland, and Pennsylvania from the Papers of Colonel W.H. Paine, 1861–1865; manuscript maps showing troop positions of the 29th Division in Europe during World War I from the Papers of Lieutenant Colonel George Stewart, Jr.; maps relating to World War II from the Papers of M. Henri Michel; maps reconstructing the Santa Fe Trail from the Papers of Hobart E. Stocking; maps of the Forbes Purchase and the town of St. Marks, Florida, from the Papers of J. Edwin White; maps relating to the Northeastern Boundary Treaty between Canada and the United States in 1842 from the Papers of Mrs. Paul H. Quigg; manuscript maps and sketches pertaining to the Pacific Railroad Surveys from the Papers of John J. Young, 1855–1873; and maps of Assam, India, annotated by the Graves Registration Service to show the location of American airplanes downed while flying the Burma Hump during World War II from the Papers of Elizabeth Gussak.

Aerial photographic negatives in NNFN taken during mapping and exploratory flights from Little America Station, Antarctica, are in the Papers of Richard E. Byrd, 1929–1930, 1934–1935 (2,612 aerial photographs). A copy of Mark Jefferson's diary, which he kept while in Paris during his work as chief cartographer of the American Commission to Negotiate Peace, 1918–1919, is in NNFD.

Motion picture films in NNSM include "War: A Headache to Map Makers" (vol. 11, No. 818), showing mapmaking at Rand McNally in 1939, "Flying Cameramen Complete World's Largest Aerial Map", showing mapping in New York with the aid of aerial photography (vol. 4, No. 52), 1932, from the Universal Film Collection of Newspaper Newsreels; and a film clip of United States Army cartographers preparing maps in Washington, D.C. during World War II from Paramount News.

RG 206: Records of the Solicitor of the Treasury. Correspondence files in NNFJ contain letters received from the Post Office Department relating to the transmittal of post route maps, 1823–1895.

RG 217: Records of the United States General Accounting Office, 1827–1837, 1922–1937.—29 maps. Charts of the Atlantic and Gulf coasts by E. and G.W. Blunt. Maps of the midwestern states annotated by the Indian Tribal Section to show military and trading posts prior to Indian title. Among the textual records in NNFG and NNFJ are correspondence files and accounts relating to the funding of nineteenth century boundary surveys.

RG 221: Records of the Rural Electrification Administration, 1939-1952.—1,285 maps. Maps of the United States and individual states prepared by the Mapping Services Section showing status of REA projects, distribution of rural telephones and electricity, location of transmission lines, and electric generating plants.

RG 226: Records of the Office of Strategic Services, 1941–1945.—9,210 maps. Thematic maps of areas throughout the world having military significance prepared by the Cartographic Section of the OSS under the direction of Arthur H. Robinson (7,500 items). A descriptive list with sample maps prepared by the Cartographic Unit, Map Section, of the Research and Analysis Branch Field Office, China Theatre under the direction of Major Herman Friis, 1945 (1 foot). Aerial photographic views in NNSP show industrial plants, urban centers, and terrain features in China, Japan, and the Philippine Islands, 1919–1943 (242 items).

Related textual records of the Research and Analysis Branch in NNMR include descriptions of maps along with map specifications and sample maps; log books of maps, 1945–1947; and map analysis files of various countries and subjects such as German cartographic and map collecting agencies, German cartographic techniques and procedures, and map procurement in the Soviet Union (2 feet). There are also manuals and correspondence relating to map cataloging and the Map Information Section, as well as an organizational manual for the Geography Division prepared by Richard Hartshorne, 1942. The textual records of the Visual Presentation Branch contain project case files relating to maps and other graphic materials prepared by the Branch, 1942–1945 (14 feet).

Motion picture films in NNSM include a film, "Military Objectives of the Axis Psychological Warfare" (226 D 195), which uses maps to illustrate these objectives.

RG 229: Records of the Office of Inter-American Affairs. Maps and correspondence found among the records of the Department of Transportation in NNFG relate to the Pan American Highway survey in Central America and Mexico, the survey of the Orinoco-Casiquiare Canal-Rio Negro Waterway connecting Venezuela and the Amazon Basin, and other railroad and highway surveys, 1943–1946 (4 linear feet). Manuscript and published maps of South American countries, cities, and seaports. Maps accompanying studies of railroads in Bolivia, Columbia, Ecuador, and Mexico, 1942–1947. Maps relating to the work of the Division of Health and Sanitation, 1942–1951. These records are described in *Inventory* 7 (1973).

RG 233: Records of the United States House of Representatives, 1828–1930.—395 maps. An incomplete series of maps and atlases published as part of the congressional serial set.

Manuscript maps are occasionally enclosed with the annual reports in NNLR which were transmitted to the House of Representatives by the President, Secretary of War, Postmaster General, Secretary of the Interior, and other executive departments and agencies. These reports were printed as part of the congressional serial set. Committee reports and papers contain a variety of subjects, including exploration of the Northwest Coast, 1825–1827, the South Seas, 1827–1829, and the American West, 1847–1849; surveys of canal routes in Massachusetts, 1825–1827; surveys of boundary lines between Missouri and Iowa, 1839–1841, Texas and New Mexico Territory, 1855–1857, and the Northwest United States and Canada, 1857–1859; the Daniel process for mapmaking submitted to the Committee on Printing, 1899-1901; lithographic maps accompanying the Presidential message, 1847; map services provided to congressmen by the General Land Office, 1861–1863; establishment of an American Prime Meridian, 1849–1851; compensation for A.R. Parker for maps prepared for the Committee on Public Lands, 1863–1865; railroad surveys of the American West, 1849–1861; surveying and calculating instruments, 1857–1859; and geological surveys of public lands, 1857–1859.

RG 234: Records of the Reconstruction Finance Corporation, 1934–1950.—2,770 maps. Detailed manuscript and blueprint maps of the United States railroads prepared by the Railroad Division from technical and economic data supplied by some 125 railroads, (2,309 maps). Manuscript and published thematic and general maps of rubber-producing areas in Brazil, Colombia, and Peru prepared by the Rubber Development Corporation, 1943–1944 (224 maps). These maps are described in *Preliminary Inventory* 173 (1973).

RG 237: Records of the Federal Aviation Administration, 1926–1952.—4,162 maps. Published maps of the United States showing commercial, military, and airmail air routes; published airway strip maps; manuscript plans and maps showing airfields and beacon light sites; plans of airports and airport improvements including details of utility and runway systems made under a Works Progress Administration project, 1935–1943 (4,000 items); and charts showing radio facilities. Field notebooks containing topographic sketches of a survey of the Washington, D.C. alternate airport, 1939–1940.

RG 238: National Archives Collection of World War II War Crimes Records, 1945–1948.—50 maps. Photostatic copies of maps in NNMR from the staff evidence analysis records of the Document Control Branch, Office of the Chief Counsel for War Crimes.

RG 239: Records of the American Commission for the Protection and Salvage of Artistic and Historic Monuments in War Areas, 1943–1946.—1,489 maps and 124 aerial photographs. Maps of provinces, regions, and cities in Europe and Asia compiled from the research files of American Council of Learned Societies Committee on the Protection of Cultural Treasures in War Areas during World War II to show cultural sites which were to be spared destruction, 1943–1946. Aerial photographs of cities in Italy, Spain, and Burma.

RG 241: Records of the Patent Office, 1791–1877.— 126,600 drawings. Includes selected patent drawings of globes, drafting tools, maps, and surveying instruments. Patent specifications are filed with the related textual records in NNFG.

RG 242: National Archives Collections of Foreign Records Seized, 1941– , 1934–1945.—22,635 maps and 8,000 aerial photographs. Maps prepared or collected by the German Army show German defenses in European countries, troop billeting, propaganda, boundary changes, views of mountain passes in Italy, and topography. Bound volumes of charts, photographs, and descriptive texts issued by the German Navy High Command relating to strategic coastal waters throughout the world, sea ice conditions along the Arctic shores of Siberia and European Russia, and oil tanker routes and facilities in Great Britain (61 volumes). Maps and aerial photographic prints comprising target dossiers prepared by the German Air Force High Command of targets chiefly in France, 1939–1940, Great Britain, 1939–1943, Italy, 1943–1944, and a few for the Balkan Countries, North Africa, the Middle East, and Iceland (22,000 items). Maps seized from Italy showing defense systems. Maps from Japanese Forces include a Japanese overprinting of a United States Coast and Geodetic Survey map of Washington, D.C., situation maps of China and the Pacific, city plans in China, Japan, and the Southwest Pacific, and charts of the Pacific showing defenses.

German aerial photographs of cities, towns, airfields, and military installations in North Africa, the Mediterranean, Great Britain, Eastern Russia, and parts of the Middle East.

Many maps are filed among the textual records in NNMR. The largest and most significant series is comprised of unique German Army operations and situation maps covering all fronts, 1939–1945 (10,000 maps). There are also maps from the records of the Reich Leader of the SS pertaining to cavern exploration in Bavaria, 1845-1945; maps and charts of Europe from the map collection of the Reich Archives, 1910–1942; twenty-one feet of records of the Mapping and Survey Branch, German High Command, 1928–1944 (Microfilm T78, Rolls 207-256); climatological maps of Russia and the Polar region prepared in connection with winter warfare, 1941–1944; German Air Force target maps; and maps relating to German colonies, 1914–1944. There are microfilm copies of the German Naval War Staff charts of U-boat operations, route charts of German patrols and cruisers prepared by U-boat commanders for their war journals (narratives of combat operations), and printed charts issued to U-boat commanders, 1914-1918, 1939-1945 (T1022). These records are described in *Guides to the Microfilmed Records of the German Navy, 1850-1945* (2 volumes). Among non-German records are Soviet situation maps of the eastern front; geodetic journals and survey notebooks from the Polish Military Geographical Institute, 1929–1939 and physiographic maps published by the Academy of Science at Cracow, 1887–1908 (stored at the Washington National Record Center); and Italian situation maps and records of army commands relating to mapping and surveying. Some of this material is available through microfilm (T733).

Motion picture films in NNSM include "Die deutsche Westgrenze", an animated propaganda map showing changes in Germany's western boundary, 1800-1936 (242 MID 2997) (Berlin, 95 minutes).

RG 243: Records of the United States Strategic Bombing Survey, 1944–1945.—2,340 aerial photographs. Aerial photographic prints of bombing targets (mainly port areas, airfields, and industrial areas) in Japan and Korea taken by the Joint Task Group and the 21st Bomber Command. Aerial photographs and maps of regions, cities, airfields, and industrial plants in Europe and Asia are also found among the textual records of British and American damage assessment reports in NNMR. Two series have been microfilmed: the final reports of the Survey (Microfilm M1013) and the tactical mission reports of the 20th and 21st Bomber Command relating to Japan (Microfilm M1159). In addition, the records of the Pacific Survey contain a collection of Japanese maps; transcripts of interrogations of Japanese intelligence officers; and Joint Army Navy Intelligence Studies (JANIS) of Siberia, Korea, China, Japan, Formosa, and several Pacific Islands, which include numbered reference maps and plans (Microfilm M1169). These records are described in *Inventory* 10 (1975).

RG 253: Records of the Petroleum Administration for War, 1942–1946.—1,135 maps. Maps showing oil pipelines, petroleum production, and oil facilities throughout the world.

RG 256: Records of the American Commission to Negotiate Peace, 1917–1919.—1,178 maps. Manuscript, published, and annotated thematic and general maps prepared or collected by the Commission's Geography and Cartography Division, under the direction of Mark Jefferson, the Economic and Statistics Division, and 9 regional divisions. These maps, designed specifically to aid in the reestablishment of national boundaries, depict geographical, ethnographic, linguistic, political, economic, topographic, and historical data primarily for Eastern Europe and Africa.

Among related textual records in NNFD are reports collected or prepared by the staff of The Inquiry under the direction of Isaiah Bowman, director of the American Geographical Society, for the anticipated peace conference following World War I (2000 volumes). The general correspondence files of The Inquiry contain letters by many prominent geographers and cartographers including Oliver E. Baker, William Morris Davis, Douglas W. Johnson, A.K. Lobeck, and Bailey Willis. Both the cartographic and textual records are described in *Inventory* 9 (1974).

RG 261: Records of Former Russian Agencies. Correspondence in NNFD relates to maps of Alaskan coastal areas prepared by the Hydrographic Office of the Russian Naval Staff, 1828 (Microfilm M11).

RG 267: Records of the Supreme Court of the United States, 1851–1946.—1,602 items. Maps, charts, aerial photographs and field notes submitted as exhibits before the Supreme Court.

RG 279: Records of the Indian Claims Commission, 1947– 1967.—1,092 maps. A variety of cartographic exhibit materials submitted as part of case files by petitioners, plaintiffs and defendants showing tribal areas, treaty and reservation boundaries, villages, routes of early explorers, mineral deposits, land ownership, and range carrying capacity.

RG 287: Publications of the United States Government, 1850–1970.—50,000 maps. An incomplete record set of published maps compiled by various Federal agencies and issued by the Government Printing Office.

RG 311: Records of the Federal Emergency Management Agency, 1975–1981.—

60,000 maps. Maps variously entitled Flood Hazard Boundary Maps, Flood Insurance Rate Maps, or Flood Boundary and Floodway Maps, and related studies published by the Federal Emergency Management Agency (FEMA) and its predecessor the Federal Insurance Administration (FIA). These are designed to show special flood-prone areas within selected counties and communities for the purpose of administering Federal flood insurance. The maps identify flood zones based on 100-year and 500-year flood occurrences and other hazard factors.

RG 313: Records of Naval Operating Forces. Records of the United States Naval Support Forces, Antarctica (Task Force 43, Operation Deep Freeze) in NNFN contain selected aerial photographs of Antarctica chiefly relating to United States logistics operations from McMurdo Station, 1957–1974.

RG 319: Records of the Army Staff, 1933–1951.—447 maps. Printed maps and overlays of Japan, plans of towns in Hungary, 1951, and map of France, 1933–1934, removed from the records of the Assistant Chief of Staff, G-2 (Intelligence). Manuscript and printed maps of various countries compiled or annotated by the Graphics Art Branch, Center of Military History, particularly for histories of World War II. The records of this office in NNMF also include the Intelligence Library ("P" Publications file) which contains cartographic materials among the military geographic studies produced by the Interservice Topographic Department of the South East Asia Command; the Strategic Engineering Studies prepared by the Intelligence Branch of the Office of the Chief of Engineers; and the War Gaming Strategic Surveys compiled by the Military Intelligence Division of the General Staff.

RG 324: Records of the Board on Geographic Names, 1890–1973.—171 cu. feet. Reports and decision lists of the Board relating to place-name decisions; files of Meredith F. Burrill, former Executive Secretary of the Board, 1943–1973; and published place-name gazetteers of foreign countries, 1955–1968. Miscellaneous manuscript, printed, and annotated maps used as reference aids for place-name studies or prepared for other government agencies, some with place-name corrections, 1943–1947. A partial description is found in unpublished preliminary inventory *NC*-123 (August, 1965).

RG 328: Records of the National Capital Planning Commission, 1791–1962.—1,500 maps and 2,390 aerial photographs. Maps and plans of the District of Columbia showing Federal property, parks, military posts, and highways within the Washington, D.C. metropolitan area. Aerial photographic prints relating to a parked-car survey in the District of Columbia and flood conditions along the Potomac and Anacostia Rivers, 1936 and 1942.

A small number of maps, survey reports, and plats are among the planning office files of commissioners and directors in NNFN, 1924–1958. The historical data files of William T. Partridge contain materials pertaining to the historical development of Washington, D.C.; typed transcripts of letters by Pierre L'Enfant; and Partridges personal recollections of his work on the McMillan Commission of 1901. Additional plats and surveyors computations are found among the land acquisition case files and appraisal reports, 1924–1956. The records are further described in PI 175 (1973).

RG 331: Records of Allied Operational and Occupation Headquarters, World War II, 1942–1945.—7,000 maps. Strategic and operational maps of Europe prepared or annotated by the Supreme Headquarters Allied Expeditionary Forces (SHAEF), of the Mediterranean region by Allied Forces Headquarters (AFHQ), of the Pacific Ocean and its islands by forces under the Commander in Chief, Pacific Ocean Area (CINCPOA), of Australia, New Guinea, and the Philippines by forces of the South West Pacific Area (SWPA), and of Japan by Supreme Commander, Allied Powers (SCAP).

RG 332: Records of United States Theaters of War, World War II, 1941–1948.—300 maps. Military maps pertaining to the China, Burma, India Theater (CBI) and the European Theater of Operations.

RG 333: Records of International Military Agencies. The records of the Korean

Armistice Agreement in NNMR contain maps and correspondence relating to the joint United States-U.S.S.R. survey of the 38th degree north parallel dividing North and South Korea, 1947.

RG 338: Records of the United States Army Commands, 1943–1952.—60 maps. Maps prepared by Service Commands and post- World War II Commands including United States Army in Europe (USAREUR), United States Army in Korea (EUSAK), United States Army Forces Far East (USAFFE), the Far East Command (FEC), and the 8th United States Army.

RG 341: Records of Headquarters United States Air Force, 1947–1963.—4,458 maps. Published aeronautical charts and special maps issued by the Aeronautical Chart and Information Center, a continuation of the series described in RG 18. Maps are also found in NNMF among the operations records, 1947–1956, and intelligence records, 1942–1956. Textual records of the Deputy Chief of Staff for Operations in NNMF contain aerial photographs and radar reconnaissance reports on Korea, 1950–1955 (5 feet); correspondence and reports relating to photographic interpretation and control of reproduction and graphic services, 1954–1955 (2 inches); and files of the Photo and Cartography Branch, 1952–1956 (3 feet).

RG 342: Records of United States Air Force Commands, Activities, and Organizations, 1945–1955.—1,010 aerial photographs. Aerial photographs of London, Dover, Paris (200 9x18 inch negatives), and other cities in northern France made by Colonel George W. Goddard following World War II. A United States Air Force exhibit of aerial photographs of cities in ten states and the District of Columbia held in New York City as part of President Eisenhower's Mutual Inspection for Peace (Open Skies) proposal for an exchange of aerial photographs that would reduce the threat of surprise attack.

RG 349: Records of the Joint Commands. Machine-readable data files in NNSR relating to National Police analysis of the Viet Cong infrastructure in North and South Vietnam include a gazetteer subfile (1971–1973) containing United States, South Vietnamese and Viet Cong place names for hamlets along with their grid coordinates.

RG 350: Records of the Bureau of Insular Affairs, 1902–1934.—57 maps. Manuscript and annotated maps of the Philippine Islands and Puerto Rico from the general classified files show communication systems, roads, trails, and railroads, forests, and harbor facilities. Maps and plats are also found among the manuscript annual reports of the Philippine Commission in NNFN, 1900–1915 (108 volumes), of the Governors General of the Philippines, 1916–1940 (118 volumes), and of the Governors General of Puerto Rico, 1909–1931 (42 volumes). A description of these records is found in *Preliminary Inventory* 130 (1960).

RG 351: Records of the Government of the District of Columbia, 1791–1955.—1,350 maps. Manuscript maps, survey plats, and survey notes by Andrew Ellicott, Thomas Freeman, Isaac Briggs, James Dermott, and Nicholas and Robert King, 1791–1815, and the Office of the Surveyor, 1803–1915; the Henry W. Brewer map collection of Georgetown, 1809–1891; maps and plans issued by the Corps of Engineers, 1876–1908; and maps prepared by the Highway Department, 1948–1955.

Related textual records in NNFN include the minutes of the Board of the Commissioners, in which plats have been inserted, 1878–1952 (42 feet); and notes and calculations, survey plats, and correspondence files prepared by the Office of Surveyor, 1804–1938 (7.5 feet).

RG 360: Records of the Continental and Confederate Congresses and the Constitutional Convention, 1781.—1 map. Manuscript map of the Yorktown, Virginia battlefield drawn by Lt. Col. Jean-Baptiste Gouvion. The papers of the Continental Congress in NNFD include the correspondence and reports of Simeon DeWitt, Robert Erskine, Thomas Hutchins, Andrew Ellicott, Rufus Putnam, Pierre L'Enfant, Absalom Martin and other early mapmakers and surveyors. The papers also contain a number of manuscript maps or references to maps, including a watercolor map accompanying John

Stuart's "Plan of the New Provinces of Vandalia and of the Cherokee Boundary Line", 1773; an unidentified map of the upper Mississippi River systems, 1784; a map of the lands between the Ohio River and Lake Erie by Nathaniel Sackett, 1785; and a sketch of British and American lines near Boston by John Trumbull, 1775.

RG 370: Records of the National Oceanic and Atmospheric Administration, 1965–1982.—45,000 maps. Published weather charts issued by the National Weather Service, nautical charts by the National Ocean Survey, and aeronautical charts by the Office of Aeronautical Charting and Cartography and their predecessors in the Environmental Science Services Administration. Nautical chart database in NNSR contains hydrographic and topographic records (from 1930 through 1976) in machine-readable form.

RG 373: Records of the Defense Intelligence Agency, 1935–1965.—79,000 maps and 4,900,400 aerial photographs. Vertical and oblique sequential aerial photographic negatives of cities, coastal and navigable inland waterways, military installations and airfields and other areas of the United States flown by the United States Air Force and Navy at scales ranging from 1:5,000 to 1:90,000, 1935–1965 (3,200,000 photographs); aerial photographic negatives of Antarctica from the United States Navy Operation High Jump, 1947–1948; German-flown mapping and combat aerial photographic prints covering England, Norway, Poland, Western Russia, the Middle East, and North Africa chiefly at scales ranging from 1:20,000 to 1:30,000, 1939–1945 (900,000 prints); mapping and reconnaissance photography flown worldwide by United States and Allied Airforces during World War II, including coverage of major military actions in Europe and North Africa such as the Normandy beaches on D-Day, many of the Pacific Island campaigns, and unique sites such as the Auschwitz Concentration Camp in Poland, Dresden, Nagasaki and Hiroshima bomb damage, and Peenemunde rocket sites in Germany (800,000 photographs); and Japanese-flown bomb-strike aerial photographic negatives of Manchuria, Shanghai and other Chinese ports, Hanoi, and oil-producing areas of Southeast Asia, ca. 1933–1943 (400 photographs). Most of these aerial photographs are accompanied by map indexes and overlays showing aerial coverage of individual photographs.

RG 391: Records of the United States Regular Army Mobile Units, 1821–1942.—50 maps. Maps made by various infantry, cavalry, and field artillery units during the nineteenth century. Textual records in NNMR contain the correspondence and reports for the 1st, 2nd, and 3rd Engineer Battalions, 1846–1918, and the 1st, 3rd-7th, 9th-11th, 21st, 27th, 29th, and 70th Engineer Regiments, 1919–1939.

RG 393: Records of United States Army Continental Commands, 1821–1920.—3,000 maps. Maps of the Seminole War, western exploration, and military operations against Indians in the West; maps of military departments and divisions; and maps and plans of military posts and reservations. The correspondence files in NNMR contain letters and reports from engineers, with subject indexes for most of the military departments and divisions from 1821–1920. In addition, the records in NNMR include a survey map of the military reservation of Fort Gibson, Creek Nation, by Capt. Nathan Boone, 1842; a subject card index to map files and a small collection of maps, sketches, and blueprints from the Department of California, 1865–1913; one volume of indexes to maps and plans of military posts, 1885, and record cards on work completed on township maps from the Department of the Columbia, 1909–1911; a series of letters received containing maps relating to forts and reservations, 1868–1875, and a series of charts and maps relating to camps of instructions and practice marches from the Department of Dakota, 1889; a military memoir with maps documenting the Florida Campaign, 1854–1858 (microfilm M-1090); an extensive special file of letters received in the Military Division of the Missouri relating to military surveys within the Division, a map of the Department of New Mexico, 1859, material on the Northwest Boundary Survey, 1873–1874, and reports and map showing the extent of the public land surveys in Kansas, 1869; maps of marches and requests for maps from the Department of the Platte, 1868–1881; twelve field notebooks of military surveys from the Department of the South and South Carolina, 1863–1865; maps relating to transportation from the Southeastern Department, 1920; reports of military reconnaissances by topographical engineers from the Department of Texas, 1849–1852; and maps of the western United States from the files of the Western Division, 1918. For further information see *Preliminary Inventory* 172 (1973).

RG 394: Records of United States Army Continental Commands, 1920–1942.—150 maps. Cartographic records include maps of Mexico and its border area by the Eighth Corps, and photomaps of military reservations and training areas by the First and Fourth Armies. Textual records in NNMF include maps and plans relating to First and Third Army maneuvers, 1934–1940; recruiting maps relating to tactical exercises of the Second Army, 1933; maps relating to joint Army and Navy exercises in Hawaii, 1931–1932; and maps of Vancouver Barracks region in Washington, 1935.

RG 395: Records of the United States Army Overseas Operations and Commands, 1898–1942.—2,239 maps. Topographic and military operation maps of Cuba and Puerto Rico prepared during the Spanish-American War, 1898; of the Philippines during the Philippine Pacification; of the defenses of Peking and the seige of Pei-Tang during the China Relief Expedition, 1900–1901; and of northern Mexico during General John J. Pershing's Punitive Expedition, 1916. Also a detailed set of 316 manuscript route maps of the Philippines compiled by Spanish troops, 1870–1892; maps of Hawaii prepared by the Military Department of Hawaii, 1912–1942; undated aerial photographs of Puerto Rico; reconnaissance and topographic maps of Panama and the Canal Zone, 1916–1942; and miscellaneous military maps of the Russo-Japanese War, French forces in Indochina, 1939, Thailand (Siam), and Guam.

Related textual records in NNMR contain correspondence and reports of the Engineer Battalion and the Chief Engineers relating to the war with Spain, 1898–1899; records of the Chief Engineer and the Military Intelligence Officer with the Army of Cuban Pacification, 1906–1909; and records of the Intelligence Officer with the Punitive Expedition to Mexico, 1916–1917. The records of the Philippine Islands Command contain a map pertaining to the Surigao operation against insurrectionists (1903), and a book of maps of towns in the Southern Philippines, 1902.

RG 401: National Archives Gift Collection of Materials Relating to Polar Regions, 1750–1976.—1,327 maps and 1,028 aerial photographs. Major collections in NNFN include the files of Meredith F. Burrill relating to his work on the U.S. Board on Geographic Names (1943–1967) and lecture notes on toponymy, 1959; surveying and topographic reports prepared by Quin Blackburn during the first and second Byrd Antarctic expeditions, 1928–1929 and 1933–1935; diaries, topographic drawings, and photographs relating to Clyde Baldwin's survey work in Southeast Alaska and the Alaska-Canadian Boundary, 1905–1910; lecture notes on cartography, materials relating to the Advisory Committee on Antarctic Names, 1947–1973, and maps prepared or acquired by Kenneth J. Bertrand; bibliographic research notes on the history of cartography and exploration, and manuscript maps (175 items) compiled by Herman R. Friis, 1920–1974; flight maps pertaining to the first Byrd Antarctic Expedition, 1928–1930, and a diary of Adolphus W. Greely (1883–1884) from the papers of William C. Haines; survey reports, maps, sketches, and other records relating to Robert E. Peary's work as a surveyor in Fryeburg, Maine (1878), with the U.S. Coast and Geodetic Survey (1879), with the United States Navy (1882–1904), with the Nicaragua Canal Survey (1884–1988) and with his Arctic expeditions, 1886–1909 (252 feet); aerial photographs by Thomas Poulter relating to the second Byrd Antarctic Expedition, 1933–1935 (300 photographs); maps and aerial photographs of the Finn Ronne Antarctic Research Expedition (1946–1947) and IGY, 1957–1958; aerial photographs, maps, reports and calculations relating to antarctic mapping programs (1929–1962) and reference files pertaining to the work of the Board on Geographic Names and the Advisory Committee on Antarctic Names (1910–1961) from the papers of Harold E. Saunders; and aerial photographs of Kainan Bay, Little America, and the Bay of Whales from the Walter R. Seelig Papers,

1939–1958; and selected aerial photographs and maps relating to the first and second Byrd Antarctic expeditions, 1928–1930 and 1933–1935, and the United States Antarctic Service Expedition, West Base, 1934–1941, from the Paul A. Siple Papers.

RG 406: Records of the Federal Highway Administration, 1967—1984.—4,000 maps. Published county and State highway maps.

RG 407: Records of the Adjutant Generals Office, 1917–, 1918—1945.—2,000 maps. Topographic, strategic, tactical, and situation manuscript and annotated maps prepared by United States Army and Navy units, 1937–1945. Included is an 1887 Coast and Geodetic multi-sheet map of Washington, D.C. overprinted in Japanese. World War II and Korean War operations reports in NNMF (8,219 linear feet) include reports of engineer topographic battalions responsible for surveying and mapping activities in the field; thousands of maps and manuscript map overlays accompanying after-action reports and reports of combat units; and map-illustrated terrain studies, terrain handbooks, and special reports published by General Douglas MacArthur's Headquarters, South West Pacific Theater, 1942–1945. NNSP holds aerial reconnaissance photographic prints of Luzon in the Philippine Islands during the Japanese occupation, 1942–1945 (ca. 1,200 prints), aerial strip mosaic prints annotated to show battlefield areas, and lantern slides of military maps relating to the Moroccan War, 1925–1927.

RG 456: Records of the Defense Mapping Agency, 1972–1984.—20,000 maps. A record set of published topographic map and nautical chart series issued by DMA.

4. *General Information Leaflet Number 26* (1984) lists 31 published inventories, special lists, special guides, and resource papers describing individual map series or map themes, and contains a map showing the location of the Cartographic and Architectural Branch. A list of all finding aids published by NARA is found in General Information Leaflet Number 3, *Select List of Publications of the National Archives and Records Service* (1982). Many record series, including some map series, are available in microfilm. These are listed in *Catalog of National Archives Microfilm Publications* [with] *Supplementary List* . . . 1974–1982 (1982). Descriptions of some records acquired by NARA since 1977 are available on microfiche in the Central Research Room and most branches. A popular introduction to the National Archives, beautifully illustrated, is Herman J. Viola's *The National Archives of the United States* (New York: Harry N. Abrams, 1984).

The quarterly journal, *Prologue: Journal of the National Archives,* contains articles based on the records, listings of recent accessions and openings, and timely news and notices concerning NARA holdings.

Note: See also K11

National Museum of American History (NMAH) (Smithsonian Institution) **See entry C8**

National Ocean Service (NOS) (Commerce Department—National Oceanic and Atmospheric Administration—Data Control Section **See entry G20, section 4**

B20 Naval Historical Center (Navy Department)—Curator Branch—Photographic Section

1 a. *Washington Navy Yard, Building 57*
9th and M Streets, S.E.
Washington, D.C. 20374-0571
(202) 433-2765

b. 9:00 A.M.–4:00 P.M. Monday–Friday

c. Open to the public, but appointments are recommended. File prints are not loaned.

d. The photographic Section does not process photographic reproduction orders for the general public. Reproductions of photographs of many of the reference prints maintained by the Photographic Section, however, can be obtained from the Department of Defense Still Media Depository (B10), the National Archives and Records Administration (B19), or the Naval Imaging Command. Researchers may also copy unclassified or unrestricted file prints using their own equipment.

2–3. The Naval Historical Center Photographic Section maintains a large collection of unique Navy photographs made prior to 1920 and reference file prints of photographs in the Department of Defense Still Media Depository and the National Archives and Records Administration Still Picture Branch. The collection numbers over 250,000 photographs and reference prints, including several thousand aerial photographs of airstrips, harbors, and military targets. For example, there are reference prints of aerial photomosaic target maps of the Buka Passage between Bougainville and the Buka Islands made during the Solomon Islands campaign in 1943 and pre-strike reconnaissance aerial photographs of Haiphong, North Vietnam, taken in 1967.

4. The file print collection is arranged by places, subjects, ships, events, organizations, and a variety of other topics.

B21 Naval Historical Center (Navy Department)—Operational Archives Branch

1 a. *Washington Navy Yard, Building 57*
9th and M Streets, S.E.
Washington, D.C. 20374
(202) 433-3170

b. 7:30 A.M.–4:30 P.M. Monday–Friday

c. Open to serious researchers. It is recommended that researchers call in advance. Some of the post-1955 materials are restricted due to national security classifications. A list of declassified and unclassified records will be furnished on request.

d. Limited duplication facilities are available. The Branch is unable to reproduce large maps.

e. Dean C. Allard, Director

2. The Operational Archives Branch collects documents relating to the combat and peacetime activities of naval fleet units and to the strategic, policy, and planning programs of naval operational headquarters. Most of the records date from 1939, with heavy

emphasis on the World War II era and the Pacific region. The records, consisting of 200,000 items, include a separate collection of some 5,400 maps. There are also related cartographic materials found in documentary series.

3 a. The map collection consists of the following series:

Charts of Submarine Sinkings, 1918.—4 maps. Manuscript charts showing the locations and names of ships sunk off the east coast of the United States by German U-Boats.

Daily Situation Charts of Combatant Vessels, 1941–1946. —2,600 charts. Plotting charts annotated on a daily basis in the Navy's Operations Plotting Room in Washington to show the approximate location of each United States, allied, and suspected enemy ship and submarine in the Atlantic, October 1941–March 1946 (1,000 charts) and in the Pacific, December 1941–April 1941 (1,600 charts).

Situation Maps of Operations in North Africa, 1942–1943.—190 maps. French chart of Casablanca and Fedala, Morocco, annotated to show mine fields, 1944; plotting chart of Atlantic Ocean annotated to show United States and Canadian air bases and air routes to Europe and North Africa; and a set of daily situation maps showing military operations in North Africa, November 9, 1942–May 14, 1943.

Coastal Chart of Sicily, 1943.—1 item. Italian coastal chart, annotated by Captain John A. Webster, operations officer for Commander, Destroyer Squadron 16, to show fire support areas and enemy batteries during the invasion of Sicily.

Detailed Strategic Engineering Study Reports for Italy and Sicily, 1944.—9 volumes. Contains printed topographic maps, aerial photographs, and coastal charts of landing beaches and adjacent areas in Calabria, Campania, Lucania, and Puglia compartimentos in Southern Italy and in Sicily prepared by the Intelligence Branch of the United States Army's Chief of Engineers (ca. 540 maps).

Maps of the Normandy Invasion and Southern France, 1944.—47 maps. A series of printed and annotated topographic maps and coastal charts of landing beaches and German defenses at Normandy compiled and printed for operation BIGOT, May 20, 1944 (35 maps), and a set of large aerial photographic mosaics, panoramic views, and maps of Utah and Omaha beaches prepared by Commander, Task Force 122, for landing boat operations, 1944 (12 items).

Track Charts Pertaining to the Pearl Harbor Attack, December 7, 1941, and the Battle of Midway, June 4–6, 1942.—24 items. Large photoprocessed and printed situation maps. These charts can also be found in the Congressional *Hearings*, Investigation of the Pearl Harbor Attack.

Strategic Historical Plot Charts, 1941–1946.—125 maps. Situation maps of the world or Pacific Ocean area annotated to show the location of United States and enemy forces during significant actions from Pearl Harbor through the early occupation of Japan.

Traffic and Decryption Intelligence Charts, 1942.—249 maps. Plotting charts of the Pacific Region showing the daily situation of the Japanese Navy as determined by decryption intelligence, January 20–May 1.

Maps of Japanese Naval and Ground Forces in the Pacific, 1942–1943.—2 maps. Photoprocessed maps of the Pacific annotated with information copied from a chart prepared by T. Ohmae to show zones of operations of Japanese naval and ground forces.

Maps of United States Navy and Air Force Searches in Pacific Region, 1942–1945.—13 maps. Colored photographic prints of maps showing air searches.

View Charts of the Aleutian Islands, 1942.—3 charts. Printed charts with perspective insets of strategic harbors and landing sites in the Aleutian Islands.

United States Hydrographic Office Charts, 1941–1945.—293 charts. Printed nautical charts, chiefly of the Pacific region and the North Sea.

United States Hydrographic Office Emergency Nautical Charts, 1943.—27 charts. Emergency printings by the United States Hydrographic Office of Australian, Japanese, and German nautical charts of the Southwest Pacific.

Maps of Marine Corps Campaigns, 1943.—8 maps. Photoprocessed maps of the Bismarck Archipelago, Bougainville Straits, Guadalcanal, New Britain, Solomon Islands, and Tulagi prepared by M-2 Section, United States Marine Corps Headquarters.

Maps of Iwo Jima, 1944.—60 maps. Series of published United States Army Map Service topographic quadrangles with aerial photographic maps on the verso (40 maps); printed special air and gunnery target maps at various scales, some measuring 4 x 6 feet (20 maps).

Maps of the Mariana and Marshall Islands, 1943–1944.—77 maps. Annotated plotting chart showing the invasion of Guam, June 1944; set of topographic and other maps of Guam, 1944 (20 items); United States Marine Corps intelligence study of Marshall Islands, 1943 (24 maps); special air and gunnery target maps of Kwajalein and Saipan (25 maps); and annotated daily situation maps of the Tinian Campaign (8 maps).

Pacific Airways Plotting Charts, 1944.—9 charts. Printed United States Hydrographic Office plotting charts for the Pacific region.

Army Map Service Combination Topographic/Aerial Photographic Maps of New Guinea, 1944.—6 maps. Set of topographic maps, with aerial photographic mosaics on verso, of strategic bays, rivers, and capes in New Guinea.

Combat Maps of the Caroline Islands, 1944.—56 maps. Printed advanced plotting maps, topographic maps, and special air and gunnery target maps prepared by the 64th United States Army Engineer Topographic Battalion for Angaur, Palau, Peleliu, Ulithi, and Yap Islands.

Maps of the Philippine Campaigns, 1944.—36 maps. A manuscript map in Japanese, which accompanied a detailed action report; printed operational maps of the Central Philippines prepared by the United States Army, 64th Engineer Topographical Battalion, 1944 (21 maps); and manuscript and photoprocessed charts of the battle of Leyte Gulf showing movements of United States and Japanese forces and extent of air searches, October 22–27, 1944 (14 maps).

CINCPAC-CINCPOA Bulletins, 1944.—24 volumes. A set of miscellaneous terrain studies, airfield surveys, air target map bulletins, air information summaries, and target analysis reports with key maps and aerial photographs for the China Coast, Formosa, Kyushu, Leyte, Palau, Tokyo Bay, and other Pacific areas (ca. 500 maps and aerial photographs).

Daily Strategic Plot Charts of Submarines, November, 1944–June 1945.—240 items. Plotting charts of the Pacific region annotated in manuscript on a daily basis to show the location of each allied submarine.

Mine Field Charts, 1944–1945.—200 maps. Printed charts of Japanese coastal areas and the West Pacific prepared by the United States Army, 949th Engineer Aviation Topographic Company showing areas mined by the United States Air Force (43 charts); captured Japanese charts showing the location of Japanese mine fields and underwater obstacles along the South China coast, Manila Bay, and the Southwest Pacific, including a mine field laid off the coast by a German auxiliary cruiser (21 maps); and manuscript maps of the Malacca Straits, Sumatra coastal areas, and Aru Bay, Ceylon, showing the location of mine fields planted by Royal Air Force Liberators (7 maps).

Intelligence Reports, Pacific Theater, 1944–1945.—2 volumes. Published intelligence studies of the Shang-Hai coastal area prepared by United States Naval Group China, 1945 (20 maps), and the Caroline Islands prepared by the Intelligence Section, United States Marine Corps, 1944 (40 maps).

Aerial photographic mosaics and target maps of Okinawa, 1945.—ca. 200 maps.

Photo Coverage Report 22, 1946–1947.—1 volume. A bound volume of 55 aerial photographic indexes showing the coverage of aerial photographs for the Western Pacific region (55 indexes).

Daily Situation Maps of Formosa Straits, 1950.—30 maps. Maps depicting the daily total shipping available along the China Coast, September 4–October 5.

Daily Situation Maps of the Korean War, 1950–1951.—229 maps. Large photographic prints of the map of Korea showing daily troop positions of United Nations and North Korean forces, December 1, 1950–January 24, 1951 (54 maps), daily situation maps of the United States Navy WESPAC fleet, September 1, 1950–January 24, 1954 (150 maps), and daily situation maps of the Inchon-Seoul region, September 14–October 10, 1950 (25 maps).

3 d. Maps and related cartographic materials are found in the following declassified records of naval commands, office files of the Naval Historical Center's Operational Archives, and records of individuals.

Action and Operational Reports of Naval Commands, 1941–1953.—1,200 feet. Includes manuscript plotting chart overlays prepared during specific actions and operations to show positions and tracks of United States, allied, and enemy ships, submarines, merchant vessels, and life boats.

Strategic and Operational Planning Documents, 1939–1950.—270 feet. Includes maps illustrating strategic and operational plans.

Miscellaneous Record Material and Publications, 1939–1950.—570 feet. Includes two pertinent series. (1) Unpublished or limited circulation World War II histories and historical reports include intelligence summaries, terrain studies, histories of naval stations, and unit histories with detailed map enclosures. Of particular note is "An Informal History of the COMSOPAC Photographic and Reproduction Unit", South Pacific Area (1945), which contains photographs, charts, and correspondence. (2) Intelligence Center, Pacific Area Ocean Area (ICPOA) and Joint Intelligence Center, Pacific Ocean Area (JICPOA) Files, 1942–1946 (466 bulletins), consist of geographic and technical intelligence bulletins produced during World War II from information obtained from captured Japanese documents or prisoner of war interrogations, as well as Allied intelligence sources. Of particular interest are air target maps and aerial photo bulletins of the Lesser Carolines, China Coast, Eniwetok, northern Formosa, Guam, Halmahera, Honshu, Jaluit, Kusaie, Kwajalein, Kyushu, Luzon, Marcus, Minor Marianas, Lesser Marshalls, Mindanao, Nauru, Nomoi, Pagan, Palau, Pescadores, Ponape, Roi, Rota, Ryukyu, Saipan, Tinian, Truk, Ulithi, Wotje, Woleai, and Yap. Other bulletins are devoted to symbols and abbreviations used on Japanese topographic maps and nautical charts, Japanese methods of aerial photographic interpretation, Japanese place names arranged by characters, amphibious mapping and terrain intelligence, the Terrain Model Unit, translation of a Japanese military topographic map of Nansei Shoto, and transliterated place name gazetteers for Amami Gunto, the China Coast, Southern Japan, Miyako Retto, Palau, and Yap. These bulletins have been microfilmed and are described in Microfilm Publication 3 (1976).

Records of the Aviation History Unit, Office of the Chief of Naval Aviation, 1943–1963.—183 feet. Includes histories of naval air reconnaissance units active during World War II and Korea.

Records of the World War II Battle Evaluation Group, Naval War College, 1933–1952.—9 feet. Includes charts and maps of all major World War II battles based on United States and captured Japanese sources.

Reports of the United States Naval Technical Mission to Japan, 1945–1946.—13 reels of 35mm microfilm. Contains reports on Japanese naval aerial photography, and the organization and operation of the Japanese hydrographic office, including data on high altitude radar maps.

Dispatches and Records from the Chart Room of the Commander in Chief, United States Fleet, 1940–1946.—70 feet. Includes 148 charts and maps relating to United States naval action at Pearl Harbor, Doolittle's raid on Japan, battle of Coral Sea, Aleutian campaigns, Operation Torch in North Africa, Japanese attack on Ceylon, Wake Island strike, Pacific island campaigns, battle of the Philippine Sea, disposition of forces in Burma, India-China land routes, initial occupation of Japan, air strikes on Japan, division of territory among allies following Japanese surrender, partition of Austria (1945), German air and submarine bases in Norway, strategic spheres of command in Europe, plans for final push to Berlin, Greenland patrols, operations in Sicily, Salerno and Anzio, Normandy invasion, and operations in Southern France. There are also target approach charts of Japan (24 items), a folder of aerial photographs relating to China, and a folder of materials relating to terrain models. A checklist is available.

Naval Facilities Engineering Command, Documents Concerning the Navy's Real Estate, 1778–1934.—27 items. Includes two maps of a Spanish land grant on Santa Rosa Sound, West Florida, now the site of the Pensacola Naval Air Station and Navy Yard, 1817 and 1844. The 1844 map is signed by President John Tyler. The collection also includes an original survey of the Naval Shipyard at Portsmouth, New Hampshire, 1800, photocopies of a map of Beaufort County, South Carolina, 1873, and a map of San Clemente Island, California, 1854. The documents are described in a finding aid. Also included is a map of Tutuila, Samoa, 1904.

Fragmentary Collections of Papers, 1902–1979.—8 feet. Papers of David Westheimer include two Japanese maps with English translations showing troop dispositions in Southern Kyushu and the counter-attack plan for the Shibushi area, 1945. Papers of Captain Thomas A. Lombardi, USNR, contain the pre-landing bombardment and target maps he used during the invasions of Iwo Jima, Okinawa, and Ie Shiwa, 1944–1945. Papers of Lieutenant Commander Edgar Bromer, USNR, include a map of Iwo Jima.

4. A card index and shelf list provide general access to the map collection and finding aids are available for most of the record groups. A partial checklist of the unpublished histories has been published under the title *World War II Histories and Historical Reports in the U.S. Naval History Division* (Naval History Division, 1977). General information about the archives is found in *Information for visitors to the Operational Archives* (1983) and *A History of the Dudley Knox Center for Naval History,* both available on request.

An excellent introduction to naval records in other repositories is *U.S. Naval History Sources in the United States* (U.S. Naval History Division, 1979), compiled by Dean C. Allard, Martha L. Crawley, and Mary W. Edmison. These are available from the Naval Historical Center as long as supplies are available.

Patuxent Wildlife Research Center (Interior Department—Fish and Wildlife Service) **See entry G12 section 3**

Smithsonian Institution Libraries (Smithsonian Institution)—Special Collections Branch **See entry C8**

B22 Smithsonian Institution (SI) Smithsonian Institution Archives

1 a. *Arts and Industries Building, Room 2135*
900 Jefferson Drive, S.W.
Washington, D.C. 20560
(202) 357–1420

b. 9:00 A.M.–5:00 P.M. Monday–Friday. Scholars planning to use the Archives before 10:00 A.M. must make arrangements in advance since the Arts and Industries Building does not open until that hour.

c. Open to qualified researchers. Advance arrangements are recommended. Researchers are required to register with building security staff and obtain a building pass before being admitted to the Archives. Access to some records is restricted.

d. A reasonable number of photocopies will be made for researchers at no cost.

e. William W. Moss, Archivist

2–3. The Smithsonian Institution Archives contains the official records of the Smithsonian's secretaries, curators, and other staff members, as well as the records of a number of professional organizations and societies closely associated with the Smithsonian. Established for the "increase and diffusion of knowledge among men", the Smithsonian has served as the center or focal point of Washington's scientific and cultural community since its founding in 1846. Reflecting these interests, the records are particularly valuable for the study of nineteenth century American science.

The records are organized and maintained in record units (RU), with official records of the Smithsonian assigned record unit numbers from 1 to 6999, and manuscript papers and archives acquired from outside the Smithsonian assigned numbers from 7000 to 9999. Unprocessed collections are identified by accession number.

Among the more than 600 record units currently in the Smithsonian Archives, the following contain some 800 maps, 1646 aerial photographs, and related materials:

RU 60. Meteorological Project, 1820-1875.—7.5 linear feet. Consists of correspondence, maps, and reports relating to the Smithsonian's effort to publish weather maps based on data collected from a nationwide network of voluntary observers. Includes a large manuscript chart of the Gulf Stream (54x74 inches) based on United States Coast Survey data, 1845–1860, and printed isothermal maps of the United States and a star chart prepared under the direction of Joseph Henry, 1866–1874. Correspondents include James Pollard Espy, Arnold Henry Guyot, Elias Loomis, and Charles Anthony Schott.

RU 69. Topographical Data Project—Walter L. Nicholson Papers, 1873-1882.—4 linear feet. Contains elevation data and several railroad maps, collected by Nicholson under the direction of the Smithsonian Institution and the United States Coast and Geodetic Survey for a hypsometrical map of the United States. Also some correspondence.

RU 87. Ethnogeographic Board, 1942–1945.—Miscellaneous map material includes two mimeographed booklets, *Glossary of Selected Map Terms Relative to Authorities, Dates, Scales, Editions, and Locations in Foreign Text Maps* (1944), and *Glossary of Russian Map Terms* (1946), both issued by the United States Army Map Service; monthly declassification lists of Office of Strategic Services (OSS) maps, 1945–1946; and a list of maps printed by the Harvard-Yenching Institute (2 folders). Also useful are the correspondence files which often contain lists or descriptions of maps sought or acquired as part of the Board's role as a clearinghouse for ethnogeographic information on non-European areas, particularly files relating to the Military Intelligence Service, Army Map Service, Joint Army-Navy letters of 1943, and Naval Intelligence, 1942–1946 (.5 linear feet); correspondence file relating to the Committee on Asiatic Geography, 1942–1946 (2 folders); country information files of specialized strategic areas, containing information on map sources or maps, 1943–1944 (.5 linear feet); a set of mimeographed bulletins, *Status of Geographic Projects,* which provides descriptions of maps or geographic materials from 13 Federal agencies which could be presented in map form, 1942–1944 (6 bulletins); and photographic negatives and prints of unidentified maps, apparently taken during a book survey (20 negatives).

RU 134. Canal Zone Biological Area, 1927-1960.—25 maps. Annotated and printed maps of the Panama Canal Zone and Barro Colorado Island.

RU 192. United States National Museum, 1877-1975.—261 linear feet. Includes administrative records relating to the Mexican-United States Boundary Commission and other Smithsonian expeditions.

RU 245. Pacific Ocean Biological Survey Program, 1963- 970.—500 maps and 1,500 aerial photographs. Correspondence and list relating to maps used in the Program's study of plants and animals on Pacific Islands and the distribution and population of the pelagic birds in that area (1 folder); manuscript and reproduced page-size outline maps of the Central Pacific and individual islands prepared specifically for the Program, some compiled from aerial photographs (ca. 200 items); and Pacific Ocean Grid Survey Charts, United States Hydrographic Position Plotting Charts or nautical charts, which have been annotated to show the direction of flight of different pelagic birds (300 charts).

RU 253. Assistant Director (Science), Smithsonian Astrophysical Observatory, 1961–1973. Includes correspondence and report on the aerial photographic survey of Stonehenge and Callanish (Outer Hebrides) project, 1966 (1 folder). These files are restricted.

RU 7001. Joseph Henry Collection, 1808, 1825–1878. Henry served as Secretary of the Smithsonian from 1846 to 1878. This collection contains his correspondence, diaries, research and lecture notes, publications, biographical material, and copies of Alexander Dallas Bache and Henry papers from other collections. A computer index, prepared by the Joseph Henry Papers, provides name and subject access to the collection (C9).

RU 7002. Spencer F. Baird Papers, 1833–1889.—28 linear feet. Include extensive correspondence and fiscal records related to several mapping and surveying expeditions, including the Ringgold-Rodgers Expedition, the United States-Mexico Boundary Survey, and the Northern Pacific Railroad Route Survey.

RU 7004. Charles D. Walcott Collection, 1851-1940.—34 linear feet. Charles D. Walcott was the director of the United States Geological Survey, 1894-1907, and Secretary of the Smithsonian Institution, 1907-1927. This collection includes relevant personal correspondence with Cleveland Abbe, William Morris Davis, Henry Gannett, Grove Karl Gilbert, Arnold Hague, William Henry Holmes, Clarence King, Jules Marcou, and John Wesley Powell, 1874–1927; speeches presented during his service as Director of the United States Geological Survey, including "Washington as an Explorer and Surveyor" 1900, and "Work of the Geological Survey in Mapping the Reserves", n.d.; United States Geological Survey correspondence, reports and related materials, chiefly 1879–1904, including reports on "Instructions Relative to Mapping Wooded Areas", 1897, "Government Topographic Surveys", by H.M. Wilson, "Reorganization Proposals of the Geological Survey", 1903, and "Geological and Topographical Surveys in the Philippine Islands", 1903 (2.5 linear feet); and a manuscript report written by Walcot, entitled "Notes on Map and Sections of the Grand Canyon Area", 1882–1883. See Smithsonian Archives *Guide Number 2*.

RU 7050. George Brown Goode Collection, 1798–1896.—10 linear feet. Contains an uncataloged series of miscellaneous biographical notes on men of science.

RU 7051. Columbian Institute and Related Records, 1791–1800, 1816–1841.—1.3 feet. Established to promote agriculture, manufacturing, and natural resources, the Institute's records include 8 papers by William Lambert relating to the determination of latitude, longitude, and the figure of the earth, 1825–28, and a map of the botanical garden plot on the Mall.

RU 7052. Jean Louis Berlandier Papers, 1876–1851.—5.3 linear feet. Consists of a printed catalog of historical and geographical manuscripts, describing manuscript maps of Mexico, which Berlandier deposited in the Smithsonian in 1853 (many of these manuscripts and maps are now in the Berlandier and Thomas Phillipps Papers in the Library of Congress Manuscript Division, see entry B15); manuscript geographical journals (in French) relating to journeys in Mexico, one of which contains many maps and elevations; and correspondence of Walter L. Nicholson, United States Post Office Topographer, concerning Berlandier, and manuscript maps of Brownsville, Texas and Matamoros, Mexico, the latter showing the location of Berlandier's house and business, 1868 (2 folders).

RU 7053. Alexander Dallas Bache Papers, 1821–1869.—3 linear feet. Includes letters of recommendation supporting Bache for the position of Superintendent of the Coast Survey, 1843, and correspondence with John J. Abert, John H. Alexander, Hartman Bache, Albert Boschke, James P. Espy, Ferdinand R. Hassler, Andrew A. Humphreys, and James Renwick.

RU 7058. National Institute Records, 1839–1863.—6.2 feet. The National Institute was organized in the nation's capital to promote the study of natural history and the physical sciences. Its collections were transferred to the Smithsonian Institution in 1862. The records contain a paper on preparing nautical charts by Matthew Fontaine Maury, 1843; ledgers of accounts and receipts relating to Charles Wilkes' United States Exploring Expedition, 1839–1858 (2 boxes); and publications, including Peter Force's "Grinnell Land: Remarks on the English Maps of Arctic Discoveries in 1850 and 1851".

RU 7067. James G. Cooper Papers, 1853–1870. A journal and two printed maps pertaining to his service as a naturalist with Isaac Stevens' Pacific Railroad Survey.

RU 7073. William H. Dall Papers, 1839–1927.—30 linear feet. Manuscript and printed maps relating to his Alaskan explorations, 1861–1898, including a hand-drawn map by George Davidson giving the astronomical position for Sitka, 1869 (40 maps); correspondence and reports concerning the Alaskan Western Union Telegraph Expedition, 1865–1867, and the United States Coast Survey Expedition, 1870–1880; correspondence by Dall pertaining to Alaskan place names, 1878, 1919; papers relating to Alaskan boundary questions; Dall's monthly reports and journals as chief of a United States Coast Survey hydrograph surveying party, 1871–1880; and correspondence with Cleveland Abbe, Marcus Baker, George Davidson, William Morris Davis, William Francis Ganong, George Gibbs, Grove Karl Gilbert, Arnold Henry Hague, William H. Holmes, Clarence King, Jules Marcou, and Justin Winsor.

RU 7074. Leonhard Stejneger Papers, 1867–1943.—18 linear feet. Manuscript and annotated maps by Stejneger, some apparently drawn for publication, show Siberia, the Bering Sea, individual islands (his map of Bering Island served as the standard for fifty years), and seal distribution, 1890s (20 maps); an exercise sketchbook containing excellent examples of hand drawn and colored maps and a map symbol legend, apparently compiled by Stan Backer; a United States Forest Service pocket instruction manual for mapmaking, dated 1912, filed with several rough manuscript map sketches; and a small manuscript chart showing direction and force of winds along a sailing route in the Bering Sea.

RU 7084. William Henry Holmes Papers, 1870–1931.—3 linear feet. Microfilm copy of his 16 volume *Random Records of a Lifetime, 1846–1931* (for original, see Library of the National Museum of American Art, C7). This includes narrative descriptions and documents relating to his work as an artist-topographer with the United States Geological Survey of the Territories (Hayden Survey), 1872–1879, and the United States Geological Survey, 1880–1889.

RU 7085. Marcus Benjamin Papers, 1886–1929.—2 linear feet. Contain biographical information, collected by Benjamin as an editor and contributor of Appleton's *Cyclopaedia of American Biography,* on George Gibbs, Ferdinand V. Hayden, Elias Loomis, John Wesley Powell, and others.

RU 7088. Charles Orcutt Papers, 1927–1929.—3 linear feet. Letters containing numerous map sketches showing flora and fauna collecting sites in Jamaica (2 folders); annotated blueprint map of Haiti; and manuscript sketch maps of Jamaica, including one in 14 sections (30 items).

RU 7148. David Crockett Graham Papers, 1925–1933.—4 maps. Manuscript maps by Graham recording his routes and places visited during expeditions to Szechuan and the China-Tibetan border.

RU 7157. Frederick Kreutzfeldt Journal, 1853.—1 volume. German and English versions of Kreutzfeldt's journal kept during Captain John W. Gunnison's Pacific Railroad Survey along the 38th parallel. Kreutzfeldt was killed by Indians along with Gunnison and his entire survey party, October 26, 1853.

RU 7177. George P. Merrill Collection, ca. 1800–1930. —10 linear feet. Photographs and autographs collected by Merrill for his work on the history of American geology and correspondence of James Hall, Ferdinand Hayden, and Merrill. The latter includes letters written by a number of geologists and others who were associated with mapping and surveying: Cleveland Abbe, John James Abert, John Alexander, Alexander Dallas Bache, Nathaniel Bowditch, Mathew Carey, G. Frederick Cuvier, George Davidson, Nicolas Desmarest, George William Featherstonhaugh, Henry Gannett, James T. Gardiner, Grove Karl Gilbert, Arnold Henry Guyot, Arnold Hague, Ferdinand Vandeveer Hayden, William Henry Holmes, Alexander von Humboldt, Clarence King, Increase Allen Lapham, Elias Loomis, Charles Lyell, William Maclure, Jules Marcou, Nils Adolph Erik Nordenskiold, David Dale Owen, John Wesley Powell, Raphael Pumpelly, Ferdinand von Richtofen, Henry Rowe Schoolcraft, and Justin Winsor.

There are also photographs of the California Geological Survey Corps, the United States Geological Survey, and the United States Geological Survey of the Territories (Hayden Survey), depicting field parties, campsites, and office staff in Washington, D.C., 1871–1877.

RU 7179. Edmund Heller Papers, ca. 1898–1918.—25 maps. Manuscript and annotated maps relating to British Columbia and Yukon Territory, including an interesting set of printed promotional hunting maps of the Cassiar Big Game District annotated to show the location and distribution of moose, mountain goats, grizzly bears, and black bears, 1897–1914; printed maps showing the routes of scientific expeditions on which Heller participated or led as a naturalist, including the Alexander Alaska Expedition, the Smithsonian African Expedition, led by Theodore Roosevelt, and the Paul J. Rainey African Expedition, 1908–1912; and annotated field maps of the Peruvian Expedition of 1915, sponsored by the National Geographic Society and Yale University.

RU 7186. United States Exploring Expedition Collection, 1838–1885.—Manuscripts, notes, and correspondence concerning the Charles Wilkes expedition to the Pacific Ocean. Includes Titian Ramsay Peale's manuscript history of the expedition.

RU 7191. George Suckley Papers, 1849–1861.—.5 linear feet. An unidentified manuscript map on tracing cloth of southwest Washington along with journals and notes made by Suckley while serving as assistant surgeon and naturalist with the Pacific Railroad Survey of the 47th and 49th Parallels, 1853.

RU 7198. John Evans Papers, 1854–1860.—1 folder. Journal pertaining to his work on the Isaac Stevens survey for a northern railroad route to the Pacific Coast.

RU 7202. Caleb Burwell Rowan Kennerly Papers, 1855–1860.—.3 linear feet. Journals and field books, prepared by Kennerly during his service as a naturalist with the United States-Mexican Boundary Survey and the Northwest Boundary Survey.

RU 7230. Department of Geology Biographical File, 1836–1958.—7.5 linear feet. Contains biographies, obituaries, memoirs, memorial service programs, addresses, and some correspondence on noted scientists and geologists, including a number associated with mapping. These are Cleveland Abbe, Henry L. Abbot, Marcus Baker, George Engleman, George William Featherstonhaugh, Henry Gannett, Grove Karl Gilbert, Arnold Hague, Ferdinand V. Hayden, Edward Hitchcock, William Henry Holmes, Jedediah V. Hotchkiss, Douglas Houghton, Thomas Jefferson, Clarence King, Increase Allen Lapham, Charles Lyell, William Maclure, David Dale Owen, John Wesley Powell, Raphael Pumpelly, Henry Darwin Rogers, Henry Rowe Schoolcraft, Charles Anthony Schott, William Smith, and Leonhard Stejneger.

RU 7242. August F. Foerste Papers, 1887–1933.—2.8 linear feet. Field notebooks, prepared by Foerste during service with the United States Geological Survey, containing topographic map sections of Massachusetts and Rhode Island annotated to show stratigraphic and petrographic information, ca. 1888–1890 (3 volumes); and United States Geological Survey topographic quadrangles and other maps of Lewis County, Kentucky, Ohio, Eastern Ontario, and Rutland, Vermont annotated to show geological information, ca. 1908–1924 (30 maps).

RU 7251. J. Brookes Knight Papers, 1928–1955.—1 map. A. Hoen and Company advance sheet with manuscript corrections of *Geologic Map of the Carboniferous Formations in the Llano Region, Texas,* by F.B. Plummer, ca. 1931–1938.

RU 7267. Vernon Orlando Bailey Papers, 1889–1941.—2 linear feet. Includes printed topographic maps of the Grand Canyon National Park, the Kaibab National Forest, and the Tusayam National Forest, Arizona, annotated by Bailey to show life zones for different fauna and flora during his service with the United States Biological Service, 1929 (8 maps).

RU 7275. William Edwin Safford Papers, 1894–1925.—.3 linear feet. Correspondence and notes concerning Joseph N. Nicollet's exploring expedition in Minnesota and his map of the region, 1836–1839.

RU 7281. William F. Foshag Collection, 1923–1965.—5.3 cubic feet. Includes manuscript, printed, and annotated aeronautical, geology, and topographic maps and profiles relating to volcanic areas in Mexico, particularly Paricutin Volcano, 1907–1946 (63 maps); series of geographic maps of Mexican States issued by the Secretary of Agriculture, 1940–1942 (21 maps); a large wall map of Mexico published by the Mexican National Railroad Company, 1881; oblique aerial photographic prints (including color) of Paricutin and Zapicho Volcanos and the Parangaricutera lava flow covering the town of San Juan, taken by Otto Fisher and the United States Navy, 1944 (14 items); and a set of vertical aerial photographic prints of Paricutin, taken by Compania Mexicana Aerofoto, South America, at an elevation of 15,000 feet, May 26, 1945 (132 photographs).

Accession 83011. Farouk El-Bay Papers, 1971–1972.—60 maps. Printed and photoprocessed maps of the lunar surface prepared by the United States Air Force Aeronautical Chart and Information Office; lunar orbital science flight charts for Apollo Missions 14, 15, and 16; and United States Geological Survey geologic sketch maps of parts of the lunar surface.

4. The collections are described in *Guide to the Smithsonian Archives* (Smithsonian Institution Press, 1983). More extensive unpublished finding aids to many of the collections are available for consultation in the search room.

B23 University of Maryland Libraries (College Park Campus)—Special Collections Division

1 a. *Theodore R. McKeldin Library*
College Park, Maryland 20742

b. Maryland Room:
8:30 A.M.–5:00 P.M. Monday–Friday
10:00 A.M.–5:00 P.M. Saturday

East Asia Collection:
8:00 A.M.–6:00 P.M. Monday–Friday

c. Open to the public. Interlibrary loan services are available for some items.

d. Photographic reproduction services are available except for material in fragile condition.

e. Donald Farren, Associate Director

2–3. The Special Collections Division consists of the East Asia Collection, the Marylandia Department, the Historical Manuscripts and Archives Department, and the Rare Books and Literary Manuscript Department. The Maryland Room (fourth floor) serves as the reading room for all departments, except the East Asia Collection.

EAST ASIA COLLECTION
Room 3115
Frank Joseph Shulman, Curator
(301) 454–2819
(301) 454–5459 (East Asia Office)

The East Asia Collection contains some 55,000 books and periodicals in the Chinese, Japanese, and Korean languages, including a small number of atlases, books on geographic names, and books on Japanese and Chinese cartography published since the 1920s. Reproductions and descriptions of early maps are also found in standard published monographs illustrating the history of Japan such as *Edo Jidai Zushi,* Tokyo, 1975–1978 (27 volumes), devoted to the Tokugawa period, 1600 to 1868, and *Meiji Taisho Zushi,* Tokyo, 1978–1979 (17 volumes), covering the Meiji period, 1868 to 1945. An important source of Japanese commercial maps published immediately after World War II is the Gordon W. Prange Collection, which contains the files of the Civil Censorship Detachment (CCD), Press Publication and Broadcasting Section of SCAP (Supreme Commander for Allied Powers). This collection includes some 60 maps submitted for censorship review as part of the overall censorship activities of CCD that involved materials being printed for commercial distribution, 1945–1949. None of these maps, which show chiefly prefectures or major cities in Japan, have been processed or cataloged, but insofar as they have been kept together, they are accessible to researchers.

The Prange Collection is described in an offprint by Frank Shulman entitled *The Gordon W. Prange Collection: Publications and Unpublished Materials From the Allied Occupation of Japan Within the East Asia Collection, McKeldin Library, University of Maryland, College Park* (6 pages).

MARYLANDIA DEPARTMENT
Maryland Room
Peter H. Curtis, Curator
(301) 454–3035

The Marylandia Department has a comprehensive collection of some 10,000 published and microfilmed maps of Maryland and the Chesapeake Bay region dating from 1590 to the present. It consists of general and special purpose maps of the state, regions, counties, cities, and towns, including about 100 dated before 1800. These include maps issued by such state organizations as the Agricultural Experiment Station, 1889–1973 (11 soil maps), Bureau of Immigration, 1896–1912 (5 economic maps), Department of Geology, Mines, and Water Resources, 1948–1964 (165 maps), Department of Natural Resources, 1976–1981 (60 maps), Department of State Planning, 1963–1982 (125 geology, census tract and congressional district maps), Geological Survey, 1834–1975 (300 topographic and geology maps), Maryland–National Capital Park and Planning Commission, 1943–1983 (310 plans), State Board of Forestry, 1910–1927 (20 maps of forested areas), State Highway Administration, 1963–1984 (50 state highway maps), State Roads Commission, 1937–1970 (70 county road maps), and State Weather Service, 1889–1921 (5 weather charts). The collection also contains original and microfilm Sanborn fire insurance maps for 132 Maryland cities and towns, 1885–1960, and Sanborn microfilm coverage for Washington, D.C., 1888–1950 (4 reels).

In addition, the Marylandia Department has custody of the deposit copies of University of Maryland College Park Campus theses and dissertations, including the following prepared under the direction of the Geography Department: Janet H. Bigbee, "17th Century Place Names Culture and Process on the Eastern Shore" (M.A. Thesis, 1970), Michael Rocco Cirino, "An Evaluation of Modern Maps Available for South America" (M.A. Thesis, 1960), Mary Clawson, "The Evolution of Symbols on Nautical Charts Prior to 1800" (M.A. Thesis, 1979), Barbara June Fegley, "Implications of Map Design on Trail Selection in Cederville Natural Resources Management Area: A Pilot Study" (M.A. Thesis, 1977), Virginia S. Gibbons, "Lithography and the City Map: Baltimore, 1850–1900" (M.A. Thesis, 1983), Catesby Thomas Jones, "Arabic Place Names in Relation to Geography" (M.A. Thesis, 1949), Annie Limpa-Amora, "An Investigation of the Modes of Cartographic Representation of Recent American Census Data" (M.A. Thesis, 1964), Kathleen Ann McCormick, "Manual vs. Computer-Assisted Cartography: The Influence of Production Method on Map Percipients Evaluation and Recall" (M.A. Thesis, 1983), Alastair Morrison, "Classification and Representation of Roads for Road Maps of North America and Western Europe" (M.A. Thesis, 1962), Victoria June Raab, "Maps for the Visually Handicapped: An Investigation of Users Problems and Suggestions for Map Program Development" (M.A. Thesis, 1983), and Thomas D. Robenhorst, "A Psychophysical Study of Area Symbols used in Choropleth and Isopleth Mapping" (M.A. Thesis, 1972).

RARE BOOKS AND LITERARY MANUSCRIPTS DEPARTMENT
Maryland Room
Blanche Ebeling-Koning, Curator
(301) 454-3035

The Rare Books Collection includes several early atlases and geographical textbooks, including Richard Blome's *A Geographical Description of the Four Parts of the World* (London, 1670), J. and P. Knapton's *Englands Gazetteer,* (London, 1751), Thomas Salmon's *A New Geographical and Historical Grammar* (London, 1758), Johann Homann's *Atlas novus terrarum orbis imperia* (Nuremberg, 1751), Thomas Keith's *A New Treatise on the Use of the Globe* (London, 1819), Robert Gibson's *A Treatise on Practical Surveying* (Baltimore, 1822), Samuel Butler's *An Atlas of Antient Geography* (Philadelphia, 1834), and Gustave Eiffel's *Atlas météorologique pour l'année 1906–1912]* (Paris, 1907–1913).

HISTORICAL MANUSCRIPTS AND ARCHIVES DEPARTMENT
Lauren Brown, Curator and University Archivist
(301) 454-2318

The University Archives contain several early maps of the University grounds, including the first manuscript plat of the University, ca. 1854, and a collection of publications issued by the Department of Geography, including *Tactual Mapping: Design, Reproduction, Reading, and Interpretation* by Joseph W. Wiedel and Paul A. Groves (1972), *An Economic and Social Atlas of Maryland,* compiled by Derek Thompson and Joseph W. Wiedel (1974), and the *Atlas of Maryland Commemorative Edition* (1977).

The collections of historical manuscripts include the John H. Alexander Papers, containing correspondence concerning the progress of surveys on the Eastern shore of Virginia, Maryland, and Delaware (1831–1848); the Milton Atchinson Reckord Papers, which contain blueprints for Camp Ritchie, Maryland; and several Maryland land plats and surveys, dated between 1664 and 1808.

4. Card catalogs are available in both the East Asia Collection and the Maryland Room. The card catalogs for the book collections are arranged by author, title, and subject; the map collection by date and subject; and the thesis and dissertation collection by university department and thereunder by author. The manuscript collections are only partly cataloged, but there are separate finding aids for the larger collections.

C Museums and Galleries

Museums and Galleries Entry Format (C)

1. General Information
   a. address; telephone numbers
   b. hours of service
   c. conditions of access
   d. reproduction services
   e. name/title of director and heads of relevant divisions

2. Size of Holdings

3. Description of Holdings
   a. maps, atlases, and globes
   b. aerial photographs and remote sensing images
   c. literature
   d. manuscript collections
   e. photographs and motion pictures
   f. instruments

4. Bibliographic Aids Facilitating Use of Collection (cartobibliographies, catalog cards, computerized retrieval systems, inventories, special lists, catalog guides)

C1 Army Engineers Museum

1 a. *Belvoir Road and 16th Street*
Fort Belvoir, Virginia 22060–5054
(703) 664–3171 (Information)

b. 10:00 A.M.–4:30 P.M. Daily, except major holidays.

c. Open to the public. Scholars should contact curator in advance.

d. Microfilm reader/copier, microfiche reader/copier, and photocopy machines available on premises.

e. James L. Kochan, Director/Chief Curator.

2–3. The Museum contains displays tracing the history of the United States Army Corps of Engineers from its founding in 1775 to the present and a limited collection of manuscripts, rare books, maps, and charts. Several maps are on display including a manuscript plan of the siege of Charleston (1780) and a manuscript French map showing the French and American positions during the siege of Yorktown in 1781. Also in the holdings are Major William Tatham's manuscript *Journal While Acting Topographical] Engineer (1814) to Gen. Jackson Commander [7th Military] District,* Lt. Col. Isaac Roberdeau's *Memoir on the Defenses,* and a French journal of the Yorktown Campaign (1781). Surveying instruments on display include a surveyors' chain, an Army sketching case (1908) and a transit used by the United States Lake Survey, 1910–1912.

4. The collection is currently being inventoried and organized (1986). A descriptive list and inventory of the archives will be available in 1987.

C2 Freer Gallery of Art Library and Archives (Smithsonian Institution)

1 a. *National Mall at Jefferson Drive and 12th Street, S.W.*
Washington, D.C. 20560
(202) 357–2104

b. 10:00 A.M.–5:30 P.M. Monday–Friday. Closed Christmas Day.

c. Open to researchers, but arrangements should be made in advance.

d. Photoduplication services are available.

e. Elizabeth Kelly, Archivist

2–3. The Freer Gallery, which houses one of the finest collections of Oriental Art in the world, maintains several collections of private papers of eminent archeologists and architectural historians that contain some 350 maps.

The Carl Whiting Bishop Collection includes seven printed maps relating to Whiting's archaeological trips to China in the 1920s, showing ancient tombs and fortification systems in Honan and Shansi Provinces.

The Ernest Herzfeld Archives includes 74 manuscript, printed, and photoprocessed maps pertaining to Herzfeld's archeological work in the Near East, particularly Iran, during the first half of the nineteenth century. Of particular note are a number of large-scale contour and general manuscript maps of the ancient Persian cities of Pasargadae and Persepolis showing ruins, blueprints of a map of the city of Shiraz made in 1306 H, and maps of other cities, including Baghdad, Damascus, Palmyra, and Samarra. The collection also contains a series of manuscript regional maps of the Middle East, some with Assyrian, Avestan and Greek place names, apparently showing the Achaemenian period, and a number of printed German maps of the Middle East, 1896–1918, some annotated by Herzfeld to show his travel routes or the routes of other expeditions.

The Myron Smith Papers contain a map of Iran showing roads and railways compiled and drawn by Smith, an architectural historian who worked in the Middle East during the 1930s and 1940s; United States Army Map Service topographic maps of Palestine, Iran, Iraq, Jordan, and Syria, 1938–1943 (144 items); maps of Iranian provinces published by the Surveyor General of India, 1910–1922, 1939–1940 (29 items); and miscellaneous printed and photoprocessed maps, some in French and Persian, showing geology, railroads, roads, and towns in Iran, chiefly 1926–1963 (94 items). A city plan of Tehran was copied from an original map in the Tehran Archives.

4. Unpublished lists of the maps are available from the archivist.

Geological Survey (Interior Department)—Visual Information Services Group **See entry G14**

C3 George Washington University—Dimock Gallery

1 a. *730 21st Street, N.W.*
Washington, D.C. 20052
(202) 676–7091
(202) 676–7157

b. 10:00 A.M.–5:00 P.M. Monday–Friday

c. Open to the public, appointment is preferred.

d. Duplication processes available.

e. Lenore D. Miller, Curator

3 a. The W. Lloyd Wright Collection of Washingtoniana and the George Washington University Permanent Collection contain 73 printed maps of the District of Columbia dating chiefly from 1793–1895. Included are 8 maps from the 1790s and the rare multi-sheet United States Coast and Geodetic map of the District, 1880–1895 (59 sheets).

4. The maps are listed in a card catalog.

Marine Corps Historical Center (Navy Department) **See entry B16**

C4 Mount Vernon Museum and Mansion House

1 a. *Mount Vernon, Virginia 22121*
(703) 780–2000

b. 9:00 A.M.–5:00 P.M. Monday–Friday, March 1–November 1.
9:00 A.M.–4:00 P.M. Monday–Friday, November 1–March 1.

c. Open to the public.

2. Mount Vernon is the restored estate of George Washington. It consists of Washington's Mansion house, completed in 1787, Museum Shop, and surrounding outbuildings and gardens.

3a–b. The map and aerial photography collections are described in entry A28.

3 f. The Mount Vernon Museum and Mansion house contain several instruments that purportedly belonged to George Washington. These include a set of drafting instruments and several telescopes and spy glasses. The museum also has custody of a measuring chain and jacob's staff and compass. The latter date from the early nineteenth century and belonged to George Washington's nephew, Lawrence. Also on display in the Mansion is John Senex's large terrestrial globe, ordered by Washington in 1789. Correspondence concerning this globe is in the Manuscript Division of the Library of Congress (B15).

4. The Museum Shop sells facsimiles of Samuel Vaughan's plan of Mount Vernon (1787) and Washington's map of the 5 farms comprising his Mount Vernon estate in 1793. The original of the latter map is in the Huntington Library. The publication *Mount Vernon: A Handbook* (1985), contains reduced reproductions of these maps as well as photographs of Washington's telescope and his collection of drafting instruments.

C5 National Air and Space Museum (NASM)—Smithsonian Institution

1 a. *7th and Independence Avenue, S.W.*
Washington, D.C. 20560
(202) 357-3133

b. 10:00 A.M.-5:00 P.M. Monday-Friday

c. Open to scholars and the public. Researchers must register and obtain a pass at the information desk. Interlibrary loan service is available for library materials.

d. Viewing equipment and duplication services are available.

2. NASM collects, preserves, and displays artifacts and documents in support of research, exhibitions, and public programs relating to aeronautics, space science, and planetary studies and exploration. The documentary materials consist of archival and research collections acquired through deposits, donations, or solicitations from individuals, aircraft and aerospace companies, the armed forces, aviation organizations, and Federal agencies. These include more than 4,000 aerial photographs, 132,000 remote sensing images, 9,000 maps, and related textual materials.

3-4. NASM archival and research collections are found in the NASM Library, Center for Earth and Planetary Studies, Records Management Division, and Aeronautics Department.

NASM BRANCH LIBRARY
Frank A. Pietropaoli, Chief Librarian (202) 357-3133
Monica Knudsen, Reference Librarian, Admiral DeWitt
Clinton Ramsey Room Collection (202) 357-3133

The NASM Library, a branch of the Smithsonian Institution Libraries, supports the research, exhibition, and public programs of the NASM. The library contains about 35,000 books, over 7,000 bound volumes of journals, as well as collections of microforms of books, journals, and technical documents covering the history of aeronautics and earth and planetary science. Included are materials on aerial photography and remote sensing imagery. The holdings of the NASM Library are accessed through the Smithsonian Institution Library's Online Catalog. The reference collection contains the *Bibliography of Aeronautics,* which was issued by various institutions, 1910, 1917-1940 (97 volumes). It includes numerous citations to aerial photography, as well as the *WPA*

Bibliography of Aeronautics, Part 30 which is devoted entirely to the subject. The Admiral DeWitt Clinton Ramsey Room, which houses rare aeronautica, contains an autographed copy of *Pioneering Years in Aerial Photography, U.S. Army and Air Force Brigadier General George W. Goddard, U.S.A.F. (Ret.),* a bound volume of reproductions of newspaper clippings, photographs, and aerial photographs relating to Goddard and the military development of aerial photography and the related field of aerial photogrammetry from 1917–1969.

CENTER FOR EARTH AND PLANETARY STUDIES
PLANETARY IMAGE FACILITY
Room 3101
Ted A. Maxwell, Facility Director (202) 357–1457
Rosemary E. Aiello, Photolibrarian (202) 357–1457

The Planetary Image Facility is one of nine similar facilities established in cooperation with the National Aeronautics and Space Administration (NASA) to provide scientists and other scholars access to the remote sensing imagery and related cartographic products generated from interplanetary probes, as well as Landsat and other terrestrial remote sensing programs. Other Planetary Image Facilities are located at the University of Arizona, Tucson, Arizona 85721; Brown University, Providence, Rhode Island 02912; Cornell University, Ithaca, New York 14853; University of Hawaii, Honolulu, Hawaii 96822; Jet Propulsion Laboratory, Pasadena, California 91109; Lunar and Planetary Institute, Houston, Texas 77058; United States Geological Survey (USGS), Flagstaff, Arizona 86001; and Washington University, St. Louis, Missouri 63130.

The facility does not provide photoreproductions of its holdings, but the photolibrarian will aid scholars who wish to order photographic copies from the National Space Science Data Center, NASA (D9). Aerial photo indices and other documentation (55 linear feet) provide information on scale, sun angle, sensor, and geographic location. Planetary images are accessed through BIRP, an online computer retrieval system that provides access to the individual frame image; terrestrial images are indexed by computer searches through the Earth Resources Observation System (EROS) network. Viewing equipment includes a zoom transfer scope and light table with stereoscope.

The following collections contain 8,240 maps and 132,070 remote sensing images:

Lunar Maps—printed USGS orthophoto topographic maps, (1:250,000 and 1:1,000,000); original NASA orbital photomaps of the Apollo landing zone prepared by the Langley Research Center (1:10,000, 1:25,000, and 1:50,000); NASA topophoto maps of the Apollo landing zone (1:250,000); geological maps (1:1,000,000), and large-scale geological maps of landing sites, 1960–1970s (ca. 7,600 maps).

Planetary Maps—printed USGS shaded relief maps, geologic maps, topographic maps, photomosaics, and lava flow maps of Mars (600 maps); printed USGS preliminary pictorial maps and high resolution controlled photomosaics of the satellites of Jupiter (40 maps); printed USGS preliminary pictorial maps of the satellites of Saturn; and printed USGS shaded relief maps and geological maps of Mercury.

Lunar Remote Sensing Imagery—Ranger, Surveyor, and Lunar Orbiter 1-5 orbital, press-release, and surface photographs (21,000 photographs); Apollo 15–17 metric (mapping camera) photographs (6,500 photographs); Apollo 8,10-17 hasselblad handheld orbital and surface color and black and white photographs (16,000 photographs); and Apollo 15-17 panoramic photographs (5x8 inches) and rectified panoramic photographs (9.5x96 inches), (9,350 photographs).

Mars Remote Sensing Imagery—Mariner 4,6-7, 9 press-release and orbital images (50 photographs); and Viking 1-2 orbital images, mosaics, and press-release photographs (50,000 photographs).

Jupiter Remote Sensing Imagery—Pioneer 10-11 press release photography (60 photographs); and Voyager 1-2 orbital images of Jupiter, Io, Ganymede, Callisto, Europa, and other satellites (10,000 photographs).

Saturn Remote Sensing Imagery—Voyager 1-2 5-inch images of Saturn, Tethys, Enceledus, Iapetus, Dione, Rhea, and other satellites (10,000 photographs).

Mercury Remote Sensing Imagery—Mariner 10 orbital photographs (5,511 photographs).

Earth Remote Sensing Imagery—Landsat multispectral scanner large color transparencies, color prints and black and white prints of Bulgaria, China, Egypt, India, Israel, Romania, and Saudi Arabia at scales ranging from 1:100,000 to 1:1,000,000, 1972–1980 (462 prints); Gemini orbital photographs (400 prints); Apollo hasselblad orbital photographs (1,400 prints); Skylab hasselblad, multispectral camera, and earth terrain camera photographs; Apollo-Soyuz test project hasselblad orbital photographs (1,350 prints); and Shuttle radar and hand-held photographs.

RECORDS MANAGEMENT DIVISION
Karl P. Suthard, Chief (202) 357–3133
Larry Wilson, Information (202) 357–3133

The Records Management Division maintains NASM's archival and research collections, some of which are housed in the Archival Support Center, 3904 Old Silver Hill Road, Suitland, Maryland 20746.

Computer-generated master index lists provide access to the largest collections. About 300,000 archival photographs are available for viewing on analog laser-read 12-inch diameter videodiscs. These videodiscs, which can be played on all laser videodisc players, may be purchased from the Smithsonian Institution Press. They are described in the Smithsonian Institution Press catalog and a division brochure.

The following collections contain more than 700 maps, 4,000 aerial photographs, and related textual materials:

Documentary Reference Collection. Consists of more than 30,000 subject files of articles, clippings, drawings, manuscripts, maps, pamphlets, photographs, and technical manuals documenting the development of aviation and space science. Many of the aerial photographs and some maps, however, have been removed from the subject files and stored on videodiscs. Some of the more pertinent subject files are listed below.

Aircraft (A)—Photography from balloons. An English translation of "Early Aerial Photography From Balloons," originally published in Paris, 1886. (1 folder).

Biography (C)—Thaddeus Lowe (2 folders).

Airlines (F1)—Airline Route Maps. Early aviation maps of commercial, airmail, and transportation routes, including a presentation map certifying the flight of a passenger aboard Transcontinental Air Transport from St. Louis to Columbus, Ohio, 1929 (41 items); United States Army Air Force, Royal Air Force, and Geographical Section, General Staff aeronautical charts and United States Army Air Force annotated weather flight charts, 1939–1957 (72 items); United States Airmail maps, 1924–1938 (7 items); and souvenir air maps, airline system maps, and route maps issued by commercial air carriers such as American, Eastern, Lufthansa, Imperial, Trans-Canada, Trans-World, and United, 1931–1980s (120 items).

Airports (F2)—Aerial photographs of airports in the United States, arranged by state (ca. 1,200 items).

Communications (G)—Mapping. Articles and reports on the role of radar and shoran in mapping and charting, 1942–1947 (1 folder).

Events (J)—Includes aerial photographs and maps of airfields, adjacent cities, and maps showing routes of air races, 1904–1980. Some early views include photographic obliques taken from a balloon during the St. Louis Air Show (23 items), an aerial photograph of Ottawa, 1911, and a map of the Great American Circuit Race in the Middle West, 1912.

Military (S)—Aerial photographs of military air bases in the United States and the Philippines, 1920s–1940s. (60 photographs).

Miscellaneous (Y)—Charts and Maps. Experimental air navigation chart, 1932, and other early charts, 1930s (10 items); Geographical Section, General Staff aeronautical charts, chiefly European coverage during World War II (275 items); and articles on aeronautical charts, aerial mapping, and chart catalogs (10 items).

Miscellaneous (Y)—Cameras. Contains clippings, instructional manuals, and vendors catalogs relating to aerial photographic cameras, 1916–1923 (26 items); United States Army Air Corps technical reports, World War II (4 items); and a British Air Ministry history of photographic reconnaissance and intelligence, 1939–1944.

Miscellaneous (Y)—Photographs. Aerial photographs, many unidentified, of United States and foreign cities, airports, natural features, field patterns, 1890s–1940s (522 prints); and photographs of United States Army and Navy aerial photographers at work (8 prints).

Collections (Z)—Aerial photographs of Washington, D.C. during World War II and New York City, 1929 (3 albums).

Space Science and Exploration Research File. Includes maps, charts, articles, unpublished professional papers, NASA press releases, Congressional staff reports, and photographs relating to planetary mapping, the Landsat program, and remote sensing, 1946–1980s (2.5 linear feet). Examples of the types of unpublished professional papers are Frederick J. Doyle, "Map of the Land From Space" (1967), and Pamela E. Mack, "A History of Landsat, 1964–1977 Politics and Technological Change at NASA".

United States Air Force Photographic Collection. Consists of some 200,000 photographic prints documenting United States Army Air Force and United States Air Force activities from the nineteenth century through the Korean War. These photographs, which have been loaned to the Museum for reproducing on video disc, are maintained in loose leaf binders and arranged in four collections: Pre-World War II, Domestic and Historical (220 binders), World War II Combat (960 binders), World War II and Post-World War II Domestic (520 binders), and Korean War Combat (200 binders). Post-Korean War material is still maintained by the United States Department of Defense Still Media Depository (B10). Preliminary shelf lists are currently available only for the World War II Combat and Pre-World War II collections.

The Pre-World War II collection contains the following major series: photographs of photogrammetric and mapping activities associated with the United States Army Schools of Aerial Photography, held at Rochester, New York, Ithaca, New York, and Langley Field, Virginia, during World War I (122 photographs); 2 volumes of photographs of maps and charts showing noteworthy flight routes during the 1920s, bird's eye views of New York City and other cities, a map comparing the flight time of an ambulance airplane with rail and auto travel between Fort Ringgold and Fort Antonio, Texas, 1927, series of maps prepared under the direction of Colonel William Mitchell, showing spheres of influence and radius of airplane action in Asia and the North Atlantic, 1924, and maps of air defenses used during lectures at the Army War College by General H.H. Arnold and other officers, 1936–1938 (120 maps); aerial photographs (air scapes) of military airfields and installations, chiefly in the United States, but also Bermuda, Bolivia, Equador, France, Italy, Mexico, and the Philippines, 1928–1940s (400 photographs); and three volumes (designated *Events/Activities–Photography–Cameras)* of photographs with captions of aerial cameras, photogrammetric equipment and their operation, pictures of military and United States Coast and Geodetic aerial photographers and photogrammetrists during training and at work, and several series of early experimental aerial photographs taken at night, at high altitudes, at long distances, and with infra-red film, 1922–1939 (300 photographs).

The World War II Combat Collection contains worldwide aerial reconnaissance and mapping photographs of airfields, ports, towns, and significant geographical features

(995 prints); photographs of maps and charts showing theaters of operations and bomb damage assessment, including a map of Japan depicting principal industrial cities destroyed by B-29 incendiary attacks, with figures showing percent of cities destroyed and size comparisons with United States cities (85 prints); and photographs of activities of photographic reconnaissance squadrons in Burma-India, China, England, France, Germany, Italy, Marianas, Marshall Islands, North Africa, and Ryukyu Retto (135 prints).

AERONAUTICS DEPARTMENT
Room 3309
E.T. Woolridge, Chairman (202) 357-2515
Kathleen L. Brooks-Pazmany, Research Assistant (202) 357-2515

The Aeronautics Department maintains the photographic collections of two very well-known aviation photographers of the 1930s-1950s.

Rudy Arnold Collection—Contains aerial photographic views of New York City, 1930s-1950s.

Hans Groenhoff Collection—Contains aerial photographic views of the Bahamas, early 1960s.

C6 National Museum of African Art Branch Library (Smithsonian Institution Libraries)

1 a. *318 A Street, N.E.*
Washington, D.C. 20560
(202) 287-3490, extension 67

b. 9:00 A.M.-5:00 P.M. Monday-Friday

c. Open to the government agencies, professional associations, scholars, and the public by appointment. Interlibrary loan service is available.

d. A photocopier is located in the library.

e. Janet L. Stanley, Chief Librarian

2-3a The National Museum of African Art Library, a branch of the Smithsonian Institution Libraries, was established in 1971 to support the research, exhibition, and public programs of the museum. In addition to a collection of more than 8,000 books, the museum contains a collection of some 131 printed and photoprocessed reference maps of Africa and individual African countries, 1860s-1980. Included among the collection are a series of topographic and geographical maps of the French Congo and French West Africa prepared in Paris by the Service Geographique de l'Armée, 1926-1938, and the Institut Géographique National, 1943-1954 (29 items), topographic maps of Egypt, Sudan, and parts of East Africa issued by the British War Office, 1917-1942 (9 items), an undated German map showing areas where carved figures and masks, metal work, fabric and rock art were produced, and a manuscript map of Kenya drawn before independence.

4. A preliminary check list of the collection is available.

C7 National Museum of American Art *and* the National Portrait Gallery (Smithsonian Institution)—Library

1 a. *Old Patent Office Building, Room 331*
8th and G Streets
Smithsonian Institution
Washington, D.C. 20560
(202) 357-1886

b. 10:00 A.M.-5:00 P.M. Monday-Friday
Closed on holidays.

c. Open to Smithsonian staff, students, and researchers in American art and related studies. Directions to the library will be given by the Guard Office. Researchers must register. The books may only be charged out to Smithsonian employees.

d. Photocopy facilities are available.

e. Cecilia H. Chin, Librarian

3 d. The library contains William Henry Holmes scrapbooks, *Random Records of a Lifetime, 1846-1931,* which are comprised chiefly of newspaper clippings, personal correspondence, reports, photographs, and pencil drawings mounted in 16 volumes. Three volumes relate to his work as a topographer and artist with the Hayden geological and topographic survey of Colorado, Idaho, Nebraska, New Mexico, Montana, and Wyoming, 1869-1875. They include correspondence with Ferdinand V. Hayden and G.K. Gilbert, typescript reports by Holmes, and photographs by William H. Jackson of field parties and individual survey members- George B. Chittenden, Henry Gannett, Hayden, and others.

C8 National Museum of American History (NMAH) (Smithsonian Institution

1 a. *14th Street and Constitution Avenue, N.W.*
Washington, D.C. 20560
(202) 357-2700

b. Generally 10:00 A.M.-5:00 P.M., but hours vary.
Monday-Friday. The Museum building does not open until 10:00 A.M.

c. Collections are open to serious researchers by appointment only. Collection curators must be contacted well in advance to ensure that the desired research materials are available. Because of security considerations, scholars are required to register at one of the information desks (located at both entrances of the Museum), where they are then escorted to the appropriate division.

d. Copiers are available in most of the collection areas. Loans are generally limited to educational institutions for exhibition purposes, and must be arranged through the NMAH Office of the Registrar.

3. The National Museum of American History is concerned with the exhibition, preservation, and interpretation of artifacts reflecting the American experience. Some 2,500 maps, 550 surveying and drafting instruments, 29 globes, 10,500 maps on stamps, and

related materials, including manuscript correspondence and exercise books, are in the custody of curators from 5 separate divisions and libraries. The materials date from 1486 to the 1970s.

Each division has responsibility for an exhibition area devoted to its field of specialization. The Division of Physical Sciences has a permanent display on the first floor devoted to the "Laying Out the Nation's Capital", which includes many of the surveying instruments used by Andrew Ellicott to survey the City of Washington in 1792. Additional surveying instruments are found on display in "1876: A Centennial Exhibition". Located in the Arts and Industries Building, this exhibit reconstructs the 1876 Philadelphia Centennial Fair and contains instruments used by the United States Navy and the United States Coast Survey, as well as instruments manufactured by the W. and L.E. Gurley Company.

Two major map exhibits were on display in 1985. The exhibition, "The Naming of America", contained Martin Waldseemuller's world map of 1507, the earliest printed map to depict the name "America". This map was on temporary loan from the castle of Fürst Franz von Waldburg-Wolfegg family in southern Germany. An exhibition brochure describing the map is available. The other exhibition, "Celestial Images: Astronomical Charts from 1500 to 1900", was on display May 16–August 23, 1985. A catalog describes the 69 charts comprising the exhibition.

Papers of Robert Mills Project, Room 5109
Pamela Scott, Associate Editor

This project is responsible for assembling, editing, and publishing on microfilm the complete papers, drawings, and maps of Robert Mills, America's first native-born professional architect. In addition to designing and constructing many of the official buildings in Washington, D.C., Mills compiled the first state atlas, the *Atlas of the State of South Carolina* (1825). Pertinent files include a computerized database listing all documents relating to Mills, 2,000 photocopies of original documents, and research files organized by subject and author. The documents include correspondence with a number of early nineteenth century mapmakers, surveyors, and individuals associated with these activities: John James Abert, Alexander Dallas Bache, Hartman Bache, William Elliot, William P. Elliot, Charles Gratiot, Andrew A. Humphreys, James Kearney, Benjamin Henry Latrobe, Fielding Lucas, Jr., Matthew F. Maury, Montgomery Meigs, David Dale Owen, James Renwick, Isaac Roberdeau, and William B. Stone.

DIVISION OF ARMED FORCES HISTORY
Harold D. Langley, Curator, United States Naval, Marine Corps, and Coast Guard History (202) 357–2249
Donald E. Kloster, Curator, United States Army Dress, Insignia, Heraldry and Graphics (202) 357–1883

The Armed Forces History Division contains materials that document the activities of the United States Army, Navy, Marine Corps, and Coast Guard. A card catalog is organized by name of donor and often contains information on date and subject of materials. Not all cartographic materials, however, are listed in the card catalog. Approximately 1,500 maps and charts are maintained by the Division, dating from 1777 to the 1970s.

SHAEF War Room Map Collection. Contains some of the maps (some original, some reproduced at a later date) that were in the War Room of the Supreme Headquarters Allied Expeditionary Force (SHAEF) in the Ecole Professionelle, Reims, France, on May 17, 1945. Also, a list of the maps and photographs of the War Room on that date showing the various maps as they were located on the walls.

Pershing Collection. Contains a map of northwestern Europe that was used by General John J. Pershing in the War Room, Allied Headquarters, showing the German and Allied battle lines, July 15–November 11, 1918 (only 6 of these maps were printed). Also, photographs of the Map Room.

Photographic Collection of Relief Models. Set of original color photographs of relief models marked to show American, British, German, and Japanese troop concentrations during military operations in Italy, 1943, and Okinawa, 1945. Some are captioned. See entry B19, RG 165.

Military History Map Collection. An unarranged collection of approximately 1,400 military maps loosely organized chronologically, with some duplication, 1777–1970s. Significant early maps include a manuscript copy of Tadeusz A. Kościuszko's situation map of the Saratoga Campaign, 1777, copied from the original in Cracow, ca. 1894; an engraved set of French maps concerning the American Revolution, published in 1807; an engraved map showing the retreat of the French Army from Moscow; a manuscript map of the Battle of South Mountain compiled by the United States Army Bureau of Topographical Engineers, September 14, 1862; a wall map of Cuba published by the Adjutant General's Office, Military Information Division, 1897; 2 photoprocessed maps of military operations in the vicinity of Manila, compiled by the United States Army Signal Corps, 1898; and an undated postal map of Alaska annotated to show locations of Russian church missions and routes between missions.

World War I maps include a set of printed and photoprocessed topographic and intelligence maps with accompanying general or field orders bound by the Historical Section of the General Staff, 2nd Division (68 maps); bound order of battle and intelligence maps concerning the First Army (ca. 240 maps); a series of printed barrage charts, artillery fire maps, and maps showing deployment of American and German artillery (39 maps); a captured German situation map concerning the St. Mihiel offensive, September 12, 1918; a series of printed maps annotated daily in the Map Room of the First Army to show army and divisional boundaries, Oct.–Nov. 1918; and a special series of overprinted maps showing military operations of the Romanian Army during World War I (4 maps).

Significant World War II maps include situation maps prepared by headquarters of the 12th Army Group to accompany G-3 reports, with some reports, August, 1944–May, 1945 (100 maps); series of 1:250,000 and 1:500,000 United States Army Map Service (AMS) and British War Office Geographical Section, General Staff (GSGS) maps, chiefly of Europe with some coverage for Manchuria and Japan, 1942–1945 (530 maps); copy of map issued to junior officers for the invasion of Guadalcanal, August 7, 1942; a printed Japanese wall map of the Pacific area; and military maps on cloth of Belgium, Burma, China, Germany, Japan, and Manchuria (16 maps).

Lt. Jonathan W. Sherbourne Collection. Contains a manuscript chart of Annapolis Harbor compiled by Sherbourne, 1818; Spanish manuscript charts of the coasts of South America drawn during the Malaspina Expedition, 1790 (5 charts); and charts of the coasts of Florida and the Carolinas published by Edmund Blunt, 1820–1827 (3 charts).

Farragut Collection. Contains a manuscript chart showing the attack on Mobile Bay by Rear Admiral D.G. Farragut, drawn by Robert Weir, 1864.

Polar Exploration Collection. Contains a lithographic map of the exploration of the *Polaris* along Grinnell Land, drawn by F. Meyers of the United States Army Signal Corp, 1870–1873; undated original engraver's copy of a National Geographic Society map of Antarctica showing Gilbert Grosvenor Trail, prepared by A.H. Bumstead; and a map of field operations of the geological sledging party of the Byrd Antarctica Expedition, 1933–1934.

DIVISION OF GRAPHIC ARTS
Elizabeth M. Harris, Curator, Printing and Topography
(202) 357—2877
Helena E. Wright, Curator, Prints and Printmaking
(202) 357-2877

The Division of Graphic Arts has custody of over 43,500 original prints, drawings, photomechanical prints, and maps that have been collected as study specimens to illustrate most printing techniques. There are also examples of tools used for paper making, etched and engraved plates, and woodblocks. A card catalog (25 drawers) provides access to the collections by name of graphic artist or printer (4 drawers), subject (2 drawers), or donor (2 drawers). Each card generally contains information on title/subject, medium, dimensions, date, artist, and provenance. An exhibition catalog, *What is a Map?* (Washington, D.C.: Smithsonian Press, 1976), illustrated with maps from the Division, describes the process of map making.

The Division also maintains an information file (32 linear feet) concerning relevant subjects and graphic artists. An incomplete check of the file revealed folders for Julius Bien, Charles Eckstein, Frederick von Egglofstein, Maps, and John Walter Osborne.

The Division has custody of approximately 400 maps dating from the sixteenth century. In addition to the major collections described below, there are maps scattered throughout the collections, including Firmin Didot's map of France, printed in relief in seven colors, with a copy of his patent specifications, 1823, and a Laurie and Whittle Atlas, with many insertions, 1806.

Bregan Collection of Maps. Study collection of small-scale hand-colored engraved maps of various countries in Europe and North America, 1558–1818 (163 maps). Map engravers and publishers represented include: Blaeu, Bonne, Emanuel Bowen, John Cary, G. Delahaye, Hondius, Kitchin, Lamarche, W.& D. Lizars, Ortelius, Sanson (31 maps), Seller, and Senex (9 maps). A checklist is available.

Francis Garvan Collection. Engraved and lithographic maps, chiefly of North America and the United States, by John Cary, Currier and Ives, Johann Baptist Homann, Romeyn de Hooghe, William Hooker, Tobias Conrad Lotter, Rowland Lyon, John Melish, Matthaeus Seutter, Cornelis Visscher, and others, 1571–1748 (59 maps).

Miscellaneous Map Collection. Contains miscellaneous page size lithographic maps and several maps prepared for the Smithsonian Institution including a relief map of China by Raphael Pumpelly, a map of the entomological provinces of North America by John L. Le Conte, and a base map of the United States by A. Lindenkohl, engraved by Julius Bien, nineteenth century, (33 maps).

John Walter Osborne Collection. One of the primary study collections in the Division, it contains over 2,500 examples of early photomechanical printing. There are maps printed by Osborne during the initial development of his photolithographic process in Australia, by the American Photo-Lithographic Company of which he was superintendent, and by other American, English, and German photomechanical printers who sent Osborne examples of their work, ca. 1855–1885 (ca. 100 maps). The latter include specimen maps by James Degotardi, Frederick von Egglofstein, J. Noone, and James Ramage.

DIVISION OF MECHANICAL AND CIVIL ENGINEERING
Robert M. Vogel, Curator (202) 357–2058

The Division of Mechanical and Civil Engineering is concerned with documenting technological advances and developments in canal and railroad building, especially bridge and tunnel engineering, power-producing machinery, and pumping and refrigeration equipment.

The following collections contain some 400 maps:

Baltimore and Ohio Railroad Collection. Contains three printed maps (one printed in color) and profiles of the B & O Railroad, 1850–1858.

Canal Records. Log book of George W. Brown, engineer for the Nicaragua Canal Construction Company, contains a manuscript sketch map of the general plan of the Company's location for a transisthmus ship canal; a manuscript and printed map of the valley of the Durama River, apparently showing the route of the Marseille Canal; and a volume containing a printed map and longitudinal profiles of the Marseille Canal issued by the Department of Bouches-du-Rhône, ca. 1874.

Conrail Collection. Printed maps of cities in the Central Atlantic and Midwestern States showing rail facilities for the Pennsylvania Railroad, 1921–1946 (128 maps).

Fine Print Collection. Contains manuscript topographic maps and profiles of the Western Railroad experimental line by H. Stebbins, and the Boston and Worcester Railroad by G.B. Parroll, 1847 (6 maps); a printed panoramic map of Lowell, Massachusetts, 1876; and a series of lithographic maps of railroad lines, chiefly in Massachusetts, by G.B. Parroll and others, 1837–1847 (12 maps).

Hudson Highland Bridge Collection. Manuscript and printed location, survey, and topographic maps relating to the vicinity of the Hudson Highland Bridge and the northeastern highlands. Manuscript right-of-way maps of the New England Railway, 1874–1904 (49 maps), showing property owners. Finding aid available.

Mechanical and Civil Engineering History Collection. Contains a few unrelated maps including 2 volumes and separate sheets of Sanborn maps of Woonsocket, Rhode Island, one heavily annotated apparently by the Royal Insurance Company of Liverpool, England, 1892, 1903; annotated maps of New York City, 1870s; and printed maps of the Erie Canal, ca. 1817, and the Mirama Railroad.

George S. Morison Collection. Contains a large number of printed and manuscript railroad location maps and profiles, topographic surveys, and city plans chiefly relating to Morison's work as a civil engineer building railroad bridges in Missouri, New York, and several other states, 1873–1903, and some maps relating to the Panama Canal, ca. 1894–1900 (ca. 150 maps). A general inventory is available.

DIVISION OF PHYSICAL SCIENCES
Deborah J. Warner, Curator, History of Astronomy and
Meteorology (202) 357-2482

The Division of Physical Sciences collects materials relating to the history of astronomy, cartography, chemistry, physics, and surveying, including over 540 made and used geodetic and surveying instruments, the largest public collection in North America. As an aid to its acquisitions and research programs, the Division maintains an extensive, unique card file containing all available information on United States and foreign instrument makers (14 file drawers) and a collection of nineteenth and twentieth century trade literature (12 linear feet). A card catalog, organized by format and subject, describes the Division's holdings of 29 globes, 40 maps, and other related materials. Pertinent collections are:

Celestial Chart Collection. Contains published charts by the following cartographers or atlas publishers: John Bevis, Johann Elert Bode, Elijah H. Burritt, Andreas Cellarius, Georg Christoph Eimmart, John Flamsteed, J. B. Homann, and Antonio Zatta, 1690–1835 (40 items). A number of these charts are described in the exhibition catalog, *Celestial Images* (Boston: Massachusetts, 1985), which describes sixty-nine celestial charts that were on display in the National Museum of American History, May 16–August 23, 1985.

Documents Collection. Contains a variety of miscellaneous materials including surveyors' notebooks dated 1783 and 1885, the latter pertaining to a United States Coast and Geodetic Survey in Alaska; water-color sketches of geodetic work in Eastport, Maine, 1887, and a plane table scene by George E. Gladwin, 1895; and United States General Land Office instructions for Deputy Surveyors for Ohio, Indiana, and Michigan with annotations, 1851.

Andrew Ellicott Collection. Consists of surveying instruments including transits, telescopes, and a portable quadrant made and used by Ellicott, 1784–1817 (10 instruments). Also, his notebook of astonomical observations concerning the United States-Spain boundary survey, 1797–1801, and an accompanying journal.

W. and L.E. Gurley Company Collection. Consists of business records relating to the work of this surveying equipment and instrument manufacturer, 1860–1920 (39 cubic feet).

Globe Collection. Contains two rare globes, an undated, unsigned Islamic celestial globe, ca. 1620, and a brass and silver celestial globe from Lahore, India, seventeenth century. Other globes include a celestial German globe, ca. 1625, pocket globe by James Ferguson, ca. 1750, and nineteenth century celestial and terrestrial globes by G. and J. Cary, Gilman Joslin, C. Lancaster, H.B. Nims, Quimby, and J. Wilson. Also, Rhodes W. Fairbridge Collection of eleven thematic globes, 1962, showing geodesy, oceanic tides, January temperatures, July temperatures, volcanoes, geomagnetism, seismology, gravimetry, jet streams and hurricane tracks, ocean currents, and January isobars.

James Griswold Collection. Surveying and drawing instruments used by Griswold during his survey of the Erie Railroad (6 items).

Instrument Collection. This collection is worldwide in scope (English, French, German, Japanese, Russian, and Swiss), but recent acquisition policy emphasizes instruments made in the United States. A large number of the instruments were used by and obtained from the United States Coast and Geodetic Survey, the United States Geological Survey, and the United States Military Academy. Each instrument is described on a catalog card and its provenance indicated, if known. Instruments in the collection used by noted American surveyors include the zenith telescope designed and used by Andrew Talcott for the Ohio-Michigan Boundary Survey in 1846, a surveying compass used by David Rittenhouse, and a measuring chain believed to have been used by Isaac Roberdeau during the original survey of Washington, D.C., ca. 1793.

The collection includes the following geodetic and surveying instruments:

Instruments	*Number*	*Dates*
Alidade and Plane Table	24	1625–1936
Aneroid Barometer	32	19th–20th century
Artificial Horizon	3	19th century
Base Bars, Chains, Tapes	41	1780–19th century
Circumferentor, Semicircle, Graphometer	25	1622–19th century
Clinometer	7	19th century
Distance Measuring Instruments	10	19th century
Geodetic Theodolite	4	1850–1892
Heliotrope, Signal Lamp	20	20th century
Land Traveler's Compass	30	19th–20th century
Level	58	19th–20th century
Odometer	24	1723–1914
Repeating Circle	3	19th century
Solar Compass	6	19th century
Survey Marker	31	17th–19th century
Surveying Accessories, Drawing Instruments	31	17th–19th century

Instruments	*Number*	*Dates*
Surveying Compass	71	1750s–1800s
Theodolite	50	1780–1942
Transit	28	1790–1913
Tripod	69	19th century–1942
Verticle Circle	2	1880s
Zenith Telescope	7	19th century

John Johnson Collection. Contains his surveying instruments, including theodolite (7 items), a set of field notes, and a manuscript map pertaining to his survey of the Maine-New Brunswick boundary, 1817–1820. Also, description of equipment used by Johnson.

United States Coast and Geodetic Photographs Collection. Relevant subjects include cartography, aerial photography, geodesy, and topography (0.5 linear foot).

NATIONAL PHILATELIC COLLECTION
Reidar Norby, Curator, World Philately and Postal History
(202) 357–1796
James H. Bruns, Curator, United States Philately and Postal History
(202) 357–1796

The National Philatelic Collection contains more than 14 million postage stamps and related materials concerning postal history and philately. It includes a unique collection of 10,579 specimen map stamps collected by Allan Lee between 1943 and 1976 and mounted in 25 volumes. This collection contains every map stamp cataloged by Scott, Minkus, and Stanley Gibbons through 1976, as well as related designs. Most are mint issues, dated between 1867 and 1976. The collection is organized by subject: world, map elements, geographic areas, nations, islands and archipelagos, genesis of United States, routes, ancient maps, political and territorial disputes, errors and varieties, miscellaneous, souvenir sheets, unused stamps, omnibus issues, marginal maps stamps, and collateral materials. Many mountings also contain detailed information concerning the cartographic design, stamp designer, type of production, and historical description.

In addition, the National Philatelic Collection has custody of the original survey journal of Hugh Finlay (1773–1774), on permanent loan from the National Archives and Records Administration (B19, RG 28), and maintains a small map collection of some 130 United States and foreign route and postal maps for exhibit and study purposes. Some of the maps are annotated. There are several early post route maps of Germany and Central Europe, engraved and published by Johann Baptist Homann, Tobias Conrad Lotter, and Matthaeus Seutter during the eighteenth century, but most were issued during the last one hundred years. Several United States postal route maps are autographed by Postmaster Generals. A few manuscript maps show historical stage and post routes in the United States for the Northeast and Far West. There are also photographic prints of a map of Archangel, Russia, prepared by the Allied Mapping Section, 1919.

The Library contains a photographic reproduction of Christopher Colles, *Survey of the Roads of the United States*, 1789 (86 maps); an autographed set of Walter Klinefelter's privately printed limited editions, *The World Minutely Mapped An Atlas on Postal Paper* (1952), and *Studies in Postal Cartography* (1962, 1969, 1973); and many postal studies which contain sketch maps of postal routes. The George Turner Collection, formerly one of the largest privately owned collections of philatelic literature, contains atlases designed specifically for stamp collectors, including copies issued by the C.H. Mekeel Stamp and Publishing Company, 1895, and the Scott Stamp and Coin Company, 1894.

The Postage Stamp Album Collection contains specimen albums which often include maps. Early examples are the *Album Timbres-Poste Orné de Cartes* (Paris, 1862) and *International Postage and Stamp Album Nineteenth Century* (New York, ca. 1908).

SMITHSONIAN INSTITUTION LIBRARIES (SIL) SPECIAL COLLECTIONS BRANCH
Dibner Library
Ellen B. Wells, Chief Librarian
(202) 257–1568

The Special Collections Branch has approximately 25,000 valuable and scarce works relating to the history of science, technology, applied art, aerospace, and natural history. About sixty percent of the holdings have been cataloged in machine-readable form and are available through on-line terminals in the various SIL library branches or through the *SIL Catalogue,* a computer-output-microfiche guide. Remaining titles are described in the SIL Union Catalog. A search of the machine-readable catalog indicated 179 works on voyages and travels, including Bernhard von Breydenbach's *Sanctaru Peregrinationu in Montem Syon* (Mainz, 1486), the first edition of the earliest illustrated travel book, with a woodcut map. Special Collections materials are not available for loan.

The most significant collection is the Dibner History of Science and Technology Collection. Collected by Dr. Bern Dibner and donated to SIL in 1974–1977, it contains 1,619 manuscripts dating from the twelfth century. A number of these unique works relate to early surveying and mapping, including a letter by Abraham Ortelius, 1597; holograph manuscript on surveying by Daniel Mayer with colored illustrations, 1607; manuscript on geometry and land measurement by Sebastianus David Louys, 1681; 2 letters by Joseph Nicolas de L'Isle, one concerning M. Kemfer's map, 1733–1741; a letter by Jean Philippe Baratier concerning determination of longitude, 1738; 4 documents by Jacque Cassini relating to compasses and funding, 1739–1747; manuscript instructional books on navigation by Joseph Barber with illustrations, including instructions on nautical chart-making and 3 charts, 1759–1761; Spanish manuscript work book on navigation with 3 navigational charts, 1758; manuscript treatise in Danish on mathematics by Christian Carl Lous containing a section on land surveying, heavily illustrated, including three topographic maps, 1770s; manuscript notes and sketch maps bound with John Hood's work on *Plotting and Calculating Surveys* (1772); correspondence by Alexander Dallas Bache concerning Charles Schott and other topics, 1837–1858 (5 items); work on geometry and trigonometry by E. Knight, including surveying, and the use of the plane table, theodolite, and circumferentor, ca. 1790; letters by David Rittenhouse, John Ewing, Robert Patterson, and Andrew Ellicott concerning John Hall, a surveyor, 1796; a bound volume of manuscript maps and sketches of canals in Pennsylvania and Maryland by Thomas Gilpin and Charles De Krafft, 1769–1770 (13 items); holograph manuscript concerning the measurement of the earth's diameter by Thomas William, ca. 1770–1788; letters and documents of Jean Dominique comte de Cassini, one concerning Didier Robert de Vaugondy's armillary sphere (5 items), 1772–1817; Italian holograph manuscript on the sphere, eighteenth century; bound French manuscript on the principles of the sphere and the universal map, eighteenth century; manuscript treatises with illustrations on geography and cosmography by Lorenzo Lagomarsino, 1711–1713; letter by Pierre Armand Petit Dufrénoy concerning a geological map, 1841; manuscript in French concerning topographic mapping, including the use of photolithography, undertaken by the Belgium War Department, ca. 1870; papers of William Smith include correspondence and a list of maps exhibited by the British Museum commemorating Smith's work in geological mapping; letter from Francis Beaufort to John Lubbock concerning the latter's gnomonic projection, 1850; letters from Adolphus Washington Greely, one with colored map of Antarctica; letter from Adolf Erik Nordenskiold concerning history of mapping in the Pacific Ocean, 1882–1890; and letters sent by Louis Charles Karpinski, 1931–1937. These materials are described in *Manuscripts of the Dibner Collection* (Washington, D.C.: Smithsonian Press, 1985), available from Science History Publications/USA, P.O. Box 493, Canton, MA. 02021.

A small map collection of some 25 printed maps includes celestial maps by Johann Baptist Homann (5 items); two atlases relating to the geology of Missouri, 1873–1874; Henry S. Tanner's wall map of the United States, 1841; and John Reid's *American Atlas*, 1796.

National Ocean Service (NOS) (Commerce Department—National Oceanic and Atmospheric Administration)—Washington Science Center Building. **See entry G20, Section 2**

C9 Smithsonian Institution—Joseph Henry Papers

1 a. *Smithsonian Institution Building, Room 149*
1000 Jefferson Drive, S.W.
Washington, D.C. 20560
(202) 357-2787

e. Marc Rothenberg, Acting Editor

2–3d. In cooperation with the American Philosophical Society and the National Academy of Sciences, this project is responsible for assembling copies of Henry's papers for the preparation of letterpress and microfilm editions of his work. Henry, one of America's leading nineteenth century scientists, corresponded with a wide range of scientists, explorers, and publishers, including a number associated with mapping and surveying. He served as the first secretary of the Smithsonian Institution from 1846–1878, and directed the compilation of weather charts by the Smithsonian Weather Service, ca. 1865–1872. Some 70,000 documents, chiefly his correspondence and diaries, will eventually be collected and published in microfilm edition, with selected annotated materials appearing in a 15-volume letterpress edition, 5 of which have been issued. The collected documents are indexed by subject and name and a hardcopy index is available in the Smithsonian Institution Archives (B22). Pertinent subject headings, with the number of citations listed in parentheses, are Army Engineers (37), Civil Engineering (127), United States Coast Survey (460), Geology (1361), Internal Improvements (36), United States Naval Observatory (148), Physical Geography (276), Surveys and Explorations (1325), Wilkes Expedition (89), and Smithsonian Weather Service (1429). Correspondents of interest include Cleveland Abbe, Henry L. Abbot, John J. Abert, John H. Alexander, Julius Bien, Edmund Blunt, George William Blunt, Mathew Carey, Richard D. Cutts, P.S. Duval, Andrew Ellicott, William Hemsley Emory, Joseph Enthoffer, George Featherstonhaugh, Henry Gannett, John D. Graham, Henry Harrisse, Ferdinand R. Hassler, Ferdinand V. Hayden, Jedediah Hotchkiss, Alexander von Humboldt, Andrew A. Humphreys, Clarence King, Pierre L'Enfant, Adolf Lindenkohl, Stephen H. Long, Elias Loomis, Jules Marcou, Matthew F. Maury, Sidney Morse, Walter L. Nicholson, Joseph N. Nicollet, David Dale Owen, John Wesley Powell, Raphael Pumpelly, C.A. Schott, Henry S. Tanner, Henry F. Walling, Gouveneur K. Warren, George M. Wheeler, and Charles Wilkes.

C10 White House—Office of the Curator

1 a. *1600 Pennsylvania Avenue, N.W.*
Washington, D.C. 20500
(202) 456-2550

b. 9:00 A.M.-5:30 P.M. Monday-Friday

c. Admission by appointment only.

d. Clement Conger, Curator

2-3. The White House serves as the official residence of the President of the United States and as a museum. In addition to architectural drawings and plans, landscape plans, and other archival collections relating to the White House and its grounds, the curatorial staff maintains a small collection of early maps of the District of Columbia, including James Thackara and John Vallance's plan of the City of Washington, 1792.

D Data Banks

Data Banks Entry Format (D)

1. General Information
   a. address; telephone numbers
   b. hours of service
   c. conditions of access
   d. name/title of director and key staff members
2. Description of Data Files (hard-data and bibliographic-reference)
3. Bibliographic Aids Facilitating Use of Storage Media

Agricultural Online Access (AGRICOLA) (Agriculture Department—National Agricultural Library) **See entry A29**

Agricultural Research Service (ARS) (Agriculture Department)—Remote Sensing Research Laboratory **See entry E1**

American Geological Institute (AGI)—GEOREF Information Services **See entry J2**

D1 BRS Information Technologies

1 a. *Crystal Gateway II*
1225 Jefferson Davis Highway
Arlington, Virginia 22202
(703) 486–5652
(800) 345–4277 (Toll Free Customer Service)

d. Paula Swope, Regional Representative

2. BRS (Bibliographic Retrieval Service) Information Technologies is a private organization that provides computer-searchable versions of products produced by leading information publishers through its BRS/SEARCH Service. BRS can provide offline printing and automatic search service whenever specified databases are updated. BRS/SEARCH Services includes more than 80 databases. The following databases contain cartographic data.

AGRICOLA.—See entry A29.

COMPENDEX.—A computerized version of the *Engineering Index* produced by Engineering Information, Inc., New York. It provides abstracts from 3,500 worldwide engineering and technical journals, reports, and books. Indexing terms include aerial photography, aviation mapping, computer graphics, geographic surveying, maps and mapping, mines and mining maps, photogrammetry, remote sensing, and surveying, 1970 to the present (1.5 million records).

DISSERTATION ABSTRACTS ONLINE.—Subject, title, and author guide to American dissertations microfilmed by University Microfilms International, Ann Arbor, Michigan, 1861 to the present (872,500 records). Also see entry A20, Microform Reading Room.

ERIC.—See entry D4.

GPO MONTHLY CATALOG.—The machine-readable version of the *Monthly Catalog of United States Government Publications,* produced by the Government Printing Office. It includes records of maps and other pertinent materials, 1976 to the present (227,300 records). See entry K8.

MEDLINE.—The National Library of Medicine online index to articles from more than 3000 worldwide journals, 1966 to the present (4,687,000 records). See entry A31.

NTIS.—The National Technical Information Service database contains unclassified research, development, and engineering reports prepared by more than 240 Federal agencies, 1964 to the present (1,122,000 records). See entry K12.

NEDS.—The National Environmental Data Referral Service Database (NEDS), produced by the National Environmental Satellite, Data, and Information Services (NESDIS) (see entry D8), contains unpublished environmental data files, data from remote sensing satellites, and publications, manuals, and catalogs including subjects such as geography.

3. The *BRS/SEARCH Service Database Catalog* is available on request. A monthly *BRS Bulletin* provides information on new databases, searching strategies, and training schedules. A *BRS/SEARCH Service Users Manual* and one page summaries and detailed guides for each database are also available.

D2 Census Bureau (Commerce Department)—National Clearinghouse for Census Data Services

1 a. *State and Regional Programs Staff*
Data User Services Division
Washington, D.C. 20233
(301) 763-1580

d. John Kavaliunas

2. This office serves as a clearinghouse for private organizations which provide informational and technical services relating to Census Bureau computerized tapes, including digitized cartographic data. Services provided by these private organizations include preparation of census map copies, address matching/geocoding services, assistance in use of GBF/DIME Files, online access to data, information or services relating to computer graphics, and training in workshops.

3. An address list provides the names of organizations registered with the National Clearinghouse along with the services they provide.

Census Bureau Data Bases (Commerce Department) **See entry G5**

Census Bureau Library (Commerce Department) **See entry A8**

Central Intelligence Agency (CIA) **See entry G6**

Computer Mapping and Special Analysis Laboratory (University of Maryland—Department of Geography) **See entry F11, section 5**

Defense Department—Defense Technical Information Center (DTIC) **See entry K6**

Defense Mapping Agency (DMA) (Defense Department)—Scientific Data Department **See entry G8**

D3 DIALOG Information Services, Inc.

1 a. *1901 North Moore Street, Suite 809*
Arlington, Virginia 22209
(703) 553-8455

b. 9:00 A.M.-5:00 P.M. Monday-Friday

d. Richard Caputo, Manager

2. DIALOG Information Services, Inc. is a commercial organization that provides online computer access to some 220 bibliographic and numeric databases containing more than 110 million records through regional offices in Palo Alto, California, New York, Boston, Houston, Washington, Los Angeles, Chicago, Toronto, London, Sydney, Tokyo, and other cities. Services provided include ordering complete text of documents on line (DIALORDER), automatic search runs following the updating of selected files (Selective Dissemination of Information Service), information searches by subject (DIALINDEX), and training sessions.

The following databases contain relevant cartographic data.

AGRICOLA.—See entry A29.

COMPENDEX.—See entry D1.

DISSERTATION ABSTRACTS.—See entry D1.

ERIC.—See entry D4.

GEOARCHIVE.—Provides an index to 5,000 geoscience serials and books by Geosystems, London, 1969 to the present (538,500 records). Approximately 100,000 geological maps from the Institute of Geological Sciences libraries (England) are currently being indexed and added to the database.

GEOREF.—The American Geological Institute index to 4,500 international journals, books, conference papers, government publications, and maps concerned with geology, geochemistry, geophysics, mineralogy, paleontology, petrology, and seismology, 1919 to the present for North American material and 1967 to the present for worldwide material (1,005,000 records). See entry J2.

LC MARC.—The Library of Congress machine-readable database, 1968 to the present (1,984,000 records). See entry A20, Computer Catalog Center.

MEDLINE.—See entries D1 and A31.

NTIS. See entries D1 and K12.

REMARC.—The Library of Congress bibliographic database for materials cataloged from 1897 to 1980 (2,409,000 records). See entry A20, Computer Catalog Center.

3. A copy of the current *DIALOG Database Catalog* is available on request.

Earth Resources Observations Systems (EROS) Data Center (Interior Department—Geological Survey) See entry E7

Earth Satellite Corporation (EarthSat) See entry E4

D4 Education Resources Information Center (ERIC) (National Institute of Education (NIE)

1 a. *1200 19th Street, N.W.*
Washington, D.C. 20208
(202) 254–7934 (Information)
(202) 254–5500 (Central ERIC)

b. 7:30 A.M.–4:30 P.M. Monday–Friday

c. Open to the public.

d. Charles W. Hoover, Chief

2. The Educational Resources Information Center (ERIC) is an information system devoted primarily to English language literature pertaining to outstanding programs and research in education. The present database contains more than 560,000 records, including a small number (107) relating to cartography. The ERIC database can be searched online through BRS/SEARCH (D1), DIALOG (D3), and ORBIT (D10). A *Dictionary of ERIC Search Services* (1981. 83 pages), listing organizations nationwide providing computerized searches of the ERIC database with fee schedules, is available on request from the ERIC Processing and Referencing Facility, 4833 Rugby Avenue, Suite 303, Bethesda, Maryland 20014 (telephone 301/656–9723).

Reproductions of the documents and articles cited in ERIC are available in microfilm or paper copy through the ERIC Documents Reproduction Service (EDRS), 3030 N. Fairfax Drive, Suite 200, Arlington, Virginia 22201, (telephone 703/841–1212).

3. A monthly journal of abstracts, *Resources in Education* (RIE), lists new research reports and educational programs. The monthly *Current Index to Journals in Education* (CIJE) provides a guide to more than 700 periodicals. The *Directory of ERIC Microfiche Collections* (1983. 67 pages) lists all organizations in the United States and overseas with a sizeable collection of microfiche.

Engineer Topographic Laboratories (ETL) (Army Corps of Engineers) **See entry E5**

D5 Federal Interagency Coordinating Committee on Digital Cartography (FICCDC) (Geological Survey—National Mapping Division)

1 a. *516 National Center*
Reston, Virginia 22092
(703) 860–6221

d. Larry L. Amos, Committee Secretary

2. The Federal Interagency Coordinating Committee (FICCDC) on Digital Cartography was established by the Office of Management and Budget (OMB) in 1983 to aid in coordinating Federal agencies' digital cartographic activities, to develop standards and specifications for the production of digital cartographic data, and to report annually on

the activities and accomplishments of the committee. FICCDC consists of a Steering Committee (Rupert B. Southard, USGS, Chairman 703/860–6231) and 5 working groups. These are the User Applications Working Group, responsible for facilitating the application of digital cartographic data (Frank Maloney, National Ocean Service, Chairman 301/443–8071), Data Requirements Working Group, charged with identifying Federal requirements for digital cartographic data and establishing appropriate coordinating and data digitizing priorities (Terry W. Gossard, Forest Service, Chairman, 703/235–8184), Data Standards Working Group, responsible for reviewing and developing digital cartographic data standards that will facilitate data interchange within the Federal establishment (Gale TeSelle, Soil Conservation Service, Chairman 202/447–5421), Technology Exchange Working Group, which monitors current methods and technologies for collecting, managing, and using digital cartographic data (Stephen Guptill, USGS, Chairman 703/860–6345), and the Reports Working Group, which collects, maintains, and reports to OMB on Federal digital data programs (Sandra Shaw, State Department, Chairman 202/647–1428).

4. The Committee publishes an *Annual Report to the Director, Office of Management and Budget,* comprising the reports of each of the working groups. It also issues an occasional newsletter, *FDC Newsletter.* Both publications are available on request from the Committee Secretary.

Fish and Wildlife Service (Interior Department)—Western Energy and Land Use Team (WELUT) **See entry G12**

D6 Geological Survey (USGS) (Department of Interior)—Office of Data Administration

1 a. *806 National Center*
12201 Sunrise Valley Drive
Reston, Virginia 22092
(703) 860–6086

b. The databases described below are available through NCIC (K12) or through the office or person cited.

d. Theodore M. Albert, Data Administrator

2. This office is responsible for coordinating and standardizing all machine-readable scientific, technical, spatial, and bibliographic databases in the USGS. The following cartographic databases are arranged by USGS divisions.

GEOLOGY DIVISION

Geologic Map Data (GEOMAPFIL), comprises a catalog of medium- and small-scale published geologic maps of the conterminous United States and Canada issued by the USGS and by State geologic surveys from 1930 to 1978. The data lists generalized features displayed on the maps such as dominant rock type, average elevation, and man-made features. For further information on this database, contact J. Nicholas Van Driel (703/860–6034).

Index to Geologic Maps (GEOINDEX), contains index data on geologic maps of the

United States and its territories obtained from published materials received by the USGS Library and the Division's Geologic Inquiries Group (GIG). Some of the maps indexed date from the 1840s. Information is available from the USGS Public Inquiries Office. (G14).

LORAN-C Map Directory (LORMAP), comprises 824 records on magnetic tape and disc of the National Ocean Service LORAN-C Map Directory. It is available from the Office of Energy and Marine Geology, Quissett Campus, Woods Hole, MA 02543 (617/548–8700).

Western Integrated Topographic Database, comprises digital data of shaded relief maps of the Western United States. This data is derived from Defense Mapping Agency digital maps at a scale of 1:250,000. Access is currently limited to the Department of Defense.

INFORMATION SYSTEMS DIVISIONS

Earth Science Information System (ESIS), is a comprehensive management information database comprising an inventory of the scientific, technical, and bibliographic automated databases and systems of USGS. These databases include information about cartography, geography, and satellite remote sensing. A brochure describing this system is available.

NATIONAL MAPPING DIVISION (NMD)

Aerial Photography Information System (APIS), contains 14,350 administrative and operational data records of aerial photography acquired for NMD's various mapping programs from 1970 to the present. The data, covering the United States, United States Territories, Antarctica, and Alaska, contains information on contract awards, acceptance and delivery of photography, camera and lens specifications, coverage and costs. Access is limited to NMD.

Aerial Photography Summary Record System (APSRS), contains 203,000 records about aerial photography of the United States, Puerto Rico, and the Virgin Islands held by various Federal, state, municipal, and local agencies, as well as private companies. The data spans the period 1935 to the present. For more information, contact the National Cartographic Information Center (E7).

Geographic Names Information System (GNIS), contains five databases that provide information on some two million names of geographic places and features in the United States and its territories. The databases include the National Geographic Names Database, the USGS Topographic Map Names Database, the National Atlas of the United States Database, and the Board on Geographic Names Database. The latter database extends back to 1890. A *Geographic Names Information System Users Guide* has recently been published (USGS Open-file Report 84-551, 1984). For further information contact Roger L. Payne (703/860–6261). A fact sheet available from NCIC provides a brief description of the different databases.

Inventory of Published Maps (T-70), comprises an inventory of maps published by NMD, the Defense Map Agency (15-Minute United States 1:50,000 scale) and the Bureau of Land Management (1:1000,000 scale) from 1884 to 1978.

Main Image File (MIF), contains more than 1,750,000 operational records of aerial photography of the United States and satellite imagery coverage of the world maintained by the EROS Data Center, Mundt Federal Building, Sioux Falls, South Dakota 57189 (605/594–6511). The file is used for research and inquiry purposes by NCIC (E7). It contains the records of the Bureau of Indian Affairs, Bureau of Land Management, Bureau of Reclamation, Department of the Air Force, Department of the Army, Department of the Navy, National Aeronautics and Space Administration, National Space Technology Laboratory, and United States Army Corps of Engineers.

Map and Chart Information System File (MCIS), comprises some 150,000 descriptor records of USGS topographic maps, National Ocean Service nautical charts, United States Army Corps of Engineer charts, and Defense Mapping Agency maps of the United States issued between 1884 and the present. For information contact Phil Guss, NCIC (703/860–6508).

National Cartographic Information Center Cartographic Catalog File, contains 38,000 bibliographic records of descriptive information about historical maps described in the Library of Congress MARC file, summary descriptions of geodetic data, digital cartographic data and aerial photographs. The information in this data file is limited to the United States and its possessions from 1722 to the present.

National Cartographic Information System Topographic Quadrangle (NCISTQ), is an operational database comprising 52,245 records of map information from the topographic quadrangle map series collected in 1978. A microfiche program is available. Contact NCIC (703/860–6508).

National Digital Cartographic Databases (US GEO DATA), include digital elevation data, available in the form of digital elevation models (DEM) of the United States at scales of 1:24,000 and 1:250,000; digital planimetric data, distributed as digital line graphs (DLG), which provide base line map information at scales ranging from 1:24,000 to 1:2,000,000; land use and land cover digital files produced and distributed at scale of 1:250,000 and 1:100,000; and GNIS, described above. Free information sheets, order forms, and price lists for any USGEO DATA are available from NCIC. These files are described in *USGS Digital Cartographic Data Standards* (USGS Circular 895), in seven separately bound chapters: (A) Overview and USGS Activities, (B) Digital Elevation Models, (C) Digital Line Graphs from 1:24,000 - scale Maps, (D) Digital Line Graphs from 1:2,000,000 - scale Maps, (E) Land Use and Land Cover Digital Data, (F) Geographic Names Information System, and (G) Digital Line Graph Attribute Coding Standards.

Worldwide Banks, comprises sequential data files providing worldwide coverage of coastlines, primary drainage, international boundaries, and some railroad lines at small map scales for the period 1966–1967 and 1973–1977. Copies of the data are available from NTIS (K12).

WATER RESOURCES DIVISION

Flood Map Inventory (FMI), is a bibliographic data file containing data for all published flood maps prepared by the Water Resources Division from 1913 to 1979. Flood-prone area maps comprise most of the file. Data is available for the United States and its territories covered by 7.5- and 15- minute quadrangles. Information on FMI can be obtained from the Water Resources Division (703/860–6872).

Full State and National Digitized Hydrological Unit Lines Databases, provide digitized hydrographic boundaries of major United States river basins by state at a scale of 1:1,000,000 for the series of uniform State Hydrologic Unit maps prepared by USGS and the United States Water Resources Council. *The Hydrologic Unit Name and Description Data Base* (Hundbase) contains the names and the descriptions of the regions, subregions, accounting units and cataloging units comprising these State Hydrologic Units. For information on these files contact the Office of Water Data Coordination (703/860–6935).

MINERALS MANAGEMENT SERVICE

Geophysical Mapping System (GMS), comprises 1,000,000 records of cartographic data for geologic, geophysical, and bottom sample base maps used for lease-tract evaluation of California, 1968 to present. Information about this system is available from Pacific OCS Region, 1340 W. Sixth Street, Los Angeles, CA 90017 (213/688–2046).

3. A basic guide to USGS data bases is *Scientific and Technical, Spatial, and Bibliographic Data Bases and Systems of the U.S. Geological Survey,* 1983 (USGS Circular 817, Revised Edition).

Geological Survey Library (Interior Department) **See entry A12**

Government Printing Office (GPO) **See entry K8**

Land Management Bureau (BLM) Interior Department—Division of Engineering **See entry G17**

Library of Congress Computer Catalog Center **See entry A20**

Machine-Readable Cataloging (MARC) Maps Database (Library of Congress—Geography and Map Division) **See entry A21**

D7 Mines Bureau (Interior Department)—Minerals Availability Division

1 a. *2401 E Street, N.W.*
Washington, D.C. 20241
(202) 634-1138

c. Open to the public.

d. Robert L. Marovelli, Chief

2. The Bureau of Mines conducts research on mineral materials and collects and analyzes mineral reserve information to help ensure that the United States has an adequate mineral supply to meet future requirements.

As part of its program, the Bureau maintains a cartographic-related database known as the Mineral Industry Location System (MILS), a location subsystem of the computerized Minerals Availability System (MAS). MILS contains information on more than 135,000 mineral locations and processing plants principally in the United States. Each entry includes such information as name(s) of the mine or plant, location, mineral commodities, type of operation, status, bibliography, map name, and cross-references. Most of this information is derived from the literature and files of the Bureau of Mines, United States Geological Survey, State geology departments, universities, mining companies, and other Federal agencies.

This data is available in two formats: magnetic computer tapes and computer-generated plastic map overlays at various scales and projections that show cluster point locations supplemented by computer printouts of site-specific data keyed to the overlay cluster points. Map overlay data can be plotted for USGS quadrangles, states, and specific commodities.

The magnetic data tapes are available from the Minerals Availability Field Office in Denver, Colorado (Harold Bennett, Chief 303/236–5200); map overlays of the east, midwest, and intermountain area of the west are available from the Intermountain Field Operation Center in Denver (George Schottler, Chief, Branch of Minerals Availability 303/236–0423); map overlays of Far Western states are available from the Western Field Operations Center in Spokane, Washington (Robert Weldin, Chief, Branch of Minerals Availability 509/439–7917); and map overlays of Alaska from the Alaska Field Operations Center, Anchorage (Donald Blasko, Chief 907/261–2455).

3. The MILS system is described in *MILS: The Mineral Industry Location System of the Federal Bureau of Mines,* by Andrew W. Berg and Fred V. Carrillo (Bureau of Mines Information Circular 8815, 1980. 24 p.). This circular contains a sample of a plastic overlay map.

National Aeronautics and Space Administration Remote Console (NASA RECON) **See entry G18, section 3**

National Archives and Records Administration (NARA)—Machine-Readable Branch **See entry B19, (RG349, 370)**

National Cartographic Information Center (NCIC) (Interior Department—Geological Survey) **See entry E7**

D8 National Environmental Satellite, Data, and Information Service (NESDIS) (Commerce Department—National Oceanic and Atmospheric Administration)

1 a. *Federal Building No. 4*
Washington, D.C. 20233
(202) 763–4690 (General Information)

b. Hours vary.

c. Open to the public. Appointments are recommended.

d. William Bishop, Acting Administrator

2–3. NESDIS is responsible for operating the civilian earth-observing satellite systems, for processing and analyzing global data bases for meteorology, oceanography, solid-earth geophysics and solar-terrestrial sciences, and for storing and disseminating the largest environmental data system in the world. 2 NOAA weather satellites transmit images of weather and surface conditions of the entire earth on a daily basis.

ASSESSMENT AND INFORMATION SERVICE CENTER (AISC)
3300 Whitehaven Street, N.W.
Washington, D.C. 20235
Joan C. Hock, Director (202) 634–7251

AISC coordinates NOAA's library and information program. The library is described in entry A33. The National Environmental Data Referral Service (NEDRES) (Gerald S. Barton, Chief 202/634–7722) maintains a publicly accessible, computer-searchable catalog and index containing descriptions of environmental data files, published data sources, data file documentation references, and environmental organizations that make data available (entry D1). The *NEDRES Database User Guide* provides a detailed description of the database.

NATIONAL CLIMATIC DATA CENTER (NCDC)
Federal Building
Asheville, North Carolina 28801
(704) 259–0682 (Information)
Kenneth D. Hadeen, Director (704) 259–0476

NCDC is the largest climatic data center in the world. It serves as the collection center and custodian for weather data generated by the National Weather Service, the Air Force and Navy, the Federal Aviation Administration, the Coast Guard, and individual observers.

Information Services Division (ISD)
Herschel L. Suits, Chief (704) 259–0680

This Division maintains a collection of some 215 million weather records, including over 4 million synoptic weather maps in more than 30 series. The major data sets and map series are described below.

Atlas of Marine Data, 1800–1969, and Surface Marine Observations, 1970 to the present.—90 magnetic tapes. Marine data from ship logs, ship weather reporting forms, automatic observing buoys, and foreign meteorological services ordered by 10-degree Marsden Square and Sub-Square. Worldwide coverage.

Atlas of Mean Winter Temperature Departures From the Long Term Mean Over the Contiguous United States, 1895–1983.—1 volume; 2 microfiche.

Atlas of Monthly and Seasonal Temperature Departures from the Long-Term Mean for the Contiguous United States, 1895–1983 (1 volume for each of the 4 seasons).

Climatic Atlas of the United States, 1931–1960.—1 volume, 231 maps.

Composite Moisture Index Charts, 1962 to the present.—21 reels, 35mm microfilm. Computer-plotted and hand-analyzed four-panel charts of the conterminous United States, southern Canada, and northern Mexico showing precipitable water, freezing level, and average relative humidity.

Constant Pressure Charts of North America and the Northern Hemisphere, 1946 to the present.—373 reels, 35mm microfilm.

Daily Weather Maps of the Contiguous United States, weekly series, January 1899 to the present.—97 reels, 35mm microfilm.

Digitized Isopleths of the World, 1800-1970.—14 magnetic tapes. Provides monthly means and standard deviations of wind speed, temperatures, air pressure, and wave heights for the world oceans.

Four-Panel Baroclinic 500—Millibar Height/Vorticity Charts, 1961 to the present.—47 reels, 35mm microfilm. Computer-produced charts of conterminous United States, Canada, and northern Mexico depicting 500—millibar contours.

Historical Climatology Series, 1839-1977.—3 publications. Daily cooperative weather observations maintained at stations in Cooperstown, New York, Yellowstone

National Park and Southeastern Iowa with pertinent topographic maps showing the location and region of each station.

Initial Wind-Wave/Swell/Combined Sea Height Charts, 1979 to the present.—4 reels, 35mm microfilm. Analyzed charts of the Northern Hemisphere.

Mariners Worldwide Guide to Tropical Storms at Sea, 1831-1973.—1 volume; magnetic tape. Supplemented with storm tracks and frequency maps. Also available from NTIS (see entry K12).

Mean Relative Humidity/Vertical-Velocity Charts, 1961 to the present.—45 reels, 35mm microfilm. Computer-produced charts of the United States, Canada, and Mexico.

North American Surface Chart, 1942 to the present.—161 reels, 35mm microfilm. Analyzed surface weather charts of the North American continent.

North Atlantic Atlas Contours, 1850–1970.—27 magnetic tapes. Monthly means and percent frequency of air and sea temperatures, relative humidity, wind speed, visibility, precipitation, cloud cover, wave heights, air pressure, and tropical cyclone occurrence for the North Atlantic Ocean Basin.

Northern Hemisphere Surface Charts, 1954 to the present.—113 reels, 35mm microfilm. Analyzed surface weather charts.

Observed Snow Cover Charts, 1966 to the present.—18 reels, 35mm microfilm. Computer-plotted charts of the conterminous United States and northern Canada.

Observed 24-Hour Precipitation Amounts Charts, 1962 to the present.—21 reels, 35mm microfilm. Computer-plotted charts of the conterminous United States, southern Canada, and northern Mexico.

Pilot Chart Data, 1850–1970.—7 magnetic tapes. 1- and 5-degree quadrangle summaries for wind speed, pressure, and temperatures worldwide. This data was used to produce the United States Navy Marine Climatic Atlas, which is available in hardcopy from NTIS (K12).

Precipitation-Frequency Atlas of the Western United States, 1973.—1 reel, 35mm microfilm. Isopluvial maps.

Radar Summary Charts, 1956 to the present.—350 reels, 35mm microfilm. Hourly analyzed charts of the conterminous Unites States showing cloud formations and precipitation types.

Rainfall Frequency Atlas of the United States, 1961.—1 reel, 35mm microfilm.

Southern Hemisphere Constant Pressure Charts, 1975 to the present.—19 reels, 35mm microfilm. Analyzed charts.

Southern Hemisphere Surface/1000-500 - Millibar Thickness Charts, 1967–1971, 1975 to the present.—16 reels, 35mm microfilm. Computer-analyzed charts.

Storm Data, monthly series, 1922 to the present.—68 microfiche. Since 1981, includes analyzed map of outstanding storms and a computer-generated climatological map of all tornadoes each month, 1916 to the present.

Synoptic Daily Weather Maps, 1899–1978.—52 reels, 35mm microfilm. Daily sea-level maps, 1899–1971, and daily 500 - millibar maps of the northern hemisphere, 1944–1971.

Tropical Cyclones Track Charts of the North Atlantic Ocean, 1871–1980.—9 microfiche; magnetic tape.

Tropical Strip Surface Chart, 1969 to the present.—35 reels, 35mm microfilm. Analyzed surface charts of the earth from 30 degrees North to 50 degrees South latitude.

Tropical Strip Upper Air Charts, 1975 to the present.— 29 reels, 35mm microfilm. Analyzed constant pressure charts covering 60 degrees North to 50 degrees South latitude.

12-Hour Maximum and Minimum Temperature Charts, 1966 to the present.—15 reels, 35mm microfilm. Computer-plotted charts of conterminous states.

United States Winds Aloft Charts, 1942 to the present.—158 reels, 35mm microfilm. Plotted 6-hourly and 12-hourly charts showing wind direction and speed.

Weather Depiction Analysis Charts, 1976 to the present.—28 reels, 35mm microfilm. Computer-plotted and manually analyzed charts of the conterminous United States, southern Canada, and Mexico depicting surface data and tide information.

Weekly Weather and Crop Bulletins, 1872 to the present.—5300 volumes. These contain weekly weather highlights maps of the United States and agricultural weather highlights maps of the world.

Satellite Data Services Division (SDSD)
5200 Auth Road
Camp Springs, Maryland
(301) 763–8111

Mailing Address:
Satellite Data Services Division
National Climatic Data Center
World Weather Building, Room 1
Washington, D.C. 20233
Telex No. RCA 248376 OBSWUR
Gregory Hunoldt, Director (301) 763–8185

This Division manages a database of environmental satellite data and derives information that includes approximately 100,000 magnetic tapes and several million hardcopy images.

This unique database has been gathered by NOAA operational environmental satellites and various experimental environmental satellites beginning with TIROS in 1960. 2 types of environmental satellites are used: polar orbiting and geostationary. Polar orbiting satellites (TIROS 1-10, ESSA 1,3,5,7, and 9, ITOS, NOAA 1-5, GEOS 3, SEASAT, TIROS-N, NIMBUS 7, NOAA 6-9), ranging in orbits from 437 to 1000 miles and circling the Earth 12 to 14 times daily, provide complete global coverage twice each day. Geostationary satellites (ATS-1 & 3, SMS 1-2, GOES 1-6) operate at a height of 22,300 miles and are synchronized with the Earth's rotation so that they provide a fixed field of view which covers 25% of the Earth's surface between 50 degrees of latitude North and South of the Equator. Although most of these data were collected for meteorological purposes, they have applications in the fields of agronomy, geology, hydrology, and oceanography.

Useful accession aids available on request from SDSD include the *Catalog of Operational Satellite Products*, the *Satellite Data Users Bulletin*, the *NOAA Polar Orbiter Data Users Guide*, *GOES Digital Data Users Guide*, and *Price List and Ordering Procedures*.

Advanced Very High Resolution Radiometer (AVHRR) data, 1979 to the present, derived from TIROS-N/NOAA operational Polar orbiter satellites, are used to produce sea surface temperature, atmospheric sounding, heat budget, and other products in digital form, or visible and IR polar stereographic and Mercator mosaic imagery of the whole Earth, and limited area imagery of Eastern North America, Alaska, Western Canada, and selected areas in Europe, Africa, and Asia in 1 kilometer resolution.

Visible and Infra-Red Spin Scan Radiometer (VISSR) data, 1976 to the present, were gathered by GOES (Geostationary Operational Environmental Satellite) satellites. A complete archive of GOES VISSR and VAS (VISSR Atmospheric Sounder) digital data is maintained. The database also includes visible and IR images of the Earth. Data are available in the form of digital sectors on magnetic tape or photographic prints and transparencies.

NATIONAL GEOPHYSICAL DATA CENTER (NGDC)
NOAA E/GC
325 Broadway
Boulder, Colorado 80303
(303) 497–6474
Michael A. Chinnery, Director (303) 497–6215

NGDC collects, analyzes, and distributes more than 300 worldwide data files relating to earthquake seismology, solid earth geophysics, geothermics, marine geology and geophysics, geomagnetics, solar activity, ionospherics, and glaciology, some of which consist of maps or may be used to generate map plots and computer graphics. NGDC staff also compiles special thematic maps based on these data files, particularly in the following program areas: gravity (David T. Dater, Group Leader 303/497–6120), topography and geothermics (Joy A. Ikelman, Project Scientist 303/497–6149), aeromagnetics (Ronald Buhman and Susan McLean, Project Scientists 303/497–6128), and tsunamis (Patricia Lockridge, Project Scientist 303/497–6337). The Marine Applications of Computer Graphics Project (Peter Sloss, Project Scientist 303/497–6119) is developing color graphics software for the production of three dimensional stereoscopic images of the ocean bottom. The Snow and Ice Information Center (Ann Brennan, Group Leader) maintains sea ice charts of the United States, Canada, Great Britain, Japan, Norway, Sweden, and Denmark.

These services are described in *National Geophysical Data Center: Annual Report, Fiscal Year 1984* (1985. 61 pages), which is free on request.

The following pertinent data files and published maps are maintained and sold by NGDC.

Data Files

Hydrographic Database. These files consist of digitized depths, bottom characteristics, and navigational features for United States, Alaska, Hawaii, and Puerto Rico coastal waters collected by the National Ocean Service, 1935 to date (35 million records). They are available on magnetic tape and as custom plots at various scales and projections.

Defense Meteorological Satellite Program (DMSP) Data File. Consists of a 10-year record of visible and thermal spectral bands high resolution images of the earth's surface. (1 million images).

Geothermal Data Files. Consists of 1,500 digital data records recording the names, geographic positions, last known eruptions, and total number of eruptions for 1,117 volcanoes which were used to print a multicolored map of world volcanoes in 1979 for the International Association of Volcanology and Chemistry of the Earth's Interior; 6,600 digitized heat-flow measurements used to publish a heat-flow map of the world in 1976; digitized data of temperatures obtained from 1,700 wells used to produce a geothermal gradient map of the conterminous United States, which was published jointly by NGDC and the Los Alamos National Laboratory; and a digital database of 6,265 thermal springs and wells in the western states recording their location, temperature, flow, depth, and other significant data used in creating state geothermal maps.

Gravity Data Files. Gravity data files compiled by the Defense Mapping Agency and the National Geodetic Survey of NOAA contain data for 3.7 million gravity observations in the conterminous United States and Alaska, with supplemental data on latitude, longitude, and elevation. Available in magnetic tape, computer printout, and geophysical data plots (gravity anomaly maps). Further information on these databases are found in *U.S. Land Gravity: Key to Geophysical Records Documentation No. 18* (1982. 24 pages), available on request from NGDC.

Digital Geomagnetic Data File. This file contains two main types of data: aeromagnetic observations and global magnetic field secular variation observations. The digital aeromagnetic file contains approximately 50% of the United States public domain data as well as international and global data. Combined with the over 17 million global ground and satellite secular variation observations obtained since 1800, the total file consists of 55 million observations. Data are described by location, elevation, and date.

Outer Continental Shelves/Exclusive Economic Zone Resource Assessment and Hazards Data Sets. Consist of data sets in the form of interpretive maps, navigation plots, reports, bathymetry and seismic records for Georges Bank, Baltimore Canyon Trough, and other offshore areas on the Atlantic, California, and Alaskan coasts and the Gulf of Mexico.

Snow and Ice Data Files. Include digital data derived from sea ice charts and satellite observations; and aerial photographs and weekly ice charts of ice on the Great Lakes, 1956 to date.

Marine Minerals Database and Bibliography. The bibliography is a computerized index to literature pertaining to present-day marine deposits of manganese, polymetallic sulfides, phosphorites, and placers/heavy minerals. The database contains geochemical and morphologic information on manganese deposits; geochemistry of sulfides, phosphorites, and placers will be added at a later date. Searches, plots, and listings are available on request to user specifications.

Trackline Geophysical Data Worldwide. Navigation, bathymetric, magnetic, gravity, and seismic reflection data from oceanographic cruises worldwide are included in this database. Data entries are in geographic coordinates and include about 45 million data points and extensive seismic sections from about 10 million track miles of cruises. Considerable foreign data are included.

Tsunami Data Worldwide. Digital data include earthquake, epicenter, magnitude, depth, date of event, source region name and code; tsunami maximum runup, magnitude, intensity, locations experiencing tsunami, local runups arrival times, travel time, destruction, and deaths. Three thousand tsunami marigrams on microfiche and 700 tsunami photographs are also available from NCDC.

Earthquake Database. This file contains information on more than 500,000 earthquakes, known or suspected explosions and associated collapse phenomena, coal bumps, rockbursts, quarry blasts, and other earth disturbances recorded worldwide for the period 2100 B.C. to the present. It includes data and origin time of the event, geographic location, depth, magnitude, maximum intensity, and related earthquake phenomena (including casualties, damage, faulting, tsunami, volcanism, and others). The file was formed from data furnished by the United States Geological Survey (in earlier years by the United States Coast and Geodetic Survey and the National Oceanic and Atmospheric Administration), the California Institute of Technology (Pasadena), the University of California (Berkeley), the California Division of Mines and Geology (Sacramento), and many other sources worldwide. Data for large historical earthquakes are included for earlier years (about 2100 B.C. to A.D. 1897).

Earthquake Intensity Data Base. This file contains about 140,000 earthquake intensity (Modified Mercalli-MM) observations gathered from many sources. The data represent 21,000 events for the period 1638 to 1982. Each listing contains date, time, and location of earthquakes (where available); name of reporting towns and their geographic locations; and Modified Mercalli intensity at each town. Principal sources used in compiling the data are: *United States Earthquakes* (for the years 1928–1981) and *Earthquake History of the United States* (for the years 1638–1980).

Topographic-Bathymetric Data Files. A global digital bathymetric database containing some 7.8 million depth values on a 5-minute grid useful for generating elevation and depth contour charts and bathymetric perspective charts. Some topographic data were resampled to 5-minute resolution from original 10-minute gridded data.

Topographic Data Files. Consist of digitized elevation and depth data derived from United States Defense Mapping Agency maps (1:250,000), NGS data, aeronautical charts, and GEOS satellite radar altimetry that can be used to generate three-dimensional topographic maps. Coverage is available for the conterminous United States, North America, and the world for areas ranging in size from 30 seconds to 1 degree. The 10-minute global elevation data set, containing 2.3 million records, is the best resolution database currently available to the public for areas not covered by Defense Mapping Agency 5-minute data.

Published Maps

Earthquake Epicenter World Map, 1963–1977. Computer-plotted.

Geothermal Map Series. Geothermal energy maps of the western United States, Alaska, northern gulf of Mexico basin 1979; geothermal maps of eighteen individual western states, 1980–1984; technical geothermal maps of California and New Mexico, 1983; and geothermal gradient map of the conterminous United States, 1982.

Miscellaneous Maps. *Significant Earthquake World Map, 1900–1979* (1980), *Map of Tsunamis in the Pacific Basin, 1900–1983* (1984), *Seismicity of Middle America Map, 1982, Seismicity of the Middle East, 1900–1983,* and *Isostatic Residual Gravity Anomaly Map of the United States, 1985.* These maps are described in fliers available on request from NGDC.

Computer-Generated Relief Maps of the Earth's Surface. A 3-sheet set of images depicting relief of the earth's surface, produced from gridded digital elevation and bathymetric databases, are entirely machine-produced using state-of-the-art computer imaging, graphics, photography, and printing. These attractive, highly accurate relief maps in color are described in announcements available on request from NGDC.

NATIONAL OCEANOGRAPHIC DATA CENTER (NODC)
2001 Wisconsin Avenue, N.W.
Washington, D.C. 20235
Gregory W. Withee, Director (202) 634–7232

NODC is the United States national facility established to acquire, process, archive, and disseminate global oceanographic data. In this role, NODC maintains the world's largest collection of oceanographic data and administers World Data Center A (WDC-A)—Oceanography, part of a worldwide system that provides for international data exchange. NODC's digital databases include data collected by Federal, state, and local government agencies, universities and research institutions, and private industry. NODC holds physical, chemical, and biological oceanographic data. Global coverage, deep ocean databases include: 1) oceanographic station data—measurements of temperature, salinity, oxygen, phosphate, phosphorous, nitrate, nitrite, silicate, and pH at the surface and serial depths; 2) temperature-depth profiles from expendable and mechanical bathythermographs; and 3) surface current (ship drift) data. NODC data holdings on the United States continental shelf include: 1) winds, waves, and ocean surface data from automated buoys; 2) current meter data; 3) measurements of hydrocarbons, metals, and other pollutants and toxic substances; and 4) data on marine organisms, including plankton, benthos, and marine birds and mammals.

Products are available from most data files in map format showing geographic location and time. An extensive *Users Guide,* free on request, provides information on NODC holdings, data products, publications, and international data exchange services.

OFFICE OF SATELLITE DATA PROCESSING AND DISTRIBUTION
Federal Office Building 4
Suitland Road and Silver Hill Road
Suitland, Maryland 20233
Russell Koffler, Director (301) 763–1564

This office processes and distributes current weather satellite data and derived products to the National Weather Service and other domestic and foreign users. Through its direct readout service program, customers can receive weather charts displayed or printed on their own equipment directly from NOAA's weather satellites.

National Geographic Society (NGS)—Geographic Names Database **See entry J7**

National Library of Medicine (NLM) (National Institute of Health) **See entry A31**

National Ocean Service (NOS) (Commerce Department—National Oceanic and Atmospheric Administration) **See entry G20**

National Oceanic and Atmospheric Administration (NOAA) Automated Library Information System (NALIS) (Commerce Department) **See entry A33**

D9 National Space Science Data Center (NSSDC) (National Aeronautics and Space Administration)

1 a. Goddard Space Flight Center
Greenbelt, Maryland 20771
(301) 344-6695 (Request Coordination Office)

Mailing Address for United States researchers:
National Space Science Data Center
Code 633.4
Goddard Space Flight Center
Greenbelt, Maryland 20771

Mailing Address for researchers residing outside the United States:
World Data Center A for Rockets and Satellites
Code 630.2
Goddard Space Flight Center
Greenbelt, Maryland 20771 U.S.A.

b. 8:00 A.M.–4:30 P.M. Monday–Friday

c Open to researchers. Appointments are recommended.

d. James Green, Director
James Vette, Senior Scientist
Patricia Voss, Manager, Request Coordination Office

2. NSSDC serves as the central government source for data and for information about data in other repositories derived from special space science investigations carried out on terrestrial and planetary spacecraft by United States, Soviet Union, Japan, and European Space Agency (ESA) scientists. The following pertinent data collections are available from NSSDC.

SATELLITE DATA FILE

Apollo 8-17, 1968–1973.—97,000 items. Lunar surface photographs, including multispectral terrain photographs, trans-earth lunar photographs, metric photographs, panoramic photographs, hand-held photographs, and stellar photographs of the earth and celestial region (photos range from 16mm microfilm to 5 x 48 inch prints); photographic data on digital magnetic tape (6 reels); and mapping camera support data. Principal cartographic investigators included the Mapping Sciences Laboratory, NASA-Johnson Space Center, and Frederick J. Doyle, United States Geological Survey.

Heat Capacity Mapping Mission, 1978–1979.—157,614 items. Visible and infrared images of the Earth in the middle northern latitudes designed to show variations in surface temperatures and used to produce thermal maps (9.5 inch film, digital magnetic data tape). The principal remote sensing investigator was W.L. Barnes, NASA-Goddard Space Flight Center.

Luna 3, 9, 13, 1959–1966.—11 items. Photos and atlas of the far side of the moon; first panoramic photographs of the lunar surface.

Lunar Orbiter 1-5, 1966–1967.—115,000 items. Lunar topographic photographs of potential Apollo and Surveyor landing sites and photographic survey covering 99 percent of the lunar surface (photos range from 35mm microfilm to 20 x 24 inch prints); and photo support data (15 reels, digital magnetic data tape). The principal remote sensing investigator was L.J. Kusofsky, NASA Headquarters.

Mariner 6-10, 1969–1974.—58,000 items. Analog and enhanced surface TV photographs of Mars (70mm and photometric data tapes); map photomosaics of 30 percent of Mars surface (432 70mm negatives); photographs and imagery data of Mercury and Venus (70mm negatives, press-release prints, and magnetic data tape). The principal investigators for the surface photography of Mars were R.B. Leighton, California Institute of Technology and H. Masursky, United States Geological Survey; for Martian mapping, G. DeVaucouleurs, University of Texas, Austin; and for telemetry photography of the encounters with Mercury and Venus, B.C. Murray, California Institute of Technology.

Nimbus 5, 1972.—45 tapes. Surface Composition Mapping Radiometer (SCMR) digital magnetic tapes of the Earth's surface. The principal investigator for this study was W.A. Hovis, National Oceanic and Atmospheric Administration.

Nimbus 7, 1978.—1,200 tapes. Data tapes from the Coastal Zone Color Scanner Experiment to map chlorophyll concentration, sediments, salinity, and temperatures of coastal waters and ocean currents; data tapes and map data matrix on microfilm from the Limb Infrared Monitor of the Stratosphere investigation designed to map the temperature profile and concentrations of ozone and water vapor in the middle stratosphere; data tapes and film matrix from a project to map the ozone content. The principal investigators were D.F. Heath, NASA Goddard Space Flight Center, and W.A. Hovis, National Oceanic and Atmospheric Administration.

Pioneer 10-11, 1973–1979.—700 items. Color press-release photographs of Jupiter and Saturn (various sizes).

Pioneer Venus 1, 1978–1980.—87 items. Radar altimeter topographic maps (4 x 5 inch prints); press-release photographs (4 x 5 inch prints); and digital map images on magnetic tape (60 reels).

Ranger 7-9, 1964–1965.—17,000 items. Lunar photographs (35mm) and atlas of lunar photographs (microfiche). The principal investigator was G.P. Kuiper, University of Arizona.

Skylab 1-4, 1973–1974.—2 items. Index to multispectral photography of regions of the earth's surface (microfiche) and volume of synoptic maps. The principal remote sensing investigators were K. Demel, NASA Johnson Space Center, and R. Tousey, United States Naval Research Laboratory.

Space Shuttle (STS 2/OSTA-1), 1981.—2,200 items. Map-like radar imagery of earth's surface designed for geological exploration (1,700 items of various formats); multispectral infrared radiometer data and imagery used for mapping rocks associated with mineral deposits (500 16mm film frames and magnetic tapes); and data for mapping the location and circulation of plankton by color patterns in the oceans (2 data tapes). The principal remote sensing investigator was C. Elachi, NASA Jet Propulsion Laboratory, Johnson Space Center.

Surveyor 1-7, 1966–1968.—170,000 items. Television photographs and panoramic photomosaics of the lunar surface taken from unmanned space vehicles in support of Apollo landing sites (35mm, 70mm, and 4 x 5 inch prints). Investigators for lunar photography were E.M. Shoemaker, California Institute of Technology, and R.M. Batson, United States Geological Survey.

Viking 1 and 2 Lander, 1976–1982.—5,000 items. Photographs, image data, and stereo photomosaics of the surface of Mars (various size negatives and prints, digital magnetic tape); topographic map atlas of landing site on Mars. Investigator for imaging was R.E. Arvidson, Washington University.

Viking 1 and 2 Orbiter, 1976–1980.—85,000 items. Photographs of Mars, including press-release photographs, rectilinear orbital photography (51,000 5 x 5 inch photographs), orthographic orbital photography (16,743 5 x 5 inch photographs); United States Geological Survey photomosaics (1,026 8 x 10 inch negatives); and imaging data on magnetic tape (100 reels). The team leader of imagery experiment was M.H. Carr, United States Geological Survey.

Voyager 1-2, 1978–1981.—138,000 items. Photographs of Jupiter and Saturn and their satellites, including press-release photographs, mosaics, systematic MTIS images (137,000 5 x 5 inch positives). Team leader for imaging was B.A. Smith, University of Arizona.

Zond 3-8, 1965–1970.—54,000 items. Lunar surface photographs and atlas of the far side of the moon (7 volumes).

NSSDC SUPPLEMENTARY DATA FILE (NSDF)

Includes digitized Earth maps of continents and bodies of water (1 digitized magnetic tape); Defense Mapping Agency lunar maps (888 hard copy and 70mm maps); geological maps of Poland (2 maps); composite spacecraft and groundbased data images of Mars (20 images); and Pennsylvania State Photograph Rectification Program (427 punch cards).

3. The most useful publication on NSSDC holdings is *NSSDC Data Listing* (latest, July, 1985. 67 p.). The *Data Catalog Series for Space Science and Applications Flight Missions Volume 4A Descriptions of Meteorological and Terrestrial Applications Spacecraft and Investigations* (latest, July, 1985. 107 p.) provides descriptions of research and development investigations and operational studies of the earth performed with earth-orbiting spacecraft and the locations of the resulting data sets. A description of each NASA space mission, including a discussion of project accomplishments and list of investigators, is found in *Satellite Handbook: A Record of NASA Space Missions: 1958–1980,* compiled by Alfred Rosenthall (NASA-Goddard Space Flight Center, 1981. 829 p.)

National Technical Information Service (NTIS) (Commerce Department) **See entry K12**

D10 ORBIT Search Service

1 a. *Systems Development Corporation (SDC)*
7925 Jones Branch Drive
McLean, Virginia 22102
(703) 790-9850
(800) 336-3313 (Toll Free)

d. Cynthia Hull

2. The Systems Development Corporation's ORBIT Search Service provides access to more than 70 online bibliographic and full-text record databases with some 55 million citations. Pertinent databases include COMPENDEX (D1), ERIC (D4), GeoRef (D3 and J2), LC/LINE and LC/PRE 84 (D3, LC MARC, and REMARC), and NTIS (D1, K12).

3. A copy of the current *ORBIT Search Service Database Catalog* is available on request.

SPOT Image Corporation **See entry E8**

The World Bank (International Bank for Reconstruction and Development—Sectoral Library) **See entry A41**

ORGANIZATIONS

E Research Centers and Referral Services

Research Centers and Referral Services Entry Format (E)

1. General Information
   a. address; telephone numbers
   b. hours of service
   c. conditions of access
   d. chief official/key resource person
2. Objectives and/or Programs
3. Collections/Research Facilities
4. Products

E1 Agricultural Research Service (ARS) (Agriculture Department)—Remote Sensing Research Laboratory

1 a. *Building 007, BARC-W*
Beltsville, Maryland 20705
(301) 344-3490

d. Galen Hart, Research Leader

2. The Remote Sensing Research Laboratory conducts basic and applied research on remote sensing imagery with respect to agriculture, particularly serving the programs of the Soil Conservation Service and the Foreign Agriculture Service of the United States Department of Agriculture.

3. The Laboratory currently maintains 2 data sets: a file of weather data tapes containing information (minimum and maximum temperature and precipitation) obtained from cooperative weather data stations in the United States, 1890s–1980 (168 tapes) and a set

of daily, growing season, ground and satellite data for 23 sites in Iowa, Nebraska, and North Dakota for 1983.

Census Bureau (Commerce Department)—International Statistical Programs Center (ISPC) **See entry F3**

Center for Earth and Planetary Studies Image Facility (Smithsonian Institution—National Air and Space Museum) **See entry C5**

E2 Coastal Zone Information Center (Commerce Department—National Oceanic and Atmospheric Administration)

1 a. *Page Building, No. 1, 3rd Floor*
3300 Whitehaven Street, N.W.
Washington D.C. 20235
(202) 634-4255

b. 8:00 A.M.–4:00 P.M. Monday–Friday

c. Open to the public.

d. Sally Cauchon, Director

2. The Coastal Zone Information Center provides advisory, reference, and referral service on coastal zone planning and management with respect to natural resources, energy facilities, outer continental shelf oil and gas, marine recreation, and land use.

3. The Center's reference collection includes 200 atlases and charts of coastal areas prepared by the National Ocean Service (G20) and the United States Geological Survey (G14).

E3 Earth Observation Satellite Company (EOSAT)

1 a. *4300 Forbes Boulevard*
Lanham, Maryland 20706
(301) 552-0500 (Information)
(800) 344-9933 (Toll-Free Information)
(800) 367-2801 (EOSAT Representative, EROS Data Center)
(605) 594-2291 (EOSAT Representative, EROS Data Center, commercial line, South Dakota and overseas)

d. Charles P. Williams, President
James Love, Manager, Customer Service
Donald Garofalo, Director, Applications Support
Raymond Byrnes, Landsat Product Manager, EOSAT Representative, EROS Data Center, Sioux Falls, South Dakota.

2. EOSAT is a partnership formed by Hughes Aircraft Company and the RCA Corporation to commercialize the operation of the Federal Government's Landsat (Land Satellite) program, which was transferred to the private sector on September 27, 1985. The Landsat system involves the remote sensing of the earth's surface from unmanned satellites equipped with special mapping sensors and the dissemination of the collected data, which has been used to map, plan and research vegetation, agriculture, mineral resources, water, pollution, and land use. EOSAT operates Landsats 4 and 5 and plans to launch Landsat 6 in 1988. Current and archival Landsat data will continue to be housed at the Department of Interior's EROS Data Center (E7) in Sioux Falls, South Dakota until 1988 and is available to all users through the EOSAT representatives at Sioux Falls or Lanham.

3. The Landsat data set consists of some 650,000 images of the earth's surface taken from an orbital altitude of approximately 570 miles by a Multispectral Scanner System (MSS) with four spectral bands and the Thematic Mapper (TM) system with seven bands. Each image covers about 115 square miles. Microimages of the Landsat photography archived at the EROS Data Center may be previewed in the Geography and Map Division of the Library of Congress (A21) and the National Cartographic and Information Center (E7).

4. Brochures describing EOSAT's functions and Landsat data purchasing procedures are available on request from EOSAT.

Earth Resources Observations Systems (EROS) Data Center (Interior Department—Geological Survey) **See entry E7, section 3**

E4 Earth Satellite Corporation (EarthSat)

1 a. *7222 47th Street*
Chevy Chase, Maryland 20815
(301) 951-0104

b. 8:00 A.M.–4:30 P.M. Monday–Friday

c. Open to scholars. Copies of photo maps and imagery may be obtained for a fee.

d. J. Robert Porter, Jr., President
Max E. Miller, Director, Technical Services Group
(301) 951-0104

2–3. The Earth Satellite Corporation is a commercial consulting firm that provides computer processed Landsat images for commercial and academic worldwide resource studies and exploration projects. Custom products are available in the form of false-color infrared prints, color-matched images, photo and digital mosaics, photomaps, and imagery scaled to particular maps.

EarthSat maintains an inventory of Landsat Computer Compatible Tapes (CCT), which provide coverage for most of the United States and some coverage for 83 foreign countries, particularly Argentina, Australia, Canada, Chile, China, Japan, Kenya, Libya, Oman, Peru, Saudi Arabia, Sudan, and Yemen.

Training packages of remotely sensed imagery covering Death Valley, California, and Paradox Basin, Utah and Colorado, are also available.

4. Several brochures are available describing EarthSat's products and fees, as well as a list of Landsat CCT coverage by country. No list of holdings which may be made available for public scholarly use has been published.

E5 Engineer Topographic Laboratories (ETL) (Army Corps of Engineers)

1 a. *Fort Belvoir, Virginia 22060–5546*
(202) 355–2634 (Public Affairs)

b. Open only to government officials and contractors with security clearance.

d. Colonel Alan L. Laubscher, Commander and Director
F. Darlene Seyler, Public Affairs Officer

2. ETL undertakes basic research and development in the fields of mapping, terrain analysis, geodesy, surveying, and military geographic information systems for the United States Army and other Federal agencies. It is comprised of 5 units. The Research Institute is responsible for basic and applied research particularly with respect to obtaining mapping and terrain data from aerial imagery with the aid of digital computers. The Computer Sciences Laboratory applies mathematics and computer science to the development of automated techniques for extracting terrain and target information from digital images. The Geographic Sciences Laboratory investigates military geographic information and reproduction systems. Current work includes the Digital Topographic Support System, a project which will give Army units access to automated terrain analysis techniques, and the Quick Response Multicolor Printer, a color copier designed for reproducing multicolor topographic maps and digital data. The Topographic Developments Laboratory develops computer programs and equipment for map production and investigates new survey techniques. The Terrain Analysis Center compiles and analyses terrain data in support of military planning and operations.

3. The Scientific and Technical Information Center (Mildred Stiger, Chief 202/355–2656) is not open to private research but books are available through interlibrary loan. The Center contains some 7,000 books and 2,000 technical reports devoted chiefly to geodesy, surveying, digital mapping, remote sensing, and computer sciences.

4. Unclassified publications may be obtained through the Department of Commerce's National Technical Information Service (K12). They are also available through interlibrary loan from the Scientific and Technical Information Center. A published bibliography with supplements, *Bibliography of In-House and Contract Reports,* is published yearly. The most recent issue, *Supplement 13* (May 1985) contains descriptions of 36 reports, 23 of which are available through NTIS, and bibliographies of 14 papers by ETL scientists published in professional journals and proceedings. In addition, this issue indexes all reports issued by ETL between 1970 and 1984 (ca. 1,126 titles).

Examples of some recent ETL reports available through NTIS are: *Advance Edit System,* describing an interactive graphic workstation and software for editing digital cartographic data; *Evaluation of Published Criteria for Identifying Metamorphic Rocks in Air Photos: Two Case Studies in the Northeastern United States; Application of Hierarchical Data Structures to Geographical Information Systems; A Sensing Array System With Image Statistics Process,* evaluating 2 types of classifiers for a set of photographic imagery by using a solid-state sensor array minicomputer system; *Vegetation and Terrain Effects on Digital Classification of Landsat Imagery; Classification of Cartographic Features Through Walsh Transforms; Applying Photogrammetry to Real*

Time Collection of Digital Image Data; and *Data Integrity Factors Affecting the Construction of the Mapping, Charting, and Geodesy Data Base.*

Current activities of ETL are described in a quarterly information exchange bulletin, *Tech-Tran.* This bulletin also lists recent ETL published reports and papers given at workshops and conferences.

E6 Environmental Photographic Interpretation Center (EPIC) (Environmental Protection Agency) (EPA)

1 a. *Vint Hill Farm Station*
Warrenton, Virginia 22186
(703) 557-3110

Mailing Address:
P.O. Box 1587

c. Open to researchers by appointment. Reproductions of the aerial photography is available through the Freedom of Information Act. Some of the film is restricted due to proprietary rights.

d. Vernard H. Webb, Director

3. The Environmental Photographic Interpretation Center has custody of some 5,000 rolls of conventional black and white and color-infrared photography acquired in support of EPA studies and monitoring programs concerning the environment, especially water pollution control and water supply, disposal of solid and hazardous wastes, and the impact of pesticides and toxic substances on fish and wildlife. There is also a small amount of thermal infrared photography. Some of the imagery is acquired from EPA photographic missions, the remainder from commercial aerial photographic companies, the National Aeronautical and Space Administration and other government agencies. The film ranges in scale from 1:2,000 to 1:80,000, but the average scale is 1:8,400. EPIC maintains coverage for specific EPA sites and study areas east of the Mississippi River. Coverage for the area west of the Mississippi River is maintained by the Environmental Protection Agency, Environmental Monitoring System Laboratory, Advanced Monitoring Division (Gene Meyer, Director, P.O. Box 15027, Las Vegas, Nevada 89114, telephone 702/789-2237).

Geological Survey (USGS) (Interior Department)—Office of Geographic and Cartographic Branch **See entry G14**

Land Management Bureau (BLM) (Interior Department)—Eastern States Office **See entry G17**

National Aeronautics and Space Administration (NASA)—Scientific and Technical Information Branch **See entry G18**

National Air and Space Museum (NASM) (Smithsonian Institution)—Center for Earth and Planetary Studies—Planetary Image Facility **See entry C5**

E7 National Cartographic Information Center (NCIC) (Interior Department—Geological Survey)

1 a. *507 National Center*
12201 Sunrise Valley Drive
Reston, Virginia 22092
(703) 860-6045

d. John Wood, Center Chief
Lyle Kemper, Chief, Branch of User Services

2. The National Cartographic Information Center collects, organizes and distributes current cartographic data in the form of maps, charts, aerial photographs, satellite images, geodetic control, and digital records. This data is acquired from the United States Geological Survey (USGS) and a broad range of Federal, state, and local government agencies as well as some commercial mapping companies. The Center will respond to general inquiries or technical questions received by letter, telephone, or personal visit. Staff members will do limited research in response to specific questions, or if necessary, will refer scholars to appropriate Federal agencies or private organizations. They will also provide assistance in using graphic and digital mapping products.

NCIC comprises a national network of information centers. There are NCIC regional centers in USGS mapping centers and 41 state affiliate offices. For addresses of regional and state affiliates, contact the National Center.

NCIC can furnish information and products on a variety of cartographic materials. It has information on 250,000 maps and charts from some 60 Federal and state agencies relating to land use, geological features, land forms, soils, mineral exploration, zoning, and taxes. These include all of the maps produced by USGS (G14). The most up-to-date large-scale topographic maps of the United States available from NCIC are USGS Advance Prints. These are manuscript, edited, or partially edited prints of topographic quadrangles or othophotoquads prepared prior to the final published map.

Through NCICs information systems, the scholar has access to information about 13 million aerial photographs of the United States produced by USGS, other Federal agencies, and private aerial photography firms. Dating from the 1930s, these photographs are available in black and white, color, or color-infrared. Low-altitude photographs (taken from 3,000 to 40,000 feet) usually range in scale from 1:20,000 to 1:24,000; high-altitude photographs (taken above 40,000 feet) have scales varying from 1:60,000 to 1:120,000. A computerized system known as the Aerial Photography Summary Record System (APSRS) provides information on the availability of photo coverage for a particular geographic area, the quality of the image, the type of film emulsion, the camera focal length, and the custodian of the film. NCIC also distributes other cartographic and geographic data in digital form (D6).

3. NCIC provides information about satellite imagery maintained in the Department of Interior Earth Resources Observations System's (EROS) Data Center in Sioux Falls, South Dakota 57198 (Thomas M. Holm, Data Services Officer 605/594-6507). The EROS Data Center is a national archive, production, and research facility for aerial photography and remote sensing data. It has custody of more than 5.7 million aerial

photographs of the United States; 650,000 worldwide images of the Earth acquired by Landsat satellites (the latter are now sold by the Earth Observation Satellite Company, EOSAT, through their representative at the EROS Data Center, see entry E3); 94,000 images from Skylab II, III, IV, Apollo/ Gemini/ Apollo-Soyuz, and Shuttle space programs; and 9,500 digital magnetic tapes of Landsat imagery. The aerial photography holdings consist of photographs from the National High-Altitude Photography Program (409,577 images), NASA high-altitude aircraft photography program (1.6 million), Bureau of Land Management (124,000 images), Environmental Protection Agency (75,000), Bureau of Reclamation (60,000),National Park Service (8,000), Bureau of Indian Affairs (7,400), Army Map Service (214,000), United States Navy (406,000), and Army Corps of Engineers (22,765).

4. NCIC has published numerous brochures, fact sheets, and catalogs to aid scholars and public users. Its *Map Data Catalog* (Second edition, 1984) provides an excellent illustrated summary of available products. A brochure entitled *National Cartographic Information Center* is a useful introduction to the services provided by the Center. The NCIC *Newsletter* provides current information on USGS products, other pertinent publications, and dates of professional meetings and conventions. Brochures relating to maps include: *Looking for an Old Map, Advance Materials,* and *How to Order Maps on Microfilm.* Recent brochures pertaining to aerial photography and remote sensing imagery include, *Looking for an Old Aerial Photograph, How to Order Aerial Photographs, Alaska From Space, The Aerial Photography Summary Record System,* and *Using APSRS Microfiche. The Sky's the Limit* describes the National High Altitude Photography Program, an interdepartmental aerial photography program coordinated by the USGS.

National Environmental Satellite, Data, and Information Service (NESDIS) (Commerce Department—National Oceanic and Atmospheric Administration) **See entry D8**

National Geodetic Information Center (National Oceanic and Atmospheric Administration—National Ocean Service) **See entry G20**

National Ocean Service (NOS) (Commerce Department—National Oceanic and Atmospheric Administration) **See entry G20**

Soil Conservation Service (SCS) (Agriculture Department)—Cartography and Geographic Information Systems Division **See entry G25**

E8 SPOT Image Corporation

1 a. *1897 Preston White Drive*
Reston, Virginia 22091-4326
(703) 620–2200

c. Open to the public.

d. Nadine Binger, Manager, Market Development

2. SPOT Image Corporation is a commercial company formed in 1982 to market SPOT (Systeme Probatoire d'Observation de la Terre) satellite data products derived from the SPOT remote sensing program initiated by the French government in cooperation with Belgium and Sweden. The first digital imagery of the Earth from SPOT satellites became available in early 1986. SPOT digital imagery provides ground resolution as high as 10 meters (33 feet) in black and white and 20 meters (66 feet) in color from an altitude of 517 miles. Each image covers an area of 1,400 square miles. The SPOT remote sensing system is especially suitable for the following applications: geological exploration and mapping, urban planning and cartography, agricultural studies and yield estimates, forestry research, wildlife habitat mapping, study of hydrologic transport processes, and recreation resource management.

4. SPOT products are available on computer-compatible tapes, films, or on paper. Access to these products is through the *SPOT Image Catalog,* an electronic database. Information on new acquisitions and services is found in the *SPOT Newsletter,* published twice yearly. The *SPOT Simulation Applications Handbook,* covering a wide range of applications in agriculture, cartography, forestry, geology, urban planning, and water resources, is available from the SPOT Image Corporation or the American Society for Photogrammetry and Remote Sensing (entry J3). A good description of the SPOT program is Michael Courtois and Gilbert Weill, "The SPOT Satellite System", *Monitoring Earth's Ocean, Land, and Atmosphere from Space-Sensors, Systems, and Applications,* edited by Abraham Schnapf (American Institute of Aeronautics and Astronautics, 1985, pp. 493–523).

F Academic Programs and Departments

Academic Programs and Departments Entry Format (F)

1. Address; Telephone Numbers
2. Chief Official and Title
3. Degrees and Subjects Offered; Programs
4. Library/Research Facilities
5. Laboratory Facilities
6. Publications

F1 Agriculture Department—Graduate School

1. 600 Maryland Avenue, Room 129
Washington, D.C. 20024
(202) 447-4419

2. Karen Niles, Director

3. The Graduate School, United States Department of Agriculture (USDA), established in 1921, offers a continuing education program for federal employees and working adults. It does not grant degrees. Classes are open to all persons eighteen years of age or older. The school offers more than 2000 courses designed to prepare participants for new careers, to continue their professional development, or to pursue personal interests. The part-time faculty is drawn from government, business, and academia. The Sciences and Engineering Program offers a course on basic cartography and a seminar on map projections and grid systems, both taught by Anthony S. Basile.

F2 The Catholic University of America—School of Library and Information Sciences

1. *Michigan Avenue and Harewood Road, N.E.*
Washington, D.C. 20064
(202) 635-5085

2. Raymond F. Vondran, Dean

3. The School of Library and Information Sciences offers two relevant graduate courses, "Map Librarianship," and "History of Maps and Map Collecting." They are currently taught by Richard W. Stephenson (202/287-8530).

4. The University library is described in entry A7.

F3 Census Bureau (Commerce Department)—International Statistical Programs Center (ISPC)

1. *Scuderi Building*
Suite 303
4235 28th Avenue
Marlow Heights, Maryland 20748

Mailing Address:
International Statistical Programs Center
Bureau of the Census
Washington, D.C. 20233
(301) 763-2832

2. Karl K. Kindel, Chief

3. ISPC conducts practical training and technical assistance programs for statisticians and technicians in developing countries particularly with respect to developing technical and organizational skills for carrying out nationwide agricultural, demographic, and economic censuses or surveys. These programs are generally sponsored by the United States Agency for International Development (AID), private foundations, or third-world countries.

TRAINING BRANCH
Kenneth Bryson, Chief
(301) 763-2860

This branch develops and conducts the overseas training programs, including a full year program in census-survey geography designed to develop mapping and airphoto interpretation skills that can be applied to national censuses and surveys; a short term program in field operations and mapping in a host country, with emphasis on the use of maps during census enumeration; and overseas workshops (of one or two weeks duration) on mapping for statistical officers at the executive level, cartographers, and field staff. Catalogs describing the overseas training workshop and the statistical training programs are available on request.

CENSUS AND SURVEY METHODS BRANCH
Carol Van Horn, Chief
(301) 763-1192

This branch conducts research on census and survey methods to be used in developing countries, conducts courses in these subjects for overseas seminars and workshops, and prepares manuals, including *Mapping for Censuses and Surveys* (1977. 30 p.) and *Cartografia para Censos y Encuestas* (1979. 351 p.) with accompanying workbooks.

6. In addition to the publications listed above, the Center publishes a brochure describing its various activities.

F4 Consortium of Universities of the Washington Metropolitan Area

Academic courses and library resources of nine colleges and universities located in the Washington D.C. area and associated through the Consortium of Universities of the Washington Metropolitan Area are available to degree candidates enrolled at any one of the participating institutions. These institutions are: American University, Catholic University, Gallaudet College, Georgetown University, George Washington University, Howard University, Mount Vernon College, Trinity College, and the University of the District of Columbia.

Defense Mapping School (Defense Department–Defense Mapping Agency) **See entry G8**

F5 George Mason University—Public Affairs Department—Geographic and Cartographic Sciences Program

1. *4400 University Drive*
   Fairfax, Virginia 22030
   (703) 323-2272

2. Mark Lindberg, Director

3. The Public Affairs Department offers a certificate program in cartography, which consists of 24 semester hours, and a MS degree program in Geographic and Cartographic Sciences. Five undergraduate and 11 graduate courses pertain to cartography. Current graduate courses include "Thematic Cartography," "Geographic Information Systems," "History of Cartography," "Analytic Photogrammetry," "Computer Applications in Cartography," "Terrain Mapping," "Geodetic Cartography," and "Map Projections and Coordinate Systems." Some of these courses are offered in the evenings.

4. The department maintains collections of hydrographic, topographic and thematic maps as well as aerial photographs, Landsat imagery, and high altitude NASA imagery. The University Fenwick Library map collections are described in entry A13.

5. The cartography laboratory is equipped with a Repromaster Camera, AMS stereoplotter, projector, and platemaker. The department also has access to the University

computer (CYBER 720), HP 2000 and 3000 HP graphics plotter and CRT display, and an APPLE II graphics system.

6. The Geography Program publishes the *Virginia Geographer,* a semiannual journal of the Virginia Geographical Society.

F6 George Washington University—Department of Geography and Regional Science

1. *2023 G Street, N.W.*
   Washington, D.C. 20052
   (202) 676–6185

2. John Lowe, Chairman

3. The Department of Geography and Regional Science offers a four-year undergraduate degree in Cartographic Science. Course offerings range from the fundamental concepts of mapmaking and practical applications in cartography to elements of remote sensing, map design, photointerpretation, and automated cartography.

4. The George Washington University Library is described in entry A14.

F7 George Washington University—School of Engineering and Applied Sciences—Continuing Engineering Education Program

1. *725 23rd Street, N.W.*
   Washington, D.C. 20052
   (202) 676–6106
   (800) 424–9773 (toll free)

2. J.W. Perkins, Director

3. The Continuing Education program offers noncredit short courses designed for practicing scientists and engineers who wish to remain current in fast-changing fields. The courses are taught by professionals from industry, government, and universities. They range in length from 2 to 5 days. Courses offered in 1985 included "Satellite Geodetic Positioning, Datums, and Datum Transformations", "Introduction to Techniques for Information Extraction From Remotely Sensed Data", "Digital Image Processing of Earth Observation Sensor Data", "Digital Geographic Information Systems", "Applying Remote Sensing Techniques to the Marine Environment", "Mapping From Space: Techniques and Applications", and "Automated Mapping Using Digital Image Classification Techniques".

4. The University Library is described in entry A14.

6. Brochures describing courses offered each year are available.

F8 Montgomery College—Rockville Campus—Applied Technologies Department

1. *51 Mannakee Street*
   Rockville, Maryland 20850
   (301) 279-5173/5142

2. Paul D. McDermott, Professor of Cartography and Computer Graphics

3. The Department offers a two-year undergraduate program in cartography, with course work in general cartography, cartographic design, and aerial photography and map interpretation.

5. The Department maintains a Cartography Laboratory and a Computer Graphics Laboratory. The latter is equipped with IBM and Apple minicomputer stations for 15 students and includes plotters, tablets, and printers.

6. A brochure describing the program is available.

F9 Towson State University—Department of Geography and Environmental Planning

1. *York Road*
   Towson, Maryland 21204
   (301) 321-2973

2. James E. DiLisio, Chairperson

3. In addition to undergraduate and graduate degrees in geography, the Department offers an 18-semester-hour program leading to a Certificate in Cartography. Pertinent courses include map interpretation, aerial photography interpretation, cartography and graphics, and a graduate-level course in remote sensing.

4. The Department serves as a map depository for United States Geological Survey and Defense Mapping Agency maps.

5. The Department maintains cartography and air photo laboratories.

F10 University of the District of Columbia

1. *4200 Connecticut Avenue, N.W.*
   Washington, D.C. 20004
   (202) 282-7300

2. Rafael Cortada, President

3. Although the University of the District of Columbia does not offer a degree program in cartography, pertinent courses are available from several departments. The Geography Department offers 2 introductory courses: map and aerial photointerpretation and graphics and cartography. The Department of Earth and Life Sciences includes a course on air photo-interpretation and remote sensing. The Civil and Mechanical Engineering

Department provides courses in engineering graphics, photogrammetry, and surveying practices. The Department of Community and Urban Planning offers two courses on urban planning graphics.

F11 University of Maryland—Department of Geography

1. *College Park, Maryland 20742*
(301) 454-2241

2. Kenneth E. Corey, Director

3. The Department offers M.A. and Ph.D. degree programs in geography, with particular emphasis on environmental systems studies, cultural studies, and metropolitan studies. In addition, the Department is developing a cartography and computer mapping applications program. Pertinent courses currently offered include maps and map use, cartographic products, principles of map design, development of cartographic technology, problems in cartography, remote sensing, computer mapping, geographic information systems, and principles of cartography.

4. The University map library is described in entry A40.

5. The Computer Mapping and Spatial Analysis (CMSA) Laboratory, an adjunct to the Division of Behavioral and Social Sciences (BSOS) Computer Laboratory, provides comprehensive mapping and graphic services and is available for student and faculty use (Ronald Linton, Director, 301/454-6659). The CMSA Laboratory is supported by a dedicated PRIME 550 mini-computer, Tektronix digitizing tablets, Tektronix computer graphics terminals, a Tektronix interactive digital plotter, and a CALCOMP 1073 plotter. Twenty-one application software packages and programs currently available for statistical analysis and spatial mapping are listed in a brochure describing the services of CMSA. The Department also has access to the University's Remote Sensing Systems Laboratory (Robert Ragan, Director, 301/454-3107).

6. The Department's *Occasional Paper Series* has included *The Atlas of Maryland.*

G United States Government Agencies

United States Government Agencies Entry Format (G)

1. General Information
   a. address; telephone numbers
   b. conditions of access
   c. name/title of director and heads of relevant divisions
2. Agency Functions and Programs
3. Agency Collections and Reference Facilities
4. Unpublished Materials
5. Publications
   a. published products
   b. published bibliographies and reference aids

In the case of large, structurally complex agencies, each relevant division/bureau is described separately in accordance with the above entry format and cross referenced in the index.

G1 Agricultural Stabilization and Conservation Service (ASCS) (Agriculture Department)

1 a. *14th Street and Independence Avenue, S.W.*
Washington, D.C. 20250
(202) 447-5237 Information

b. Open to the public.

c. Everett Rank, Administrator

2. Since 1935, ASCS has used rectified-to-scale aerial photographs to determine acreage for farm program compliance purposes. Land to be filmed is recommended by state and county Agricultural Stabilization and Conservation Committees. After approval by the Deputy Administrator for State and County Operations (Roy T. Cozart 202/447–3175), filming contracts are awarded to aerial photographic firms by competitive bids. All major cropland areas, representing approximately 80 percent of the total land area of the United States, has been filmed. Since 1978, the prime source of new aerial photography for ASCS has been the National High Altitude Photography Program (NHAP). This program is a cooperative interagency effort to provide aerial photographic coverage of the contiguous United States in a consistent and systematic manner. Photographs are taken at an altitude of about 40,000 feet from 2 cameras exposed simultaneously. One camera provides black-and-white panchromatic film images at a scale of 1:80,000 for use primarily for map revision and orthophoto mapping; the other camera provides color-infrared (CIR) images at a scale of 1:58:000, useful for inventorying and monitoring natural resources.

3. The ASDS Aerial Photography Field Office (APFO) (Customer Service 801/524–5856, 2222 West, 2300 South, Post Office Box 30010, Salt Lake City, Utah 84130) holds more than 50,000 rolls of aerial photography film acquired for ASCS, the Forest Service (FS), and the Soil Conservation Service (SCS). The film dates from 1945. This collection includes ASCS conventional black-and-white aerial film, ranging in scale from 1 inch equals 4833 feet to 1 inch equals 200 feet; NHAP 1:58,000 CIR film (NHAP 1:80,000 is available from the EROS Data Center, entry E7); FS and SCS conventional black-and-white aerial film varying in scale from 1:6000 to 1:120,000; NASA high-altitude photography of Alaska (1969); Skylab 2, 3, and 4 imagery; and Landsat false-color infrared mosaics and black-and-white photographs of the United States and Alaska.

4. ASCS aerial photography dated prior to 1945 has been transferred to the National Archives and Records Administration (B19, RG 145).

5. A loose-leaf publication *Comprehensive Listing of Aerial Photography Libraried at the United States Department of Agriculture, ASCS Aerial Photography Field Office*, provides information on coverage by state for ASCS, SCS, FS, and NHAP photography. It is available from ASCS county offices or APFO. An index map of the United States showing coverage of the NHAP program is available from the National Cartographic Information Center (E7). APFO also provides a useful brochure, *ASCS Aerial Photography,* which contains a brief description of its products, services, and ordering procedures.

G2 Army Center of Military History (Army Department)—Graphics Art Branch

1 a. *Pulaski Building, Room 4220 C*
20 Massachusetts Avenue, N.W.
Washington, D.C. 20314
(202) 272–0345

b. Open to the public by appointment.

c. Arthur S. Hardyman, Chief

2. The Graphics Art Branch prepares locational and situational maps to illustrate historical manuscripts published by the United States Army Center of Military History and

classified studies prepared for Army commands. About 50 to 75 new page-size or single-sheet maps are produced each year. Each one is based on primary source documents such as after-action reports, contemporary journals, oral histories, battle maps, and aerial photographs. More than 50 percent of the Branch's current work is devoted to mapping battle sites and troop support activities in Vietnam for a planned multi-volume series on the Vietnam War. Other work in progress includes a series of maps showing the geographical boundaries of medical commands and the locations of troop hospitals for a work on American Military Medicine, 1818–1865, and 9 maps showing the location of MASH units for a book on medical services in Korea.

3. See Army Center of Military History (B5).

4. Some of the manuscript base maps pertaining to World War II and Korean actions have been transferred to the National Archives and Records Administration (B19, RG 319).

5. No lists of the maps published by the Branch have been maintained since its inception in 1956. The published maps are not issued separately but are available only with the books that they illustrate. Major series, supplemented with these unique maps, include the official United States Army in World War II (78 volumes with three in preparation), the United States Army in the Korean War, and the United States Army in Vietnam. These books are sold through the United States Government Printing Office (K8). A published list, *United States Army Center of Military History Publications,* with ordering information, is available from the Center or the Superintendent of Documents, Department 6030, United States Government Printing Office, Washington, D.C. 20402.

G3 Army Corps of Engineers (Defense Department)

1 a. *Pulaski Building*
20 Massachusetts Avenue, N.W.
Washington, D.C. 20314
(202) 272–0010 (Public Affairs)

b. Open to the public by appointment.

c. Lt. Gen. Elvin R. Heiberg III, Commanding Officer

2. The United States Army Corps of Engineers manages and conducts engineering, construction, and real estate programs for the Army and Air Force, and a civil works' program of research and development, planning, design, construction, operations and maintenance, and research and development related to domestic rivers, harbors, and waterways. It also administers laws protecting navigable waters and wetlands. The Corps has a long association with map making dating from the establishment of the Bureau of Topographical Engineers during the War of 1812. Today, it continues to prepare a variety of maps in support of its many activities. At the same time, remote sensing technology plays an increasing role as a data source for the Corps.

Mapping and remote sensing activities are decentralized and carried out by division and district field offices located throughout the country. For the Washington, D.C. area, the Baltimore District of the Corps archives several types of maps. At the Office of the Chief of Engineers, M.K. Miles, Engineering Division, Engineering and Construction Directorate (202/272–8885), serves as point of contact for those interested in engineering and general maps. A point of contact for water transportation maps is Richard Schultz (202/272–8572).

The Water Resources Support Center (Colonel George R. Kleb, Commander and Director, 703/355–2250, Casey Building, Fort Belvoir, Virginia 22060) produces water transportation maps and co-manages the civil works' remote sensing program. The Center's Institute for Water Resources under the direction of James R. Hanchey, 703/355–2015, has produced two sets of specialized maps relating to national studies. One set, produced as part of the National Waterways Study, consists of a series of United States and regional maps showing the physical system of waterways and ports and international and domestic commodity flows (Dave Grier, 703/355–2438). The other set, produced as part of the National Hydroelectric Power Resources Study, consists of a national index map and regional (Electric Reliability Council Regions) maps. They identify hydroelectric power sites and generating capacity by categories of existing, incremental, and undeveloped (Darrell Nolton, 703/355–3084).

The Center's Data Collection and Management Division produces port series reports, which contain detailed maps of commercial piers, wharves, docks, and related facilities for coastal, Great Lakes, and inland waterway ports. The Port Facilities Branch (John Vetter, Chief, 703/355–2495) also maintains a map and photograph collection of port facilities with some items dating back to the 1920s.

The Division also serves as the principle point of contact for researchers interested in the civil works' remote sensing resources of the Corps of Engineers (David Lichy, Remote Sensing Technical Specialist, 703/355–3052). The Water Resources Support Center also organizes a symposium on remote sensing, which is held every other year. The proceedings of the symposium are published and available from the Center.

Basic and applied research in remote sensing and mapping is conducted by the United States Army Engineer Topographic Laboratories (E5).

3. For a description of the United States Corps of Engineer School Library, see entry A5.

4. The Corps of Engineers district offices have transferred many of their more recent non-current records to regional Federal Records Centers, including large scale maps and aerial photographs (B19). The majority of non-current maps and aerial photographs, however, have been transferred for permanent retention to the National Archives and Records Administration (B19, RG 77). There are also related materials in the Corps of Engineers' Historical Division (B6).

5. In addition to the published maps listed above, the Army Corps of Engineers issues a series of 6 regional maps of the United States showing lakeside recreational areas along reservoirs and a map of the United States depicting Army Engineer civil works' activities. Both are available from the Office of Public Affairs. Bound navigational charts of major inland waterways such as the Mississippi, Ohio, and Missouri Rivers and their major tributaries are available from Army Engineer division field offices.

The only published source of information for the remote sensing activities of the Corps is the *Remote Sensing Applications Guide* (Washington, D.C., Engineer Pamphlet 70-1-1, October 1979). Although dated, this three volume work provides a good overview to planning and managing a remote sensing program. Volume 3 contains a summary of the available remote sensing imagery in the 36 Corps of Engineers' district offices. This publication may be requested from the Corps of Engineers' Publications Depot (Hyattsville, Maryland, 301/436–2063).

Current remote sensing and mapping activities of the Corps of Engineers are described in *The Military Engineer,* a bimonthly journal published by the Society of American Military Engineers (K10) and *Engineer: The Magazine for Army Engineers* (K7). Histories of individual Corps of Engineers' district offices, which include maps and aerial photographs illustrative of the type of cartographic materials prepared by these field offices, are available from the Government Printing Office. These publications are listed in GPO Subject Bibliography SB-261, United States Army Corps of Engineers (K8).

G4 United States Board on Geographic Names (BGN)

1 a. *Executive Secretary*
Defense Mapping Agency
United States Naval Observatory, Building 56
Washington, D.C. 20305
Richard R. Randall (202) 254–4453

Executive Secretary
BGN Domestic Geographic Names
United States Geological Survey National Center (523)
12201 Sunrise Valley Drive
Reston, Virginia 22092
Donald J. Orth (703) 860–6331

2. The United States Board on Geographic Names (BGN) is an interdepartmental agency that has legal responsibility for standardizing place names used on Federal maps and in other official government publications. Established in 1890, the Board is comprised of representatives of 9 Federal agencies, appointed for 2-year terms, who review all new names, name changes, or name conflicts submitted by public or private persons or organizations. This work, which results in standardized names, is carried out by four committees—Domestic Names Committee, Foreign Names Committee, Executive Committee, and the Publications Committee. In addition, advisory committees comprised of non-BGN name experts assist the Board in areas having special kinds of names problems. These include Antarctic names and undersea features names.

3. The Board is provided with research and administrative support by the Geological Survey's Branch of Geographic Names (G14), for domestic names, and the Defense Mapping Agency's Name Branch (G8), for foreign names. Both agencies have extensive research facilities and libraries. Telephone inquiries about domestic names can be made at (703) 860–6256; for foreign names, (301) 227–2360.

4. The original minutes of the BGN from 1890 to 1940, the minutes of the Domestic Names Committee, 1947 to the present, and the decision cards and case briefs relating to domestic place names are in the Geological Survey's Branch of Geographic Names. Decision cards and case briefs relating to foreign names from 1890–1972 have been transferred to the Cartographic and Architectural Branch of the National Archives and Records Administration (B19, RG 324). Data prepared since 1972 are held at the Defense Mapping Agency.

5. BGN publishes some 175 gazetteers listing approved place names for all areas of the world outside the United States. The Executive Secretary, BGN Domestic Geographic Names, compiled a list of names of authorities in the United States, Canada, and Mexico that was published by the United States Geological Survey under the title *Official Authorities and Other Organizations Involved With Geographic Names—1984 United States Canada Mexico.* (United States Geological Survey Open File Report 83-881).

G5 Census Bureau (Commerce Department)—Field Operations

1 a. *Federal Center Number 3*
Suitland Road and Silver Hill Road
Suitland, Maryland

Mailing Address: Washington, D.C. 20233

Map Information (301) 763–7818

Computer Graphics and Computer Mapping Information
Frederick Broome (301) 763–7818

Map Orders
Jeffersonville, Indiana (812) 288–3213

Computer Tape Orders
Data Users Services Division (301) 763–4100

b. Open to the public, but scholars should call ahead to make arrangements since work hours vary for individual staff members. A shuttle bus is available from the main Commerce Building in Washington, D.C.

c. Ronald H. Moore, Associate Director (301) 763–7247

2. The Census Bureau collects, tabulates and publishes a wide variety of basic statistical data about the people and economy of the United States through its decennial censuses of population and housing and more frequent surveys of agriculture, industries and other subjects. The Office of Field Operations assists in this endeavor by providing geographic and cartographic support. Among its basic functions are determining the correct geographic location for each housing unit or business establishment in the United States and its territories, classifying each geographic location according to the tabulation units chosen for a particular census or survey, and producing map products for planning purposes (field maps), for illustrating data collected (maps in reports), and for data display (thematic maps).

The major programs and support divisions are described below.

3. The Geography Division maintains a reference library of unpublished documents relating to the mapping program of the Division. These include hard-copy files described below. The library also contains complete microfilm sets of both the 1970 and 1980 basic outline maps showing block and enumeration district boundaries (60,000 maps); various series of control lists and operation manuals which the Geography Division followed in preparing its various computerized file bases described below; and a computer inventory (MAPPER) of the individual sheets comprising the current United States Geological Survey quadrangle set housed in Jeffersonville, Indiana. For information about the holdings of the Division's library contact Lawrence Taylor (301) 783–5720.

4. Noncurrent unpublished maps showing enumeration boundaries for the bicennial censuses from 1890–1960 have been transferred to the Cartographic and Architectural Branch of the National Archives and Records Administration (B19, RG 29). There are also a few enumeration district maps scattered throughout the title collection of the Geography and Map Division of the Library of Congress (A21).

Some 32,000 outline base maps were prepared for the 1980 census. Those maps that show boundaries for urbanized areas down to the block level have been published ("Block Statistics Map Series" described below). The remaining 21,000 maps covering less populated areas have not been published. Referred to as "Non-Block Statistics

Maps", they portray boundaries down to the level of the enumeration district. The original Non-Block Statistics Maps remain on file in the Jeffersonville, Indiana, Geography Branch (see below). Microfiche copies of these maps can be obtained from the Geography Division. A complete set of the microfiche Non-Block Statistics Maps are also available for viewing at the Geography and Map Division of the Library of Congress and the Cartographic and Architectural Branch of the National Archives and Records Administration.

5. Cartographic products are currently available in the form of maps, digitized data files used for computer mapping, and printed reports. They are described in more detail in a brochure, *Factfinder for the Nation: Census Geography Concepts and Products* (1982. 8p.), for sale by Customer Services, and, *Bureau of the Census Catalog 1984* (June 1984), available from the U.S. Superintendent of Documents, United States Government Printing Office, Washington, D.C. 20401.

The maps and reports listed below are available from the Superintendent of Documents. Some maps may also be obtained from Jeffersonville, Indiana. Computer tapes are sold by the Data User Services Division.

MAPS

Outline Maps.—These maps accompany final reports of various series relating to the census of population and housing. They include map series showing congressional district boundaries of the 98th Congress by states; county subdivision boundaries by states; extent of blocked numbered areas by Standard Metropolitan Statistical Areas (SMSA); extent of block numbered areas and SMSAs by states; boundaries of Standard Consolidated Statistical Areas (SCSAs), SMSAs, counties, and selected places by states and territories; boundaries of SCSAs and SMSAs on a single map of the United States and Puerto Rico; boundaries of urbanized areas and their subdivisions; and boundaries of census tracts.

Block Statistics Maps Series.—Consists of 11,383 map sheets showing boundaries in all areas with numbered blocks, that is, urbanized areas and places of 10,000 or more population. These maps are available both in print and microfiche formats. They were designed to be used with a series of 374 microfiche reports of *Block Statistics* for SMSAs and states. These reports provide population and housing data by block-numbered areas. Special series of block statistic maps are available by counties, SMSAs (Metropolitan Map Series), urban concentration outside of SMSAs (Vicinity Map Series), nonmetropolitan incorporated and census designated places (Place Map Series, Place-and-Vicinity Map Series).

Indian Reservation Maps.—Consist of 85 sheets covering 20 reservations. These maps show boundaries for minor civil divisions or census county divisions, places, Indian reservations and Alaska native villages, census tracts, and enumeration districts (G15).

Data Display Maps (GE-50) Series.—These are thematic maps of the United States which show demographic and economic census data by county at scales of 1:5 million or 1:75 million. Thus far, the following GE-50 series maps have been produced: United States County Outline Map, Standard Consolidated Statistical Areas and Standard Metropolitan Statistical Areas Map, Congressional Districts of the 98th Congress Map, 1977 Per Capita Retail Sales by Counties Map, and Metropolitan Statistical Areas of the United States and Puerto Rico Map.

Congressional District Atlas.—Contains maps of the states and territories showing the boundaries and number of the congressional districts of the 99th Congress (1985).

International Map Series.—Prepared for the Agency for International Development in 1980. Includes four world maps showing the year of the latest census by country, fertility rate by country in 1978, population growth by country in 1978, and mortality rate by country in 1978.

DIGITIZED DATA FILES

Geographic Base File/Dual Independent Map Encoding (GBF/DIME) Tape File.—Provides digitized cartographic data for 278 metropolitan areas. It includes address ranges, ZIP codes, place codes, streets, railroads, streams, and political boundaries. This file and related software packages are described in *GBF/DIME System: A Tool for Urban Management and Planning*. Paper or diazo map sheets (CUE maps) showing the nodes (street intersections) and their identifying number are available for each metropolitan area.

County Boundary Tape File.—Contains a set of digitized county boundary coordinates in latitude and longitude and land, water and total area information for each state and county in square miles and kilometers.

Geographic Identification Code Scheme Tape File.—Records census geographic names and numeric codes. This is also available in printed form as *1980 Census of Population and Housing. Geographic Identification Code Scheme* (1983).

Master Area Reference Tape File (MARF).—Provides a computerized master list of population and housing data by states, counties, minor civil divisions/census county divisions, places, census tracts/block numbering areas, and block group/enumeration districts.

PICADAD.—A digitized list of 70,000 place names or key points with coordinates which allow one to determine distances between almost any two points in the United States.

PRINTED REPORTS

1980 Census Tract/Street Address Indexes.—Computer printouts that provide alphabetic listings of street names and their address ranges within census tracts for 277 SMSA's.

Boundary and Annexation Survey 1970–1979.—Contains information on all boundary changes from 1970–1979 for incorporated places of 2,500 or more persons.

GEOGRAPHY DIVISION
Robert W. Marx, Chief (301) 763-5636

Operations Division
Silla Tomasi, Chief (301)763-5702

This division is responsible for recording and updating nationwide geographic base files which are comprised of geographic area data and individual addresses (geocoding) linked by geographic classification codes, for preparing thematic and statistical maps, for conducting research on current traditional and cartographic methods, and for monitoring mapping operations at the Jeffersonville, Indiana facility. The Geographic Assistance Branch (Donald Herschfeld, Chief 301/763-5720) provides assistance to public users of geographic information and data and maintains the division library.

Planning Division
Joseph J. Knott, Chief (301) 763-1794

The Planning Division defines and develops standards and specifications for the Census Bureau's political and statistical geographic areas. It also prepares plans for the geographic support activities within the Census Bureau.

Geoprocessing Division
Jerome M. Glynn, Chief (301) 763-7880

This division performs planning and development work for the Topologically Integrated Geographic Encoding and Reference System (TIGER), a unified geographic information system, designed for the 1990 decennial census, which records all available data about an area in a single computer file. In the TIGER system, the computer assigns residential and business addresses to the current geographic location, performs data tabulation for geographic units, and produces census maps for field operations and publications. This Division also is responsible for planning and preparing specifications for the acquisition of source materials, for updating the map base and address reference portion of TIGER, and for recording the geographic points, boundaries, and related geographic data in the computer files.

FIELD DIVISION
Lawrence T. Love, Chief (301) 763–5000
Federal Building 3, Room 2037

This division organizes and conducts the Census Bureau's various field data collection programs through regional offices. Its Geographic Support Branch (Darren Althouse, Chief 301/763–1494) provides coordination between regional offices and the Geography Division. The Geographic Support Branch also is responsible for acquiring and evaluating new map sources for future censuses.

DATA PREPARATION DIVISION
Don L. Adams, Chief (812) 288–3344
Jeffersonville, Indiana

This division conducts pre-computer statistical processing operations for current and special censuses. Through its Geography Branch (J. Gary Doyle, Chief 812/288–3212), the division prepares the basic outline maps (32,000 map sheets for the 1980 decennial census) that show boundaries for all counties, cities, townships, census tracts, and block areas or enumeration districts in the United States and its territories.

G6 Central Intelligence Agency (CIA)

1 a. *Langley, Virginia*
(703) 351–1100 (Information)
(703) 351–7676 (Public Affairs)

Mailing Address:
Washington, D.C. 20505

b. Access is restricted to authorized persons with national security clearance.

2. The Central Intelligence Agency is responsible for the collection of foreign intelligence, conducting counterintelligence abroad, and for the research and development of technical collection systems. Cartography, by its very nature, plays an important role in intelligence work, and this is particularly true for the CIA. The Cartography, Design and Publishing Group prepares thematic maps of foreign areas, some of which are available to the general public. The National Photographic Interpretation Center processes and analyzes remote sensing imagery.

3. The CIA map and remote sensing collections consist of national classified materials and are not accessible to private researchers.

4. Declassified, noncurrent maps of the Office of Strategic Services (OSS), the predecessor of the CIA, have been transferred to the National Archives and Records Administration (B19, RG 226). Partial sets of printed copies of OSS maps are also found in the

University of Maryland Map Library (A40) and the Geography and Map Division of the Library of Congress (A21).

5. Unclassified selected maps, atlases, and data bases which have been released for public sale to the general public are available from the Government Printing Office (K8) and the National Technical Information Service (K12). Since January, 1982, NTIS stocks all unclassified maps produced by CIA. Reproductions of out-of-stock selected CIA maps may be obtained through the Library of Congress, Photoduplication Service, Washington, D.C. 20540 (202/287–5650). A subscription to all available current CIA publications may be obtained from the Document Expediting Project (DOCEX), Exchange and Gifts Division, Library of Congress, Washington, D.C. 20540, telephone 202/287–9527). The unclassified published CIA maps and atlases, received through DOCEX, are also found in the Library of Congress (A21), George Mason University (A13), and the University of Maryland (F11).

The following series of unclassified cartographic materials have been released by the CIA:

General Reference Maps of Foreign Countries.—These are multicolored maps showing transportation systems, populated places, and terrain features accompanied by thematic maps of population density, economic activity, ethnic groups, and other significant aspects of each county, 1969–1983 (93 maps).

Atlases.—Includes atlases on the Indian Ocean (1976), Middle East (1973), People's Republic of China (1976), Polar Region (1978), U.S.S.R. Agriculture (1974), and U.S.S.R. Energy (1985).

Regional Reference Maps.—Single-sheet multicolored maps of Southwest Asia, Persian Gulf, Afghanistan, China (Pinyin Edition), Middle East, Middle East Airfields and Facilities, and Central America.

Street Guides.—Pocket-sized guides of Moscow and Leningrad.

Digital Data.—A cartographic data base *World Data Bank II,* containing 6 million points of natural and manmade features, and the related *Cartographic Autonomic Mapping Program,* are availalble from NTIS.

The World Factbook.—An annual publication containing regional maps showing current political boundaries as well as geographical, political and economic data for each country.

G7 Defense Intelligence Agency (DIA) (Department of Defense)

1 a. *The Pentagon*
Washington, D.C. 20301
(202) 695–7353 (Information)
(202) 373–3910 (Freedom-of-Information)

b. Access is restricted to those with national security clearance.

2–3. The Defense Intelligence Agency (DIA) coordinates the foreign military intelligence-gathering activities of the United States Army, Navy, and Air Force, and serves as the major repository for the intelligence and mapping aerial photography film taken by these services. While the majority of the collection is classified, there is a fairly large amount of unclassified imagery dating back to World War II which has been turned over to the National Archives.

4. On a continuing basis, imagery is reviewed for intelligence/historical value with declassified aerial photographs being transferred to the National Archives and Records

Administration (B19, RG 373). The scholar desiring aerial photography of a foreign area should begin his search at the Cartographic and Architectural Branch of NARA, particularly for earlier date coverage. In some instances, if the film has been declassified and is no longer required for official business, DIA will release it to NARA to satisfy a researcher's request.

5. Because of the sensitivity of this collection, no public list of the film coverage is available. An important book, based in part on this collection and written by a former employee of the agency is Roy M. Stanley's *World War II Photo Intelligence* (New York: Charles Scribner's Sons, 1981).

G8 Defense Mapping Agency (DMA) (Defense Department)

1 a. *Building 56*
United States Naval Observatory
Washington, D.C. 20305
(202) 653-1131 (Public Affairs)

Office of Distribution Services
6101 MacArthur Boulevard
Brookmont, Maryland 20315-0020
(202) 227-2816 (Customer Service and Sales)

2. The basic functions of the Defense Mapping Agency (DMA) are to provide mapping, charting, and geodetic support and services to the Department of Defense for military operations, and to furnish nautical charts and marine navigational data to commercial vessels of the United States for maritime activities. DMA was established in 1972 through the consolidation of the major mapping, charting, and geodetic production facilities of the Army, Navy, and Air Force, including the Mapping, Charting, and Geodetic Directorate of the Defense Intelligence Agency, the Army Topographic Command (the former Army Map Service), the hydrographic charting element of the Naval Oceanographic Office (the former United States Hydrographic Office), the Air Force Aeronautical Chart and Information Center, the 1381st Geodetic Survey Squadron of the Military Airlift Command, the mapping element of the Strategic Air Command's 15th Reconnaissance Technical Squadron, the Inter-American Geodetic Survey, and the Department of Topography of the Army Engineer School.

The major programs and departments are described below.

3. The DMA libraries are discussed under the heading, Scientific Data Department.

4–5. Unpublished and published materials are generally restricted to Department of Defense personnel and contractors with security clearances, but some information and products are available. Researchers should consult with the Public Affairs Office or the Scientific Data Department described below. The mission and functions of DMA are described in *MC & G...A Brief History of U.S. Military Mapmaking - and the First Decade of the Defense Mapping Agency* (July, 1982). Products available to the public through the DMA Office of Distribution Services are described in their Public Sale Catalog. Specific products and publications are listed below.

DMA HYDROGRAPHIC/TOPOGRAPHIC CENTER (HTC)
6500 Brookes Lane
Brookmont, Maryland 20315
(202) 227-2006 (Public Affairs)

This center produces up to 3,000 new or revised topographic maps and nautical charts each year, as well as precise position data and cartographic data in digital form for millions of square miles of the earth's surface.

Topography Department

The Topography Department prepares topographic maps at various scales, including the standard operational topographic map (1:50,000); overlays showing cross-country movements, cover concealments, soil types, and vegetation; terrain elevation data; and feature analysis data for use in missile and navigation systems. Smaller scale topographic map series which are available to the public through the Office of Distribution Services include Area Outline Maps (1:20,000,000), showing major areas of the Earth in 27 sheets; Europe (1:2,000,000), showing major regions of Europe, the Mediterranean, and the Eastern Soviet Union in 6 sheets; Middle East Briefing Map (1:1,500,000); Africa (1:2,000,000), comprising a set of 36 sheets; Administrative Areas of the USSR (1:8,000,000); USSR and Adjacent Areas (1:8,000,000); Arabian Peninsula (1:2,250,000); Southeast Asia Briefing Map (1:2,000,000); and United States (1:3,500,000), showing administrative boundaries and major installations of the Army, Air Force and Navy. Unclassified superceded maps published by the Topography Department and its immediate predecessor, The Army Map Service, are found in the collections of the Geography and Map Division of the Library of Congress (A21) and the Cartographic and Architectural Branch of the National Archives and Records Administration (B19, RG 77). The official, unpublished topographic maps prepared by the United States Army before World War II are also in the National Archives and Records Administration.

Hydrography Department

This department is responsible for producing port and harbor approach charts, coastal charts, and bottom contour charts of foreign waters. These charts are available for sale to the public from the Office of Distribution Services and several commercial outlets in the Washington, D.C. area. DMA nautical charts are decribed in *Defense Mapping Agency Catalog of Maps, Charts, and Related Products Part 2 - Hydrographic Products*, issued in ten volumes by geographic area. Complete sets of these hydrographic charts dating from about 1841 are in the Geography and Map Division of the Library of Congress and the Cartographic and Architectural Branch of the National Archives and Records Administration.

Scientific Data Department
(202) 227-2380 (Topographic and Hydrographic Information)
Stephen Webb, Hydrographic Desk
John Lau, Topographic Desk
(202) 227-2109 (Inquiries Section for Library Materials)

The Scientific Data Department collects, catalogs, stores, analyzes, and evaluates cartographic materials of a worldwide nature. The department's Support Division operates and maintains the DMA libraries and performs geographic names research. The department's Analysis and Evaluation Division carries out extensive research on current cartographic and textual documents obtained from foreign and domestic sources. Questions concerning these materials should be directed to the Hydrographic and Topographic Desks or the Inquiries Section, which will either provide unclassified information directly, or refer researchers to appropriate specialists within the Department in response to specific questions. In general, information concerning hydrographic data is unclassified while topographic data is restricted.

The Map and Chart Library contains the most recent published editions of some 500,000 maps and 30,000 nautical charts, as well as 80,000 books and periodicals, 14,000 magnetic tapes of digital data of terrain elevations, feature analysis, terrain analysis, and catalogs of official charting agencies in foreign countries. Many of the foreign charts in French, German, Japanese, and Spanish have been translated into English. Since about 1951, the superceded maps and charts have been removed from the collection and sent to the Geography and Map Division of the Library of Congress. In 1980, for example, some 400,000 unclassified maps and charts captured during World War II by American military forces were transferred to the Library of Congress.

The Geodetic Library contains some 900,000 geodetic positions worldwide and some textual materials.

The Bathymetric Data Library has unclassified smooth sheets dating from about 1960, navigation logs, survey reports, and special tide studies. Smooth sheets prepared before World War II are in the Cartographic and Architectural Branch of the National Archives; those compiled between World War II and the 1960s are stored at the Washington National Records Center in Suitland, Maryland, and are serviced by the Information and Records Management Systems Division (202/227–2389). Boat sheets have been retained by the United States Oceanographic Office, NSTL Station, Bay St. Louis, MS 39522 (601/688–3390–Information). Some 7.5 million soundings of unclassified data have also been digitized.

The Foreign Place Names Library contains some 5 million place names used in support of mapping and charting activities.

The Names Branch carries out research on foreign place names and publishes the United States Board on Geographic Names' Foreign Gazetteers (G4). These gazetteers contain names for places and features. Each name is further defined by designations indicating the type of place or feature, latitude and longitude, area code, and Universal Transverse Mercator (UTM) grid coordinates. A list of foreign name gazetteers currently available is found in the DOD *Public Sale Catalog*.

DMA AEROSPACE CENTER
St. Louis Air Force Station
St. Louis, Missouri 63118

This center is responsible for producing aeronautical charts, digital data, flight information publications, and space mission charts for the Armed Forces.

DEFENSE MAPPING SCHOOL (DMS)
Fort Belvoir, Virginia 22060

At DMS, military personnel, civilian members of Federal agencies, and foreign nationals are trained in basic map preparation, geodetic surveying, terrain evaluation, map printing, and optical survey instrument repair.

DMA INTER AMERICAN GEODETIC SURVEY (IAGS)
Fort Sam Houston, Texas 78234

IAGS was established in 1946 to assist cartographic agencies in Latin America in performing long-range mapping, charting, and geodetic projects. These cooperating countries include Bolivia, Brazil, Chile, Columbia, Costa Rica, Dominican Republic, Ecuador, El Salvador, Guatemala, Honduras, Mexico, Paraguay, Peru, Panama, and Venezuela.

IAGS personnel assigned to each country provide technical guidance and training in field work, and map production and distribution. A brochure describing the program is available.

G9 Federal Aviation Administration (FAA)—(Department of Transportation)—Air Traffic Service

1 a. *800 Independence Avenue, S.W.*
Washington, D.C. 20591
(202) 426–3666

b. Open to the public by appointment.

c. Walter S. Luffsey, Associate Administrator for Air Traffic

2. FAA regulates air commerce in the United States, constructs and maintains air navigation facilities, and manages airspace and air traffic. Within the Air Traffic Service, the National Flight Data Center (202/426–3288) develops national standards for format, symbolization, and content of United States aeronautical charts and navigational publications, which are compiled and published by the National Ocean Service (G20).

3. The Cartographic Standards Section of the National Flight Data Center maintains a reference collection of approximately 2500 United States Geological Survey topographic quadrangles and National Ocean Service aeronautical charts.

G10 Federal Emergency Management Agency (FEMA)—Federal Insurance Administration (FIA)—Risk Assessment Office

1 a. *500 C Street, S.W.*
Washington, D.C. 20472
(202) 646–2769

b. Open to the public.

c. Brian R. Mrazik, Assistant Administrator

2. FEMA administers and coordinates national programs concerned with nationwide security emergencies and major domestic disasters. It also works closely with state and local governments, providing guidelines and furnishing technical and financial support for their emergency management programs.

The National Flood Insurance Program (NFIP), administered by the Federal Insurance Administration, has an important map component administered by the Office of Risk Assessment. Since 1973, individual Flood Insurance Rate Maps (FIRM), Flood Hazard Boundary Maps (FHBM), and Flood Boundary and Floodway Maps (FBFM) have been published for some 19,000 flood-prone communities. The FIRM delineates flood boundaries, base (100 year) flood elevations, coastal high hazard areas, and risk zones. It is used primarily by communities, insurance underwriters and lending institutions. The FHBM is a preliminary map, depicting approximate special flood hazard areas. The

FBFM shows the limits of the floodplain and floodway and is used by state and local officials for floodplain management and enforcement purposes. Since April 1985, FIA has begun publishing new Flood Insurance Rate Maps (FIRM) consolidating the information formerly found on the separate FIRM and FBFM maps. In addition, the new maps contain an alphanumeric grid system, an index of flood-prone streets and roads, and the addresses of the local map repository.

3–4. The Office of Risk Assessment, through its contractor, maintains active and archive files of all FIRM, FHBM, and FBFM maps. One copy of each map has also been transferred to the Cartographic and Architectural Branch, National Archives and Records Administration (B19, RG 311).

5. Publications include *Map Initiative Project Final Report* (1985), *How to Read a Flood Insurance Rate Map* (1977), and *How to Read Flood Hazard Boundary Maps* (1976).

G11 Federal Highway Administration (FHWA)—(Transportation Department)

1 a. *400 7th Street, S.W.*
Washington, D.C. 20590
(202) 426–0660 (Public Affairs)

b. Open to the public by prior appointment only.

c. Ray A. Barnhart, Administrator

2. FHWA is responsible for administering the Federal-Aid Highway Program, which provides for the planning, design, and construction of the National System of Interstate and Defense Highways and other Federal-Aid highways. In 1934, the Federal-Aid Highway Act included funds, not to exceed 1.5 percent of the amount apportioned for any year, to any state for surveys, plans, and engineering investigations for future road construction projects. In 1936, state highway departments began to prepare a series of county general maps as part of each state's highway planning program.

3. The Property Services Branch (James Kabel, Chief 202/426–0550) maintains a collection of some 2,500 recent copies of state and county road maps issued by state highway departments.

4. FHWA requires each state to deposit one signed copy of each new or revised county map as a record copy in the Cartographic and Architectural Branch, National Archives and Records Administration (B19, RG 30). Copies of the county and general highway maps are also deposited in the Geography and Map Division, Library of Congress (A21).

5. The Interstate Management Branch, Federal Aid Division (Curtis L. Shufflebarger, Chief 202/426–0404) publishes semi- annually a small map of the national system of interstate and defense highways showing their status.

Published copies of state highway maps may be obtained from state highway departments.

A large wall map (65 x 42 inches) of the Federal-Aid Highway System is available from the Department of Interior/United States Geological Survey (United States Geological Survey, Western Distribution Branch, Box 25286, Federal Center, Denver, Colorado 80225). For faster processing, the order number, US-5563, should be specified.

G12 Fish and Wildlife Service (Interior Department)

1 a. *18th and C Streets, N.W.*
Washington, D.C. 20240
(202) 343–5634 (Public Affairs)

b. Open to the public.

c. Frank Dunkle, Director

2. The United States Fish and Wildlife Service is responsible for conserving, protecting, and enhancing fish, wildlife, and their habitats. It manages over 400 national wildlife refuges for migratory birds, endangered species, and other wildlife, and operates national fish hatcheries. The agency also conducts scientific research programs to aid in the conservation and management of fish and wildlife resources. Two of the programs are associated with mapping. The Patuxent Wildlife Research Center also maintains a small but important map collection.

OFFICE OF NATIONAL WETLAND INVENTORY
1375 K Street, Room 415
William Wilen, National Coordinator (202) 343–1626

This office is responsible for the National Wetlands Inventory (Ross Pywell, Senior Mapping Specialist, 813/893–3872, 101 Monroe Building, 9720 Executive Center Drive, St. Petersburg, Florida 33702), a program that involves the aerial photographing and mapping of acquired and potential wetland habitat areas in the United States and Alaska. The following series of maps are prepared: Wetland Maps, showing different habitat types, compiled at scales of 1:24,000, 1:62,000, 1:100,000 or 1:250,000; National Wildlife Refuge Maps, varying in scale and size; acquisition and property maps showing land parcels purchased by tract; and status maps showing boundary surveys. These maps may be obtained from the address above or from the National Cartographic and Information Center (E7).

WESTERN ENERGY AND LAND USE TEAM (WELUT)
Division of Biological Sciences
Creekside One Building
2627 Redwing Road
Fort Collins, Colorado 80526–2899
Ralph Morgenweck, Team Leader (303) 226–9402

WELUT developed and maintains a computer-assisted geographic information system for natural resource management and planning, including vegetation/terrain mapping in Alaska, suitability mapping, analysis of land use, and simulation mapping of the quality of wildlife habitats. It is composed of the Analytical Mapping System (AMS), a software component for digitizing and editing maps and aerial photographs for entry into a digital data base; the Map Overlay and Statistical System (MOSS), the data analysis component of the geographic information systems which allows the retrieval, analysis, and display of maps and other spatial data; and the Cartographic Output System (COS) for enhancing and plotting maps.

3. A collection of more than 1,000 maps, originally assembled by the United States Biological Survey, is maintained at the Patuxent Wildlife Research Center (Kheryn Klubnikin 301/498–0496, Planning and Development Section, Patuxent Wildlife Research Center, Route 197 and Powder Mill Road, Laurel, Maryland 20708). It consists

of a wide variety of printed and manuscript topographic, geological, road, and thematic maps of areas and regions in Canada, Mexico, and the United States, 1850s–1960s. Many of the printed maps are annotated to show locations of game preserves and bird sanctuaries and the distribution of birds and animals. Noteworthy series include annotated and manuscript route and field maps prepared by C. Hart Merriam, founder of the Bureau of Biological Survey, Vernon Bailey, Merritt Cary, E.A. Goldman, E.W. Nelson, Walter P. Taylor, and other early Bureau scientists relating to the Death Valley Expedition, Olympic Mountains Expedition, and reconnaissance work in Alaska, Puerto Rico, Wyoming, South America, and the Southwest, 1891–1927 (ca. 105 maps); set of annotated and manuscript maps of the United States, Arizona, Oregon, and Washington showing the ranges of individual bird, animal and tree species, ca. 1910–1930 (100 items); a set of transparent overlay maps, the Distribution Map Series, prepared by the United States Biological Survey in 1935 to show the original and present range of wildlife (wild turkey, sage grouse, blue grouse, etc.) and waterfowl (American Eider, Wood Duck, etc.), and bird breeding locations (157 maps); 2 bound books of maps, some annotated, showing chiefly the life zones of North America areas mapped by Bailey, Cary, Merriam, and Nelson; and printed distribution maps of mammals, ungulates, carnivores, birds, reptiles, and plants, 1890–1927 (317 maps); and a set of maps of the Mississippi River relating Duck Food Studies with locations of vegetation and names of marshes and lakes, 1892–1894 (36 maps).

G13 Forest Service (FS)—Engineering Staff

1 a. *Rosslyn Plaza*
1611 and 1621 North Kent Street
Arlington, Virginia

Mailing Office
P.O. Box 2417
Washington, D.C. 20013
(202) 235–8035

b. Open to the public, 8:15 A.M.–4:45 P.M. Monday–Friday

c. Walter Furen, Deputy Director (703) 235–8098

2. This office is responsible for coordinating all mapping work for the Department of Agriculture, producing maps and aerial photographs of national forests, grasslands, and wilderness areas, serving as the principal point of contact for remote sensing activities within FS, providing technical liaison and training in remote sensing techniques through the Nationwide Forestry Application Program, and developing and distributing technical information on cartography, remote sensing, geodesy, and photogrammetry. An official of the Engineering Staff also represents the Secretary of Agriculture on the United States Board on Geographic Names (G4).

TECHNICAL APPLICATIONS AND SUPPORT
Harold Strickland, Assistant Director (703) 235–8046

Geometronics Development
Terry Gossard, Supervisor (703) 235–8187

This section is responsible for developing policies, procedures, standards, and specifications for the Services' national mapping program and for developing guidelines and procedures for the production of FS maps. Currently, it is investigating a national geographic data system that will involve automated cartography.

National Remote Sensing Coordinator
Ray Allison (703) 235–2138

The coordinator serves as the Forest Service's contact point with the public and government officials for questions concerning standard aerial photography, high altitude photography, satellite data, and other aircraft sensor systems. The Forest Service acquires conventional aerial photographic coverage of areas greater than 100 square miles through the United States Agricultural Stabilization and Conservation Service (ASCS) - Aerial Photography Field Office (APFO) (G1), who plan, contract, and inspect the film; photography coverage for areas less than 100 square miles is obtained on contract through the FS regional, station, or area director.

Administrative Support and Data Retrieval
A.L. Colley, Supervisor (703) 235–1425

This branch maintains a limited quantity of technical reports and maps through its Technical Information Center and Maps and Atlas Unit to meet the official needs of the FS headquarters.

GEOMETRONICS SERVICE CENTER
2222 West 2300 South
Salt Lake City, Utah 84119
Peter Hager, Manager (801) 524–4296

The Geometronics Service Center is responsible for producing all FS maps. These include: 1) Primary Base Series (PBS), which consists generally of 1:24,000 7.5-minute or 1:25,000 metric quadrangle maps from the United States Geological Survey to which FS information has been added; 2) Secondary Base Series (SBS) which is prepared at a scale of 1:126,720 or 1:100,000 metric, and covers a total or partial forest; and 3) Regional Base Series, produced at a scale of 1:500,000. The Primary Base Series are not normally published, but regional foresters will often supply black and white diazo prints to the public for the cost of reproduction and handling.

3. The Maps and Atlas Branch (Lewis G. Glover, Supervisor 703/235–8071) maintains a collection of some 10,000 map sheets, consisting of forest visitor maps published by the FS and USGS quadrangle maps that cover forests, grasslands, and wilderness areas administered by FS. The use of this collection is limited to FS employees and other government agencies, but its staff will answer questions concerning the collection and the availability of maps for individual forests.

The Technical Information Center (Constance Connally, Supervisor 703/235–3111) maintains an extensive collection of technical reports and books, many published by the FS, including works on photography and remote sensing. The latter also includes the *Remote Sensing Applications in Forestry* series, prepared under the auspices of the Forestry Remote Sensing Laboratory, Berkeley, California.

The Aerial Photography Field Office (USDA-ASCS, 2222 West 2300 South, P.O. Box 30010 Salt Lake City, Utah 84130, telephone 801/524–5294) maintains the collection of original film of all FS aerial photography less than forty years old of national forests, grasslands, and wilderness areas, including black and white, color, and color infrared. Status maps showing FS aerial photographic coverage for each state are available through the Field Office. It also maintains national coverage of the 1:58,000 scale color infrared photography obtained through the National High Altitude Photography (NHAP) Program.

4. A multi-volume atlas of forest maps and related records, compiled and formerly maintained by the Map and Atlas Branch as a source of information on the boundaries of National Forests, other early maps compiled or acquired by the FS, and aerial photographs of national forests taken by FS prior to about 1945, have been transferred to the National Archives and Records Administration (B19, RG 95).

5. The FS publishes a *National Forest Index Map* of the United States, and a *National Forest Wilderness and Primitive Areas Map.* It also sells lithographic reproductions of its Secondary Base Series, usually in the form of *Forest Visitor Maps,* which depict detailed information on individual National Forests, and *Wilderness and Special Designated Area Maps.*

Finally, the Service offers complimentary copies of *Forest Visitor and Regional Guides* which contain maps showing recreation areas and trails. Maps published by the FS can only be obtained from the Regional and Field Offices. A brochure listing these addresses is available.

G14 Geological Survey (USGS) (Interior Department)

1 a. *12201 Sunrise Valley Drive*
National Center
Reston, Virginia 22092
(703) 648–4460 (Public Affairs Office)
(703) 648–6892 (Public Inquiries Office and Sales)(PIO)

Public Inquiries Office (PIO)
Rm. 1028 General Services Bldg.
18th & F. Sts., N.W.
Washington, D.C.
(202) 343–8073 (Information and Sales)

Maps and Text Products (Mail Order Sales)
Now only available from:
Western Distribution
United States Geological Survey
Box 25286, Federal Center
Denver, Colorado 80225
(303) 236–7477

b. Open to the public. The Public Inquiries Office (PIO) is open 8:00 A.M.–4:00 P.M. Hours vary for Departments and Offices.

c. Dallas L. Peck, Director

2. Established in 1879 to classify the geological structure of the public lands and inventory their mineral and other natural resources, the responsibilities of the United States Geological Survey have been broadened to include a wide range of geographical research, hazard studies, topographic and geological mapping, and water resources assessments. The Survey has primary responsibility for the domestic topographic and geologic mapping and surveying of the continental United States, Alaska, and Hawaii. During fiscal year 1984, the Survey produced over 5,265 new and revised topographic, hydrologic, and geologic maps. It is a nationwide organization with major field offices at Reston, Virginia; Denver, Colorado; and Menlo Park, California, and a network of some 200 smaller field and special-purpose offices.

The major programs and support divisions are described below.

3. The USGS library, reference facilities, and data bank facilities are discussed in entries A12, E7, and D6, respectively. The Branch of Geographic Names Library and researh facilities are described below.

4. The earliest unpublished noncurrent records, program reports, manuscript maps, project files, and photographs have been transferred to the National Archives and Records Administration (B19, RG 57). Copies of some 20,000 unpublished scientific reports, maps, and water-resource investigation materials may be obtained from the Open-Files Services Section (Western Distribution Branch, Box 25425, Federal Center, Denver, CO 80225), the National Cartographic Information Center (E7), or directly from Geological Survey Field Offices. Some copies may also be available for inspection in the USGS Library (A12), the PIO in Washington, or the United States Department of Interior, Natural Resources Library (A19). Open-File Reports are announced in the USGS monthly list of publications. A list of reports released from 1938 to April, 1974, is available on microfiche from the Open-Files Services Section. Reports released since April, 1974, are listed in the yearly *Publications of the Geological Survey.*

The Survey maintains some 50,000 "map jackets", each of which contain original hand-drawings from field or photogrammetric measurements on paper, metal-mounted boards (1930 to 1955), mylar mounts (1955 to 1980) and other materials; stereoplotting sheets; information concerning the production and revision of maps; place name information; and related correspondence, memoranda, and map control lists. These are currently maintained by the four mapping centers described below. The original field survey notebooks recording field measurements and descriptions of the geodetic control stations are also stored in the appropriate mapping center. Most of these notebooks have been reproduced on 35mm microfilm and microfiche, copies of which are in the Cartograhic and Architectural Branch of the National Archives and Records Administration.

Motion picture films of cartographic activities are maintained by the Visual Information Services Office, described below.

5. The Survey publishes many brochures and reports describing its activities and products. A useful introduction is *A Guide to Obtaining USGS Information* (Circular 900). A free monthly catalog *New Publications of the Geological Survey* lists both maps and publications. This list has also been available on an annual basis since 1971. For earlier products, two cumulative catalogs list all maps and publications prepared by USGS for the periods 1879–1961 and 1962 to 1970. The published maps and publications described in these lists are found in the USGS Library and the Library of Congress. Publications currently available from the Survey include *Professional Papers,* which report on the results of topographic, hydrologic, geologic, cartograhic and remote sensing studies; *Bulletins,* which provide studies generally limited in scope relating to topographic and geologic investigations and descriptions of Survey instruments and mapping techniques such as map projections; and *Circulars,* which provide briefer treatment of geoscience research such as USGS digital cartographic data standards and mapping activities in Antarctica.

An annual yearbook describing the goals and accomplishments of the Survey is sold by the Superintendent of Documents, United States Government Printing Office, Washington, D.C. 20402 and the Survey. A helpful brochure is *Visitors Guide to the National Center U.S. Geological Survey* (1984) which contains a map of routes to the National Center.

The best description of the maps produced by USGS is Morris A. Thompson's *Maps for America: Cartographic Products of the United States Geological Survey* (1982). The basic series are described below.

Topographic Maps, show the natural and cultural features of an area. They are published at various scales to serve different users. The standard formats are the 7.5-minute 1:24,000 topographic quadrangle series (covering 7.5 minutes of both latitude and longitude) and the 15-minute 1:62,500 series. Some quadrangles are also available in photoimage format (orthophoto maps). Other series of topographic maps include:

1:50,000 Scale County Maps
1:100,000 Scale Quadrangle, County, or Regional Maps
1:250,000 Scale Quadrangle Maps
1:500,000 Scale State Maps
1:1,000,000 Scale United States Maps
1:2,000,000 National Atlas Sectional Maps
1:2,500,000 Scale United States Wall Maps
National Park Maps at various scales
Antarctica Maps at various scales

National Atlas of the United States (1976), consists of thematic and general reference maps. Some of the maps are available as separate sheets.

Landsat Image Maps, are maps produced from the multispectral images sent back to Earth from Landsat (Land Satellite) and converted to a graphic image. Maps are available for some states and geographic regions.

Geologic Quadrangle Maps, show bedrock, surficial or engineering geology. These maps are issued in 7.5 or 15-minute quadrangle units. Scale is 1:24,000 or 1:62,500.

Geophysical Investigation Maps, show subsurface structures of economic or geologic significance. They generally cover a state or larger region. Scale varies.

Miscellaneous Investigations Maps, emphasize geoscience studies but also include topographic maps of the Moon and Mars.

State Hydrologic Unit Maps, provide relevant information on drainage, culture, and hydrography for major river basins in the United States. They contain Federal, state and county hydrologic unit cataloging codes which assist researchers in using data from the Survey's automated National Water Information systems. Scale is 1:500,000.

Miscellaneous Field Studies Maps, relate to mining, mineral deposits, environmental studies, and wilderness mineral investigations. Scale varies.

Coal Investigation Maps, show bedrock geology, stratigraphy and structured formations of coal areas. Scale varies.

Oil and Gas Investigation Charts, show stratigraphic information for certain oil and gas fields and other areas having hydrocarbon potential.

Mineral Investigation Resource Maps, show geographic distribution and classification of minerals. Scales range from 1:250,000 to 1:5,000,000.

State Geologic Maps. Scales 1:250,000 and 1:500,000.

Hydrologic Investigation Atlases, show geohydrologic data at scales of 1:24,000 or 1:250,000.

Land Use and Land Cover Maps, depict 37 different levels of urban or built-up lands, agricultural lands, rangelands, forest level lands, water areas, wetlands, barren lands, tundra, and perennial snow or ice. These maps can be used with associated maps showing political, hydrologic units, census county subdivisions, and federal land ownership. Scales are 1:250,000 or 1:100,000. A brochure is available.

NATIONAL MAPPING DIVISION (NMD)
Lowell E. Starr, Chief (703) 648–5748
Frederick J. Doyle, Research Cartographer (703) 648–5752
VACANT, Scientific Advisor Geography (703) 648-5754
Gene A. Thorley, Research Physical Scientist (703) 648–5755

The NMD is responsible for preparing general-purpose base maps and thematic maps, maintaining a digital geographic/ cartographic data base, conducting basic geographic and cartographic research, and coordinating Federal topographic, mapping, and digital cartographic activities. The Division designs and prints the *National Atlas of the United States* and plays a leadership role in the development and advancement of cartography in the Federal Government. Through its operation of 10 nationwide Public Inquiries Offices and the National Cartographic Information Center, and its Distribution Center, the NMD makes its products and research activities available to the general public.

OFFICE OF RESEARCH
Joel Morrison, Assistant Division Chief
(703) 648–4639
Alden P. Colvocoresses, Research Cartographer,
(703) 648–4641

Office of Geographic and Cartographic Research
David A. Nystrom, Chief (703) 648–4522

This office conducts basic and applied research in geography and cartography. In its Branch of Analysis, geographers and cartographers carry out studies in geodesy, cartographic design, lithography, space systems, spatial data handling, automated cartography, geographic information systems, and thematic map data. The Branch of Applications investigates various methods and media for improving the representation and communication of spatial data. It also devises technical standards and procedures pertaining to the collection and handling of geographic and cartographic data in NMD. Recent research activities of NMD and the Office of Geographic and Cartographic Research are summarized in *Research, Investigations and Technical Developments National Mapping Program 1983–1984* (USGS Open-File Report No. 85-304). Reports of earlier geographic research projects, including those prepared under contract, are briefly described in *Geographic Research in the U.S. Geological Survey Bibliography 1966–1980* (USGS Circular 865).

The Branch of Geographic Names (Donald J. Orth, Chief (703/648–4506) conducts toponymic research with respect to the United States, Guam, American Samoa, Midway Islands, Puerto Rico, and the Virgin Islands. It also maintains the official domestic names information files and the records of the United States Board on Geographic Names (BGN) (G4). These files include place name decision cards, 1890–1940 (34 linear feet); place name cards prepared by Marcus Baker for Alaska (14 linear feet); published BGN decision lists, 1890 to the present; working cards, 1890 to the present (250,000 cards); and place name subject folders containing correspondence, supporting documents such as plats, maps and aerial photographs, petitions, and case history briefs, 1890 to the present (330 cubic feet). The Branch also maintains place name files donated by scholars or organizations that have carried out special toponymic studies. These include H.F. Raup's work cards for Ohio place names (35 linear feet), work cards prepared by the Massachusetts State Board on Geographic Names (9 linear feet), the Ramsey file containing more than 10,000 names for the state of Missouri, and the Steel file relating to the United States in general (52 linear feet of cards). In addition, the Branch maintains a reference book collection of early state gazetteers, United States

Postal Guides (1886 to the present), and a collection of topographic quadrangle maps published by the USGS. This historical map collection contains probably the most complete set of USGS topographic quadrangles in Washington D.C.

The Branch of Geographic Names maintains the automated Geographic Names Information System (GNIS) (entry D6). Information from GNIS is also available in the form of spiral bound computer printouts for 33 states and the District of Columbia, as unedited computer printouts, and on microfiche. Specialized searches will be done on request. This data base of some 2.5 million place names can also be accessed directly through online computer terminals at the NCIC Headquarters Office and the PIOs. Eventually the Branch plans to publish the GNIS as the *National Gazetteer of the United States of America* (USGS Professional Paper 1200). The only states to have been published thus far under this program are Delaware, Kansas and New Jersey. For information about this data base, contact the GNIS Manager, Roger Payne (703/648–4544).

Office of Systems and Techniques Development
Paul E. Needham, Chief (703) 648–4693

Through its staff branches and field center techology offices, this office conducts research in hardware and software systems and develops technical standards for cartographic and geographic programs. The Branch of Applied Sciences provides aerial camera calibrations for both governmental and contractor organizations.

OFFICE OF PLANS AND OPERATIONS
Richard E. Witmer, Chief (703) 648–4611

Office of Plans and Coordination
VACANT, Chief (703) 648–4160

This office is responsible for long range program planning and for coordinating these plans within USGS, the Department of the Interior, the Office of Management and Budget, congressional committees, and other Federal mapping agencies. Through its Branch of Requirements, it works with Federal, state, and other users of cartographic and geographic data to evaluate existing mapping products and services and to identify future requirements.

Office of International Activities
Clifton J. Fry, Jr., Chief (703) 648–5110

This office coordinates and facilitates NMD's participation in international activities relating to geography, cartography, surveying, and remote sensing. It manages overseas technical assistance programs and arranges for tours and training assignments for foreign geographers and cartographers. The office also serves as liaison with the National Science Foundation for planning and developing Antarctic programs with respect to mapping projects.

OFFICE OF INFORMATION AND DATA SERVICES
Gary W. North, Chief (703) 648–5780

Public Inquiries Headquarters Office (PIO)
Ernestine Jones, Chief (703) 648–6885

This office manages a network of ten information offices located throughout the United States including Washington D.C. The PIO provides information about the various programs and products of USGS. Information specialists will provide general assistance in map interpretation and geoscience investigations. They will also refer scholars to appropriate scientific offices for more technical information. PIO maintains limited copies of open-file reports, catalogs, map indexes, and circulars for reference or free distribution. Each office also provides over-the-counter sales service for professional papers and thematic and topographic maps. Many USGS books no longer available from the Superintendent of Documents can be obtained from the PIO. A brochure provides the addresses of each PIO and a list of the states for which they have maps and book reports. The PIO at the National Center in Reston, Virginia has maps and reports for all states; the PIO in the General Services Building, Washington,D.C. has maps for all states and book reports for states east of the Mississippi River.

National Cartographic Information Center
John T. Wood, Chief (703) 648–5963

The National Cartographic Information Center (NCIC) exists to help researchers find maps of all kinds and much of the data and materials used to compile and to print them. NCIC collects, sorts and describes all types of cartographic information from Federal, state and local government agencies and, where possible, from private companies in the mapping business. It is the public's primary source for current cartographic information. For a full description, see entry E7.

EASTERN MAPPING CENTER
K. Eric Anderson, Chief (703) 648–6003

The Eastern Mapping Center is 1 of 4 regional Mapping Centers. These centers perform geographic investigations, produce all the maps issued by NMD, and provide information services. The other Mapping Centers are: Mid-Continent, 1400 Independence Road, Rolla, Missouri 65401 (Lawrence H. Borgerding, Chief (314/341–0880); Rocky Mountain, Denver Federal Center, Denver, Colorado 80225 (Merle E. Southern, Chief (303/236–5825); and Western, 345 Middlefield Road, Menlo Park, California 94025 (John R. Swinnerton, Chief (415/323–2411).

GEOLOGIC DIVISION (GS)
Robert M. Hamilton, Chief Geologist (703) 648–6600

This division conducts geologic, geophysical, and geochemical surveying, mapping, and remote sensing programs as part of its responsibility to appraise mineral resources and to determine the geologic processes affecting the land and continental shelves of the United States. A good introduction to the Division is *Organization, Programs, and Activities of the Geologic Division, U.S. Geologic Survey* (USGS Circular 1000, 1985).

Office Of Regional Geology
Eugene H. Roseboom, Jr., Chief (703) 648–6959

Most of the mapping of the Geologic Division is carried out by this office. The Branch of Eastern Regional Geology (Gregory S. Gohn, Chief, 703/860–6404) prepares and distributes multipurpose geologic maps and regional geologic studies of the Eastern States, Puerto Rico, and the Virgin Islands.

Office of Scientific Publications
John M. Aaron, Chief (703) 648–6077

This office directs USGS scientific-publications programs. Staff editors review all manuscript maps prepared by GS geologists but the final preparation and printing of GS maps are done by the National Mapping Division. This Office also manages the USGS Library (A12).

Geologic Inquiries Group (GIG)
Viriginia L. Major, Chief (703) 648–4380

The GIG will respond to letter, telephone, and visitor inquiries about geologic maps in general and those related to the geologic mapping programs of the Geologic Division. GIG maintains a computer-generated Geologic Map Index (D6).

Visual Information Services Group
Sherman W. Harris, Chief (703) 648–4357

This group prepares exhibits and motion picture films pertaining to cartography and surveying. A permanent exhibit tracing the development of USGS mapping is located outside of the Public Inquiries Office at the USGS National Center. It displays original field surveying instruments, photogrammetry equipment, copper plates, specialized map engraving tools, photographs showing the various processes of engraving and printing, lithographic printing stones, offset lithographic processes, scribing tools, plastic scribe sheets, and current printing processes.

The following motion picture films are available through short-term loans to professional and technical societies: "Supplemental Control for Topographic Mapping", 1952 (29 minutes); "Negative Scribing for Map Reproduction", 1953 (22 minutes); "Topographic Mapping by Photogrammetric Methods", 1961 (21 minutes); "Preparation of Topographic Manuscripts for Reproduction", 1952 (30 minutes); "Tellurometer", 1959 (12 minutes); "The 1923 Surveying Expedition of the Colorado River in Arizona", 1979 (24 minutes); "Introduction to Photo Interpretation of Geologic Resources", 1960 (34 minutes); "Aerial Photo Interpretation of Forest Resources", 1960 (39 minutes); "Aerial Photo Interpretation of Hydrological Resources", 1961 (35 minutes); "Aerial Photo Interpretation of Soil Resources", 1961 (36 minutes); "Eros: Response to a Changing World", 1975 (14 minutes); and "Earth Resources: Mission 73", 1969 (18 minutes). The films are briefly described in a brochure, *Motion Picture Film Services of the U.S. Geological Survey.*

G15 Indian Affairs Bureau (Interior Department)

1 a. *18th and C Streets, N.W.*
Washington, D.C. 20240
(202) 343–4576 (Public Information)

b. Open to scholars by appointment.

c. John W. Fritz, Assistant Secretary

2. The Bureau of Indian Affairs (BIA) is responsible for working with Native Americans in developing and implementing programs to further their educational opportunities, social welfare, economic advancement, and natural resources development. The BIA also serves as trustee for Native American lands held in trust by the United States.

The Office of Rights Protection (Howard Piepenbrink, 202/343–5473, 1951 Constitution Avenue, Washington, D.C. 20245) maintains working copies of maps of Indian and Native Alaskan reservations. Printed copies of these maps are availalble from the Census Bureau (entry G5, section 5).

The Transportation Division (James Ball, Acting Chief, 202/343–6043, 1951 Constitution Avenue) compiles and updates the *BIA Highway System Atlas* (3 volumes), which consists of published maps of some 300 Indian reservations and 200 Alaskan native villages. These maps show Indian reservation boundaries, road systems, and other geographic features, generally at a scale of one-half inch to the mile.

3. The Natural Resources Library, Interior Department, entry A19, serves as the Bureau of Indian Affairs' library.

4. Noncurrent maps are transferred to the National Archives and Records Administration (B19, RG 75).

G16 Interior Department - Surface Mining Reclamation and Enforcement Office (OSMRE)

1 a. *1951 Constitution Avenue, N.W.*
Washington D.C. 20240
(202) 343-4953
(202) 343-4719 Public Affairs

b. Open to the public.

c. Jed D. Christensen, Director

2. OSMRE is responsible for establishing standards and regulations to ensure that the coal mining industry maintains sound environmental practices and reclaims the land during and after mining. The agency also collects funds from coal companies to be used for reclamation of lands abandoned before the surface mining law was passed. As part of the agency's permit application procedure, mining companies are required to submit maps of the land areas involved, showing all manmade features and significant archeological sites, names of present owners of record, and cross sections of the actual area to be mined.

3. Some 200,000 maps of mines and mining areas in the United States acquired through the application process described above and from interested mining engineers, geologists, mining companies, consultants, and Federal and state government agencies are maintained in microfilm format. Maps of mines in states east of the Mississippi are housed in the Mine Map Repository, Office of Surface Mining Reclamation and Enforcement, Federal Building, Room 1 B, 1000 Liberty Avenue, Pittsburgh, Pennsylvania 15222 (Michael Bursic, Supervisor 412/644-2769); printed mine maps for sites west of the Mississippi are housed in the Mines Plan Library, Office of Surface Mining Reclamation and Enforcement, Western Technical Center, Brooks Towers, 1020 15th Street, Denver, Colorado 80202 (Betty Thalhofer 303/844-3194).

A computerized index provides a list of all maps on file in the Map Mine Repository. The use of some maps is restricted due to proprietary information.

5. A useful publication is *The Mine Map Repository—A Source of Mine Map Data,* compiled by Curtis D. Edgerton (Bureau of Mines Information Circular 8657, 1974. 9 p.)

G17 Land Management Bureau (BLM) (Interior Department)

1 a. *U.S. Department of the Interior*
18th and C Streets, N.W.
Washington, D.C. 20240
(202) 343-9435 (Public Affairs Office)

b. Open to the Public. Hours Vary for Divisions and Offices.

c. Robert F. Burford, Director

2. The Bureau of Land Management (BLM) is the oldest mapping agency in the Federal Government. Its origin can be traced to the Land Ordinance Act of 1785 which initiated the surveying and plotting of the public domain states in Eastern Ohio under the direction of Thomas Hutchins in an area known as the Seven Ranges. Thereafter, Surveyors General were appointed independently to survey and map new areas of the public lands as they were needed until 1836 when they were placed under the jurisdiction of the General Land Office (GLO). In 1946, the GLO was consolidated with the Grazing Service to form the BLM. The mission of the BLM is the total management of 341 million acres of public lands, chiefly in the Far West and Alaska, and with respect to minerals, an additional 165 million subsurface acres. This includes resources management of timber, minerals, oil and gas, geothermal energy, wildlife habitat, endangered plant and animal species, rangeland vegetation, recreation and cultural values, wild and scenic rivers, designated conservation and wilderness areas, and open space; development and use of public lands; management of watersheds; and the sale and lease of public lands. In support of these programs, BLM has primary Federal government responsibility for surveying and platting the legal boundaries of public lands, subdivisions, and mineral deposits or ore-bearing formations situated on the public domain.

The major programs and support departments are described below.

3. The Natural Resources Library of the Department of Interior serves as BLM's library in Washington, D.C. (A19, RG 49). BLM maintains a separate library in its Denver Service Center which serves as the official repository for all BLM publications.

4. The original GLO map collection and noncurrent correspondence files, surveying contracts, instructions to surveyors, and other related records have been transferred to the National Archives and Records Administration (B19, RG 49). The original cadastral survey township plats and field notes of public lands have been dispersed (see below, Eastern States Office, Cadastral Survey Branch).

Certain pertinent surveying records are maintained in Federal Records Centers for disposal, permanent retention, or transfer to the National Archives and Records Administration at a later date. These include mineral surveyors records; United States mineral and location monuments records; group survey records (agricultural, land, mineral) containing instructions, reports, costs, and related documents; reports and maps documenting airborne and surface geophysical surveys; and survey records and maps prepared during mineral land classification surveys. For access to these records, the researcher must contact the records manager in the appropriate state office for approval and for the Federal Records Center accession number and location.

Other unpublished records are described below.

5. BLM publishes a number of basic works on cadastral surveying. A general introduction, *Surveying Our Public Lands,* is available from the Superintendent of Documents, United States Government Printing Office, Washington, D.C. 20402 (K8). Among more technical works are *Manual of Surveying Instructions* (1973), *A History of the Rectangular Survey System* (1983), and *Surveys and Surveyors of the Public Domain 1785-1975* by Lola Cazier (1976), which also can be obtained from the Superintendent of Documents; *Glossaries of BLM Surveying and Mapping Terms* (1980), available from the National Technical Information Service (K12); and *Mineral Survey Procedures Guides, Surveying Our Public Lands, Selected Computations of Astronomical Observations,* and *Typical Field Notes and Classified Excerpts,* available from the Denver Service Center (Survey and Mapping Development, D-416, BLM, Denver Federal Center, BLDG. 50, Denver, Colorado 80225).

Technical and scientific studies covering a wide range of topics are published as part of BLM *Technical Notes* series. Among these are several which describe the preparation, storage, and handling of field maps. These include "Map Carrying Book", describing a method for carrying maps in the field; "Field Maps", providing information about sensitized cloth materials on which maps can be printed; "Map Storage Cabinet"; "Map Carrier"; and "Map Filing System". *Technical Notes* may be obtained from the Denver Service Center.

BLM's quarterly illustrated journal, *Our Public Lands,* periodically contains brief, popular articles on the surveying and mapping activities of the Bureau. It can be obtained from the Office of Public Affairs or the Superintendent of Documents.

Several standard map series are published by BLM. Most of these maps portray western states and are produced in BLM offices located in those states, with the exception of the Surface Minerals Management Status Maps.

Surface Management Status Maps, show public lands administered by BLM, other Federal agencies, states, Indian tribes, and private companies. These maps are available by quadrangle for western states and northern Minnesota and Wisconsin at a scale of 1:100,000 from the United States Geological Survey (USGS) (G14) or BLM state offices. An index map of the United States showing the status of this program is also available.

Surface Minerals Management Status Maps, show the extent of Federally owned mineral rights overprinted on the Surface Management Status Map edition. Also available from USGS.

Land Status State Maps, generally show public lands, state lands, Indian Reservations, National Forests, National Wildlife Refuges, Military Reservations, and National Parks. Available at scales of 1:500,000 and 1:1,000,000 for Arizona, California, Colorado, Idaho, Montana, Nevada, New Mexico, Oregon, Utah, Washington, and Wyoming. These maps are available either through BLM state offices or the Superintendent of Documents.

Wilderness Status State Maps, show lands designated as wilderness or primitive areas, lands endorsed as suitable for wilderness areas, and wilderness study areas by the BLM, the United States Forest Service, the National Park Service, and the Fish and Wildlife Service. These are available for western states at a scale of 1:1,000,000 through the BLM Division of Recreation, Cultural and Wilderness Resources (Gary Marsh 202/343–6064).

In addition, large fold-out special purpose printed maps often accompany *Environmental Impact Statements* and *Technical Notes.* BLM publication, *Classification of the California Desert for Geology-Energy-Mineral Resource Potential: A Geostatistical Classification* (Technical Note 359), for example, contains five fold-out maps of the California Desert Conservation area showing iron potential, copper-lead-silver-zinc potential, gold potential, and reported occurrences of geology-energy-mineral resources, respectively.

TECHNICAL SERVICES
Suite 309
1129 20th Street, N.W.
Washington, D.C. 20036

Mailing Address
USDI- BLM- 720
18th and C Streets, N.W.
Washington, D.C. 20240

Division of Cadastral Surveys
Bernard W. Hostrop, Surveyor General (202) 653–8798

This Division is responsible for managing the Public Land Survey System, including cadastral surveys of public lands, surveys of offshore areas, and mineral surveys. It prepares the *Manual of Instruction for the Survey of the Public Lands of the United States.* Through state offices, BLM and contract surveyors prepare about 1200 approved survey plats each year, of which 600 are resurveys (conterminous United States) and 600 are original surveys (Alaska). These are available in 35mm microfilm and microfiche in public rooms located in state offices. The public contact for technical questions concerning cadastral surveys is Keith Williams (202/653–8798).

Division of Engineering
John D. Tabb, Chief (202) 653–8811
David Meier, Chief Cartographer (202) 653–8798
David Allen, Scientific Systems Manager (202) 653–8853

In addition to providing program direction for BLM's engineering activities, this division is responsible for cartography, aerial photography, and remote sensing. The Chief Cartographer is responsible for developing policies, establishing standards, and coordinating the Bureau's thematic mapping, photogrammetry, cartographic surveys, resource aerial photography, and high altitude photography. The Scientific Systems Manager is responsible for the Bureau's remote sensing programs (Landsat and Advanced Very High Resolution Radiometer -AVHRR) and Geographic Information Systems (GIS). The Geographic Information Systems consist of a large number of digital data bases derived from field data and Landsat imagery unique to BLM. A list of these data bases is in preparation.

EASTERN STATES OFFICE (ESO)
350 South Pickett Street
Alexandria, Virginia 22304
Curtis Jones, Director

The Eastern States Office is one of twelve BLM offices at the state level. BLM state offices are responsible for managing public lands and resources under their jurisdiction, conducting cadastral surveys of public lands, providing cartographic and mapping services, and releasing information to the public from survey records and maps. ESO has responsibility for the 31 states adjoining and lying east of the Mississippi River. Through its Federal Minerals Management Mapping Program (FMMMP), ESO produces Surface Minerals Management Status Maps covering the eastern region. A brochure, *BLM Maps For Eastern Lands and Minerals* contains an index map showing the sheets of this series which are currently available.

Public Room
Open to the public, 7:30 A.M.–4:00 P.M. Monday–Friday.
(703) 274–0074

The Public Room maintains the current public land status records for the Eastern States area, copies of which can be purchased. These include the *Historical Index* (HI), which records chronologically all actions that affect title to Federal lands; the *Master Title Plat* (MTP), which is a graphic representation or map of each township displaying all action affecting title; and the *Oil and Gas Plat* (OGP), which shows all oil and gas leases.

Cadastral Survey Branch
Lane Bowman, Chief (703) 274–0235

The Cadastral Survey Branch maintains some 140,000 original manuscript township plats and 7500 volumes of field notes of public lands in the Cadastral Records Section (Gary Johnson 703/274–0235). The plats show section and subdivision boundary lines, roads, streams, and lakes. They were prepared in triplicate. The original copy was retained by the Surveyor General. In the midwest, the original copy was transferred to the state. Some of these copies are now in state archives. The original plats of western states are in BLM state offices with the exception of Oklahoma, which is in the Cadastral Records Section of the Eastern States Office. The Cadastral Records Section also has custody of the original land survey plats and field notebooks prepared by GLO Deputy Surveyors for Alabama, Arkansas, Florida, Louisiana, Michigan, Minnesota, Mississippi, and Wisconsin and duplicate copies of original plats for western states and Alaska, dated 1804 to the present. The duplicate copies for Iowa, Illinois, Indiana, Ohio, Kansas, and Missouri are in the National Archives and Records Administration (B19, RG 49). Some of the third copies, which were often heavily annotated at the GLO district office to show the disposition of individual land parcels, have also been transferred to the National Archives and Records Administration; others are in state archives.

The official approved field notes from which the township plats were prepared are in state archives or BLM field offices (western states). Certified transcripts of the field notes, which were sent to the GLO Commissioner in Washington, D.C. are available from the National Archives and Records Administration (Iowa, Illinois, Indiana, Kansas, Ohio, Missouri) or the Cadastral Records Section (remaining public land states).

The Cadastral Records Section also has about 100 townsite plats of towns chiefly in Alabama, Florida, Illinois, and Iowa, ranging in date from 1760–1927. The Cadastral Records Section will provide reproductions of plats and field notes (35mm microfilm and oversize electrostatic copies) pertaining to the eastern states only. For copies of the original land survey records of the western states and Alaska, the researcher must contact the appropriate BLM state office. Copies of plats and field notes may also be certified for a small fee. While there is no charge for visitor assistance, there is a research fee for letter requests.

In addition, the Cadastral Record Branch has two rolls of microfilm recording the general instructions for Deputy Surveyors relating to the survey of the public lands (1815–1856), special instructions for mineral surveys (1879–1909), and manuals of instructions (1855–1902).

DENVER SERVICE CENTER
Building 50
Denver Federal Center
Denver, Colorado 80225
(303) 236-2329

The Denver Service Center provides technical support to the BLM Headquarters Office in Washington, D.C. and to the field offices. The Division of Records Systems operates the BLM Library, the official depository for all BLM publications. The Division of Survey and Mapping Systems provides nationwide BLM cartographic, photogrammetric, and surveying services and produces most of the maps published by the Bureau. Current aerial photographic coverage is available in natural color, color infrared (CIR), and black and white for BLM lands in Arizona, California, Colorado, Idaho, Montana, Nevada, New Mexico, North Dakota, Oregon, South Dakota, Utah, and Wyoming at scales varying from 1:12,000 to 1:31,680. BLM has compiled a catalog of map indexes showing coverage by state, in a looseleaf publication, *Summary of BLM Aerial Photography Information,* which is updated yearly. For specific information, the scholar should contact Lawrence Cunningham (303) 236–7991. Also useful are two other BLM publications, *Aerial Photography Specifications* (1983) and Wallace A. Crisco's *Interpretation of Aerial Photographs* (1983).

WESTERN STATES OFFICES

Bureau of Land Management maps of western states and Alaska may be obtained from the following state offices:

State Or Area Of Jurisdiction	*Address*
Alaska	Alaska State Office 701 C Street, Box 13 Anchorage, Alaska 99513 (907) 271–5555
Arizona	Arizona State Office 3707 North 7th Street Phoenix, Arizona 85014 (603) 261–5544
California	California State Office Federal Office Building Room E-2841 2800 Cottage Way Sacramento, California 95825 (916) 484–4724
Colorado	Colorado State Office 1037 20th Street Denver, Colorado 80202 (303) 837–4481
Idaho	Idaho State Office Federal Building, Room 398 550 West Fort Street P.O. Box 042 Boise, Idaho 83724 (208) 334–1770
Montana, North Dakota South Dakota	Montana State Office Granite Tower, P.O. Box 30157 222 North 32nd Street Billings, Montana 59107 (406) 657–6561
Nevada	Nevada State Office Federal Building, Room 3008 300 Booth Street, P.O. Box 12000 Reno, Nevada 89520 (702) 784–5311
New Mexico, Oklahoma, Texas	New Mexico State Office United States Post Office and Fed. Bldg. So. Federal Place, P.O. Box 1449 Santa Fe, New Mexico 87501 (505) 988–6316
Oregon, Washington	Oregon State Office 729 NE Oregon Street P.O. Box 2965 Portland, Oregon 97208 (503) 231–6277

State Or Area Of Jurisdiction	*Address*
Utah	Utah State Office 324 South State Street Salt Lake City, Utah 84111 - 2303 (801) 524–4227
Wyoming, Kansas, Nebraska	Wyoming State Office 2515 Warren Avenue P.O. Box 1828 Cheyenne, Wyoming 82001 (307) 778–2220

G18 National Aeronautics and Space Administration (NASA)

1 a. *400 Maryland Ave., S.W.*
Washington, D.C. 20546
(202) 453–1000 Information

b. Open to the public, but appointments are recommended.

c. James C. Fletcher, Administrator

2. NASA was established in 1958 to conduct research on extraterrestrial flight, undertake exploration of space, and support basic scientific and engineering studies in aeronautical and space activities. One of the important by-products of the satellite program has been the development of remote sensing from satellites. Between 1972 and 1978, NASA launched 3 Earth-observing satellites (Landsat) that radioed back images of the earth's surface from a nominal altitude of 570 miles. Experimental photographs and imagery have also been taken from the Apollo, Gemini, Skylab, and Shuttle manned spacecraft programs, as well as conventional NASA Aircraft.

Six offices plan, direct, and manage the research and development programs of NASA. The Office of Aeronautics and Space Technology documents and disseminates the results of NASA research and technology programs (Debra J. Rahn, Public Affairs Office, 202/453–2754). The Office of Space Flight plans and manages space transportation systems (Charles Redmond, Public Affairs Officer, 202/453–8536). The Office of Space Science and Applications directs all space flight programs concerned with scientific research and development that has applications to the broader scientific community, including remote sensing imagery (James F. Kukowski, Public Affairs Officer, 202/453–1549). The Office of Space Station manages the Space Station Program, whose goal is to develop a permanently manned space station by the early 1990s. The Office of Space Tracking and Data Systems tracks launch vehicles and space craft and distributes technical and scientific data acquired by them (Debra Rahn, Public Affairs Officer). The Office of Commercial Programs assists commercial space ventures (Azeezaly S. Jaffer, Public Affairs Officer, 202/453–1922).

NASA manages space flight centers, research centers, and other installations scattered throughout the United States. These include the Ames Research Center, Moffett Field, California 94035 (415/694–5091); Goddard Space Flight Center, Greenbelt, Maryland 20771 (301/344–6255); Jet Propulsion Laboratory, 4800 Oak Grove Drive, Pasadena, California 91109 (818/354–5011); Lyndon B. Johnson Space Center, Houston, Texas 77058 (713/483–5111); John F. Kennedy Space Center, Kennedy Space Center, Florida 32899 (305/867–2468); Langley Research Center, Hampton, Virginia 23665 (804/865–2932); Lewis Research Center, 21000 Brookpark Road, Cleveland, Ohio 44135 (216/

433–2900); Marshall Space Flight Center, Huntsville, Alabama 35812 (205/453–0034); and National Space Technology Laboratories, Mississippi 39529 (601/688–3341), located near Bay St. Louis, which manages research and development programs in remote sensing techniques and applications.

Scientific and Technical Information Branch (STIB)
Reporters Building, Room 826
300 7th Street, S.W.
Washington, D.C. 20546

Van A. Wente, Chief (202) 453–2910
Kay E. Voglewede, Head, Technical Publication Section
(202) 453–2906

Charles W. Hargrave, Head, Acquisition and Dissemination
Section (202) 453–2912

STIB manages NASA's Scientific and Technical Information Program, which is responsible for acquiring, indexing, announcing, and retrieving current aerospace literature for its scientific and technical staff. It maintains a collection of aeronautic and space-related documents at its Scientific and Technical Information Facility described below, and it provides for the distribution of NASA research and development reports and other special publications, prepares technical translations, publishes abstract journals and continuing bibliographies, and oversees a computerized data base containing citations for some 2 million documents.

An excellent description of NASA's scientific and technical information services and products is *The NASA Information System ... And How to Use It*, which is available from STIB.

History Office
Reporter's Building, Room 706
300 7th Street, S.W.
Washington, D.C. 20546
Sylvia D. Fries, Director (202) 453–2999

This office conducts research and prepares publications concerning the history of NASA, and will assist and support research in all phases of the history of astronautics, aeronautics, and space science. It also maintains an agency archives for the preservation of significant records and artifacts. The office has on file some 200 published and unpublished histories prepared under its support, including a dissertation, "The Politics of Technical Change: A History of Landsat", prepared by Pamela Etter Mack in 1983. A useful publication available from the Office is *A Guide to Research in NASA History*, compiled by Alex Roland (NASA HHR-50, January, 1984). It provides information on preparing research proposals for contract writing, NASA resources, procedures for conducting research, and potential book and dissertation subjects.

3. The NASA Scientific and Technical Information Facility (STIF) (Herman W. Miles, General Manager 301/859–5300, ext. 374, Mailing address: P.O. Box 8757, Baltimore-Washington International Airport, Maryland 21040) is not open to the public. It maintains a collection of 1,250,000 research documents pertaining to aerospace activities. More than 100,000 technical reports, patents, journal and periodical articles, books, pamphlets, conference proceedings, professional papers, translations, and dissertations are added to this collection each year, making it the largest collection of aerospace information in the world. The documents are acquired from government agencies, universities, research laboratories, commercial corporations, and publishers in more than

200 countries. These documents are controlled by a central computerized file and accessed by keywords based on the *NASA Thesaurus*, a comprehensive description of some 18,000 subject entries.

Although this collection is made available only to NASA employees and contractors and to certain affiliated organizations, some 60,000 of the most important, unclassified documents are indexed and abstracted twice monthly in *Scientific and Technical Aerospace Reports* (STAR), an abstract journal produced by STIB, and in *International Aerospace, Abstracts* (IAA), compiled by the Technical Information Service of the American Institute of Aeronautics and Astronautics (AIAA) (555 West 57th Street, 12th Floor, New York, New York 10019). *STAR* describes technical reports; *IAA* lists aerospace-related journal articles and similar forms of published literature. *STAR* and many of the NASA and other documents announced in *STAR* may be consulted in NASA Center libraries and regional Government Printing Office depository libraries. They can also be purchased from the Superintendent of Documents, United States Government Printing Office, Washington, D.C. 20402 (K8). Microfiche copies are available on a subscription basis from NTIS (K12). *IAA* and IAA publications are available from AIAA.

The citations are arranged according to 94 subject categories, 3 of which are pertinent - 35, Instrumentation and Photography, which includes remote sensors; 42, Geosciences (General), and 43, Earth Resources, which includes remote sensing, photogrammetry, and aerial photography. Subject category number 43, Earth Resources, is also described separately in *Earth Resources: A Continuing Bibliogrpahy With Indexes,* which has been issued quarterly by STIB since June, 1974. The annotated references, selected from both *STAR* and *IAA,* are grouped according to these categories: agriculture and forestry, environmental changes and cultural resources, geodesy and cartography, geology and mineral resources, oceanography and marine resources, hydrology and water management, data processing and distribution systems, instrumentation and sensors, and general. The subject index of a recent issue contained the following number of entries for aerial photography (22), computer-aided mapping (3), computer graphics (2), geodesy (6), geodetic coordinates (1), geodetic surveys (10), geographic information systems (6), ice mapping (1), image analysis (19), Landsat Satellites (50), mapping (26), maps (1), photogrammetry (22), photo interpretation (21), photomapping (17), photomaps (1), radar maps (1), remote sensing (111), satellite imagery (87), Seasat satellites (8), soil mapping (4), thematic mapping (51), thermal mapping (1), and topography (15).

Earth Resources and two bibliographies covering earth resource abstracts prepared between 1962 and 1973, *Remote Sensing of Earth Resources* (1970), and *Earth Resources* (1975), are available from NTIS.

NASA RECON (REmote CONsole), a computerized, online, interactive system provides rapid access to some 2 million documents in *STAR, IAA,* NASA Contracts Data File, NASA tech Briefs, the NASA Library Collection, and other sources. A search for remote sensing literature through NASA RECON revealed 82 pertinent citations for the period 1964–1983 including such works as K.A. Zvonarev, "The Transfer of the Contents of Satellite Pictures into Geographic Maps" (Leningrad, 1976); Noel G. DeSouza, "Interpreting the Environment from Aerial and Space Images" (Sydney, 1978); United Nations, *Aircraft and Satellite Remote Sensing for Developing Nations* (Rome, 1971); and Otto Kolbl, "Combined Evaluation of Satellite and Aerial Photographs for Topographic Mapping" (dissertation, in German language, Universtat Karlsruhe, 1973).

The Goddard Space Flight Center Library, Greenbelt, Maryland 20771, (Adelaide Del Frate, Head 301/344–6244) is open to United States citizens from 8:00 A.M. to 4:40 P.M., Monday through Friday. Limited interlibrary loan service is provided. A photocopier is available, without charge. The library has 70,000 books, 40,000 journals, and subscribes to 1,000 current journals.

The Broadcast and Audiovisual Branch (Joseph Headlee, Chief 202/453-8594, Room

6035) maintains a photolibrary of press-release color photographic prints, including 2200 selected space photographs from Apollo 7 through 17, Mariner VI through IX, Pioneer 10 and 11, Skylab 1 through 4, Viking 1 and 2, Space Shuttle and Gemini. They are organized by country. There are also 200 NASA aircraft conventional aerial photographic prints of the United States. These photographs are available for examination only, reproductions are limited to the media.

The NASA Headquarters Library (202/453–8545, Room A 39, 600 Independence Avenue, S.W., Washington, D.C. 20546) is open to the public from 8:00 A.M. to 4:30 P.M., Monday through Friday, but readers should contact the library in advance to determine security regulations. Interlibrary loan is available and there is no charge for photocopies. The library has some 30,000 books, journals, NASA publications, including *STAR* and *IAA*, and publications of the National Advisory Committee for Aeronautics, a predecessor of NASA. It also contains NASA reports in microfiche form. Access to the library collection is through a card file or NASA RECON, which can be searched by date, subject, author, and contract number. NASA RECON is available only to NASA employees and contractors and other government agencies.

The National Space Science Data Center is described in entry D9.

4. The NASA Headquarters History Office Archives (Lee D. Saegesser, NASA Archivist, 202/453–8303) contains approximately 900 cubic feet. Pertinent series include Congressional Documents, consisting of committee reports, hearings and special studies (25 feet); Unmanned Programs, Projects, and Satellites (46 feet), containing correspondence, news releases, clippings, articles, brochures, mission operations reports, and translations relating to Earth Resource Satellite (3 feet), Landsat (4 feet), and Seasat; and Manned Spaceflight (75 feet), including French SPOT.

Some 150,000 cubic feet of noncurrent records from NASA Headquarters, Goddard Space Flight Center, and Langley Research Center are stored in the Washington National Records Center, 4205 Suitland Road, Suitland, Maryland. For assistance in using these records, the researcher should contact the NASA Records Officer (Nina K. Letaw, 202/453–2918). Unclassified records may be viewed at Suitland or recalled by the NASA Archivist for examination in the NASA Archives.

5. NASA disseminates the results of its scientific and technological investigations and studies through Special Publications (SP), Reference Publications (RP), and Conference Publications (CP). All the books published by NASA through 1983 are listed in *Records of Achievement NASA Special Publications* (Washington, D.C., 1983). Current announcements are listed in the bimonthly *Scientific and Technical Aerospace Reports* (STAR). Two important NASA publications for the analysis of remote sensing imagery are Nicholas M. Short's *The Landsat Tutorial Workbook: Basics of Satellite Remote Sensing* (RP 1078, 1982), and Nicholas M. Short's *Mission to Earth: Landsat Views the World* (SP 360, 1976). NASA publications are printed and sold through the Government Printing Office or the National Technical Information Service (K12).

G19 National Capital Planning Commission (NCPC)—Carto/Graphic Division

1 a. *1325 G Street, N.W.*
Washington, D.C. 20578
(202) 724-0211–0212

b. Open to the public. 8:00 A.M.–5:00 P.M. Monday–Friday

c. Francis H. Deter, Jr., Director

2. NCPC is the central planning agency for the Federal government in the National Capital Region, which includes the District of Columbia and the adjacent counties of Montgomery and Prince George's in Maryland and Fairfax, Loudon, Prince William, and Arlington in Virginia. The Commission is responsible for developing and coordinating a comprehensive plan and program for the growth and development of the National Capital, reviewing regional, area, and project master plans, zoning regulations and map change proposals, and for scheduling, coordinating, and implementing the Federal Capital Improvements Program. In support of these programs, the Carto/Graphic Division produces the required publications, maps, and other visual materials, and maintains a map collection.

3. The Carto/Graphic Division has custody of approximately 180,000 maps and drawings submitted to the Commission for review on 35mm microfilm, as well as maps compiled by NCPC. This file includes project master plans, site plans, landscape plans, traffic-flow maps, jurisdictional boundary maps, survey plats, urban renewal plans, project area base maps, socio-economic and demographic maps, land-use maps, and road maps. The collection dates from 1940 to the present.

The Carto/Graphic Division also has a set of Sanborn insurance atlases covering Washington, D.C., which is updated yearly (11 volumes) and a set of Baist atlases of the city, 1956 (4 volumes), both of which delineate buildings, property lines, and streets.

4. Unpublished materials include eighteen series of planimetric and photogrammetric reproducible mylar base maps and rectified aerial photographs of the District of Columbia and the National Capital Region, ranging in scale from 1 inch equals 200 feet to 1 inch equals 10,000 feet. The most significant series includes coverage of the entire District of Columbia at a scale of 1 inch equals 200 feet, 1981 (115 sheets). There are also urban renewal area maps, a census tract map, and a multisheet District of Columbia zoning map. A list of these map series, with reproduction information, is available on request.

Noncurrent cartographic materials have been retired to the National Archives and Records Administration (B19, RG 328).

5. The *NCPC Quarterly* provides a summary of Commission actions on projects and programs and other information relating to the development of the National Capital Region. It is available from the Public Affairs Office (202/724-0174). Some of the work of the Carto/Graphic Division is described in Francis H. Deter, Jr., "Urban Renewal Mapping", *Revista Cartografia,* volume 36 (December, 1979), pp. 71-80.

G20 National Ocean Service (NOS) (Commerce Department —National Oceanic and Atmospheric Administration) (NOAA)—Office of Charting and Geodetic Services

1 a. *Washington Science Center Building 1*
6001 Executive Boulevard
Rockville, Maryland 20852
(301) 443-8204
(301) 443-8031 External Affairs Staff, Office of the Assistant Administrator, NOS
(202) 377-8090 (Public Information)

Chart Sales Office (301) 443-8005

Distribution Branch (Mail-order sales and over-the-counter sales).
6501 Lafayette Avenue
Riverdale, Maryland 20737

Information (301) 436–6900
Chart Sales Office (301) 436–6980

b. Open to the public, but hours vary. Appointments are recommended.

c. RADM John D. Bossler, Director

2. The oldest scientific agency in the Federal Government, NOS traces its origin to the Survey of the Coast, which was established by Thomas Jefferson in 1807 to chart the coastal waters of the United States. In 1836 the agency was renamed the United States Coast Survey and in 1878 renamed the Coast and Geodetic Survey (C&GS) when geodetic responsibilities were added by Congress. The C&GS was expanded again in 1970 and its name changed to the National Ocean Survey when it assumed responsibility for charting the Great Lakes. At that time it became part of the National Oceanic and Atmospheric Administration (NOAA). Its present organization and name dates from November 1, 1982. Within NOS, the Office of Charting and Geodetic Services is responsible for compiling and preparing marine charts and related products for United States coastal waters and the Great Lakes, domestic aeronautical charts, and a nationwide geodetic control network that provides a framework for local, state, and national mapping and charting. See the individual entries below.

The External Affairs Staff of NOS coordinates activities with user groups, designs and implements marketing strategies for the NOS, and provides editorial, publication, and graphics services. This office also maintains the Display Center located in the Washington Science Center Building 1, which traces the history of the surveying and charting activities of NOS and its predecessors. The Display Center contains nineteenth and twentieth century surveying and engraving instruments, including Ferdinand R. Hassler's 1815 theodolite; portraits of Hassler and Alexander Dallas Bache; early surveying books dating from the eighteenth century; manuscript and printed charts prepared by the Coast Survey and the C&GS; and copper plates engraved by Survey engravers, including a copper plate engraved by James McNeil Whistler about 1854. The exhibit also contains the original copper plate of Andrew Ellicott's plan of Washington, D.C., engraved by Thackara and Vallance, 1792, and copper plates from the Charles Wilkes Exploring Expedition, 1838–1842. For information concerning specific surveying instruments or charts on display, or the history of NOS and its predecessor agencies, contact William A. Stanley (Deputy Chief, External Affairs Staff, 301/443–8031).

3. See NOAA Library and Information Services Division (A33), Physical Sciences Services Section (A32), and National Geodetic Survey Library below.

4. Noncurrent textual records and a record set of published aeronautical and nautical charts have been transferred to the National Archives and Records Administration (B19, RG 23). The Geography and Map Division, Library of Congress, also maintains series of NOS charts (A21). Unpublished cartographic records have been retained by NOS. They are described below.

Hydrographic and Topographic Surveys, 1834 to the present.—23,000 sheets. Hydrographic survey sheets are the unpublished compilation sheets that store all of the primary hydrographic data in graphic form including soundings, bottom contour lines, locations of navigation aids, and shorelines. For this reason, they provide more detailed information on survey areas than the final published charts. Hydrographic survey sheets are identified by the prefix "H". They range in scale from 1:5,000 or 1:10,000 for harbor areas to smaller scales for offshore surveys. Topographic survey sheets are identified by the prefix "T" for surveys compiled before 1969 and "TP" (Topographic Photogrammetry) for later surveys. Topographic surveys may show only the shoreline and adjacent features or they may depict elevations, property lines, houses, roads, and vegetation as far as 5 miles or more inland. From 1834–1927 topographic surveys were made by plane table, since 1927 they have been compiled from aerial photographs and ground survey data. The scale of most topographic survey sheets are 1:10,000 or 1:20,000. Map indexes are available in the form of large nautical charts annotated to show the most recent coverage and page size sheets (8.5 x 11 inches). The indexes and an incomplete 210mm microfilm browse file of individual H and T series may be examined in the Data Control Section, (George H. Mastrogianis, Chief 301/443–8408), which is open to the public, 8:00 A.M.–4:30 P.M., Monday–Friday (Washington Science Center Building 2, Room 151). Reproductions of the individual page-size indexes and the H and T series may also be obtained from the Data Control Section; copies of the TP series are available from the Photo Map and Imagery Information Unit (Robert S. Kornspan, Chief, 301/443–8601, Room 526).

Descriptive Reports, 1834 to the present.—Narrative documents accompany most of the hydrographic and topographic surveys. They provide important information on the quality and accuracy of survey work and serve as an index to records relating to the survey. These reports are also available from the Data Control Section.

Soundings Data.—Prior to 1964, soundings data were hand recorded from hydrographic surveys and compiled in Soundings Volumes. Since that time, primary depth data obtained from echo sounders has been collected in digital form and maintained as digital survey records. Graphic depth records or fathograms are depth records that have been recorded manually. They provide graphic or analog records of bottom profiles of virtually every sounding line undertaken by NOS since World War II. Information about soundings data can be obtained from the Hydrographic Surveys Branch (301/443–8231).

Aerial Photographs.—Aerial photographs of coastal areas used in support of nautical charting programs are available in color, color infrared, panchromatic, and black and white infrared. These photographs date chiefly from the 1940s to the present, but a few were made as early as the 1930s. The scales vary from 1:10,000 to 1:40,000. Aerial photographic indexes and individual aerial photographs may be obtained from the Photo Map and Imagery Information Unit. A brochure, *History of Photogrammetry at the National Ocean Service,* briefly describes the contribution of NOS to the development of aerial photography and photogrammetry.

5. A guide entitled *National Ocean Service Products and Services* provides an introduction to NOS and its publications. More detailed information is found in the *National Ocean Survey Products and Services Handbook. May 1982 (Second Edition).* Specific products and publications are described below.

Aeronautical Charts.—NOS produces a large variety of types and scales of aeronautical charts which are listed in its *Catalog of Aeronautical Charts and Related Publications,* available from the Distribution Branch. The most thorough coverage is provided by 55 section charts covering the United States, Alaska, Hawaiian Islands, and Puerto Rico at a scale of 1:500,000. Designed for visual navigation of slow to medium speed aircraft, section charts portray topographic features and distinctive landmarks such as populated places, roads, rivers, and railroads. In addition to publishing and distributing aeronautical charts of the United States, NOS also sells charts of foreign areas published by the Defense Mapping Agency Aerospace Center (G8). These include worldwide coverage for Operational Navigation Charts and Jet Navigation Charts, which are also listed in the NOS *Catalog* along with a list of authorized agents who sell these charts.

Bathymetric Maps and Special Purpose Charts.—Prepared for scientific and engineering studies offshore, this category includes bathymetric maps (topographic maps of the sea floor which depict the size, shape, and distribution of underwater features), geophysical maps, marine boundary maps, offshore mineral leasing area maps, and storm evacuation maps. These maps are listed and described in *Map and Chart Catalog No. 5: Bathymetric Maps and Special Purpose Charts.* Additional information about these maps can be obtained from the Bathymetric Mapping Group (301/443-8855).

Nautical Charts.—These include published harbor charts (1:50,000 and larger), coast charts (1:50,000 to 1:1,000,000) used for offshore navigating, and small craft charts of American coastal waters. These charts and their prices are listed in four regional Nautical Chart Catalogs.

United States Coast Pilot.—A series of nine books that provide supplemental navigational information not found on nautical charts.

NATIONAL GEODETIC SURVEY DIVISION (NGS)
11400 Rockville Pike
Rockville, Maryland 20852
William M. Kaula, Chief (301) 443–8100

NGS is responsible for the establishment and maintenance of the National Geodetic Reference System which consists of more than one million geodetic control points that provide the common reference base for mapping and charting throughout the United States.

Geodetic Research and Development Laboratory
Bruce C. Douglas, Chief (301) 443–8858

This Laboratory carries out research and development in geodesy and the related fields of photogrammetry, astronomy, oceanography, and computer sciences with respect to improving point positioning systems, refining the geoid, and designing specialized geodetic instruments.

Horizontal Network Branch
Elizabeth B. Wade, Chief (301) 443–8168

The Branch is involved in the automation and analysis of archival and new observational data, adjustment of arc and area triangulation, traverses and trilateration, vertical angle adjustments to determine trigonometric elevations, analysis of the strength and internal accuracy of the basic National Geodetic Horizontal Network and preparation of specifications and standards of accuracy for surveys in order to maintain the National Geodetic Reference System.

Vertical Networks Branch
Gary Young, Acting Chief (301) 443–8567

This Branch is responsible for computing and adjusting the vertical component of the National Geodetic Reference System. The Vertical Projects Section maintains current files of vertical observational data and descriptions and calibration data of vertical survey equipment. The Geodetic Leveling Section maintains a current file of reset vertical control points. The Vertical Analysis Section provides technical assistance to the public with respect to vertical control adjustments and storage and retrieval systems.

Gravity Astronomy and Space Geodesy Branch
Benjamin W. Remondi, Acting Chief (301) 443–8171

This branch conducts practical and theoretical studies in gravity, and astronomic and space geodesy. The Gravity Section maintains an operational gravity data base and answers technical questions concerning this data.

Systems Development Branch
John Gergen, Chief (301) 443–1286

This branch conducts systems analysis and planning to identify NGS requirements in computing hardware and software, and performs program design and implementation on existing in-house computers. It is responsible for the design and implementation of the NGS integrated database which will enable a user to access almost all NGS geodetic data in a uniform mode.

Operations Branch
Gerald C. Saladin (301) 443–8792

This branch manages the NGS field parties engaged in network surveys. It also provides training in geodetic control surveys to state and local governments and foreign nationals. The Instrument and Equipment Section at Corbin, Virginia (703/925–2029), tests and evaluates geodetic instruments and equipment.

National Geodetic Information Center (NGIC)
John F. Spencer, Jr. (301) 443–8281

NGIC collects, publishes, and maintains information concerning NGS networks. The Horizontal Data Section maintains an inventory of all horizontal control data. The Vertical Data Section has a similar inventory for vertical data.

The Geodetic Reference Service Group (301/443–8316) maintains a geodetic library containing technical publications, arranges for retrieval of archival geodetic records, and researches historic geodetic data upon request. Through an arrangement with the Superintendent of Documents, United States Government Printing Office (GPO) (K8), the Geodetic Reference Service Group is also responsible for distributing all geodetic publications by NGS and its predecessors. Published information includes horizontal and vertical geodetic control network data and diagrams; astronomic and satellite surveying information; geodetic survey specifications, and geodetic data base specifications and formats. A list of these publications and their cost are found in *Publications of the National Geodetic Service*.

Computer programs for geodetic applications, written in FORTRAN, ASSEMBLY, or PL/1, are available on 9-track tapes for use on an IBM main frame computer. Additional geodetic application programs are available for the HP-41 CV and HP-97 programmable calculators. NGIC also distributes NGS digital databases for horizontal, vertical, and gravimetric control in the form of 9-track tapes and computer listings. For further information contact (301) 443–8623.

NAUTICAL CHARTING DIVISION
Capt. J. Austin Yeager, Chief (301) 443–8660

This division is responsible for managing a national program of marine mapping and nautical charting, and providing an up-to-date chart and map database. The division constructs and maintains some 1500 nautical charts and marine maps and related publications; conducts hydrographic and photogrammetric surveys; and designs, develops, and evaluates new and improved survey acquisition and chart production systems. The Chief Geographer (Charles E. Harrington 301/443–8360) maintains an extensive file of place names and related information pertaining to United States coastal waters and maritime boundaries.

Marine Chart Branch
Cdr. Donald E. Nortrup, Chief (301) 443–8741

This branch is responsible for compiling, editing, and maintaining conventional and small-craft nautical charts, bathymetric maps, topographic/bathymetric maps, and the United States Coast Pilots. The Chart Information Section maintains record files of hydrographic and related source materials.

Photogrammetry Branch
Ronald K. Brewer, Acting Chief (301) 443–8744

This branch conducts aerial photographic surveys, acquires remote sensing data, performs photogrammetric aerotriangulation, and compiles topographic, planimetric, orthophoto, and photobathymetric manuscripts by graphic and stereoscopic instrument procedures. The Photo Map and Imagery Information Unit maintains the aerial photographic collection, photogrammetric field records, photogrammetric surveys, and planimetric maps, copies of which are available for purchase. The unit will also provide technical information and other research assistance concerning these records.

Hydrographic Surveys Branch
Cdr. Roy K. Matsushige, Chief (301) 443–8231

This branch is responsible for NOS hydrographic, bathymetric, and oceanographic surveys. The Data Control Section maintains the nautical chart archives described above.

AERONAUTICAL CHARTING DIVISION
Frank W. Maloney, Acting Chief (301) 443–8717

The Aeronautical Charting Division plans and directs the aeronautical chart services program, directs the operation of a lithographic printing plant for the reproduction of NOAA charts and other publications, and directs the distribution of aeronautical and other NOAA publications.

Aeronautical Chart Branch
Ronald M. Bolton, Chief (301) 443–8075

This branch constructs and maintains aeronautical charts in response to requirements from civil and military aviation. The Aeronautical Information Section maintains files of aeronautical navigation information.

Reproduction Branch
George F. Berner, Chief (301) 443–5780

This branch plans and directs NOAA's production facility for the reproduction of maps, charts, and related publications utilizing lithographic processes.

Distribution Branch
Kenneth H. Moyer, Chief (301) 436–8301

This branch distributes charts, maps, and related publications to local sales offices, public subscribers, national and foreign commercial vendors, intergovernmental exchange programs, national defense emergency stockpiles, and college and university libraries.

The Physical Sciences Services Section (Henry Carter, Chief 301/436–5766) serves as the contact point for public inquiries concerning technical and historical questions about NOS cartographic products. It also maintains the NOS Map Library and Archives, a data file of aerial photography for coastal mapping activities, and the copperplate collection and printing facility (A32).

G21 National Park Service (NPS) (Interior Department)

1 a. *18th and C Streets, N.W.*
Washington, D.C. 20240
(202) 343–4747 (Public Inquiries)

b. Open to the public.

c. William Penn Mott, Director

2. NPS administers the National Park System which comprises more than 330 parks, monuments, historic sites, battlefields, seashores, lakeshores, and recreation areas. Cartographic products are produced and deposited at a number of locations as follows:

NATIONAL REGISTER OF HISTORIC PLACES
1100 L Street, N.W. 20013-7127
Carol Shull, Chief

This office maintains the official list of districts, sites, buildings, structures, and objects deemed significant in American history, architecture, archaeology, and culture. It also maintains a collection of 42,000 nomination files submitted by Federal agencies and state historic preservation officers, each of which includes a United States Geological Survey (USGS) map annotated to show the location of the historic district, site, building or structure.

HISTORIC AMERICAN BUILDING SURVEY AND HISTORIC AMERICAN ENGINEERING RECORD DIVISION
National Park Service
P.O. Box 37127 (429)
Washington, D.C. 20013–7127
Robert Kapsch, Chief (202) 343–9606

This division administers the Historic American Building Survey (HABS), established in 1933, and its companion program, the Historic American Engineering Record (HAER), created in 1969, to document significant American historic architecture and engineering sites. Under the direction of HABS and HAER, teams of architects, engineers, historians, and photographers have prepared measured drawings, formal photographs, and written data of over 20,000 sites and structures in the United States, the Canal Zone, the District of Columbia, and Puerto Rico. The measured drawings sometimes include large-scale site plans or maps showing the location of an individual structure or complex of several structures, such as a community or farm, located within an historic district.

The majority of the HABS and HAER records have been transferred to the Prints and Photographs Division, Library of Congress (A23). A list of the measured drawings maintained by the NPS and the Library of Congress is found in *Historic American Buildings, Structures, and Sites* (Library of Congress, 1983), which is available from the Superintendent of Documents, Government Printing Office, Washington, D.C. 20402 (K8).

HARPERS FERRY CENTER
Harpers Ferry
West Virginia 25425
(304) 535–6371 (Information)
Marc Sagan, Manager (304) 535–6211

The Division of Publications (Vincent L. Gleason, Chief 304/535–6311) produces current informational folders for the 330 areas comprising the National Park System. Each folder contains regional/area locational and interpretive maps prepared by the cartographic staff (Bill von Allmen, Senior Cartographer 304/535–6320).

3. The Office of Land Use Coordination, National Capital Region (Norbert Erickson, Chief 202/426–6724, 1100 Ohio Drive, S.W. Washington, D.C. 20242) maintains a working file, commonly referred to as the Map Room, of 200,000 landscape architectural drawings, engineering designs, plans, survey plats, and maps pertaining to the Washington, D.C. vicinity and its monuments and park system. The maps consist chiefly of United States Geological Survey quadrangles, United States Corps of Engineers topographic maps, copies of maps submitted for permits, United States Coast and Geodetic maps from the 1890s, mylar overlays of Washington, D.C. during the Civil War, and copies of early maps of the City of Washington dating from the 1790s.

The Denver Service Center (Gerald D. Patten, Manager, telephone 303/776–8729, 755 Parfet Street P.O. Box 25287 Denver, Colorado 80215) maintains a collection of some 300,000 35mm microfilm aperture cards of plans, architectural drawings, and maps relating to national parks, recreation areas, monuments, and historic buildings and building sites. Most of the drawings date from World War II although some of the maps were drawn in the nineteenth century.

4. Noncurrent manuscript and photoprocessed maps relating to the National Capital Parks system and published sets of maps pertaining to national parks have been transferred to the National Archives and Records Administration (B19, RG79).

G22 National Science Foundation

1 a. *1800 G Street, N.W.*
Washington, D.C. 20550
(202) 357-9730 (Public Affairs)

b. Open to the public.

c. Erich Bloch, Director

2. NSF provides support for basic and applied research in engineering, mathematics and the physical, biological, behavioral, and social sciences. The following programs assist cartographic-related research. The Instrumentation, Sensing and Measurement Program, Electrical Communications and Systems Engineering Division (Norman Caplan, Program Director 202/357–9618) supports fundamental research in remote sensing, pattern analysis, and image processing. Within the Social and Economic Science Division, the Geography and Regional Sciences Program (Ronald F. Abler, Program Director 202/357–7326) promotes research projects concerning artificial intelligence in computerized map systems; the Measurement Methods and Data Improvement Program (Murray Aborn, Director 202/357–7913) encourages projects that improve the usefulness of existing databases and develops new methods and models for analyzing social data; and the History and Philosophy of Science Program (Ronald J. Overmann, Director 202/357–9677) supports research relating to the nature and development of science and technology. The Information Technology Program, Information Science and Technology Division (Harold Bamford, Jr., Director 202/357–9554) provides assistance to researchers designing information processing systems emphasizing the generation, integration, transfer, retrieval and display of information in the form of text, numbers, and pictures.

5. NSF publishes an annual *Guide to Programs,* available from Forms and Publications, NSF, Washington, D.C. 20550 (202/357–7861). Program changes and notices of program brochures are announced in the *NSF Bulletin,* available from the Editor, *NSF Bulletin,* National Science Foundation/Public Affairs, Washington, D.C. 20550.

G23 National Weather Service (National Oceanic and Atmospheric Administration) (Commerce Department)—National Meteorological Center

1 a. *5200 Auth Road*
Camp Springs, Maryland 20233
(301) 763–8016
(301) 427–7622 (Public Affairs)

b. Not open to the public. Limited access by appointment.

c. William D. Bonner, Director

2. The National Weather Service provides weather forecasts for the United States and its possessions from over 100,000 observations collected daily by NOAA from surface and upper-air observing stations, weather radar facilities, ocean data buoys, ships, environmental satellites, and volunteer observers. This observational data is brought together by the National Meteorological Center where it is processed, analyzed, and distributed in the form of manual and computer generated maps by the Meteorological Operations Division (Harlan K. Saylar, Chief 301/763–8026). Three categories of maps are produced: operational weather charts, daily weather maps, and forecast products.

Operational Weather Charts. This series consists of a wide variety of charts produced on a daily basis and distributed in small numbers by facsimile transmitters to other NOAA departments, the Department of Defense, and private users. These include composite moisture index charts of North America and the Northern Hemisphere, baroclinic 500-millibar height/vorticity charts of the United States (twice daily), initial wind-wave/swell/combined sea-height charts of the Northern Hemisphere (twice daily), mean relative humidity/vertical-velocity charts of the United States, Canada, and Mexico (twice daily), North American surface charts (four times daily), observed snow-cover charts for the United States, computer-plotted precipitation chart of the United States, radar summary chart of the United States (hourly), Southern Hemisphere constant pressure chart (twice daily), Southern Hemisphere surface chart (twice daily), tropical strip surface charts (4 times daily), tropical strip upper air charts (twice daily), 12 hour maximum and minimum temperature charts of the United States (twice daily), wind direction charts of the United States (twice daily), and weather depiction analysis charts of the United States (eight times daily).

Daily Weather Maps, Weekly Series. This series, which is published weekly, consists of four daily weather maps of the conterminous United States showing surface weather 500- millibar constant pressure, highest and lowest temperature, and precipitation.

Forecast Products. Consists of computer generated analysis products such as upper-air and surface forecast maps.

4. The Meteorological Operations Division maintains operational weather maps as part of their working files for sixty days after which they are added to the data files of the National Climatic Data Center (D8). The forecast products are maintained by the Technical Support Section for five years (Robert G. Derouin 301/763-8096).

5. The *Daily Weather Maps, Weekly Series* is printed and sold by the Division of Public Documents, United States Government Printing Office, Washington D.C. 20402 (K8).

G24 Public Health Service (Department of Health and Human Services)

1 a. *200 Independence Avenue, S.W.*
Washington, D.C. 20201
(202) 245-6867

b. Open to the public.

c. Donald Ian Macdonald, Acting Assistant Secretary

2. The Public Health Service is responsible for assisting the development of state and community health resources, improving the delivery of health services at the national level, conducting and supporting medical research, and administering national programs for the prevention and control of communicable diseases.

EPIDEMIOLOGY AND BIOSTATISTICS PROGRAM
National Cancer Institute
Landow Building
9000 Rockville Pike
Bethesda, Maryland 20205
Joseph F. Fraumeni, Jr., Associate Director (301) 496–1611
William J. Blot, Chief, Biostatistics Branch (301) 496–4153
Robert N. Hoover, Chief, Environmental Epidemiology Branch (301) 496–1691
Thomas J. Mason, Chief, Population Studies Section (301) 496–6425

The Epidemiology and Biostatistics Program employs computerized mapping techniques for the depiction and analysis of the distribution of mortality in the United States from cancer and other diseases. Data files used in the preparation of these maps include a computerized National Death Index maintained by the National Center for Health Statistics (Manning Feinleib, Director 301/436–7016, 3700 East-West Highway, Hyattsville, Maryland 20782), which contains information on each death in the United States from 1933 to 1980 (age, sex, race, residence, primary and secondary cause of death); United States Census Bureau population data; and United States county and state boundary files.

DIVISION OF SURVEILLANCE, HAZARD EVALUATIONS
AND FIELD STUDIES
National Institute for Occupational Safety and Health
(NIOSH)/Centers for Disease Control
Robert A. Taft Laboratories
4676 Columbia Parkway
Cincinnati, Ohio 45226
James Melius, Director (513) 841–4428
Todd M. Frazier, Chief, Surveillance Branch (513) 841–4303

The Surveillance Branch (Contact person: David Pedersen, Industrial Hygienist 513/841–4491) generates county level computer maps as part of its nationwide hazard and mortality surveillance program to describe geographic distribution of work-related chemical exposures and causes of mortality. Five types of maps have been developed: (1) a county-level map of the United States that shows the locations of worksites where there is a high likelihood that such toxic substances as inorganic lead are used; (2) a county-level map of the United States that displays the distribution of workers potentially exposed to specific agents such as formaldehyde; (3 & 4) county-level maps of the United States or of individual states that illustrate the proportion of the workforce exposed to a particular agent; and (5) a map of the United States that shows the causes of selected deaths by county. Two data bases are maintained by the branch to generate these maps: the National Occupational Hazard Survey (NOHS), which contains 5 million records about chemical and physical agents, occupations, and industries gathered from visits to 4,500 industrial sites in 1972 to 1974, and a commercially available listing of national worksites.

5. The National Cancer Institute's mapping program is described briefly in Linda Williams Pickle and Thomas J. Mason's, "Mapping Cancer Mortality in the United States", *Proceedings of the First International Symposium on Geochemistry and Health* (London, 1985). The following atlases issued by the National Cancer Institute are available from the United States Government Printing Office (K8): *Atlas of Cancer Mortality for U.S. Counties: 1950–1969* (1975), *Atlas of Cancer Mortality Among U.S. Nonwhites: 1950–1969* (1976), and *An Atlas of Mortality From Selected Diseases* (1981).

The NOSH mapping program is described in Todd M. Frazier, Nina R. Lalich, and David H. Pedersen's, "Uses of Computer-Generated Maps in Occupational Hazard and Mortality Surveillance", *Scandinavian Journal of Work and Environmental Health,* vol. 9 (1983), pages 148–154. Another version appeared in the *Centers for Disease Control Morbidity and Mortality Weekly Report* (Vol. 33/no. 255), available from the Public Health Service, Centers for Disease Control, Atlanta, Georgia 30333.

G25 Soil Conservation Service (SCS) (Agriculture Department) —Office of Assessment and Planning

1 a. *14th Street and Independence Avenue, S.W.*
Washington, D.C. 20250
(202) 447-3712 (Public Information)

b. Open to the public.

c. Richard L. Duesterhaus, Deputy Chief

2. SCS provides technical assistance to individuals, organizations, and local and state governments concerned with soil and water conservation, conducts national natural resource surveys, and aids communities in resource protection and development. In support of these programs, the Office of Assessment and Planning administers major national cartographic and remote sensing programs.

SOIL SURVEY DIVISION
Richard W. Arnold, Director (202) 382-1819

This Division administers the soil survey program. In cooperation with state agricultural experiment stations and other federal and state agencies, the Department of Agriculture has prepared soil surveys with maps for more than 1600 counties since the inception of the program in 1899. Each survey contains detailed maps showing the distribution of the soils based on a classification system that considers their texture, structure, chemical composition, depth, slope, degree of erosion, and other physical characteristics. Since 1957, most soil maps are printed on an aerial photobase at scales of 1:24,000, 1:20,000 or 1:15,840. More than 3,500 soil maps have been published since 1899.

The Soil Geography Staff (William V. Reybold, National Leader for Soil Geography, 202/382-1825) prepares national standards and procedures for the soil scientists who compile the county soil maps. This staff also maintains a worldwide set of World Aeronautical Charts (1:1,000,000) annotated to show soil classification for the period

1950–1965. This series is currently being updated with the aid of Landsat imagery and soil maps obtained from other countries. The staff is also compiling a new 1:250,000 soil map of the United States for a digital geographic soil database.

CARTOGRAPHY AND GEOGRAPHIC INFORMATION SYSTEMS DIVISION (CGIS)
Gale W. TeSelle, Director (202) 447–5420

This Division is responsible for developing and coordinating cartographic, remote sensing, and geographic information systems within SCS. It also serves as the point of contact with other agencies and private contractors. The National Cartographic Coordinator (George Rohaley, 202/447–5405) coordinates cartographic development and projects within SCS and other federal agencies. Current efforts include technical assistance for the preparation of soil maps of Saudi Arabia, development of maps for the Chesapeake Bay and Colorado River Salinity Projects, standardization of base maps for the Resource Conservation Act Report, and development of national SCS watershed maps. The National Geographic Information Systems (GIS) Coordinator (Edward Chapman 202/447–5381) coordinates the effort of map digitizing, automated map plotting, and duplicating digital geographic files in SCS national technical centers and state offices. CGIS is developing and testing several GIS pilot projects and is currently working with the Soil Survey Division and the USGS to develop a national geographic digital soil data base which can be used for the production of soil maps of the United States at 1:250,000.

The National Remote Sensing Coordinator (Olin D. Bockes 202/447–5322) coordinates acquisition of conventional, national high altitude photography (NHAP), orthophotography, and satellite imagery which is used by SCS state offices to produce county land use and erosion maps, watershed maps, and soil survey maps. In general, Landsat imagery is used to produce general soil maps of the states at a scale of 1:250,000 while high altitude color infrared photographs are used for larger scale maps.

NATIONAL CARTOGRAPHIC CENTER (NCC)
South National Technical Center
Soil Conservation Service
Fort Worth Federal Center, Building 23
Felix and Hemphill Streets
P.O. Box 6567
Fort Worth, Texas 76115
Richard Folsche, Chief (817) 334–5292

NCC performs the cartographic, remote sensing, and geographic information systems production activities of SCS. This includes the compilation and printing of some 100 new soil maps each year for the National Cooperative Soil Survey; photographic reproduction of maps for conservation plans on farms and ranches (about 60,000 per year); preparation of planimetric and topographic maps for watershed projects and flood hazard maps for potential flood areas; publication of *Important Farmland Maps,* which delineate prime and unique farmlands for more than 1,200 counties; issuance of general administrative, operational, and status maps showing the progress of SCS programs; and acquisition and reproduction of aerial photograph and remote sensing imagery.

3. Current SCS conventional and high altitude aerial photography is maintained by the Agricultural Stabilization and Conservation Service Aerial Photography Field Office (G1). A published set of bound maps showing the status of SCS aerial photography coverage by state is available from that office. A large published map of the United States showing coverage of national high altitude photography is available from the National Cartographic and Information Center (E7).

4. Non-current manuscript SCS soil maps and conventional aerial photographs filmed from 1936 through 1947 have been transferred to the National Archives and Records Administration (B19, RG 114).

5. County soil survey maps published by SCS are listed by county and date in *History of Published Soil Surveys: January 1985* along with a directory of state conservationists who can provide copies of the maps as well as information on the current status of new soil surveys. No list exists for other maps published by SCS. Soil maps can be obtained from state or local offices of the Soil Conservation Service, county agents, congressional offices, and the United States Government Printing Office (K8).

G26 State Department—Intelligence and Research Bureau—Office of the Geographer

1 a. *21st Street and Virginia Avenue, N.W.*
Washington, D.C. 20520
(202) 647-1428–2022–2156

b. Open to the public by appointment.

c. George J. Demko, Director

2. The Office of the Geographer (GE) is responsible for the preparation of analytical studies associated with geography, the law of the sea, United States maritime issues, international land and maritime boundaries and jurisdictional problems, refuge affairs, and environmental issues.

The Cartography and Automated Geoprocessing Division (Sandra H. Shaw, Chief and Special Assistant on Foreign Geographic Names, telephone 202/250–8551) produces maps for the State Department and reviews maps and charts produced by other Federal agencies to ensure consistency in nomenclature and in matters of sovereignty.

3–4. Current geographic and cartographic files are not open to the public, but assistance regarding the availability of information may be obtained by contacting the Office. Non-current textual and cartographic records have been transferred to the National Archives and Records Administration (B19, RG 59).

5. Standard cartographic product series issued by the Office of the Geographer are listed below.

Geographic Notes.—A quarterly publication, heavily illustrated with maps. It provides current information and analysis about changes in international and maritime boundaries, changes in foreign geographic names, general geopolitical issues, and a list of recent publications by the Office of the Geographer.

Geographic Research Study.—Unclassified geographic studies issued as needed. A recent example is *National Maritime Claims: 1958–85* (No. 20, October 21, 1985. 50 p.), with fold-out world map displaying the 200 nautical mile maritime claims as of May, 1985.

Guide to International Boundaries Map.—World map showing international boundaries, international boundaries in dispute, indefinite international boundaries, other land and water separation lines, boundary disclaimers, and geographic names disclaimers.

International Boundary Studies.—Brief studies of specific boundaries, generally between 2 countries. Each study generally contains a boundary brief, geographical and historical background information, a boundary analysis, list of pertinent treaties, and maps illustrating the boundary. Since 1961, 175 boundary studies have been released.

An index with map is available on request. The most recent studies have dealt with the China-Mongolia boundary, the Brazil-Colombia boundary, and the Brazil-Venezuela boundary.

Limits in the Seas.—Brief studies of maritime boundaries, issued on no fixed schedule. Since 1970, 104 *Limit in the Seas* studies have appeared. An index with map is available. Recent topics include the Cuba-Mexico maritime boundary, the Colombia straight baselines, the Burma-Thailand maritime boundary, and Fiji's maritime claims.

Miscellaneous Maps.—Small scale, page-size maps published as required for Department of State publications. Recent examples include maps showing population distribution in the Senegal River Basin, disputed area along the China-India border, countries of the Caribbean Basin, and location of the Kazakh S.S.R. within the Soviet Union.

Status of the World's Nations.—Published list of all nations with a separate foldout political map of the World, issued every 2-to-3 years. Available from the Government Printing Office (K8).

Thematic Maps.—Maps devoted to special themes such as large world map showing maritime production and transportation of petroleum (1981). No set schedule.

United States Foreign Service Posts and Department of State Jurisdictions Map.—Wall map showing locations of foreign service posts and geographical jurisdictions of the Bureau of African Affairs, Bureau of Inter-American Affairs, Bureau of East Asian and Pacific Affairs, Bureau of Near Eastern and South Asian Affairs, and Bureau of European and Canadian Affairs. Issued annually.

G27 World Agricultural Outlook Board (WAOB) (Agricultural Department)

1 a. *12th Street and Independence Avenue, S.W.*
Washington, D.C. 20250
(202) 447–5447

b. Open to the public.

c. James R. Donald

2. The WAOB is responsible for coordinating and developing the Department of Agriculture's official estimates and forecasts concerning domestic and world agriculture, which are based in part on remote sensing data; coordinating weather and climate forecasts within the Department; and overseeing remote sensing activities, particularly with respect to food and fiber estimates. The Remote Sensing Coordinator (Richard C. McArdle, 202/447–5913) serves as a focal point for all remote sensing activities within the Department of Agriculture and functions as the executive secretary of the Department's Remote Sensing Coordination Committee.

The Department of Agriculture has participated in two recent remote sensing interagency programs—Large Area Crop Inventory Experiment (LACIE) and Agricultural and Resources Inventory Surveys Through Aerospace Remote Sensing (AgRISTARS). LACIE was a feasibility study designed to monitor wheat production in eight countries from 1974 to 1978. AgRISTARS was a five year research program (1980 to 1985) whose major objective was to provide more accurate commodity production forecasts, but it was also used to classify and estimate land cover. The program was tested in Argentina, Australia, Brazil, Canada, India, the U.S.S.R. and the United States.

3. Published AgRISTARS program and program related documentation are available in the National Agricultural Library (A29).

4. The LACIE data files are still maintained by the Department of Agriculture in the Washington National Record Center (B19); the AgRISTARS data files are maintained by the Goddard Space Center (G18).

5. Reproductions of some AgRISTARS documents are available from the National Technical Information Services (NTIS) (K12). AgRISTARS documents, with NTIS numbers, are listed in the annual *AgRISTARS Research Report*.

H State and Local Government Agencies

State and Local Government Agencies Entry Format (H)

1. General Information
   a. address; telephone numbers
   b. condition of access
   c. name/title of director and heads of relevant divisions
2. Agency Functions and Programs
3. Agency Collections and Reference Facilities
4. Unpublished Materials
5. Publications
   a. published products
   b. published bibliographies and reference aids

H1 City of Alexandria—Office of Planning and Community Development—Zoning Administration

1 a. *Room 201 A*
320 King Street
Alexandria, Virginia 22314
(703) 838-4688

b. Open to the public 8:00 A.M.–5:00 P.M. Monday–Friday

c. Charles B. Moore, Director
Ralph Pond, Cartographer

2. The Zoning Administration is responsible for compiling and maintaining the official real estate assessment maps (tax maps) for the City of Alexandria. The Division also

prepares topographic and special purpose maps for various city departments, some of which are published.

5. The following published maps of Alexandria are currently available at a scale of 1 inch equals 1200 feet: street map, 1985, street map with 1980 census tract boundaries, 1984; long range land use plan, 1981; existing generalized land use map, 1986; and zoning map, 1985. Real estate assessment maps are available in a reproduced atlas format from REDI Corporation (2398 N.W. 119th Street, Miami, Florida 33167, telephone 305/685-3625).

H2 District of Columbia

1 a. *District Building*
1350 Pennsylvania Avenue, N.W.
Washington, D.C. 20001
(202) 727-1000 (Information)

b. Open to the public.

c. Marion Barry, Jr., Mayor

2-3. The District of Columbia was created in 1791 from lands ceded by Virginia and Maryland and permanently established as the nation's capital in 1800. Surveying and mapping activities played important roles in the development of the city from the time of its origin in 1791, when the Board of Commissioners for the District of Columbia was appointed to plan and construct the new capital. Today, these activities are carried out by a number of departments and offices.

OFFICE OF THE SURVEYOR
Potomac Building, Room 605
614 H Street, N.W.
Ralph B. Sheaffer, Surveyor (202) 727-1104

The Office of the Surveyor prepares and maintains the official cadastral plats and subdivisions of public and private property within the District of Columbia, conducts field surveys of real property boundaries, and establishes and maintains the survey control system for all property surveys. This office maintains some 211,000 real property records dating from the establishment of the Office in the 1790s. These include field surveys (Survey Jackets) and related "working maps," original subdivision plats and plats for street and alley closings (Red Band Jackets), miscellaneous maps and plats, including highway plans, an extensive system of index cards that provide access to surveys and plats by lot, subdivision, and street, and map indexes (13 drawers) indexed by square and parcel number.

DEPARTMENT OF PUBLIC WORKS
11th Floor
613 G Street, N.W.
(202) 727-0215

The Department of Public Works maintains and makes available basic black and white topographic and aerial photography multiple sheet quadrant maps of the city (scale one inch equals 200 feet), base maps, special purpose maps, and transportation maps.

OFFICE OF PLANNING
Urban Design Unit, 4th Floor
420 7th Street, N.W.
David W. Colby, Chief (202) 727–6504

The Urban Design Unit is responsible for a variety of design activities, including developing general design guidelines for large areas within the Capital, providing site planning and design functions for District of Columbia projects and facilities, and providing cartographic and graphic design support to the Office of Planning and Zoning Commission.

The Urban Design Unit will make the following maps available to the public: topographic maps of the District of Columbia by quadrant (scale one inch equals 100 feet and one inch equals 400 feet)), ward maps (scale one inch equals 600 feet), city map with wards (scale one inch equals 1400 feet), and downtown map (scale one inch equals 250 feet).

4. Some of the earlier maps and plats have been transferred to the National Archives and Records Administration (B19, RG 42 and RG 351). The original manuscript plan of the City by Pierre Charles L'Enfant (1791) and the manuscript map of the District of Columbia (1793) by Andrew Ellicott, along with a few other maps compiled by the City Surveyor in the 1790s, are in the Geographic and Map Division of the Library of Congress (entry A21).

5. Typescript copies of *Services Provided by the Office of the Surveyor of the District of Columbia* (1983, 4 p.) and *Real Property Records System of Information in the Office of the Surveyor, D.C.* (1983, 14 p.) are available on request. A published copy of the detailed *Washington, D.C. Transportation Map* is available free of charge from the District of Columbia Department of Transportation, 415 12th Street, N.W. Room 519, Washington, D.C. 20004 (202/727–6562).

H3 Fairfax County—General Services Department, Communications Division—Mapping and Geographic Services

1 a. *4103 Chain Bridge Road 3rd Floor*
Fairfax, Virginia 22030

Maps, Publications, and Products Sales
Floor 1, Massey Building
4100 Chain Bridge Road
Fairfax, Virginia 22030
(703) 691–2974

b. Open to the public.
8:00 A.M.–4:30 P.M. Monday–Friday.

c. Property Map and Overlay Branch
Frederick Beales, Senior Supervisor
(703) 691–2714

Large Area Mapping and Graphics Branch
Melvin Mauck, Senior Supervisor
(703) 385–5296

2. The Mapping and Graphics Services unit is responsible for the official mapping of Fairfax County, Virginia. The Property Map and Overlay Branch prepares and publishes large scale cadastral maps; the Large Areas Mapping and Graphics Branch designs and compiles special maps, street maps, and land use maps at smaller scales.

3–4. The Property Map and the Overlay Branch maintains several unique series of surveying and mapping records that are used for compilation and reproduction work as well as for reference purposes. The Branch has a complete set of vertical aerial photographs covering Fairfax County for the years 1937, 1953, and 1960 through 1984, at even year intervals.

The most recent photography was flown at an altitude of 6,000 feet, with an 80% forward overlap, requiring more than 800 images to cover the county. Since 1976, aerial photographs have been taken in color as well as black and white. Orthophotographs (1 inch equals 200 feet), prepared in 1984 and overprinted with the Virginia State Grid, are also available. A new topographic overlay is also being compiled at 1 inch equals 200 feet at 5 foot intervals. Continuous tone reproductions of aerial photographs can be purchased at scales of 1 inch equals 200 feet (1986) and 1 inch equals 500 feet (1968–1986).

Property identification maps, which show each residential and commercial lot on 444 sheets, are maintained at scales of 1 inch equals 200 feet and 1 inch equals 500 feet (mylar transparencies). Zoning, soil, topographic, major utility, and geography maps are also available at similar scales. In addition, the Branch has 90 cubic feet of original subdivision plats which have been submitted by private surveyors; some Landsat prints of the county; open-file reports from the United States Geological Survey (USGS) relating to geology and minerals within the county (G14); USGS flood plain maps prepared at a scale of 1 inch equals 100 feet in 1972; a set of property identification maps prepared yearly from 1961 to the present; and a set of 444 county zoning classification overlay maps, which is updated daily. A complete zoning history is also available from 1941 to the present.

5. A price list of the maps produced by the Fairfax County Mapping and Graphics Services may be obtained from the Map and Publication Sales Counter. These include individual *Real Property Identification Map Book* (1986), *Individual Zoning Map Book* (1986), *Soil Identification Map Book, Bicycle Routes in the Washington Area, Street and Area Designation Atlas 1985, Street Maps* (at various scales), *Commercial and Industrial Map, Fire and Rescue Service Map, Magisterial District Map, Public Park Map, Planning Areas and District Map, Public School Map* (1983), *Public School Atlas* (1984–1985), *Solid Waste Refuse Collection Map, Sanitary Sewer Map, Sub Census Map* (1983), *Water and Gas Distribution Map* (1974), *Voting Precincts Map, Water Shed Map*, and *Postal Zip Code Map*.

H4 Maryland—National Capital Park and Planning Commission (M-NCPPC)

1 a. *Montgomery County Planning Board*
Regional Office Building
8787 Georgia Avenue
Silver Spring, Maryland 20907
(301) 279–1000 (Information)

Prince George's County Planning Board
County Administration Building, 4th Floor
14741 Governor Oden Bowie Drive
Upper Marlboro, Maryland 20772
(301) 952–3514 (Information)

b. Open to the public.

2. The Maryland—National Capital Park and Planning Commission is responsible for the comprehensive planning and development of a regional system of parks and for the preservation of open spaces in Montgomery and Prince George's Counties.

MONTGOMERY COUNTY PLANNING DEPARTMENT
Richard E. Tustian, Director (301) 495–4500

The Drafting Section (Marie Elaine Lanza, Supervisor 301/495–4584) compiles the primary mylar base maps of Montgomery County showing streets, lots, blocks, and parcels at a scale of 1 inch equals 200 feet (1,290 sheets); clear acetate overlays of base maps showing house numbers at a scale of 1 inch equals 200 feet (1,290 sheets); mylar and sepia base maps showing existing and proposed zoning at a scale of 1 inch equals 200 feet (1,285 sheets); mylar topographic maps at a scale of 1 inch equals 200 feet (319 sheets); mylar flood plain maps showing existing land use and ultimate land use at a scale of 1 inch equals 200 feet (628 sheets); local area vicinity street maps at a scale of 1 inch equals 1,000 feet (16 sheets); county wide map at a scale of 1 inch equals 3,000 feet with overlays for planning areas, citizen associations, zip-codes, census tracts, traffic zones, approved and adopted master plans, and generalized existing zoning area master and sector plans, in addition to functional maps of bikeways, highways, open spaces, water sheds, and historic sites. Printed or reproducible copies of these mylar maps are available through the Records and Information Office (David R. Hudgel, Jr., Supervisor 301/495–4610). A list of these maps may be obtained on request.

PRINCE GEORGE'S COUNTY PLANNING DEPARTMENT
John F. Downs, Jr., Director (301) 952–3594

The Drafting Department (Ward Bourgondien, Supervisor 301/952–3108) compiles the primary mylar base map of the county showing streets, lots, and blocks at a scale of 1 inch equals 200 feet (1,200 sheets), mylar topographic maps at scales of 1 inch equals 200 feet and 1 inch equals 400 feet, county wide map at a scale of 1 inch equals 3,000 feet with overlays for schools, hospitals, and public agencies, zoning maps and master plans. The Department also maintains a set of transparent aerial photographs of the county at a scale of 1 inch equals 400 feet (176 sheets). The zoning maps are available through the Zoning Information Office (Rick Jenson 301/952–3195).

4. Non-current maps compiled by the Montgomery County Drafting Room and the Prince George's County Drafting Department, as well as subdivision plans, record plats, site plans and project plans submitted to the Commission for regulatory review, are maintained by the Records Management Section of the Department of Administration (Carol Piper, Archivist 301/942–4859 or 301/853–3300, 12751 Layhill Road, Wheaton, Maryland).

5. In addition to the sources cited above, reproducible and printed copies of M-NCPPC maps are found in the Geography and Map Division of the Library of Congress (A21) and the Montgomery County Library (A27).

H5 Metropolitan Washington Council of Governments (COG)

1 a. *1875 Eye Street, N.W.*
Washington, D.C. 20006
(202) 223–6800

b. Open by appointment.

c. Walter A. Scheiber, Executive Director

2. COG is a regional organization of local Washington area governments that is concerned with issues such as public safety, the environment, human services, transportation, and community and economic development. It also functions as a regional planning organization for the Washington metropolitan area.

3. The Information Center (Jeneane Johanningmeier, Manager, Suite 200, 202/223–6800, ext. 230) has custody of some 3,000 photoprocessed and printed maps of the Metropolitan Washington area dating from 1937. These include maps of natural features (geology, physiography, minerals, landforms, and topography), community facilities (post offices, utilities, gas and oil lines, sewer and water systems), roads and streets, social-economic conditions, and population.

4. The Information Center also maintains and sells mylar reproducible copies of large scale maps of the Washington Metropolitan area. These include a regional base map drawn at the scale of 1 inch equals 8,000 feet and 9 sectional maps of the region at the scale of 1 inch equals 3,000 feet. These maps were prepared for COG's Transportation Planning board in 1982. The Center also offers two census tract maps (1980), one inside the beltway and one outside the beltway, at a scale of 1 inch equals 3,000 feet, and a regional atlas (at the same scale) of 28 sheets.

5. A large map, *Bicycle Routes in the Washington Area*, printed by COG in 1983, is available from the Information Center.

H6 Prince George's County—Assessment and Taxation—Mapping Department

1 a. *15100 Buck Lane*
Upper Marlboro, Maryland 20772
(301) 952–4850

b. Open to the public. 8:30 A.M.–4:30 P.M.

c. Lawrence Prevatte, Drafting Supervisor

2. The Mapping Department maintains an up-to-date set of property maps of the county showing boundary lines of all properties and roads. This set consists of 185 mylar sheets, each sheet measuring 24 x 36 inches. Reproducible copies are available.

I Embassies and International Organizations

Embassies and International Organizations Entry Format (I)

1. General Information
   a. address; telephone numbers
   b. conditions of access
   c. name/title of director and heads of relevant divisions
2. Major Organizational Functions, Programs, and Research Activities
3. Libraries and Reference Facilities
4. Publications

Introductory Note

Two sources of maps unique to the nation's capital are embassies and international organizations. In addition to assisting individual scholars who wish to contact mapping organizations within their respective countries, embassies are important sources for tourist maps. The following embassies indicated that they provide tourist or other maps of their countries on request: Bahamas, Barbados, Bulgaria, Costa Rica, Denmark, Dominica, Ghana, Guyana, Hungarian Peoples Republic, Kenya, New Zealand, Norway, Philippines, Somali Democratic Republic, South Africa, Sri Lanka, Sweden, Yemen Arab Republic, and Syrian Arab Republic.

I 1 American Geophysical Union (AGU)

1 a. *2000 Florida Avenue, N.W.*
Washington, D.C. 20009
(202) 462-6903

b. Open to the public.

2. The American Geophysical Union (AGU) is an international scientific society devoted to the geophysical sciences. Through its extensive publishing program and sponsorship of scientific meetings, the AGU provides a forum for some 16,000 scientists from more than 100 countries.

4. In addition to preparing foldout maps that accompany geophysical monographs on earthquake prediction, geological research in the Eastern Alpine-Himalayan area, the continents, East Asian tectonics, and Antarctica, the AGU has published three large, full color wall maps of the geology of the Indian Ocean (1972), the geology of the Sultanate of Oman (1981), and the tectonic elements of the Rio Grande Rift and Southeastern Colorado Plateau, New Mexico and Arizona (1983). A catalog describing these monographs and maps is available on request.

I 1a Embassy of Brazil

1 a. *3006 Massachusetts Avenue, N.W.*
Washington, D.C. 20008
(202) 745-2700

b. 9:00 A.M.–1:00 P.M.; 3:00 P.M.–5:00 P.M. Monday–Friday

3. The embassy maintains a well stocked 3,000 volume public reference library. Map materials are available for the researcher.

I 2 Embassy of Canada

1 a. *1746 Massachusetts Avenue, N.W.*
Washington, D.C. 20036
(202) 785-1400

Library:
1771 N Street, N.W. 3rd Floor
Washington, D.C. 20036
(202) 785-1400 #212

b. Merle Fabian, Head Librarian

3. The library has two recent national atlases which are printed in both English and French. They include aerial photographs of the ice regions. Road maps and political maps are also available.

I 3 Embassy of Chile

1 a. *1732 Massachusetts Avenue, N.W.*
Washington, D.C. 20036
(202) 785–1746

b. 9:00 A.M.–5:00 P.M. Monday–Friday

3. A 2,000 volume public reference library includes several atlases, one produced by the National Geographic Society of Chile.

I 4 Embassy of Colombia

1 a. *2118 Leroy Place, N.W.*
Washington, D.C. 20008
(202) 387–8338

b. 9:30 A.M.–5:30 P.M. Monday–Friday

3. A small reference library contains several recent atlases.

I 5 Embassy of the Dominican Republic

1 a. *1715 22nd Street, N.W.*
Washington, D.C. 20008
(202) 332–6280

b. 9:00 A.M.–4:00 P.M. Monday–Friday

c. Antonio Rodriguez, Cultural Counselor

3. No public reference collection is maintained. However, a large (4 x 5 feet) wall map of "Ciudad Trujillo" produced in 1960 is on display. Also available for examination is an atlas, *Mapas y Planos de Santo Domingo*, showing the growth of the country for the past 400 years. It includes copies of old Spanish maps and architectural and engineering plans of the island and the capital. Aeronautical charts are available for private pilots, and a book with aerial photographs is available for reference.

I 6 Embassy of Finland

1 a. *3216 New Mexico Avenue, N.W.*
Washington, D.C. 20016
(202) 363–2430

b. 8:30 A.M.–3:45 P.M. Summer: June 1–August 31
8:30 A.M.–4:45 P.M. Winter: September 1–May 31

c. Maria Guercin, Press Section

3. A recent wall map prepared by the Land Survey of Finland is on display. Five atlases are in the collection, the earliest dated 1925. Many general information government maps are available for examination.

I 7 Embassy of France

1 a. *4101 Reservoir Road, N.W.*
Washington, D.C. 20007
(202) 944–6000

Library of the Press Division
(202) 944–6063

c. Madeline Cousin

3. The library contains a small number of black and white aerial photograps of Paris and a large (3 x 3 feet) atlas published in 1967, which pertains to French transportation, commerce, industry, and business centers.

I 8 Embassy of India

1 a. *2107 Massachusetts Avenue, N.W.*
Washington, D.C. 20008
(202) 939–7000
(202) 939–7046 Library

b. 9:30 A.M.–5:30 P.M. Monday–Friday

3. The library's 10,000 item collection includes government publications on census reports, maps, and charts.

I 9 Embassy of the State of Kuwait

1 a. *2940 Tilden Street, N.W.*
Washington, D.C. 20008
(202) 966–0702

3. Sets of aerial photographs and a color topographical map produced in 1980 by the Survey Department of Kuwait Municipality at a scale of 1:250,000 are available for reference.

I 10 Embassy of Malaysia

1 a. *2401 Massachusetts Avenue, N.W.*
Washington, D.C. 20008
(202) 328–2700

b. Closed on Thursday
9:00 A.M.–1:00 P.M.; 2:00 P.M.–5:00 P.M.

2. Miss Madhu Arya, Librarian

3. An atlas of Malaysia (1970s) and some 8 x 10 inch aerial photographs are available for inspection.

I 11 Embassy of the Netherlands

1 a. *4200 Linnean Avenue, N.W.*
Washington, D.C. 20008
(202) 244–5300

b. 9:00 A.M.–5:30 P.M. Monday–Friday

4. The embassy will provide on request a wall map, a geographic book, and a small atlas of the Netherlands published by the Information Documentation Centre for the Geography of the Netherlands (1983). Designed as a source of information to persons outside of the Netherlands, these items are available in twelve languages.

I 12 Embassy of Turkey

1 a. *1606 23rd Street, N.W.*
Washington, D.C. 20008
(202) 387–3200

Office of the Press Counselor:
2010 Massachusetts Avenue, N.W.
Washington, D.C. 20036
(202) 833–8411

b. 9:30 A.M.–6:30 P.M. Monday–Friday

3. There are 4 rolled maps (4 x 10 feet) produced by the Turkish Military Map Organization available for examination. One is regional showing city limits, another shows landforms and other physical characteristics, and the last 2 are road and highway maps.

I 13 European Community Information Service

1 a. *2100 M Street, N.W.*
Washington, D.C. 20037
(202) 862-9500

b. 9:00 A.M.–5:00 P.M. Monday–Friday

c. Open to the public.

d. Barbara Sloan, Head of Public Inquiries

2. The European Community Information Service provides information and documentation on the activities and policies of the European Communities. The Communities' member states are Belgium, Denmark, Federal Republic of Germany, Greece, France, Ireland, Italy, Luxembourg, Netherlands, Portugal, Spain, and United Kingdom.

3. The library contains a small collection of thematic maps, including maps published by the European community.

4. The European Community Information Services publishes three maps: a wall map of Europe showing the member states (except Spain and Portugal, which joined the European Community on January 1, 1986) and administrative units (102 x 136 centimeters), a map showing the woodlands of the member states, and a map depicting their agricultural areas. The maps are available in Danish, Dutch, English, French, German, Greek, and Italian. There is a charge for these maps.

I 14 Island Resources Foundation, Inc.

1 a. *1718 P Street, N.W., Suite T-4*
Washington, D.C. 20036
(202) 265-9712

b. Open to the public by prior arrangement.

c. Edward Towle, Director

2. The Island Resources Foundation is an independent and educational organization established to improve resource assessment and planning, prepare development strategies, and provide technical assistance to small tropical islands. Since 1971, it has carried out some 90 programs in insular ecology, environmental planning, transportation studies, education, cultural and economic resource development, and island resource management. These have included an inventory, mapping and evaluation program of vegetation in the United States Virgin Islands and surveying and mapping in the Eastern Caribbean as part of an environmental planning program.

3. The Foundation maintains a small collection of maps in its Washington office and several thousand maps of the Caribbean region in its Caribbean Headquarters (Red Hook Box 33, St. Thomas, United States Virgin Islands 00802, telephone 809/775-6225).

4. A list of contract reports, technical studies, planning guides, and articles sponsored, produced, published, or distributed by the Foundation is available on request. Many of the reports and guides contain maps.

I 15 Organization of American States (OAS)

1 a. *1889 F Street, N.W.*
Washington, D.C. 20006
(202) 789-3000 (Public Information)

b. Open to the public by appointment.

c. João Clemente Baena Soares, Secretary General

2. The OAS is the oldest international regional organization in the world. Established in 1890, it provides a forum for political, economic, social, and cultural cooperation and development for 31 member countries in the Western Hemisphere.

The Pan American Institute of Geography and History (PAIGH), a specialized organization within the framework of the OAS, coordinates and publicizes geographic, historic, and cartographic studies relating to the member states. Located in Mexico City, (Ex-Azobisbabo 29, Col-Observatorio, 11860 Mexico, Z.S. Mexico, telephone 515-1901 or 277-5888), PAIGH promotes mapping projects and the teaching of history and geography. It has also been involved in establishing standards of accuracy for cartography, geodetic surveys, and photogrammetric interpretation.

In the OAS General Secretariat, the Department of Regional Development (Kirk Rodgers, Director 202/789-6242) compiles and publishes maps treating natural resources, transportation, and allied subjects, based on remote sensing imagery, aerial photography and field surveys.

3. See Organization of American States Columbus Memorial Library (A36).

4. A manual, designed for training Latin American technicians in collecting and evaluating natural resources data, *Physical Resource Investigations For Economic Development, A Casebook of OAS Field Experience in Latin America* (Washington, D.C.: OAS, 1969. 439 p.), contains chapters on the use and preparation of aerial photographs and maps for geological, soil, forest, land use, reconnaissance, and cadastral surveys. Another manual, *Integrated Regional Development, Guidelines and Case Studies from OAS Experience* (Washington, D.C., 1984, 230 p.) provides a methodology for conducting integrated development studies, placing heavy emphasis on environmental considerations. Published maps currently available from the Department of Regional Development include three separate series on hydrology and climatology, natural resources, and special topics issued under the title *Cuenca del Rio de la Plata: Estudio para su Planificación y Desarrollo,* 1969-1972 (37 maps); thematic maps accompanying the report *República de Nicaragua: Descentralización y Desarrollo de la Región del Pacífico,* 1978 (13 maps); thematic maps issued with the study, *República de Panama: Proyecto de Desarrollo Integrado de la Región de Panama-Darien,* 1978 (5 maps); and *El Salvador: Sistema de Información de El Salvador,* 1977 (3 maps).

The work of the PAIGH is described in Instituto Panamericano de Geografia e Historia, *Instituto Panamericano de Geografía e Historia, Instituto Especializado de la Organización de los Estados Americanos* (Mexico, 1973, p. 1-8), and Pan American Institute of Geography and History, *American Institute of Geography and History, 1928-1978* (Mexico, 1978).

I 16 World Bank—Printing and Graphics Division—Cartography Section

1 a. *1818 H Street, N.W.*
Washington, D.C. 20433
(202) 676–0248

b. Not open to the public.

c. Ron Day, Division Chief (202) 676–0223
Ulrich Boegli, Section Chief

2. The World Bank consists of the International Bank for Reconstruction and Development and the International Development Association. It promotes ecomomic and social progress in developing nations by providing financial and technical assistance in such areas as agriculture and rural development, energy, education, transportation, telecommunications, industry, mining, urban development, water supply, population, health and nutrition. The Cartography Section contributes to these goals by preparing on request some 1,000 maps yearly for World Bank staff members who wish to convey geographical information in various internal reports and research publications. Since these maps are prepared to accompany confidential internal Bank materials, their reproduction is restricted.

4. Although most publications and accompanying maps issued by the World Bank are restricted, some are available to the public from the Bank's Book Store (600 19th Street, N.W., Washington, D.C. 202/473–2939), its European Office Book Store (66, avenue d'Iéna, 75116 Paris, France) or from publishers, booksellers, or distributors in some 60 countries. The names and addresses of the latter are listed in the Bank's annual *Catalog of Publications*. The World Bank's publication, *Directory of World Bank Depository Libraries* (1983. 56 p.), lists some 300 libraries in 93 developing countries which provide free access to most of these publications and accompanying maps.

The World Bank publishes *The World Bank Atlas* (1985. 32 p.), which provides data on population, gross national product, gross national product per capita, life expectancy, infant mortality, and primary school enrollment for 189 countries and territories. This atlas may be obtained from the Bank's Book Store.

J Associations and Societies

Associations and Societies Entry Format (J)

1. Address and Telephone Numbers
2. Chief Official and Title
3. Programs and Activities Pertaining to Cartography
4. Library, Archives, and Databases
5. Publications

J1 American Congress on Surveying and Mapping (ACSM)

1. *210 Little Falls Street*
Falls Church, Virginia 22046
(703) 241-2446

2. John C. Uehlinger, Executive Director

3. The American Congress on Surveying and Mapping (ACSM) was founded in 1941 to advance the science of surveying and mapping through public education, academic teaching, and a program of publications. ACSM consists of 3 member organizations totaling more than 10,000 members: the American Cartographic Association (ACA), the National Society of Professional Surveyors (NSPS), and the American Association For Geodetic Surveying (AAGS). It holds annual conventions in the spring and fall, one of which is usually held in Washington, D.C. ACSM sponsors some 30 short courses in surveying and mapping each year. Since 1974, ACA has conducted an annual map design contest for all mapmakers in the United States and Canada. The winning entries, following their exhibition at the annual convention, are donated to the Geography and Map Division of the Library of Congress for permanent retention (see entry A21). Copies of the winning entries are available for a fee in 35mm slide sets from ACSM.

5. The official technical journals of ASCM are *Surveying and Mapping,* published quarterly and devoted primarily to surveying and large scale or cadastral mapping, and *The American Cartographer,* issued quarterly with emphasis on thematic and computer mapping. The *ACSM Bulletin,* which appears bi-monthly, includes briefer articles and news of the Society. Useful features of the *ACSM Bulletin* are "Map Information", which lists new public land survey plats issued by the Bureau of Land Management, and "Distinctive Recent Maps", a bibliographic list of new maps cataloged by the Geography and Map Division, Library of Congress.A special issue of *The American Cartographer,* devoted entirely to the *U.S. National Report to ICA, 1984,* described mapping programs and activities in the United States for the period 1980 through 1983 (Supplement to volume 11, Summer 1984). In addition, ACSM also publishes the technical papers presented at the fall and spring conventions and a wide variety of other publications, including the *Directory of Current Cartographic Research.*

J2 American Geological Institute (AGI)

1. *4220 King Street*
Alexandria, Virginia 22302
(703) 379–2480

2. Marvin Kauffman, Executive Director

3. The American Geological Institute (AGI) is a federation of seventeen professional societies founded to provide information services to earth scientists and geoscience information specialists throughout the world.

4. The Institute operates GeoRef, a computer-based information system providing worldwide online access to geoscience information through DIALOG, ORBIT, and CAN/OLE (see entries D3 and D10). The GeoRef database file contains more than 1 million bibliographic references to pertinent material, including some 10,000 separately published maps and map related books, monographs, and reports. It is updated monthly.

5. The *Bibliography and Index of Geology,* which is photocomposed monthly from citations in GeoRef, contains a section on "Areal Geology, Maps and Charts". Also available are *Maps and Geological Publications of the United States: A Layman's Guide* (1978) and the *Proceedings of the Nineteenth Meeting of the Geoscience Information Society—Maps in the Geoscience Community* (1985. 209 p.). AGI's monthly magazine, *Geotimes,* includes a listing of new geological maps in each issue.

J3 American Society for Photogrammetry and Remote Sensing (ASPRS)

1. *210 Little Falls Street*
Falls Church, Virginia 22046
(703) 534–6617

2. William D. French, Executive Director

3. The American Society for Photogrammetry and Remote Sensing (ASPRS) is a professional organization with 8,000 members whose goal is to advance the development of the photogrammetric sciences and remote sensing technology through education and publication. It holds 2 technical meetings each year in the spring and fall. Four divisions

provide programs for more specific interests: Photogrammetric Applications Division (Ronald K. Brewer, Director, National Ocean Service, 6000 Executive Boulevard, Rockville, Maryland 20852), Primary Data Acquisition Division (Elizabeth A. Fleming, Director, Topographical Survey, Surveys and Mapping, EMR, 615 Booth Street, Ottawa, Ontario, K1A OE9, Canada), Professional Practice Division (Francis H. Moffit, Director, 721 San Luis Road, Berkeley, California 94707), and Remote Sensing Applications Division (Robert A. Ryerson, Director, Box 1125, Manotick, Ontario, KOA 2NO, Canada).

4. The Society maintains a small library devoted to works on photogrammetry and remote sensing. It also has the earliest aerial photograph of Washington, D.C. (1918).

5. A monthly professional journal, *Photogrammetric Engineering and Remote Sensing,* contains feature articles, abstracts, notes, and book reviews. The Society also publishes the two definitive works on photogrammetry and remote sensing: *Manual of Photogrammetry* (1980. 2 v. 1056 p.), which includes sections on principles of stereoscopy, plotting instruments, and planimetric and topographic mapping; and *Manual of Remote Sensing* (1983. 2 v. 2440 p.), containing topics on general and specific applications. Other publications include the *Technical Papers* of the semi-annual meetings; *Multilingual Dictionary of Photogrammetry and Remote Sensing*; *Auto-Carto V Preceedings: Environmental Assessment and Resource Management* (1983. 738 p.); the proceedings of the International Symposium on Computer-Assisted Cartography; and *Renewable Resources Management Applications of Remote Sensing* (1984. 774 p.).

The Society also sells two films (16mm, cassettes): "Vegetation Assessment: The Use of Remotely Sensed Data," and "Mineral Exploration: The Use of Remotely Sensed Data."

J4 Association of American Geographers (AAG)

1. *1710 16th Street, N.W.*
Washington, D.C. 20009
(202) 234–1450

2. Robert T. Aangeenbrug, Executive Director

3. The Association of American Geographers (AAG) is a national professional association for geographers. It promotes professional studies in geography and encourages geographic research in education, government, and business. An annual meeting is held in April or May, where members present papers and participate in symposia, workshops, and field trips. The AAG has a variety of specialty groups including groups for geographers interested in cartography and remote sensing.

The Cartography Specialty Group (CSG) (David J. Cuff, Geography, Temple University, Philadelphia, Pennsylvania 19122) promotes education and research in cartography and map use, with special emphasis on thematic maps and their use in the spatial analysis and communication of geographic concepts. The Remote Sensing Specialty Group (Vincent G. Ambrosia, Research Scientist, M/S 242-4, NASA, Ames Research Center, Moffett Field, California 94035) fosters the application of remote sensing science in geographic research. The AAG Middle Atlantic Division (Donald C. Dahmann, Chair 202/554–4504), which serves geographers in the states of Virginia and Maryland and the District of Columbia, sponsors special programs, field excursions, and an annual meeting.

4. The noncurrent records of the AAG have been transferred to the American Philosophical Society. They are described in Ralph Ehrenberg's "The Archives of the Association of American Geographers", *Professional Geographer* (May 1976).

5. The AAG publishes two scholarly journals, the *Annals* which features major articles, book reviews, and commentaries, and *The Professional Geographer,* which contains brief articles, reports, and reviews. The *AAG Newsletter* provides information on current activities, programs, and exhibits of interest to geographers. The AAG also produces *Resource Publications in Geography,* a series of original works on topics not readily accessible in the current literature. These are designed for instructors, students, and interested professionals. Pertinent titles include: James B. Campbell, *Mapping the Land: Aerial Imagery for Land Use Information* (1983. 96 p.); James R. Carter, *Computer Mapping: Progress in the 80's* (1984. 86 p.); and Mark S. Monmonier, *Maps, Distortion, and Meaning* (1977. 51 p.). Also available is the *Proceedings of the First International Symposium on Maps and Graphics for the Visually Handicapped,* edited by Joseph W. Wiedel (1983).

Selected thematic maps, published by the AAG between 1965 and 1976, are available from the Program Director in Geography, George Mason University, Fairfax, Virginia 22030. These include population maps of East Africa, Morocco, and Taiwan, an ethnolinguistic map of South American Indians, a landform map of the World, land use maps of Northeast China and the Southwestern United States, historical maps of parts of the United States, and an urban map of Moscow.

A list of publications is available on request.

J5 Association of American Railroads

1. *50 F Street, N.W.*
Washington, D.C. 20001
(202) 639–2525

5. The Office of Information and Public Affairs publishes a list of railroad maps of the United States and railroad map sources for persons interested in obtaining such maps.

J6 National Computer Graphics Association (NCGA)

1. *2722 Merrilee Drive*
Fairfax, Virginia 22031
(703) 698–9600

2. Stephanie A. Kenworthy, Editorial Office

3. The National Computer Graphics Association (NCGA) is a professional and trade association concerned with promoting computer graphics and improving the applications of computer graphics in business, industry, government, science, and the arts, including cartography.

5. The NCGA publishes *Computer Graphics Today,* a monthly tabloid containing industry news and *Graphics Network News,* a bi-monthly newsletter providing information about the Association and local chapters. The February 1986 issue of *Computer Graphics Today* featured several interviews and articles devoted to computer mapping. These included an interview with a leading manufacturer of computer mapping systems

and articles on the production of computer-generated weather maps for television news stations, the use of a computer system with a graphical database of map-like structures to locate and repair street lights by the department of city planning in New York City, and the role of computer mapping in the oil industry in evaluating potential oil sites.

J7 National Geographic Society (NGS)

1. *17th and M Streets, N.W.*
   Washington, D.C. 20036
   (202) 857-7000 (Information)
   (202) 921-1200 (Map, Atlas, and Globe Information)

2. Gilbert M. Grosvenor, President

3. The National Geographic Society was established in 1888 for the increase and diffusion of geographical knowledge. Its Cartographic Division (John B. Garver, Jr., Chief Cartographer) compiles and produces the well-known supplemental and page size maps for the *National Geographic Magazine,* physical and political globes, world and regional atlases, and mural maps.

4. The Society's map collection and related cartographic material are described in entry A30. A recently developed computerized Geographic Names Data Base (GNDB) will eventually contain more than 250,000 place names.

5. More than 110 separate maps, 3 atlases, and 5 globes are currently available from NGS. Major map series include traveler's maps of the Alps, the British Isles, and Spain and Portugal; Close-Up U.S.A. and Canada series, consisting of two sets of detailed regional maps of the United States and Canada; *Our Peoples* series, a set of maps of the Arctic, China, South Asia, Southeast Asia, and the Soviet Union showing distribution of major ethnic-linguistic groups; and *U.S. Historical Geography* series, a set of 17 regional maps of the United States showing the historical geographical development of each region. A list of these maps is availalble on request. Atlases include *World Atlas* (1981), *People and Places of the Past: Illustrated Cultural Atlas of the Ancient World* (1983), and *Atlas of North America: Space Age Portrait of a Continent* (1985).

J8 Potomac Appalachian Trail Club (PATC)

1. *1718 N Street, N.W.*
   Washington, D.C. 20036
   (202) 638-5306

2. Warren Sharp, President

3. The Potomac Appalachian Trail Club (PATC) publishes maps and guide books for the network of trails that it maintains as part of the Appalachian Trail from the Susquehanna River in Pennsylvania to Waynesboro, Virginia. An article, "The Potomac Appalachian Trail Club's Maps and How They Grew" *(Special Libraries Association Geography and Map Division Bulletin* vol. 72, June, 1968), describes the development of the PATC map series and contains a list of 105 maps issued between 1931 and 1968. Most of these maps are found in the Geography and Map Division, Library of Congress (see entry A21).

J9 Society of Women Geographers

1. *1619 New Hampshire Avenue, N.W.*
   Washington, D.C. 20009
   (202) 265-2669

2. Ellen F. Schou, Executive Secretary

3. The Society of Women Geographers, established in 1925, is a professional organization of some 500 women worldwide whose common research interest is the exploration of little-known or unique places and people in the world. Organized Groups are located in Chicago, Los Angeles, San Francisco, and other regions. The Society provides fellowship funding to aid young women in the advanced study of geography.

4. The Society maintains an archives and library, including the personal papers and publications of some members associated with cartography.

J10 Special Libraries Association (SLA)

1 a. *1700 18th Street, N.W.*
Washington, D.C. 20009

2. David Bender, Executive Director

3. The Special Libraries Association is a national library organization comprised of 21 subject divisions, one of which is the Geography and Map Division (Joanne Hansen, Chairperson 313/487–3191). The mission of the Geography and Map Division is to promote map librarianship and facilitate the exchange of information in the fields of cartography and geography. The Geography and Map Division holds an annual meeting in the spring in conjunction with the Special Libraries Association annual conference. A local affiliate, the SLA Washington, D.C. Chapter, Geography and Map Group (Susan Fifer-Canby, Chairperson 202/857–7785), meets four or five times each year.

5. The Geography and Map Division publishes a quarterly *Bulletin* featuring original articles, book reviews, and reports on map librarianship, geographic information systems, cartographic collections, and other aspects of cartographic and geographic literature (Mary Murphy, Editor, 8102 Birnam Wood Drive, McLean, Virginia 22102, telephone 202/356–5614). Other publications include *Map Collections in the United States and Canada: A Directory* (1985. 178 p.), compiled by David K. Carrington and Richard W. Stephenson; *Introduction to Map Libraries,* a Slide/Tape Presentation available from Anita K. Oser, Hunter Library, Western Carolina University, Cullowhee, North Carolina 28723 (704/227–7362); *Directory of Map Catalogers in the United States* (1983), available from Mary Galnader, Arthur H. Robinson Map Library, 310 Science Hall, University of Wisconsin, 550 North Park Street, Madison, Wisconsin 53706, and *Federal Government Map Collecting: A Brief History* (1969. 60 p.), available from SLA Geography and Map Group, 5422 Marsh Hawk Way, Columbia, Maryland 21045.

J11 Washington Map Society

1. *5100 Barto Avenue*
   Camp Springs, Maryland 20746

2. Nancy G. Miller, Secretary

3. The Washington Map Society was founded in 1979 as an informal organization of persons interested in the history of cartography and collecting antique maps. Membership is open to anyone in the Washington, D.C. area who shares these common interests. The Society meets approximately five times a year featuring speakers on various aspects of the history of cartography and map collecting, as well as visits to map collections and cartographic exhibits.

5. A newsletter, *The Portolan* (Jonathan T. Lanman, Editor), contains information about meetings, brief articles and notes on map collections, the history of cartography, and current exhibitions.

K Publishers, Publications, and Media

Publishers, Publications and Media Entry Format (K)

1. Address and Telephone Numbers
2. Publisher, Chief Official, Editor or Key Staff Member
3. Publications, Frequency of Issues, Content

K1 Alexandria Drafting Company

1. *6440 General Green Way*
   Alexandria, Virginia 22312
   (703) 750-0510

2. Thomas Sutton, President

3. The Alexandria Drafting Company is a commercial map publisher. It produces maps for local, state, and Federal agencies and under its own imprint. The latter includes a series of detailed street atlases for cities, counties, and regions in Delaware, Georgia, Maryland, Pennsylvania, and Washington, D.C., and a series of fishing maps for reservoirs and coastal areas in Maryland, North Carolina, Pennsylvania, South Carolina, and Virginia.

K2 American Automobile Association (AAA)—National Travel Department—Cartographic Services Division

1. *8111 Gatehouse Road*
   Falls Church, Virginia 22047
   (703) 222-6141

2. Kenneth Porter, Director

3. The Cartographic Services Division produces and updates annually all maps used by the 26 million members of AAA. These include state highway maps, regional highway maps, 25 city and vicinity maps, 670 strip maps of United States highways, and page size maps illustrating the Association's tour books of states and provinces in North America, state camp books listing approved camp grounds, and travel guides for Europe, Mexico, and the Caribbean.

K3 American Forces Information Services (Defense Department)

1. *1735 North Lynn Street, Room 210*
Arlington, Virginia 22209–2086
(202) 696–5294

3. The American Forces Information Service publishes *Defense,* a monthly journal issued by the Department of Defense (DOD) to provide official and professional information on Defense policies and programs. Recent issues have contained articles on new developments at the Defense Mapping Agency (G8). *Defense* is available from the United States Government Printing Office (K8).

K4 American Petroleum Institute (API)

1. *1220 L Street, N.W.*
Washington, D.C. 20005
(202) 682–8000 (Information and Publications)

3. API publishes a set of 6 detailed maps of the United States showing crude oil pipelines, product pipelines, and related facilities.

K5 American University — Foreign Area Studies

1. *5010 Wisconsin Avenue, N.W.*
Washington, D.C. 20016
(202) 885–8516-

2. Richard Nyrop, Director

3. The Foreign Area Studies program is operated under a contract between The American University and the United States Department of the Army. Its major purpose is to prepare the *Area Handbooks* series, now entitled *Country Studies*. More than 100 books have been published, each describing and analyzing the economic, military, political, social, and cultural systems and institutions of a particular foreign country. The books are illustrated with maps and other graphic materials. The maps are prepared by the Graphics Department (Harriet Blood, Graphic Artist/Cartographer 202/885-8502), which maintains the original art work and negatives.

Current *Country Studies* are available from the Government Printing Office (K8). Out-of-stock copies may be obtained in microfiche form from the National Technical Information Service (K12). A list of available *Country Studies* and a booklet, *The Area Handbook Program* (1975. 18 p.) are available from FAS.

K6 Defense Technical Information Center (DTIC) (Defense Department)

1. *Cameron Station, Building 5*
Alexandria, Virginia 22314
(703) 274–7633)

2. Kurt N. Molholm, Administrator

3. The Defense Technical Information Center is the central repository for some 1.5 million national security classified and unclassified scientific and technical research reports and documents produced or funded by the Defense Department. It is open, however, only to Department of Defense (DOD) employees and authorized staff members of DOD contractors, potential contractors, and other United States government agencies and their contractors. Most of the DTIC collection can be searched through online computers by qualified users. Researchers who do not qualify for direct access to DTIC data banks may obtain unclassified DOD technical reports and bibliography information through the National Technical Information Service (NTIS) (K12). DTIC routinely releases unclassified material to NTIS where it may be accessed through NTIS's, *Government Reports Announcements and Index,* and the NTIS Bibliographic Data File. The unclassified reports include items produced by the Army Engineer Topographical Laboratories (E5) and the Defense Mapping Agency (G8).

K7 *Engineer: The Magazine for Army Engineers*

1. *Mailing Address:*
ATZA-TD-P Stop 291 D
Fort Belvoir, Virginia 22060–5291
(703) 664–3082

2. Marilyn Fleming, Editor

3. The *Engineer,* published quarterly by the United States Army Engineer Center at Fort Belvoir, Virginia, promotes the professional development of the Army engineer community by feature articles and notes pertaining to engineering activities, training programs, and career opportunities. Recent issues have contained articles on the work and organization of Fort Belvoir's 30th Engineer Battalion (Topographic) (Army), particularly with respect to computer graphic mapping. The *Engineer* is available through the Superintendent of Documents (see entry K8).

K8 Government Printing Office (GPO)

1. *Main Bookstore*
723 North Capitol Street, N.W.
Washington, D.C. 20401
(202) 275–2051

Mail Orders:
Superintendent of Documents
U.S. Government Printing Office
Washington, D.C. 20402

2. Ralph E. Kennickell, Jr. Public Printer

3. The Government Printing Office (GPO) is the principal printing agency of the Federal government. It is responsible for printing or contracting commercially the printing of books, maps, and other publications requested by Congress and the agencies of the Federal Government. These publications are sold and distributed by the Superintendent of Documents (SupDocs), which also administers the Federal Depository Library program through which selected publications, including maps, are made available at no cost to some 1,200 libraries nationwide. The Depository Administration Branch (Barbara Appel, Chief 202/275-1071) supervises the general distribution program of selected government maps to Federal Depository Libraries including the Government Printing Office/United States Geological Survey/Defense Mapping Agency (GPO/USGS/DMA) Map Project, which pertains to USGS and DMA maps. A *Fact Sheet* (2 pages), describing the latter program, and a list of Federal depository libraries by state and city (27 pages) are available on request.

The SupDocs currently handles the sale of 168 maps and atlases. These include census and population maps compiled by the Census Bureau (G5); environmental atlases; political atlases and maps of foreign countries prepared by the State Department (G26) and Central Intelligence Agency (G6); angler's guides to fish, fishing grounds, and fishing facilities of the United States Atlantic and Pacific coasts; maps and atlases of waterways and wetlands; world and national weather and climatic charts including the weekly daily weather map publication, issued by the National Weather Service (G23); and atlases of maps and photomosaics of Mars and Mercury prepared by the National Aeronautical and Atmospheric Administration (G18). These maps, atlases, and related cartographic publications are described in a subject bibliography entitled *Maps and Atlases (United States and Foreign)*, which is revised annually and is available on request. Another helpful subject bibliography is *Surveying and Mapping*, which lists government handbooks, instructional manuals, and histories devoted to aerial photography, mapmaking, and surveying.

The *Monthly Catalog of U.S. Government Publications*, the most comprehensive listing of publications issued by Federal agencies, is available on a subscription basis (202/783-3238). The *GPO Sales Publications Reference File*, a subscription service which lists all publications and subscriptions currently offered for sale, is available in microfiche on a monthly basis. Both the *Monthly Catalog* and *Publications Reference File* may also be accessed online through BRS/Search Service (D1) and DIALOG (D3).

K9 *Mapping Sciences and Remote Sensing*

1. *V.H. Winston and Sons, Inc.*
   7961 Eastern Avenue
   Silver Spring, Maryland 20910
   (301) 587-3356

2. Joel L. Morrison, Editor-in-Chief

3. *Mapping Sciences and Remote Sensing* is published quarterly in cooperation with the American Congress on Surveying and Mapping, the American Society of Photogrammetry, and the American Geophysical Union. It contains English translations of selected substantive articles on cartography and remote sensing from Soviet and Eastern European periodicals, as well as from manuscripts and papers from other sources.

K10 *The Military Engineer*

1. *607 Prince Street, P.O. Box 180*
   Alexandria, Virginia 22313–0180
   (800) 336–3097

2. John Kern, Editor

3. *The Military Engineer* is published bimonthly (except for September and October) by The Society of American Military Engineers. In addition to occasionally featuring an article pertaining to military cartography, each issue contains an informational section "Geodesy, Mapping, Oceanography", which is devoted to current surveying and mapping news of Federal agencies.

K11 National Archives and Records Administration—National Audiovisual Center (NAC)

1. *8700 Edgeworth Drive*
   Capital Heights, Maryland 20743–3701
   (301) 763–1896 (Information Services)

2. John H. McLean, Director.

3. The National Audiovisual Center is the central information and distribution source for more than 8,000 audiovisual programs produced by or for the United States Government. Materials are made available for sale or rent on a self-sustaining basis at the lowest prices possible. The Center's *Media Resource Catalog 1986* (Washington: National Archives and Records Administration, 1986) lists and describes 2,700 of the latest and most popular programs. Also available is *Cadastral Survey Training*, a brochure describing a multimedia series produced by the United States Bureau of Land Management (G17) for surveyors, cartographers, and civil engineers.

The following titles represent a list of relevant available films. Additional earlier films produced by Federal agencies are found in the National Archives and Records Administration's Motion Picture, Sound, and Video Branch (B19, RG 29, RG 111, RG 226, and RG 242).

Aerial Navigation. Map Reading. United States Air Force. 1945. 21 min. Sound. B & W. 16 mm.

Air Masses and Fronts - Fronts and the Surface Weather Map. Department of the Air Force, 1962. 10 min. Sound. Color. 16mm.

Basic Map Reading, Part 1, Map Symbols. Department of the Army, 1967. 20 min. Sound. Color. 16mm.

Basic Map Reading, Part 2, Grid, Distance, and Elevation. Department of the Army, 1967. 29 min. Sound. Color. 16mm.

Basic Map Reading, Part 3, Direction, Orientation, and Location Without a Compass. Department of the Army, 1967. 30 min. Sound. Color. 16 mm.

Basic Map Reading, Part 4, Direction, Orientation, and Location With a Compass. Department of the Army, 1967. 30 min. Sound. Color. 16mm.

Basic Map Reading, Part 5, Photos and Photo Maps. Department of the Army, 1967. 31 min. Sound. Color. 16mm.

Bathymetry—Discovering the Ocean Floor, Charting the Ocean Bottom. United States Navy. 1970. 16 min. Sound. Color. 16 mm.

Cadastral Survey Monumentation. Bureau of Land Management, 1980. 74 min. Color. 432-2x2 slides. 4-Audio-cassettes.

Cadastral Survey Plat Preparation. Bureau of Land Management, 1980. 239 min. Color. 1464–2x2 slides. 12-Audio-cassettes.

Charting the Oceans. United States Navy, 1972. 28 min. Sound. Color. 16 mm. History and Production of charts.

Charts. United States Navy, 1942. 18 min. Sound. B & W. 16 mm. Describes Mercator, Gnomonic, and Lambert projections.

Flying the Weather Map, Part 2., The "Howgozit" Chart. United States Navy, 1944. 13 min. Sound. Color. 16 mm. (Rental only) Plotting fuel consumption with aeronautical chart.

Hydrographic Surveying Operations of the Navy - A Series. United States Navy, 1951. 2 films. Sound. 16 mm.

Images of Life. Agency for International Development/ National Aeronautics and Space Administration, 1976. 25 min. Sound. Color. 16 mm. Landsat capabilities.

Land For People, Land For Bears. NASA, 1972. 15 min. Sound. Color. Videocassette and 16 mm. Landsat satellites furnish new kind of data for land use and wildlife habitat mapping.

Mapping Adventure. United States Army, 1964. 29 min. Sound. Color. 16 mm. Army engineers and Latin Americans mapping in South America. Not available for public sale.

Maps and Records Offices. National Wildlife Coordinating Group, 1980. Multimedia Kit.

Modern Geodetic Surveying. United States Navy, 1967. 18 min. Sound. Color. 16 mm.

Multiplex Mapping, Part 1. United States Army Corps of Engineers, 1949. 25 min. Sound. Color. 16 mm. Preparation of topographical maps from aerial photographs at United States Army Map Service.

Observations, Maps, and Forecasts. United States Navy, 1949. 15 min. Sound. B & W. 16 mm. Analysis of a weather map.

Obstacle Problems in Public Land Surveying. Bureau of Land Management, 1980. 39 min. 229–2x2 slides. Color. 2-Audiocassettes. Use of solar transit.

Orientation to National Cadastral Survey Training. Bureau of Land Management, 1980. 11 min. 50–2x2 slides. Color. 1-Audiocassette.

Pathfinders to Progress. United States Air Force, 1963. 25 min. Sound. Color. 16 mm. Story of 1370th Photo-Mapping Wing.

Remote Possibilities. National Aeronautics and Space Administration, 1977. 15 min. Sound. Color. 16 mm. Remote sensing is explained.

The Storage and Care of Maps. Department of Health, Education and Welfare, 1979. 8 min. Color. 69–2x2 slides. 1-Audiocassette.

Survey Records Investigation. Bureau of Land Management, 1981. 74 min. Color. 334–2x2 slides. 2-Audiocassettes.

VMCJ. United States Marine Corps, 1970. 15 mm. Sound. Color. 16 mm. Story of aerial photographic reconnaissance squadron in combat.

K12 National Technical Information Service (NTIS) (Commerce Department)

1. *Operations Center*
   5285 Port Royal Road
   Springfield, Virginia 22161
   (703) 487–4600 (Information)
   (703) 487–4640 (Bibliographic Search Service)

NTIS Information Center and Bookstore
Main Commerce Department Building
14th Street between Constitution Avenue and E Street, N.W.
Washington, D.C. 20230
(202) 377-0365 (Information)

2. Joseph F. Caponio, Director

3. The National Technical Information Service serves as the central Federal clearinghouse for the public sale of United States Government sponsored scientific, technical, and engineering information, as well as foreign technical reports and other special materials prepared by national and local government agencies. Its information collection totals nearly 2 million titles (6 million documents), with more than 70,000 new reports added each year.

Unlike the Government Printing Office (GPO) (entry K8), NTIS material is permanently available to researchers since single copies of any research title will be printed on request in hardcopy or microform when paper copies are no longer in stock. Maps, cartographic technical reports, and cartographic software produced by a wide variety of Federal agencies, research institutions, and universities are part of the collection maintained by NTIS.

Maps are available as part of technical reports, either as a foldout sheet or as individual maps. The latter are usually maintained as paper copy shelf stock and may or may not be available in microfiche or blow-back copy when the stock is depleted, depending upon their legibility after filming.

The most important published research aid for cartographic materials is *The Published Searches Master Catalog* (1985. 152 p.), which lists some 3,000 topical subject bibliographies prepared by NTIS subject specialists. Each subject bibliography, issued as *Published Searches,* contains from 50 to 350 complete technical summaries. Examples of cartographic *Published Searches* include *Aerial Photography: Its Use in the Study of Coastal Erosion and Pollution,* 1974–1985 (301 entries), *Agronomy: Remote Sensing and Evaluation,* 1975–1984 (62 entries), *Computer Aided Mapping,* 1982–1984 (233 entries), *Oil Pollution Detection and Sensing,* 1976–1983 (267 entries), *Photogrammetry: Equipment and Image Processing,* 1975–1985 (253 entries), *Remote Sensing of Agricultural Resources,* 1973–1984 (330 entries), *Remote Sensing Applied to Geology and Minerology,* 1973–1984 (327 entries), *Remote Sensing Applied to Urban and Regional Planning,* 1964–1985 (135 entries), and *Surveying Instruments,* 1970–1985 (306 entries). Twenty-two cartographic software programs are listed in a published list entitled *NTIS Software Products.*

Access to bibliographic research summaries of current cartographic technical reports is provided by the weekly *Natural Resources and Earth Sciences Abstract Newsletter* and the biweekly *Government Reports Announcements and Index* (GRA&I) journal, both of which are available on an annual subscription basis. A recent issue of the latter journal contained summaries of map related reports and maps published by the Artificial Intelligence Laboratory, Massachusetts Institute of Technology, Cambridge ("Constructing a Depth Map from Images"); the Army Engineer Topographic Laboratories ("Mapping Applications of Video Disc Technology"); Technische Universität, Graz, Austria ("Activities Report on the Project DESBOD, a geographical and land database); and the Central Intelligence Agency (map of the distribution of religious groups in Lebanon).

The NTIS Bibliographic Database, a machine-readable version of GRA&I, is available online through DIALOG (D3), SDC (D10), Bibliographic Retrieval Services (D1), and Mead Data Central (1828 L Street, N.W. Washington, D.C. 20036, telephone 202/785-3550) in the United States, EURONET in Europe, and CISTI in Canada. The Federal Research in Progress (FEDRIP) database, which provides information about ongoing Federal research in science and engineering, is available in the United States through DIALOG and Mead Central. Both processing services are available from NERAC, Inc., Storrs, Connecticut. A specialized computer bibliographic search service (NTISearch) is also avaialable for a fee.

A descriptive brochure, *General Catalog of Information Services*, is available on request.

K13 *Navy Civil Engineer*

1. *Naval Facilities Engineering Command*
 Alexandria, Virginia 22332

2. Les Helsdon, Editor

3. The *Navy Civil Engineer,* published quarterly, occasionally contains articles relating to cartography. The Spring/Summer issue 1985, for example, carried a feature article on the Graphics Engineering and Mapping Systems (GEMS) being developed for the Navy by the Naval Facilities Engineering Command. GEMS is being used to produce computer-aided real estate existing condition maps and summary maps. The *Navy Civil Engineer* is sold by the Superintendent of Documents, United States Government Printing Office (see entry K8).

K14 *Professional Surveyor*

1. *Harrison Communications, Suite 410*
 918 F Street, N.W.
 Washington, D.C. 20004
 (202) 628-9696

2. Clifford A. Thorpe, Jr., Publisher

3. The *Professional Surveyor* is published bimonthly by the American Surveyors Publishing Co., Inc. and is distributed to members of the surveying and mapping community. Each issue includes several articles on surveying and mapping; information on new surveying products, surveying appointments and contracts, and professional meetings. A special feature, "Collectors Corner", written by Silvio A. Bedini, contains comments in response to questions concerning historical surveying instruments. Recent feature articles of interest include "Mapping Maya Civilizations", by Boyd Dixon; "The Mason-Dixon Story", by Bob Karolevitz; and "Digital Design for Using Information", by Jury Konga.

K15 Roloc Color Slides and Pictorial Research

1. *326 South Pickett Street*
   Alexandria, Virginia 22304
   (703) 751–8668

   Mail:
   P.O. Box 9026
   Alexandria, Virginia 22304

2. Lt. Col. M.W. Arps, Retired, Owner

3. Roloc Color Slides and Pictorial Research is a commercial business that serves as a source of transparencies of maps, aerial photographs, and views for teachers, publishers of textbooks and encyclopedias, and producers of educational filmstrips and audiovisual productions. Roloc maintains a stock of over 1,000,000 slides, including several hundred transparencies of maps of cities and countries produced by national tourist offices, topographic maps prepared by the Army Map Service, and aerial photographs and remote sensing imagery from various sources, including NASA. Representative examples include a slide of an aerial view of Algiers, a pictorial map slide of Rio de Janeiro, a sketch map slide of Brasilia, a map slide of Havana, issued by the Cuban Tourist Commission, a map slide of France, a pictorial map slide of the valley of the Loire in France, a map slide of India, furnished by the Information Service of India, a slide of an aerial view of Saigon, and a slide map of Dubrovnik, Yugoslavia, showing the old walled city.

A free general information brochure provides a list of 83 transparency maps of large geographic areas and countries. In addition, there are catalogs for 105 countries which list additional maps and aerial photographs.

K16 *U.S.A. Today*

1. *1000 Wilson Boulevard*
   Arlington, Virginia 22209
   (703) 276–3400

2. John C. Quinn, Editor

3. *U.S.A. Today* is a national newspaper published daily, except Saturdays, Sundays, and general legal holidays. Each issue contains a half-page detailed color-coded weather map of the United States.

K17 *The Washington Post*

1. *1150 15th Street, N.W.*
   Washington, D.C. 20071
   (202) 334-6000 (Information)

2. Benjamin Bradlee, Executive Editor
   Howard Simons, Managing Editor

3. *The Washington Post* is a daily newspaper which makes extensive use of general location, interpretation, and travel maps to illustrate and explain news stories. The News Art Department (Michael Keegan, Director, 202/334-7383, David Cook, cartographer, Richard Furno, computer cartographic specialist) is developing digitized cartographic databases.

K18 Williams & Heintz Map Corporation

1. *8119 Central Avenue*
   Capital Heights, Maryland 20743
   (301) 336-1144

2. Richard L. Heintz, President
   Albert D. Schmitz, Production Manager

3. The Williams & Heintz Map Corporation is one of the largest commercial cartographic firms in the United States, producing maps and charts for some forty states and Federal agencies. They specialize in large-scale multicolor complex technical maps, particularly geological maps, topographic maps, soil maps, zoning maps, land use maps, aeronautical charts, vegetation maps, bathymetric charts, county highway maps, environmental maps, and satellite maps. A wall display, illustrating the major types of maps produced by Williams & Heintz, and a leaflet describing the Corporation's services are available on request.

APPENDIXES

I Map Stores and Distributors of Maps

The following map stores and other distributors in the Washington area stock current and out-of-print maps, atlases, and related materials. A map source unique to the Nation's Capital is foreign embassies, a number of which are described in section I.

Entry Format

1. Address and Telephone Number
2. Stock

Alexandria Drafting Company

1. 6440 General Green Way
   Alexandria, Virginia 22312
   (703) 750-0510

2. For description, see entry K1.

Defense Mapping Agency (DMA)—Office of Distribution Services

1. 6101 MacArthur Boulevard
   Brookmont, Maryland 20315-0020
   (202) 227-2816

2. The Defense Mapping Agency publishes and sells current small scale topographic and outline maps of major world regions and countries and worldwide nautical charts. For a description of maps available, see entry G8.

Fairfax County—Maps, Products and Publications Sales Office

1. Massey Building, Floor 1
   4100 Chain Bridge Road
   Fairfax, Virginia 22030
   (703) 691-2974

2. The Maps, Products and Publications Sales Office sells a wide variety of official maps relating to Fairfax County produced by the County's Mapping and Geographic Services. A list is found in entry H3.

Geological Survey (USGS)—Public Inquiries Office and Sales

1. General Services Building, Room 1028
   18th and F Streets, N.W.
   Washington, D.C
   (202) 343-8073

   12201 Sunrise Valley Drive
   National Center
   Reston, Virginia 22092
   (703) 648-6892

2. The Geological Survey publishes and sells the basic topographic and geologic quadrangle maps of the United States, and a wide variety of other general and special purpose maps of regions, counties, and smaller areas. These maps are further described in entry G14.

Government Printing Office (GPO) Main Bookstore

1. 710 North Capitol Street, N.W.
   Washington, D.C. 20402
   (202) 783-3238

2. The Government Printing Office sells current maps published by the Bureau of Land Management (entry G17), Census Bureau (entry G5), Central Intelligence Agency (entry G6), National Weather Service (entry G23), and the State Department (entry G26).

Library of Congress—Sales Shop

1. Thomas Jefferson Building
   1st Street, S.E.
   Washington, D.C. 20540

2. The Sales Shop sells Library of Congress publications, including facsimiles of early maps from the Library's collections.

The Map Store, Inc.

1. 1636 I Street, N.W.
Washington, D.C. 20006
(202) 628-2608

2. The Map Store, Inc. stocks an extensive selection of business reference maps, travel maps and guides, globes, atlases, aeronautical and nautical charts, and topographic maps.

Maryland—National Capital Park and Planning Commission (M-NCPPC)

1. Montgomery County Planning Board
Records and Information Office
8787 Georgia Avenue
Silver Spring, Maryland 20907
(301) 495-4610

Prince George's County Planning Board
14741 Governor Oden Bowie Drive
Upper Marlboro, Maryland 20772
(301) 952-3514

2. For a description of maps of Montgomery and Prince George's Counties published and sold by the Maryland—National Capital Park and Planning Commission, see entry H4.

National Geographic Society—Sales

1. 17th and M Streets, N.W.
Washington, D.C. 20036
(202) 921-1200

2. For a description of maps and atlases published and sold by the National Geographic Society, see entry J7.

National Ocean Service (NOS)—Chart Sales Offices

1. Washington Science Center, Building 1
6001 Executive Boulevard
Rockville, Maryland 20852
(301) 443-8005

6501 Lafayette Avenue
Riverdale, Maryland 20737
(301) 436-6980

2. The National Ocean Service publishes and sells aeronautical charts of the United States, nautical charts of coastal areas of the United States, and offshore bathymetric and special charts. For a description of these charts, see entry G20.

National Technical Information Service (NTIS)

1. Commerce Department Building
14th Street between Constitution Avenue and E Street, N.W.
Washington, D.C. 20230
(202) 724-3382

2. For a description of maps available through NTIS, see entry K12.

Old Newspaper and Map Mail Auction

1. 5614 Northfield Road
Bethesda, Maryland 20817
(301) 657-9074

2. The Old Newspaper and Map Mail Auction stocks a wide variety of out-of-print maps.

Old Print Gallery

1. 1220 31st Street, N.W.
Washington, D.C. 20007
(202) 965-1818

2. The Old Print Gallery carries the largest selection of early, rare maps in the Washington, D.C. area.

Potomac Appalachian Trail Club (PATC)

1. 1718 N Street, N.W.
Washington, D.C. 20036
(202) 638-5306

2. The Potomac Appalachian Club publishes and sells maps and guide books pertaining to the Appalachian Trail. See entry J8.

Travel Books Unlimited

1. 4931 Cordell Avenue (off Old Georgetown Road)
Bethesda, Maryland 20814
(301) 951-8533

2. Travel Books Unlimited specializes in current travel maps and guide books.

The Washington Ear, Inc.

1. 35 University Boulevard East
Silver Spring, Maryland 20901

2. The Washington Ear, Inc. sells tactile and large print maps and atlases of Washington, D.C. and Maryland.

Waverly Auctions

1. 7649 Old Georgetown Road
Bethesda, Maryland 20814
(301) 951–8883

2. Waverly Auctions sells a wide variety of nineteenth century and earlier maps through consignments and auctions.

II Map Collections by Size

Estimates of the largest map collections located in the Washington, D.C. area are provided below.

More than 4 Million Maps

Library of Congress (A21, A23, A24, B15)

1–2 Million Maps

National Archives and Records Administration (B19)
National Oceanic and Atmospheric Administration (A32, A33, G20)

500,000–1 Million Maps

Defense Mapping Agency—Scientific Data Department (G8)

400,000–500,000 Maps

Geological Survey (A12, G14)

200,000–300,000 Maps

District of Columbia—Surveyors Office (H2)
National Park Service (G21)

100,000–200,000 Maps

Land Management Bureau (G17)
National Capital Planning Commission—Cartographic Services (G19)
National Geographic Society Library (A30)
University of Maryland Libraries (A40, B23)

50,000–100,000 Maps

Census Bureau (G5)
Federal Emergency Management Agency (FEMA) (G10)

10,000–20,000 Maps

George Mason University—Fenwick Library (A13)
George Washington University—Gelman Library (A14)
National Agricultural Library (A29)
World Bank—Sectoral Library (A41)

5,000–10,000 Maps

Army Military History Institute (B7)
Forest Service—Engineering Staff (G13)
Martin Luther King, Jr. Memorial Library (A25)
Maryland-National Capital Park and Planning Commission (H4)
National Air and Space Museum (Smithsonian Institution) (C5)
National Anthropological Archives (Smithsonian Institution) (B18)
Naval Historical Center (Navy Department)—Operational Archives Branch (B21)

III Remote Sensing Imagery Collections by Size

Estimates of the largest available remote sensing imagery collections located in the Washington, D.C. area are provided below.

7 million–8 million Remote Sensing Images
National Archives and Records Administration (B19)

5 million–6 million Remote Sensing Images
National Cartographic Information Center (E7)

2 million–3 million Remote Sensing Images
Library of Congress (A21, A23, B15)

500,000–1 million Remote Sensing Images
Earth Observation Satellite Company (EOSAT) (E3)
Environmental Photographic Interpretation Center (Environmental Protection Agency) (E6)
National Space Science Data Center (D9)

100,000–150,000 Remote Sensing Images
National Air and Space Museum (Smithsonian Institution) (C5)

50,000–100,000 Remote Sensing Images
National Agricultural Library (A29)

10,000–15,000 Remote Sensing Images
Defense Department Still Media Depository (B10)
National Ocean Service (G20)

IV Housing, Transportation, and Other Services

This section is prepared to help outside scholars who come to Washington, D.C., for short-term research, to find suitable housing. It also contains data on local transportation facilities and information services. Prices quoted are current as of February 1986.

HOUSING INFORMATION AND REFERRAL SERVICE

For persons interested in leasing an apartment or house, *Apartment Shoppers' Guide and Housing Directory* (ASGHD) (updated every 3 months) is a valuable source of information. The directory, which quotes current rental prices, terms of leases, and directions to each of the facilities listed, is available at People's Drug Stores in the Washington area. It is published by ASGHD (301/588-0681), located at 1110 Fidler Lane, Suite 410, Silver Spring, Maryland, 20910. The staff provides housing-referral service, for a fee, from 9:00 A.M.–5:30 P.M. Monday–Friday.

Faculty at local colleges and universities who are planning sabbaticals are sometimes willing to rent their homes to other scholars for periods of 6 months to a year. Using The American University as one example, contact the College of Arts and Sciences, Gray Building, Room 107, Washington, D.C. 20016, and ask for a copy of *Connections,* a typed newsletter that lists names, addresses, and conditions of houses available for rent.

Scholars can also obtain assistance from the following local university housing offices:

George Washington University Off-Campus Housing
Resources Center
2121 I Street, N.W. (Rice Hall), 4th Floor
Washington, D.C. 20052
(202) 676-6688
Summer: 8:30 A.M.–6:00 P.M. Monday–Friday
Winter: 8:30 A.M.–5:00 P.M. Monday–Friday

This office has listings of apartments and other housing in the Washington area. Open to the public, the office also distributes the *Apartment Shoppers' Guide and Housing Directory* (see above), maps of Washington, D.C., and a *Guide to Off-Campus Housing* (annual), prepared for students by the office.

Georgetown University Off-Campus Housing Office
Healy Building Basement, Room G08
37th and O Streets, N.W.
Washington D.C. 20057
(202) 625–3026
1:00 P.M.–4:00 P.M. Monday–Friday
Open to the public, this office offers services similar to those at the George Washington University Off-Campus Housing Resources Center.

Catholic University of America Off-Campus Housing Office
University Center East
Washington, D.C. 20064
(202) 635–5618
9:00 A.M.–5:00 P.M. Monday–Friday
Open to the public, this office provides services similar to those of the other schools listed above.

Northern Virginia Community College
Annandale Campus Housing Board
Student Activities Office
Godwin Building, Room CG103
8333 Little River Turnpike
Annandale, Virginia 22003
(703) 323–3147
8:30 A.M.–5:00 P.M. Monday–Friday
The board maintains a listing of rooms available in private homes.

NOTE: The off-campus housing offices of the American University, Howard University, and the University of Maryland handle inquiries and requests from their own students and faculty members only.

Short-Term Housing

For those scholars who intend to stay for a short period of time—a few days to a few weeks or months—the following facilities may be useful:

International Guest House
1441 Kennedy Street, N.W.
Washington D.C. 20011
(202) 726–5808
Rates: $13.70 per bed per day, or $82.70 per week (breakfast and evening tea with shared rooms); half-price for children 6 to 16 years of age.

International Student House
1825 R Street, N.W.
Washington, D.C. 20009
(202) 232–4007
Rates: $370.00 to $550.00 per month (minimum, one-semester stay) for room and board (2 meals, 7 days). Single rooms and shared double or triple rooms are available. The house maintains a nationality quota policy that permits no more than 10 Americans or 3 citizens from any one foreign country at any time.

The Woodner Hotel Apartment Buildings
3636 16th Street, N.W.
Washington, D.C. 20010
(202) 328–2800
The hotel has furnished efficiency and one-bedroom apartments. Rates per month: $355–$400 for an efficiency; $455–$600 for 1-bedroom.

The Capitol Park
800 4th Street, S.W.
Washington, D.C. 20024
(202) 479–6800
(Near the Library of Congress)
Rates: Furnished 1-bedroom apartments, $55 single, $65 double, Monday through Thursday, and $55 single or double, Friday through Sunday; and monthly, $700 single and $800–$900 double.

Long-Term Housing

Individuals wishing to rent an apartment or house for one year or more should consult not only the *Apartment Shoppers' Guide and Housing Directory* and the local university housing offices, but also the following rental agencies:

Millicent Chatel	(202) 338–0500
Lynch Realty	(202) 232–4100
Nyman Realty Co.	(301) 474–5700
Edmund Flynn Co.	(202) 537–1800
H.A. Gill	(202) 338–5000
Shannon and Luchs	(202) 659–7000
Norman Bernstein	(202) 331–7500
Snider Bros. P.M.I.	(301) 986–9500

Home and apartment rents vary greatly from area to area around Washington. Normally, rents are lower in suburban Virginia and Maryland than in Washington, D.C. One should also remember that it is difficult to find furnished apartments in the Washington area through regular real estate agents. People who need furnished quarters may have to take unfurnished apartments and rent furniture through furniture rental agencies listed in the D.C. area phone books.

TRANSPORTATION

In preparing for a visit to Washington, D.C., scholars should consider purchasing a copy of the *Washington, D.C. and Vicinity Street Map* from the Alexandria Drafting Company, 417 Clifford Avenue, Alexandria, Virginia, 22305. Free maps of the Washington metropolitan area, depicting streets and metro subway routes, are available from the District of Columbia Department of Transportation Map Office at Room 519, 415 12th Street, N.W., Washington, D.C. 20004. The office is open from 8:15 A.M.–4:45 P.M., Monday through Friday (telephone 202/727–6562). For mail requests, include a stamped (88 cents for U.S.A. delivery), self-addressed, 7" x 10" envelope. Other area street maps are available for purchase at any number of People's Drug Stores.

In general, the Metro subway and buses are the most preferable and inexpensive means of traveling in and around the city. For persons using automobiles, parking space in-town is not only limited but also relatively expensive. Commercial lots are, however, available. Metered parking is sometimes available for periods up to two hours. Many streets have restrictions for parking during rush hour (7:00–9:30 A.M. and 4:00–6:30 P.M.). Regulations are strictly enforced and violators can expect to be ticketed or towed.

To National Airport

Public transportation to and from National Airport includes Metrobus No. 11, which leaves from 10th Street and Pennsylvania Avenue, N.W., and a Metro subway train that can be accessed from various downtown stations. A bus and train leaves every 10 minutes or less. A limousine service runs between the airport and the Capital Hilton Hotel, 16th and K Streets, N.W. daily until 11:15 P.M. For further information, call the hotel (202/393–1000).

To Dulles International Airport

Buses to Dulles International Airport leave from the Capital Hilton Hotel, 16th and K Streets, N.W. once every hour in the morning starting at 5:15 A.M., every 30 minutes in the afternoon from 2:15 until 8:15 P.M., and sporadically thereon until 11:45 P.M. There is a single Metrobus to Dulles that departs each day at 8:25 A.M. from 11th and E Streets, N.W., and arrives at Dulles Airport at 9:45 A.M.

To Baltimore-Washington (Friendship) International Airport

Buses to Baltimore-Washington (Friendship) International Airport leave from 16th and K Streets, N.W., making one stop at Greenbelt Station, Maryland. For further information, call (301) 441–2345.

Trains and Buses

The terminal for all passenger trains serving Washington, D.C., is located in-town at 50 Massachusetts Avenue, N.E. An on-site subway station is there as well. The Library of Congress is within walking distance from the station. The Trailways and Greyhound bus terminals are located near Metro subway stops.

Taxi

Taxi fares in Washington, D.C. are based on a zone system and are reasonable. Taxi fares that cross into and out of Maryland and Virginia are fairly expensive. The major cab company phone numbers are:

Capital Cab	(202) 546–2400
Checker Cab	(202) 484–7888
Diamond Cab	(202) 387–6200
Yellow Cab	(202) 544–1212

Metro Subway System

The Metro subway system is a regional transportation system, which links Maryland and Virginia with the District of Columbia, and, although still under construction, is for the most part completed. All Metro station entrances are identified by pylons with a clearly marked "M" on all sides. In the station below, large maps of the entire Metrorail System and maps showing the surrounding neighborhood are illuminated. Information booths are also available. Trains operate every ten minutes during non-rush hours and every five minutes during rush hours (6:00–9:30 A.M. and 3:00–6:30 P.M.). Metrorail is in operation Monday through Friday from 6:00 A.M. to midnight, Saturday from 8:00 A.M. to midnight, and Sunday from 10:00 A.M. to 6:00 P.M. Many of the organizations listed in the present study are accessible using the system. Individuals may wish to obtain a free copy of *All About Metro* by writing to Washington Metropolitan Area Transit Authority, Consumer Department, 600 5th Street, N.W., Washington, D.C. 20001, or by telephoning (202) 637–2437 from 6:00 A.M. to 11:30 P.M., seven days a week. Copies are also available at various Metro stops.

Local Bus Systems

Almost every area of Washington, D.C. and vicinity is linked by the Metrobus system. Brochures on individual routes, including express bus service, current information on fares, and hours of normal and holiday service are available at Metro headquarters, as well as at local public libraries. Individuals may want to pick up a copy of *Metrobus Guide to Washington, D.C. and Suburban Maryland* from the Washington Metropolitan Area Transit Authority (address and telephone cited above). An important point to remember: Exact fare is required on Metrobus; operators do not give change.

Montgomery County, Maryland maintains its own ride-on bus system, and is inexpensive. For route and fare information, call (301) 251–2225 from 7:30 A.M. to 5:00 P.M., Monday through Friday.

The city of Fairfax, Virginia, maintains a commuter express bus service between the city of Fairfax and Washington, D.C., with an intermediate stop at the Pentagon. Passengers must obtain a farecard to use the city's bus system. For information and a brochure citing route and fare information, call (703) 385–7859 or write to Public Information, Room 308, City of Fairfax, Virginia 22030.

OTHER SERVICES

Foreign Student Service Council of Greater Washington (FSSC)
1623 Belmont Street N.W., Washington, D.C. 20009
(202) 232–4979
The Foreign Student Service Council provides services to foreign students living in or visiting Washington, D.C. Arrangements for board, seminars, program assistance, information on travel and lodging, and various productions are some of the services provided by FSSC.

NOTE: Because there are a large number of foreign students attending area colleges and universities, some of the schools have established offices for disseminating information of all types to foreign students.

International Visitors Information Service (IVIS)
733 15th Street, N.W. Suite 300, Washington, D.C. 20005
(202) 783–6540 (24 hour service)
The International Visitors Information Service consists of some 78 independent groups that assist international visitors in the Washington, D.C. area. Services and programs are varied, including a 24-hour telephone answering service available to international visitors for emergency problems after business hours and a multilingual referral service which includes information, maps, and brochures. All services are provided free by volunteers. A reception center is available at the above address and also at Dulles International Airport.

Washington International Center
Meridian House
1630 Crescent Place, N.W.
Washington, D.C. 20009
(202) 332–1025
The Washington International Center, established in 1950, by the American Council of Education, provides services to international visitors in Washington, D.C.

OTHER SOURCES OF INFORMATION

There are a number of excellent publications, which cite additional organizations that provide assistance to foreign visitors in the nation's capital: *The Directory of Resources for Cultural and Educational Exchanges and International Communication* (1979), published by the United States International Communications Agency; the directory lists both government and private organizations. Various indexes help facilitate the use of this *Guide*. See also *Directory of Community Organizations Serving Short-Term International Visitors* (1985–1986), published by the National Council for International Visitors. Additional guides for dining out in Washington, as well as for places to see, are available at most area bookstores.

V Federal Government Holidays

Federal government offices are closed on the following holidays:

New Year's Day	January 1
Martin Luther King's Birthday	Third Monday in January
Washington's Birthday	Third Monday in February
Memorial Day	Last Monday in May
Independence Day	July 4*
Labor Day	First Monday in September
Columbus Day	Second Monday in October
Veterans Day	November 11*
Thanksgiving	Fourth Thursday in November
Christmas	December 25*

*If this date falls on a Saturday, the holiday is on Friday; if the date falls on a Sunday, the holiday is on Monday.

The public areas of the Smithsonian Institution are open on most holidays.

VI Standard Entry Formats

A-C. Libraries; Archives and Manuscript Repositories; Museums and Galleries Entry Format

1. General Information
   a. address; telephone numbers
   b. hours of service
   c. conditions of access
   d. reproduction services
   e. name/title of director and heads of relevant divisions
2. Size of Holdings
3. Description of Holdings
   a. maps, atlases, and globes
   b. aerial photographs and remote sensing images
   c. literature, current and rare books
   d. manuscript collections
   e. photographs and motion pictures
   f. instruments
4. Bibliographic Aids Facilitating Use of Collection
   (cartobibliographies, catalog cards, computerized retrieval systems, inventories, special lists, catalog guides)

D. Data Banks Entry Format

1. General Information
   a. address; telephone numbers
   b. hours of service
   c. conditions of access
   d. name/title of director and key staff members
2. Description of Data files (hard-data and bibliographic-reference)
3. Bibliographic Aids Facilitating Use of Storage Media

E. Research Centers and Referral Services Entry Format

1. General Information
   a. address; telephone numbers
   b. hours of service
   c. conditions of access
   d. chief official/key resource person
2. Objectives and/or Programs
3. Collections/Research Facilities
4. Products

F. Academic Programs and Departments Entry Format

1. Address; Telephone Numbers
2. Chief Official and Title
3. Degrees and Subjects Offered; Programs
4. Library/Research Facilities
5. Laboratory Facilities
6. Publications

G–H. United States *and* State and Local Government Agencies Entry Format

1. General Information
   a. address; telephone numbers
   b. conditions of access
   c. name/title of director and heads of relevant divisions
2. Agency Functions and Programs
3. Agency Collections and Reference Facilities
4. Unpublished Materials
5. Publications
   a. published products
   b. published bibliographies and reference aids

   In the case of large, structurally complex agencies, each relevant division/bureau is described separately in accordance with the above entry format and cross referenced in the index.

I. Embassies and International Organizations Entry Format

1. General Information
   a. address; telephone numbers
   b. conditions of access
   c. name/title of director and heads of relevant divisions
2. Major Organizational Functions, Programs, and Research Activities
3. Libraries and Reference Facilities
4. Publications

J. Associations and Societies Entry Format

1. Address and Telephone Numbers
2. Chief Official and Title
3. Programs and Activities Pertaining to Cartography
4. Library, Archives, and Databases
5. Publications

K. Publishers, Publications and Media Entry Format

1. Address and Telephone Numbers
2. Publisher, Chief Official, Editor or Key Staff Member
3. Publications, Frequency of Issues, Content

BIBLIOGRAPHY

Bibliography

Reference sources consulted for identification of collections and organizations included in this *Scholars' Guide.*

Bhatt, Purnima M. *Scholars' Guide to Washington, D.C. for African Studies.* Washington, D.C.: Smithsonian Institution Press, 1980.

Cahill, Nancy, ed. *Federal Executive Directory.* Washington, D.C.: Carroll Publishing Company, 1985

Carrington, David K. and Richard W. Stephenson, eds. *Map Collections in the United States. A Directory.* 4th ed. New York: Special Libraries Association, 1985.

Claassen, Lynda Corey. *Finders' Guide To Prints and Drawings in the Smithsonian Institution.* Washington, D.C.: Smithsonian Institution Press, 1981.

Dillon, Kenneth J. *Scholars' Guide to Washington, D.C. for Central and East European Studies.* Washington, D.C.: Smithsonian Institution Press, 1980.

Directory of Archives and Manuscript Repositories in the United States. Washington, D.C.: National Archives and Records Service, 1978.

Directory of Federal Historical Programs and Activities. Washington, D.C.: Society for History in the Federal Government and American Historical Association, 1984.

Dorr, Steven R. *Scholars' Guide to Washington, D.C. for Middle Eastern Studies.* Washington, D.C.: Smithsonian Institution Press, 1981.

Grant, Steven A. *Scholars' Guide to Washington, D.C. for Russian/Soviet Studies.* 2nd ed., rev. by Bradford P. Johnson and Mark H. Teeter. Washington, D.C.: Smithsonian Institution Press, 1983.

Grow, Michael. *Scholars' Guide to Washington, D.C. for Latin American and Caribbean Studies.* Washington, D.C.: Smithsonian Institution Press, 1979.

Hanford, Sally, comp. and Susan Stein, ed. *Architectural Research Materials in the District of Columbia.* Washington, D.C.: American Institute of Architects Foundation, 1982.

Jennings, Margaret S., ed. *Library and Reference Facilities in the Area of the District of Columbia.* 11th ed. Washington, D.C.: American Society for Information Science, 1983.

Kim, Hong N. *Scholars' Guide to Washington, D.C. for East Asian Studies.* Washington, D.C.: Smithsonian Institution Press, 1979.

Lesko, Matthew. *Information U.S.A.*. New York: The Viking Press.

Mayerchak, Patrick M. *Scholars' Guide to Washington, D.C. for Southeast Asian Studies.* Washington, D.C.: Smithsonian Institution Press, 1983.

Olson, Judy M. ed. *Special Issue U.S. National Report to ICA, 1984. The American Cartographer.* supplement to vol. 11 (Summer, 1984). Falls Church, Virginia: American Society on Surveying and Mapping, 1984.

Pitschmann, Louis A. *Scholars' Guide to Washington, D.C. for Northwest European Studies.* Washington, D.C.: Smithsonian Institution Press, 1984.

Rahim, Enayetur. *Scholars' Guide to Washington, D.C. for South Asian Studies.* Washington, D.C.: Smithsonian Institution Press, 1981.

Santerre, Patrick J. and David G. Burke. *Maryland Cartographic Information Directory.* Annapolis, Maryland: Maryland Department of Natural Resources, 1982.

Thompson, Morris M. *Maps for America. Cartographic Products of the U.S. Geological Survey and Others.* Washington, D.C.: United States Government Printing Office, 1982.

United States National Archives and Records Service. Office of the Federal Register. *The United States Government Manual, 1984–85.* Washington, D.C.: Government Printing Office, 1984.

INDEXES

I. Personal Names Index

This index contains the names of aerial photographers, cartographers, engravers, surveyors, and others appearing in the collections cited in this *Guide*. It also includes the names of persons whose personal papers contain this cartographic material. The researcher should bear in mind that this list provides only a representative sampling of the mapmakers and related professionals found in the collections and organizations described, and that it is weighted in favor of smaller collections. Since the massive collections of the Library of Congress' Geography and Map Division and the National Archives and Records Administration are not generally indexed by personal name, one can assume that many of the names listed below are represented in these two institutions, even when they are not cited. In those cases where the spelling of a personal name differs among institutions, I have generally followed the spelling as it appears in *Tooley's Dictionary of Mapmakers,* compiled by Ronald Vere Tooley (New York and Amsterdam. 2 volumes). (This list does *not* include the names of persons responsible for administering the collections and organizations described in this volume.)

II Subject Index

This index covers broad catagories of subject headings.

III Geographic Index (Remote Sensing Images)

This index covers categories of geographic headings for aerial photographs and satellite images. Worldwide coverage provided by satellite remote sensing imagery is indexed by the heading "World."

IV Geographic Index (Maps)

This index contains geographic headings for maps. Generally, geographic headings are limited to major political entities or physical features, but prominent places or places associated with important historical events have occasionally been cited. The researcher should also bear in mind that this list provides only a sample of the geographic coverage found in the collections and organizations cited in this *Guide*.

V Organizations and Institutions Index

The following index includes entries to all organizations and institutions listed in this *Guide*. Italic names, letters and numbers indicate entry headings.

Entry symbols correspond to the following sections of the text:

- A—Libraries
- B—Archives and Manuscript Repositories
- C—Museums and Galleries
- D—Data Banks
- E—Research Centers and Referral Services
- F—Academic Programs and Departments
- G—United States Government Agencies
- H—State and Local Government Agencies
- I—Embasssies and International Organizations
- J—Associations and Societies
- K—Publishers, Publications and Media

The author, Ralph E. Ehrenberg, is currently Assistant Chief of the Geography and Map Division at the Library of Congress. Following service with the United States Navy as an aerial photographer, he earned degrees in history and geography at the University of Minnesota (B.A. 1963, M.A. 1968). Mr. Ehrenberg worked as a cartographer at the Aeronautical Chart and Information Center, United States Department of Defense, St. Louis, Missouri (1964–1966) and as a cartographic archivist at the National Archives and Records Service (1966–1979), where he served as Chief of the Cartographic and Architectural Branch from 1973. In 1972 and 1973, Mr. Ehrenberg was awarded a Council on Library Resources Fellowship to study cartographic archives in Canada, England, Scotland, and the United States. He has published a number of books and articles on the administration of cartographic collections, cartographic and geographic resources, and the history of cartography, including *Mapping of America* (with Seymour Schwartz) (New York: Harry N. Abrams, Inc., 1980) and *Archives & Manuscripts: Maps and Architectural Drawings* (Chicago: Society of American Archivists, 1982).

Alan K. Henrikson, who wrote the prefatory essay, "Frameworks for the World," is at present (1986–1987) the Lloyd I. Miller Visiting Professor of Diplomatic History at the United States Department of State's Foreign Service Institute (FSI) and also the Scholar-in-Residence at the FSI's Center for the Study of Foreign Affairs. He is also a Visiting Scholar at the Center for International Affairs, Harvard University. He teaches American and European diplomatic history at The Fletcher School of Law and Diplomacy, Tufts University. He is a former Fellow at Woodrow Wilson International Center for Scholars (1978–1979). He received A.B., A.M., and Ph.D. degrees in history from Harvard University and B.A. and M.A. degrees in philosophy-politics-and-economics from Oxford University (Balliol College), which he attended as a Rhodes Scholar. He is editor of *Negotiating World Order: The Artisanship and Architecture of Global Diplomacy* (Wilmington, DE: Scholarly Resources, Inc., 1986) and writes often on geographical aspects of foreign policy.

Consultant John A. Wolter is the Chief of the Geography and Map Division of the Library of Congress. He attended the University of Minnesota (M.A. 1965; Ph.D. 1975) where he served as map librarian and assistant to the Director of Libraries. He also taught in the geography departments at the University of Minnesota and University of Wisconsin—River Falls. Dr. Wolter served as general editor for the International Federation of Library Associations' *World Directory of Map Collections* (München, New York, etc: K.G. Saur, 1986).

Consultant Joseph Wiedel is an associate professor of Geography at the University of Maryland. He was director of the University's Cartographic Services Laboratory (1959–1975) and is a member of the American Congress on Survey and Mapping Design Committee (1978 to the present). Mr. Wiedel has worked as a consultant on Cartographic Design and Production for the World Bank (1983–1985) and the National Atlas Project, United States Geological Survey (1985–1986). He is the author and editor of many maps, atlases, articles, and books.

Series editor, Zdeněk V. David has been Librarian of the Woodrow Wilson International Center for Scholars since 1974. He attended Wesleyan University (B.A. 1952), Harvard (Ph.D. 1960), and Rutgers (M.L.S. 1970), and he taught history at Harvard, the University of Michigan in Ann Arbor, and Princeton, as well as library science at Rutgers University. He served as Slavic Bibliographer of the Princeton University Library from 1966 to 1974. He is coauthor of *Peoples of the Eastern Habsburg Lands, 1526–1918* (1984), and of *Bibliography of Works in the Philosophy of History, 1978–1982* (1984).